CW01033024

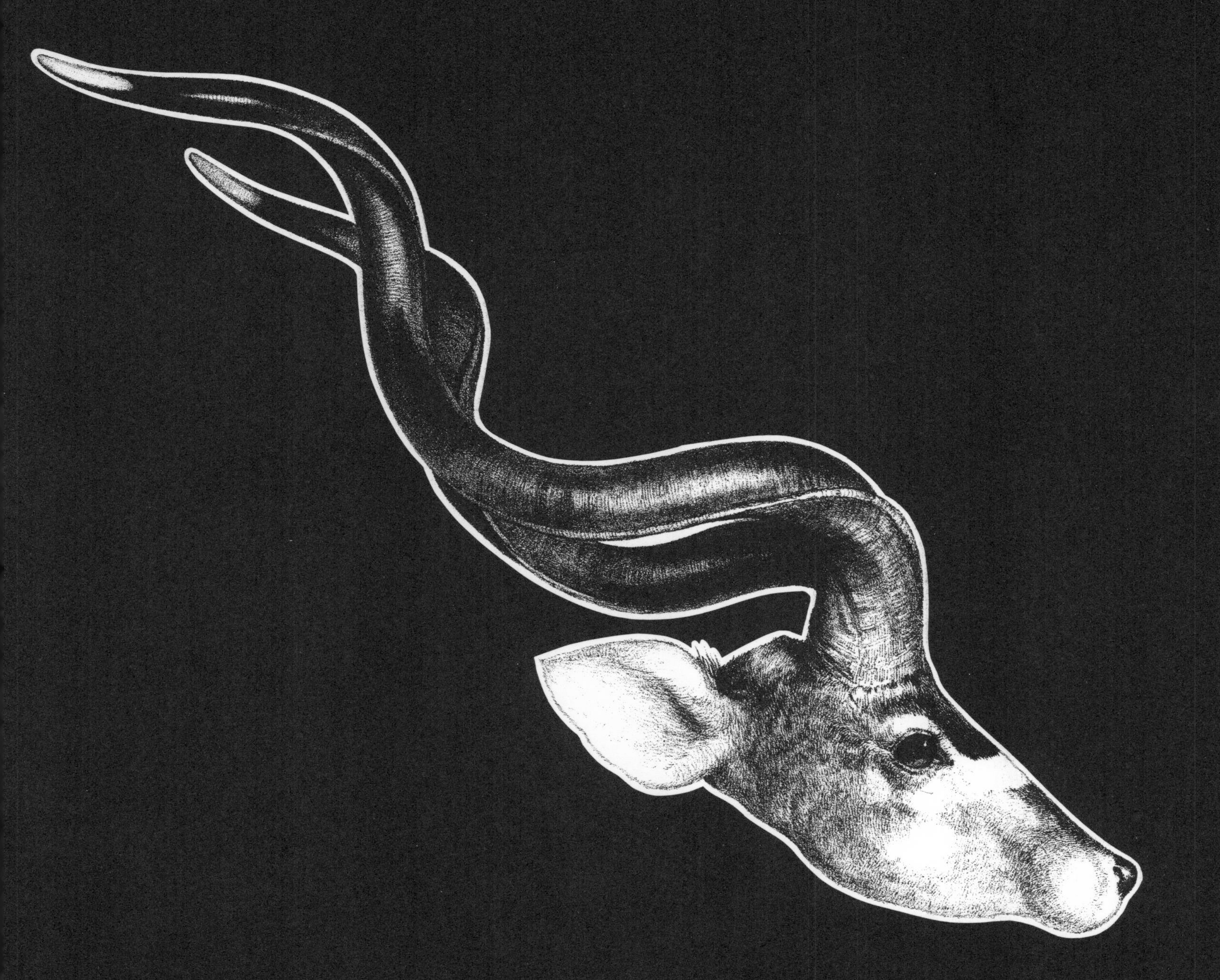

To Nick & Penny

July 9th 1993

Blantyre

Malaŵi

Helen & [illegible]

Best Wishes
Janet & Ian

Very best wishes and love - Rosalie

Best wishes. Enjoy life back in Bristol
Ann & Malcolm

Chris & [illegible] Ferguson.
Keep in touch!

Best of British for you both
Keith [illegible]

Best wishes
Richard. (X)

All the best!
Sue Cumberland.

Great to have had you as neighbours for 3 years - see you again for sure.
Seff xx

Good to have known you
George & Val

See you soon,
Pat

have a lovely time in BRISTOL
Love from Katy.

See you in Katmandu
Wiggy.
Have fun - Chris.

Best wishes,
Sue x.

Hope to see you both (or all) in America soon
Carol & Heather & Luke

Love
John + Liz

See you soon - you'll be sorely missed as a friend and colleague
[illegible]

All The George Jones best. Keep eating the grasshoppers & keep it in your [illegible]. Edward.

All the best
love Jane.

Have you got a pen, Pen? Good Luck. Enjoy.
Love, Hilary

When I have perfected the colouring in I will come for a few "big bangs and smells" lessons! All the best
Helen

Best wishes for a great life back in Downend with some wonderful African memories.
Much love Vicky x

Portraits of the Game and Wild Animals of Southern Africa

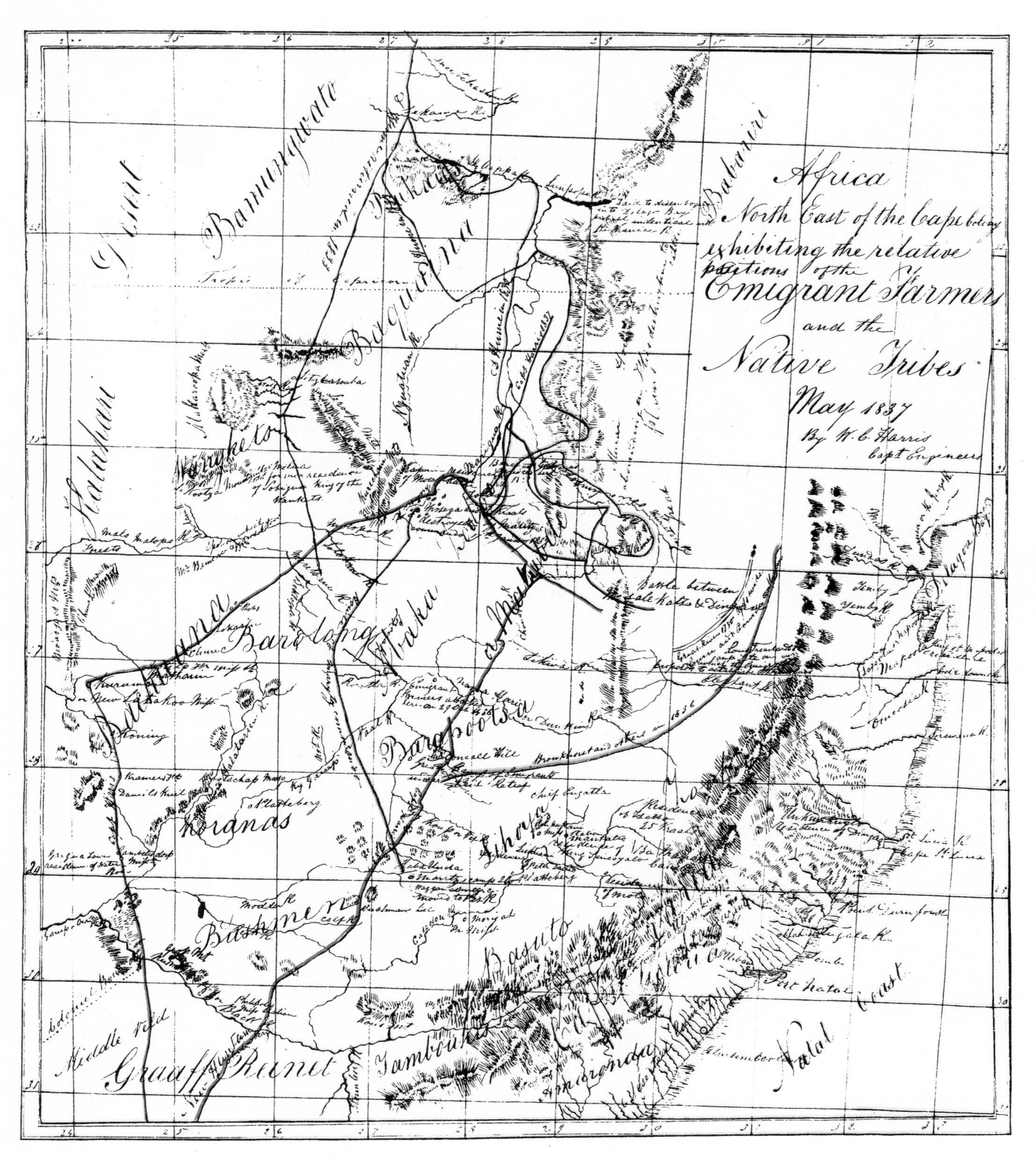

Captain Cornwallis Harris' map of his 1836 journeys in southern Africa, showing the relative positions of the settlements established by emigrant boer farmers during the Great Trek and of the native tribes

From the original water colour by O. Oakley 1845
By kind permission of Johannesburg Africana Museum

MAJOR SIR WILLIAM CORNWALLIS-HARRIS

PORTRAITS

OF THE

GAME AND WILD ANIMALS

of

SOVTHERN AFRICA

Delineated from Life in their Native Haunts

BY

CAPTAIN W. CORNWALLIS HARRIS

Hon.ble E. I. C. Engineers, Bombay.

Drawn on Stone by Frank Howard.

Sæpè diem noctemque, et totum ex ordine mensem
Pascitur itque pecus longa in deserta sine ullis
Hospitiis: tantùm campi jacet! Omnia secum
Venatorius Afer agit, tectumque, laborem
Armaque, Amyclæumque canem, Cressamque pharetram.

Virgil

London. Published for the Proprietor.

1840

1986

Galago

Foreword

Imagine Africa one and a half centuries ago, in 1836. North Africa had been well known to the civilised west since Roman times and before, but south of the great desert, other than the coastal settlements on both the east and west coast, it was truly the dark continent; vast, mysterious and unknown.

On the southern tip of the continent lies the Cape of Good Hope, described by Sir Francis Drake during his voyages, as the 'fairest cape of all'. Here was the Cape Colony, established by the Dutch East India Company as a provisioning station in 1652. But by 1836 it was in British hands. The Great Trek northwards into the hinterland by Boer settlers, who considered they had been unjustly treated by the British Government, had commenced.

Hunters, mostly Boers, but some Englishmen as well, had undoubtedly penetrated far north into the interior, but either because they couldn't or were just not interested, few had left written records of their travels and even fewer still had left behind artistic records.

Stories of the wildlife paradise that the plains of southern Africa were, had filtered through to the outside world, but there were minimal specimens to be found in the natural history museums and even less live ones in the zoos to confirm the existence of these many wonderous species. A Frenchman, M Le Vaillant, had, towards the end of the 18th century, included sketches of the giraffe in his book; but he was derided in Europe as a charlatan.

Captain William (later Sir William) Cornwallis Harris, an Indian Army officer, led a party into the interior in September 1836. His prime purpose, as can be read in the pages of this book, was to hunt and this he most certainly did. His actions in killing during the chase, a vast number and variety of game animals, would, in this a different age, be frowned on — but times were not the same then and no one would have believed most species of African game animals would one day face extinction.

Captain Harris was an accomplished writer and an observant and reliable naturalist, as can be seen by the remarkable detail in the comprehensive captions to his portraits, as well as being the first really competent wildlife artist to appear on the southern African scene. He was the first to bring to the attention of the western naturalists the existence of the sable antelope called for some time afterwards, Harris' buck.

While some of his paintings, particularly that of the elephant and the hippopotamus are undoubtedly not completely accurate depictions, it must be remembered that some were only painted after the completion of his hunting trip; and few mounted museum specimens existed to jog his memory, while the camera hadn't been invented.

The map he drew of his travels, which is reproduced in these pages, is the only one that exists to show the contemporary situations of the early settlements established by the Voortrekkers during the Great Trek.

The record of southern Africa that he left behind is a unique and marvellous slice of time depicting an era that has disappeared for ever. The raw veld he once trod, where only the cough of the lion or the call of the jackal was heard at sundown, now echoes with the roar of the Witwatersrand rush-hour traffic.

The first edition of this book published in 1840, consisted of a mere five hundred copies. Its beauty has made it the rarest, most sought after, as well as the most expensive piece of Africana ever published. Since 1840 two further limited editions have been published - expensive editions for the specialist collector — which has ensured this outstanding work on African wildlife has remained virtually unknown to the average man in the street, to whom the heritage of Africa must truly belongs.

The text of this wonderful book has not been produced facsimile. The text of the first edition was widely spread and difficult to read. For this reason it has been carefully edited to eliminate some words of archaic usage which would deter the modern reader, while keeping the old spellings of the various game animals, African tribes and place names, which, the publishers believe, add a great charm and a spirit of the times to this undying classic.

Peter Stiff

ISBN 0 947020 12 8

First published by the author in 1840
This edition first published by Galago July 1986
Galago books are published by Galago Publishing (Pty) Ltd
P O Box 404, Alberton 1450 RSA

Computer-set in 10½/12 Times Roman by Galago.
Interfaced by Citygraphics

Colour transparencies by Citylab

Colour reproduction by Klaus D Könlein of Citygraphics

Reproduction of line drawings by Citygraphics

Printed and bound by CTP Book Printers

BOOK DESIGN: PETER STIFF AND FRANCIS LATEGAN

Author's Introduction

Hunting, from the earliest antiquity, has formed no less the favourite pastime of the mightiest monarchs, than the chosen exercise of the most exhalted heroes. Poets and minstrels have made the 'merrye greene-wode' the theme and burthen of their wild song. Philisophers and sages have lauded the sylvan craft, as combining exercise to the body, with delight and entertainment to the mind; whilst painters and sculptors have made it the subject of the noblest creations of their skill and genius. The ancient schools instructed those who were destined for deeds of high emprize, to contest with the swiftest of the wild beasts in speed, with the boldest in strength, and with the most cunning in craft and subtlety; *certare cum fagacibus feris, cursu; cum audacibus, robore; cum callidis, astu.* Victories gained over the savage tenants of the forest constantly formed the prelude to heroic exploits in war; and the splendid monuments which transmitted to after ages the military achievements of the Emperors of Rome, not infrequently blended with their most celebrated triumphs, the glories of the chase.

Of those who have taken up the unpretending narrative of my recent adventures in the wilds of southern Africa, to which the present volume may be considered to form an amplification, few will deny that to wander through a fairyland of sport, among the independent denizens of the wide wilderness, realising, as it were, a new and fabled creation amid scenes never before paced by civilised foot, is in itself so truly spirit-stirring and romantic, that in spite of the many hardships and privations which are inseparable from a campaign directed against *farae naturae,* the witchcraft of the desert must prove irresistible. Nor will anyone who reflects that the regions I traversed were either totally depopulated, or very sparingly inhabited, complain, that my attention should have been so exclusively directed to the brute creation, which presented to the traveller the most prominent as well as the most engrossing objects of contemplation. In a region 'where the grim lion prowls monarch of all he surveys', my interviews with the wild races of the human species were necessarily few and far between; and it seldom fell to my fortune to have opportunities of studying the natural history of those primitive children of the desert.

Africa, it is well known, is the great nursery of many of the most noble and interesting forms that exist in the animal kingdom. Her southern regions, which extend into the temperate zone, are surrounded on three sides by the ocean; and being divided from the milder climates of the northern hemisphere by the torrid belt that intervenes, are tenanted by a vast nation of indigenous quadrupeds. The grizzled monarch of the forest — the stupendous elephant — and the shapeless river horse — the mailed rhinoceros — the gaily painted zebra — and the richly arrayed ostrich — all claim alike some portion of her savage soil as the lot of their inheritance. An endless variety of grotesque and bulky ruminants also, offer to the keen disciple of 'the mighty Hunter', *quarrees* no less glorious than eccentric. The towering giraffe, by whose lofty side man dwindles to the stature of a pygmy — the malevolent and stately buffalo; the mild, though ponderous eland, enveloped in a goodly garment of its own fat; the fantastic gnoo, with its scarcely less terrific looking congener — the unicorn-resembling oryx and the regal koodoo; the proud group of *aigoceri,* and the graceful family of star-eyed gazelles; together with a whole host of subordinates, descending by fair gradations, link by link, to that tiniest of sylvan denizens, the *caerulean* antelope and collectively filling the place which in other countries is occupied by the cervine race — all advance their hereditary title to a share in the trackless plateau of that mighty portion of the earth.

The extensive field that yet remains unexplored of the great and mysterious continent of Africa, doubtless contains a rich mine of hidden treasure, which in the progress of gradual development, will no doubt be one day fully exhausted. By the indefatigable exertions of modern travellers, the repositories of science have been already enriched with some of the choicest *exuviae* of most of the interesting forms with which we are yet acquainted: and the enterprise of others, also, has stocked our menageries, like the ark of Noah, with living specimens of nearly every variety. Widely different, however, is the graceful free-born of the desert, bounding exultingly in light and liberty over his native prairie, from the pampered cripple, pining in sad captivity, with sinews relaxed under the restraint of a prison-house. Yet is from stunted subjects such as these, or worse still, from mummies and stuffed monstrosities, that the most popular illustrations of the African fauna have heretofore been principally derived; and so little likeness do some of the abortions and absurdities thus produced, bear to the brave originals, that it is frequently difficult, if not impossible, to trace in them the most remote resemblance to the actual works of the creation.

With the design, if possible, of supplying in some measure this palpable defect in our zoological galleries, the portraits contained in the present series were originally undertaken. How manifold so ever their imperfections, if viewed as productions of art, they can boast at least of being adorned with the beauties of truth, having all been delineated from living subjects, roaming in pristine independence over their native soil. 'To study animals with accuracy,' says the observant Buffon, 'we ought to view them in their savage state; to accompany them into the retreats which they have chosen for themselves; to follow them into the deep caverns, and to attend them on the frightful precipices where they enjoy unbounded liberty.' Devoted to woodcraft from the cradle, my predilection for sylvan sports has afforded me all the opportunities, alluded to by the great naturalist, of waxing intimate with the dappled denizens of the grove and waste to an extent, which abler artists and more finished zoologists have necessarily been denied. I have beheld the venerable and half-reasoning elephant browsing in native majesty among his own contemporary trees, 'in his huge strength impregnable;' have torn the much prized ivory from his giant jaws, and plucked the horn from the saucy nose of the rhinoceros. I have stripped the proud *spolia* from the shaggy shoulder of the 'king of beasts, who clears the desert with his rolling eye' — have humbled the haughty head of the forest bull; — and though 'she scorneth the horse and his rider,' have despoiled the fleet ostrich of her costly plumes. More — I have dragged forth *Behemoth,* 'whose ribs are like bars of iron,' from his hiding place under the shady trees, in the covert of the reed and fens, — and have ridden familiarly by the side of the towering *Zamor,* the colossal glory of the wilderness, long classed with the wild chimeras of men's brain.

The leading features of my expedition, undertaken chiefly for these purposes, in the company of an esteemed and valued friend, have already been placed before the public in the narrative above referred to; and it is therefore only necessary for me now to remark, that throughout the following views, which were all executed on that occasion, my object has been to combine to the fullest practicable extent, information which might prove acceptable to the naturalist, the sportsman and the lover of wild scenery. Adapted to one standard, and corrected by actual measurement, they comprise faithful portraits of every game quadruped yet known to inhabit southern extra-tropical Africa, including one which has been pronounced an unique and splendid discovery of my own; [sable antelope] and, as neither the relative size of the animals, the characteristics of their favourite haunts, nor their manner of congregating, has in any instance been lost sight of, the series will be found to convey an accurate and tangible idea, not only of the ordinary bulk of each and of its gregarious, monogamous, or solitary habits, but also of the aspect and geographical features of the region to which it is restricted.

Those of my readers who, like myself, have been accustomed to the trappings and luxurious magnificence of Indian hunting expeditions, and who have enjoyed the sumptuous accommodation afforded by oriental tents and retinue, can form but a feeble conception of the ten thousand difficulties, distresses and drawbacks — the toils, trials and troubles, that beset the wanderer in the African desert. He who would accomplish his object under the manifold disadvantages that there exist, must be well impressed with the maxim: *Omnia vincit labor, labor enim ipse voluptas;* and I claim some share of merit for having in the domains of savage nature, not been disheartened from the exercise of the pencil under so many disadvantages. All the first sketches of my drawings were commenced either in the open air with the animal before me, in the scene of slaughter, or under the shelter of some neighbouring bush and were completed upon my knees in the waggon, often amidst rain and wind. The indolence and apathy of our Hottentot attendants, who resemble the wild beasts as nearly in habits as in features, invariably obliged me to carry the appliances for drawing, as well as the embryo portraits upon my person; and that they should have been preserved to assume their present shape will probably excite surprise, when I add, that I often wended my solitary way from the sporting field, not only encumbered with my weapons and hunting gear, but also laden with venison and staggering under the weight of the ponderous trophies which had fallen to my rifle.

Before concluding this introduction, I feel a proud satisfaction in publicly acknowledging the enthusiastic reception which has been accorded to my narrative by my brother officers in India, with whom I have the gratification of knowing it has exalted me in credit and consideration; nor must I omit to express my obligation to the critics of Europe for the favourable manner in which my work has been received in my native land.

From those kindred and congenial spirits, however, to whom especially I have inscribed the following pages — and who will not fail to interpret aright the intent of my dedication — I feel confident of approval. They, I know, will accord to their ancient ally, that fellow feeling of which others may be niggard or unsusceptible — neither amongst my brother votaries of the chase, shall there be found one, who turning over these leaves, will fail to participate in the enviable feelings of liberty and excitement which pervaded my breast, whether 'pricking at a righte merrye pace' with my fellow-voyager, over the broad bosom of the flower-decked prairies of southern Africa, or engaged in 'chance medley' with the four-footed giants that divide amongst themselves the empire of that hunter's *Elysium.*

Contents

1

Gnoo

But soon, 'mid Afric's landscape lone,
Old reminiscences are gone:
Soon we raise the eye to range
O'er prospects wild, grotesque, and strange —
Beasts of mix'd, and monstrous birth,
Creations of some fabled earth,
Bursting like whirlwind through the waste,
With clattering hoofs, and headlong haste.

A more whimsical compound than the gnoo could scarcely have been thrown together, or a monster imagined of more fanatistical and anomalous exterior. At the first glance, a stranger to the African fauna would conclude that the shaggy head of the American bison had been tacked, centaur-like, upon the shoulders of a pony; the equine similarity of the arched neck and well rounded crupper, being materially enhanced by the neatly clipped mane, and long flowing tail; whilst the legs, which are slender, vigorous, and well knit, are no less singly cervine. Exhibiting this absurd combination of characters, each in itself the peculiar feature of some other quadruped, naturalists have ever been greatly perplexed in deciding upon the legitimate position which should be assigned to so singular an animal. Originally, it was classed with the antelopes, between which and the buffalo, it unquestionably forms the link; but, possessing in general aspect, figure and motions, as well as in the texture and taste of the flesh, attributes which most strongly partake of the bovine character, zoologists have at length become unanimously agreed upon the propriety of transferring it to a genus more closely allied to the taurine group.

The supposed identity of the gnoo, with the terrific animal referred to by Aelian under the title of *catoblepas,* has latterly led to the adoption of that classical, and far more appropriate nomenclature. Inhabiting Ethiopia near the sources of the Nile, the *catoblepas* is described by Pliny, as 'a savage and sluggish beast resembling a bull, but endowed with a more fierce and terrible aspect; its eyes red with blood like those of an ox, surmounted by large and elevated brows, and having their deadly glance directed obliquely towards the earth, *nomen unde derivatur;* its ponderous head, which it carries low, furnished with a flowing mane, which descends over the forehead, and so covers the face, as to impart additional terror to its appearance.' That the ancients should have invested, with something of the marvellous, so whimsical a creature as the subject of the annexed portrait, is by no means surprising; and Pliny's description, although obviously vague and extravagant, is altogether far from being inapplicable to the gnoo, the limits of whose range are undefined, and a variety of which may not improbably have been seen by the Romans, when they had carried their conquest towards the more central regions of the African continent. In habits also, as well as in appearance, the gnoo is of all quadrupeds perhaps the most awkward and grotesque. Nature doubtless formed him in one of her freaks, and it is scarcely possible to contemplate his ungainly antics without laughter. Wheeling and prancing in every direction, his shaggy and bearded head arched between his slender and muscular legs, and his long white tail streaming in the wind, this pantomimic, and ever wary animal, has at once a ferocious and a ludicrous appearance. Suddenly stopping, showing an imposing front, and tossing his grizzled head in mock defiance, his wild red sinister eyes flash fire, and his snort, resembling the roar of a lion, is repeated with energy and effect. Then lashing his pillowed flanks with his floating tail, he plunges, bounds, kicks up his heels with a fantastic flourish, and in a moment is off again at speed, making the dust fly behind him as he sweeps across the plain.

'His eyes are jet, and they are set, in crystal rings of snow,
But now they stare, with one red glare, of brass upon their foe;
Low to his knee, his head holds he, his nostrils snuff the wind,
To his heel doth trail, his silvery tail, swinging his flanks behind.

Although daily becoming more rare, wilde beests, or wild cattle, as these eccentric quadrupeds are designated by the Dutch Boers, may still be found on the desert tracts called Karoo, as well as in some of the most remote and unfrequented districts of the Cape Colony. Gregarious, fretful, and of extremely restless habits, although seeming to be alike regardless of water, herbage and shade, the gnoo migrates from place to place, according to the season; and large troops are constantly to be seen by the traveller, grazing in the society of the quagga and springbok, or scouring the broad and verdant plains of the interior, in wide extended circles — moving usually in single files — butting, capering, and curvetting, in the performance of the most intricate and fanciful manoeuvres, their track followed by ascending columns of dust which their heels have raised; a goodly knot of giant ostriches, the independent tenants of the same wilds, tricked out in their holiday plumes, not infrequently enacting the part of reviewing general and staff, with such grave propriety, as forcibly to remind the spectator of a cavalry parade. Seen roaming singly during the season of rutting, or careering over the broad daisied prairie, jerking its long switch tail, and uttering at intervals that deep hollow moan which may best be expressed by dwelling on the two final letters of its Hottentot appellative (gnoooo), the appearance of a furious old bull is abundantly imposing, and is precisely that of a shaggy black-maned lion. But, as is too often the case,

'tis distance lends enchantment to the view;'

on nearer inspection the dreadful delusion vanishes, and the imposture becomes as palpable as that practised in days of yore upon the wild beasts, by the ass in the lion's spoils. Whilst crossing the boundless plains of the Vaal River, we had an opportunity of remarking the very similar appearance of the two animals, in twice witnessing the animating but abortive pursuit of a herd of gnoos, by an enormous lion, rendered perfectly furious by the qualms of hunger, and still more desperately frantic at the disappointment entailed by the slippery heels of his intended victims, who, on both occasions, left their grim pursuer far

I. CATOBLEPAS GNOO – THE GNOO.

behind, puffing and blowing, to grumble over the loss of the morning repast which he had vainly promised himself.

Extremely vicious and pugnacious amongst themselves, and possessed of that swiftness of foot which might be inferred from their compact and vigorous conformation, these ungainly beasts are nevertheless shot from horseback without much difficulty, and can scarcely be pronounced formidable, except in external appearance. The eyes are louring, and expressive of great ferocity: the solid casque of horn by which their beetling brows are overshadowed, greatly heightening their aspect of suspicion and vindictiveness. Like other animals possessing dispositions far more gentle and tractable, the gnoo is naturally prone to charge in self defence, when wounded, or forced into a corner; but after fracturing its leg, I have repeatedly driven a reluctant individual up to the wagons, either to escape the trouble of carrying his sirloin, or because I had expended the last bullet in my pouch. In the wild districts bordering on the Colony, where a succession of level plains are traversed by low ranges of bare stony hills, prancing troops, consisting of from fifteen to thirty gnoos of various sizes, are to be seen engaged in the most wanton frolics, and may easily be hemmed into a valley and compelled to run the gauntlet. At Vogel's valley, north of the Sneeuwbergen, with the thermometer down to eighteen degrees [fahrenheit], we first secured three shaggy fellows in this fashion, during a heavy fall of snow. Solitary individuals not infrequently grazed near our drove of oxen, without exhibiting the smallest symptom of uneasiness, and on the arrival of the cafila at some scanty pool — perhaps the only oasis within many a league — three or four that appeared to be performing the duty of vedettes, after executing the most ridiculous capers, and ungainly flourishes, would charge down to the water's edge, as if bent upon disputing to the death, with the thirsty cattle, every drop of so precious an element.

The curious and inquisitive disposition of the gnoo, often induces the herd to discontinue their giddy gambols, and slowly to approach the passing caravan with an air of laughable defiance, formed in a compact square, goring, menacing, stamping with their slender fore feet, and at length halting within rifle range to scrutinise the bold intruders upon their lone and hereditary pastures. On such occasions they were readily shot from the wagons, which, upon necessity, could invariably produce from ten to a dozen loaded barrels, in addition to those which encumbered the brawny shoulders of our followers. Although very indifferent marksmen, not one of our Hottentot attendants ever missed an opportunity of warming his flat Chinese nose, by burning a handful of coarse powder under it, through the agency of a rude apparatus of flint and steel. On the line of march, therefore, a quarter of an hour seldom elapsed without the booming of overloaded firearms, each volley being instantly followed by a general retreat of every wild quadruped that happened to be within earshot — herds of gnoos, amongst various other species of game, whisking their long white tails and scampering off in every direction, but rarely leaving any of their number to attest the accuracy of the practice. During bright moonlight nights, also, curiosity often prompted a clump of gnoos to approach within a few yards of our bivouac, where they would stand for hours in the same position, staring wildly, lashing their dark flanks, and uttering a subdued note resembling the harsh croaking of a frog; the shadowy aspect they were wont to wear on those occasions being so truly spectral and hobgoblinish, that the stoutest heart might have quailed thereat. Unyoking late one evening hear a muddy puddle on the plains of the Vaal River, I shot a noble old bull from the box of the pack wagon, and following it on foot as it limped away, actually inflicted four more gunshot wounds without realising the quarry, although from loss of blood it was frequently obliged to sit down. Night closing in, I was fain to return to the camp; but there being no flesh in the larder, I sallied forth again as soon as *bright Cynthia showed her horns,* and after a tedious moonlight pursuit, was at length enabled to perform the last ceremonies of the chase. A dense fog coming on, the Hottentot, Andries, who accompanied me, contrived to lose his reckoning, and we both wandered about the wilderness during the greater part of the night, encumbered with a load of meat, and more and more puzzled at every step what course to steer; until, towards morning, after losing each other at least a dozen times, the cracking of wagon whips and the reports of musketry, which, owing to the density of the atmosphere, had been transmitted to a very short distance only, fortunately enabled us both to stumble upon the encampment.

The cows, or female gnoos, seldom produce more than one at a birth; the young calves, which are nevertheless exceeding numerous, being at first of a pure white or cream colour, which gradually assumes a tinge of reddish grey. The latter associate with the herd apeing all the whims and antics of the adults, uttering a nasal murmur, and looking, if possible, still droller deformities than those that gave them birth. We constantly rode them down, as well for the sake of the delicious veal they afforded, as to counteract the shyness of the herd to which they belonged, by inducing the skittish mothers to slacken their baffling pace, and take heed of their offspring. Dismounting from my horse to administer the *coup de grace* to a savage old cow, whose diminutive calf I had previously captured and bound, she charged me upon her knees, distending her flabby nostrils, snorting and bellowing so lustily, that my steed became alarmed, and both my hands being encumbered, at the same time that the clumsily patched sole of my untanned leather buskin became entangled in the stirrup, I fell helpless on my back. Away galloped the horse without further ado, the bellowing of the gnoo ringing fresh in his ears; and being fully impressed with the belief, that a lion at least, was hanging to his heels, he passed the advancing caravan at speed — his nervousness yet more increased by the yells and shouts of the followers — and dragged me a sufficient distance

Plate I: Catoblepas gnoo — gnoo — *wilde beest or wild ox of the Cape colonists — gnoo of the Hottentots — impatoomo* of the Matabili

Generic Character — Adult male upwards of four feet high at the shoulder, and nine in extreme length. General contour very muscular, and exhibitive of great energy. Head heavy and square. Muzzle large, spread out and flattened, with narrow linear nostrils. Above it, on the chaffron, is seated a conspicuous tuft of black bristling hairs, radiating laterally, and resembling a blacking brush. A tuft of similar hair seated beneath each eye, concealing a gland, which distills a viscous humour. Eye wild and fiery; surrounded by a star-like fringe of white bristles, diverging as the radii of a circle. Numerous stiff white bristles scattered over the upper lip. Ears small and pointed. Horns arising from a basal mass which expands over the forehead so as to form a solid helmet furrowed upon the summit: scarcely advancing from the head, they taper out sideways over the eyes, and uncinate up into a pointed hook, sweeping with a regular curve, and producing an aspect, sinister, suspicious and vindictive. Shoulder deep. Neck resembling that of a high-fed bull, with heavy crest, and much arched. Carcase round. A cushion of fat seated on either haunch. Legs slender and long, shaped like those of a stag. Hoofs of a blue-black colour, and pointed. A full vertical mane on the summit of the crest, wearing the appearance of a neatly trimmed hog, and consisting of quantities of upright wiry white hair, tipped with brown, so as to form a dark border. A bushy black beard flowing from the chin and dewlap; and a full bush of shaggy black wavy hair descending betwixt the forelegs from the brisket, and extending some distance along the belly. Tail equine, white, and sweeping to the ground. General complexion of the hair a deep umber-brown, ranging upon black.

Female similar, but smaller, and exhibiting less depth of colour. Her horns slighter and less expanded, and their bases less approximated. Has an udder with four mammae. Very gregarious. Abundant on the open plains of the Vaal River, and still occurring in some parts of Cape Colony.

over the sharp stones, to grind the whole of the clothes, and a very ample portion of the natural covering also, from my lacerated shoulders; lashing out at intervals, to the imminent peril of my teeth, and kicking me very severely upon the knee and ankle, before I could contrive to extricate myself from my very unpleasant position.

In common with the ox and buffalo, the gnoo has an unconquerable aversion to scarlet-pawing the earth and becoming perfectly furious at the sudden display of that colour. In situations where these whimsical animals had been rendered more than usually wild by the incessant persecutions of the border colonists, I frequently found it requisite, in order to allure the herd within range, to hoist a red pocket handkerchief upon the muzzle of my rifle. This exhibition invariably produced the most violent tumult and excitement, and caused the whole troop to charge past in single file — *with mane erect and blazing eye* — following their leader, flinging out their taper heels, whisking their streaming tails, butting with their horns in so menacing a manner, and displaying emotions of such violent frenzy, that I was fain to strike my colours, and have recourse to my weapons — when they instantly wheeled, and pranced confidently round at a safer distance, headed by their swarthy chief:

Fierce on the hunter's hostile band
He rolls his eye of burnished glow:
Spurns with black hoof and horns the sand,
And tosses high his mane of snow.

De jagt van de wilde beest forms a favourite diversion of the Dutch colonists, and occupies a very large portion of the apparently valueless time of the trek-boers, or nomad farmers, who graze their overgrown flocks and herds on the verdant meadows lying beyond the borders of the sterile colony. The carcase of a full grown wilde beest, even when broken, forms a fair load for a pack-horse; the flesh, which is very insipid and usually quite destitute of fat, resembling very coarse beef in quality. A joint is therefore never dressed by the good *vrouw* without having first been garnished with huge lumps of sheep fat, a *sine qua non* in Dutch cookery, dexterously thrust with the point of the thumb into perforations carved for their reception; which done, it is placed in the iron oven, with abundance of lard, and literally baked to rags! On account of its leanness, however, it is generally cut into strips, and converted into biltong, by being dried in the sun. The silky tail of the gnoo, which is in great demand for making chowries, forms an article of export; and the hide, when brayed, is employed by the colonists for riems, or thongs, with which to harness oxen in the team, and indeed for every purpose to which hempen rope, twine and string, are usually applied in other countries.

When captured young, the gnoo, may be reared by the hand upon cow's milk, with little difficulty, and although uncertain in temper, may readily be induced, in its domesticated state, to herd with the cattle on the farm; daily going out to, and returning with them from pasture, and exhibiting no inclination to resume its pristine liberty. Amongst its other eccentricities and peculiarities, however, it is said to be liable to a cutaneous eruption of the skin, which generally proves fatal, and is so apt to be communicated to its bovine companions, that the farmer will not often admit of its presence. In common with its congener, the brindled gnoo, and some few other tenants of the African wilderness, hereafter to be noticed — whose horns are invariably placed on a high ridge upon the summit of the frontals — a certain cavity above the brain is literally crammed with a large description of fatty white bot, numbers of which are expelled whenever the animal snorts; the whole coming voluntarily away after its death, through the channel of the nostrils, which are covered with a muscular valve or flap, shutting down like a trap door so as to close the apertures. This phenomenon, to which I was not disposed to afford credit until I had actually witnessed it some twenty times, may possibly account for the petulant freaks and hair brained caprices of this absurd quadruped; the irritation caused by the maggots no doubt frequently bringing on a kind of furor which may even cause its dissolution. In a single heap I have seen so many as two or three hundred mouldering skulls; and forming an opinion from the numerous skeletons in all stages of decomposition, with which the lone pastures in the interior are everywhere strewed, the mortality amongst the species must be very great — numbers falling before the poisoned shafts of the diminutive Bushman, as well as under the talons of the prowling lion — man, beast and insect alike, proving the enemy of this most whimsical of nature's vagaries.

Head of the gnoo, as preserved by Captain Harris

2

Quagga

Who hath sent out the wild ass free? or who hath loosed the bands of the wild ass?
Whose house I have made the wilderness, and the barren land his dwellings.
He scorneth the multitude of the city, neither regardeth he the crying of the driver.
The range of the mountains is his pasture,
And he searcheth after every green thing. Job 39:5-8.

Adequately to portray upon paper the magnitude of the measureless landscape which meets the eye of the traveller in many parts of southern Africa, is beyond the limits of possibility, but some idea of the naked and remarkable scenery of the less sterile plains may be gleaned from the view annexed. A region — to the perception as vast and trackless as the ocean, and, like it, presenting an undisturbed horizon — is spread out for hundreds of miles into one level and treeless expanse of serene and sunny plain. In vain we there seek for the bewitching variety of hill or dale, forest or glade, which constitutes the chief charm of landscape; the eye wanders on, without the smallest check, over interminable flats, which are utterly wearisome from their extent and monotony:

All, all is plain,
Plain as the strand, sea lav'd, that stretches far
Beneath yon rocky shore.

Yet nature has endeavoured, in some measure, to atone for other deficiencies, by decking them out in her gaudiest colours, and in some of the most eccentric and attractive forms that exist in the vegetable world. Endless meads, clad in a vernal and variegated robe of gay, but scentless flowers, in whose presence the very desert would seem to smile, exhibit the motley variety of a Turkey carpet. With the vernal spring, the branching chandelier plant, the purple amaryllis, the golden crocus, and a thousand other splendid bulbs, push forth their blossoms and green leaves, amid trailing geraniums; and, combined with various species of the fleshy cactus, and an endless variety of the succulent greenhouse plant, styled the Hottentot fig, which there grow wild in profusion, literally impart to the waste the semblance of a flower garden. Daisies, buttercups, tulips, pinks and marigolds — white, yellow, purple and crimson, spread themselves out into beds and borders of many acres in extent:

So wondrous wild, the whole might seem
The scenery of a fairy dream.

Now may be described some reed encircled fountain, around which hosts of quaggas and other wild animals have congregated to slake their thirst — fetid and stagnant ponds covered with flowering water lilies, and surrounded by a broad belt of flags and rushes, which conceal a chain of treacherous pitfalls dug by those brown dwarfs, the wily Bushmen, for the purpose of entrapping the unwary game. Next, a string of frosted salt-pans present themselves to the view, white and hoar, with divers antelopes licking up the saline efflorescence, in which they delight; and sometimes, though rarely, may be seen an isolated tumulus, riding, like a ship at her cable, in a floating sea of deceitful mirage, which causes the gay glittering coats of the quagga of sparkle like mica. Above, through a sky of pure and delicious blue, 'spread out like a molten looking-glass,' and rarely visited by a cloud, shines the sun with matchless refulgence; and during his meridian blaze over this level expanse, in many part, so strongly impregnated with salt, the delusion of the treacherous vapour is no where more perfect. Looming as though 'the parched ground had become a pool, and the thirsty land springs of water,' optical lakes which are stretched around on every side like a white tablecloth, impart to the wanderers fevered with thirst, the torments of Tantalus:

Still the same burning sun, no cloud in heaven,
The hot air quivers, and the sultry mist
Floats o'er the desert with a show
Of distant waters, mocking their distress.

Entitled only to scanty showers during the summer months, insufficient of themselves 'to satisfy the desolate and waste ground,' although they may 'cause the bud of the tender herb to spring forth,' the face of nature thus beautifully arrayed in herbage and flowers, would appear to be kept fresh and verdant by nightly dews and humid mists, rather than by the partial and niggard showers by which it is occasionally visited; yet neither is the debilitating fervor of an Indian sun experienced in these regions, nor the country being characterised by extreme aridity, is any baneful effect experienced from these nocturnal fogs, by the wayfarer who, ensconced in his leathern mantle, may be compelled to stretch his weary limbs upon the ground with the starry firmaments for his canopy, and a stone for his pillow.

Although thinly populated by skulking broods of Bushmen, and by the starving remnants of nomadic pastoral tribes, which have been broken up by war and violence, this is a land in which no man permanently abides — neither is the soil accounted any man's property, being abandoned as water and fuel fail. Nearly all the rivers by which it is traversed are periodical, and the scanty pools that exist, being exhausted at certain seasons, the miserable wretches whose existence depends upon the wild animals, migrate with them to distant parts, keeping within the verge of expiring verdure. At length, however, the monotony of this extraordinary wilderness is broken in upon by the Wittebergen, part of a broad basaltic parallel to the eastern coast, and dividing Kaffraria from Bechuana land. This wild chaos of rocks and cliffs — of barren ridges and towering peaks worn by time into castellated fortresses, and other fantastic shapes, resembles the ruins of a world. Intersected by yawning chasms, it presents an impassable barrier; but its wild fastnesses afford shelter to various broken tribes, who have been driven by war's alarms from the land of their inheritance. Amongst the savage nations of southern Africa as elsewhere, a principle of extinction has for ages past been in active operation. Regions now silent and deserted, once contained their busy throng, whose numbers and strength have been gradually

II. EQUUS QUAGGA.— THE QUAGGA.

brought down by war and want. Whole tribes have been rooted out from their hereditary homes, and have either disappeared from off the face of the earth, or pursued by the gaunt and bony arm of famine, still wander with fluctuating fortunes over these measureless tracts. For hundreds of miles, therefore, the eye is not greeted by the smallest trace of human industry, nor by any vestige of human habitation — the wild and interminable expanse ever presenting the same appearance — that of one vast, uninhabited solitude.

Amongst the many peculiarities presented by the animal creation of southern Africa, are three distinct and elegant species of the solidungulous family, which belong exclusively to that quarter of the world. The true zebra, or daow, which is styled by the Cape colonists, the wilde paard or wild horse, is exclusively confined to mountainous regions dwelling in 'craggy castles on the hill tops', from which it rarely, if ever, descends; but the extensive and sequestered plains above referred to, abound with two other members of the equine genus, which are still more closely allied to the horse, and are never to be found but in the lowlands. These are the quagga, delineated in the annexed portrait, and the striped or bonti quagga, better recognised as Burchell's Zebra. The former, it will be remarked, is of a fulvous bay complexion, streaked or brindled with brown over the head, neck and forehead. Burchell's Zebra again, is adorned over every part, the legs alone excepted, with broad black single or double bands, detached from a dorsal stripe, and elegantly contrasted with a pale yellow ground; whilst the veritable zebra, which was known to the Romans under the title of *hippotigris,* is completely covered with alternate stripes of pure black and white, continued singly over the fetlocks, down to the very coronets.

It is now some years since the Zoological Gardens were first graced by living specimens of each of these elegant exotic species, some of which have even bred successfully in their captive state; but the period is not very remote when the greatest confusion existed in the minds of natural historians, respecting the external distinctions of the African solidungula. Disguised in a tail borrowed from the rump of the domestic ass, the subject of the annexed portrait sat for its picture to M.Buffon and may be found in the voluminous works of that eminent author, doing duty for a female zebra! Even the Baron Cuvier has fallen into the error of describing the quagga to be the proprietor of an asinine tail — a mistake which is the more surprising, since it is stated by the same author in his *Regne Animal* that 'amongst the equipages occasionally exhibited in the gay season in Hyde Park, and other fashionable places of resort, may be seen a curricle drawn by two couaggas, which seem as subservient to the curb and whip as any well trained horses'. Hereafter, in its proper place, a similar fact will be adduced with regard to the zebra or wilde paard, many of which beautiful species are annually taken in the mountainous districts of the Colony of the Cape of Good Hope, and shipped to the Isle of France, where they are not uncommonly driven in harness.

The geographical range of this species of the quagga does not appear to extend to the northward of the River Vaal. The animal was formerly extremely common within the Colony, but vanishing before the strides of civilization, is now to be found in very limited numbers, and on the borders only. Beyond, on those sultry plains which are completely taken possession of by wild beasts, and may with strict propriety be termed the domains of savage nature, it occurs in interminable herds; and although never intermixing with its own more elegant congeners, is almost invariably to be found ranging with the white tailed gnoo, and with the ostrich, for the society of which bird especially, it evinces the most singular predilection. Moving slowly across the profile of the ocean-like horizon, uttering a shrill barking neigh, of which its name forms a correct imitation, long files of quaggas continually remind the early traveller of a rival caravan on its march. Throughout the Scriptures, the inspired poets make frequent allusion to the similar habits of the Asiatic congeners of this animal; and in the vivid and startling picture of the effects of drought, given in the book of Jeremiah, we are told that 'the wild asses did stand in the desolate places; they snuffed up the wind like dragons and their eyes did fail because there was no grass'. Bands of many hundreds are thus frequently seen during their migration from the dreary and desolate plains of some portion of the interior which has formed their secluded abode, seeking for those more luxuriant pastures, where, during the summer months, various herbs thrust forth their leaves and flowers, to form a green carpet, spangled with hues the most brilliant and diversified.

In this native character, the quagga appears to be social and peaceable, living carelessly, sometimes in troops not exceeding twenty or thirty, but oftener in much larger communities. The average standard both of the males and females, is from twelve to thirteen hands. Compact, strong and muscular, with clean bony limbs, and a foot which might serve as a model to the veterinary student, this *petit cheval* cannot fail forcibly to remind us in all its form and proportions, of the horse in miniature. Doubtless, it might readily be subdued by bit and bridle, and if not capable of universal distribution, would in its native regions at least, where food and climate are congenial, reward fourfold by its services, the trouble attendant upon its education. Foals have indeed occasionally been reared, when thrown accidentally into the hands of the peasant; but no systematic attempt has yet been made on the part of the indolent colonists, to reduce the species to a state of domesticated subjection; and the carnivorous savage tribes occupying the regions which now form its habitat, regard it in common with the rest of the animal creation, only as furnishing them with an ample repast when slain. By the roving clans of Bechuana huntsmen, and the voracious Bushman hordes, its disgustingly oily and yellow flesh is even esteemed a delicacy; and the lion, which invariably follows the tide of migration towards new pastures, is not infrequently driven from his prey at the assegai's point, by these two-legged devourers of carrion. The flesh is never used by the colonists, except for the purpose of feeding their tame Bushmen, but the hides are valuable for making sacks to contain grain; and the thicker portions which cover the angle of the hocks, are greatly esteemed for the manufacture of shoe soles.

'When we consider', observes M Cuvier, 'that this species is capable of highly beneficial services in a domesticated condition;

Plate II: *Equus quagga* — quagga or *couagga* of the Cape colonists

Generic Character — Adult male stands four feet six inches, high at the wither, and measures eight feet six inches in extreme length. Form compact. Barrel round. Limbs robust, clean and sinewy. Head light and bony; of a bay colour, covered on the forehead and temples with longitudinal, and on the cheeks, with narrow transversal stripes, forming linear triangular figures between their eyes and mouth. Muzzle black. Ears and tail strictly equine; the latter white, and flowing below the hocks. Crest very high, arched, and surmounted by a full standing mane, which appears as though it had been hogged, and is banded alternately brown and white. Colour of the neck and upper parts of the body, dark rufous brown, becoming gradually more fulvous, and fading off to white behind and beneath; the upper portions banded and brindled with dark brown stripes, stronger, broader and more regular on the neck, but gradually waxing fainter, until lost behind the shoulder in spots and blotches. Dorsal line dark and broad, widening over the crupper. Legs white, with bare spots inside above the knees.

Female precisely similar. Has an udder with four mammae. Still found within the Cape Colony. Inhabits the open plains south of the Vaal River in immense herds.

that its natural courage is evinced in its wild state by the manner in which, according to the report of travellers, it repels the hyena and the wolf, an endowment which would be of great value to the animal if completely subjected to man; that this species is an inhabitant of the hottest parts of the earth, and is therefore likely to be of service where the horse loses its capabilities by climate; we may naturally be surprised that the couagga [quagga] has been suffered by us to retain its liberty so long. Naturalists now however, have discovered the pliability of its disposition, in conjunction with its physical powers; and practical men will probably in time take advantage of the discovery, by adding the couagga [quagga] to the number of species subdued to the general profit, convenience and pleasure of mankind.'

Judging from its low and somewhat laboured pace, the inactive spectator would pronounce the quagga to be a slow and heavy galloper; but it is only necessary to follow its flight a few yards on horseback to be convinced of the rate at which it covers the ground. Singly, in a stern chase, it can laugh at the miserable, conditionless hacks, upon which it is usually hunted by the Boers and Griquas; but when congregated in dense masses, nothing is easier than to turn the flank of the troop, which then immediately sounds the halt, and fronting the pursuer: gazes for a few seconds with distended nostrils, before again neighing the retreat. On nearing their heels, stones, dust and pebbles fly at a surprising rate, periling the eyes and teeth of the pursuer; and when wounded, they prove especially ugly and vicious customers. Amongst other sporting anecdotes with which one of our Hottentot followers occasionally favoured us, when in an amiable humour, was a touching account of the death of his only and beloved brother, Phoebus Cockerlockie, from a fracture of his skull inflicted by the heels of a half disabled quagga, that he had incautiously approached with hostile designs. Had the cranium of the luckless deceased possessed but one third the solidity of that of his surviving relative, this catastrophe could scarcely have occurred. I have myself narrowly escaped from many a well directed salute, and once saw a wretched savage, every finger of whose dexter hand had been stripped off by the long yellow teeth of a wounded male. Of the many specimens killed by us, all the males were entire; no instance coming under my notice of the mutilation which is of such common occurrence amongst those of the *Khur-Guddrey* or wild ass of India, chiefly found on the Runn, or desert of Cutch, and of which nine tenths are actually gelt by the teeth of the jealous sire, the moment they are foaled. If not entitled to a full share of the extravagant eulogiums that have been lavished upon the *Dziggtai* of the wilds of Tartary, 'who snuffeth up the wind at its pleasure', and can distance the fleetest Arabian courser that ever scoured the desert, the quagga, nevertheless, responds to that animal in the distinct zoological regions of southern Africa, no less than to the Asiatic species now referred to; and the habits of each of these elegant solipedal varieties, as well as those which will hereafter be noticed are alike comprehended in the poetical and beautifully graphic description of the wild ass, which has already been quoted at the head of this chapter, from the oldest Book of the world.

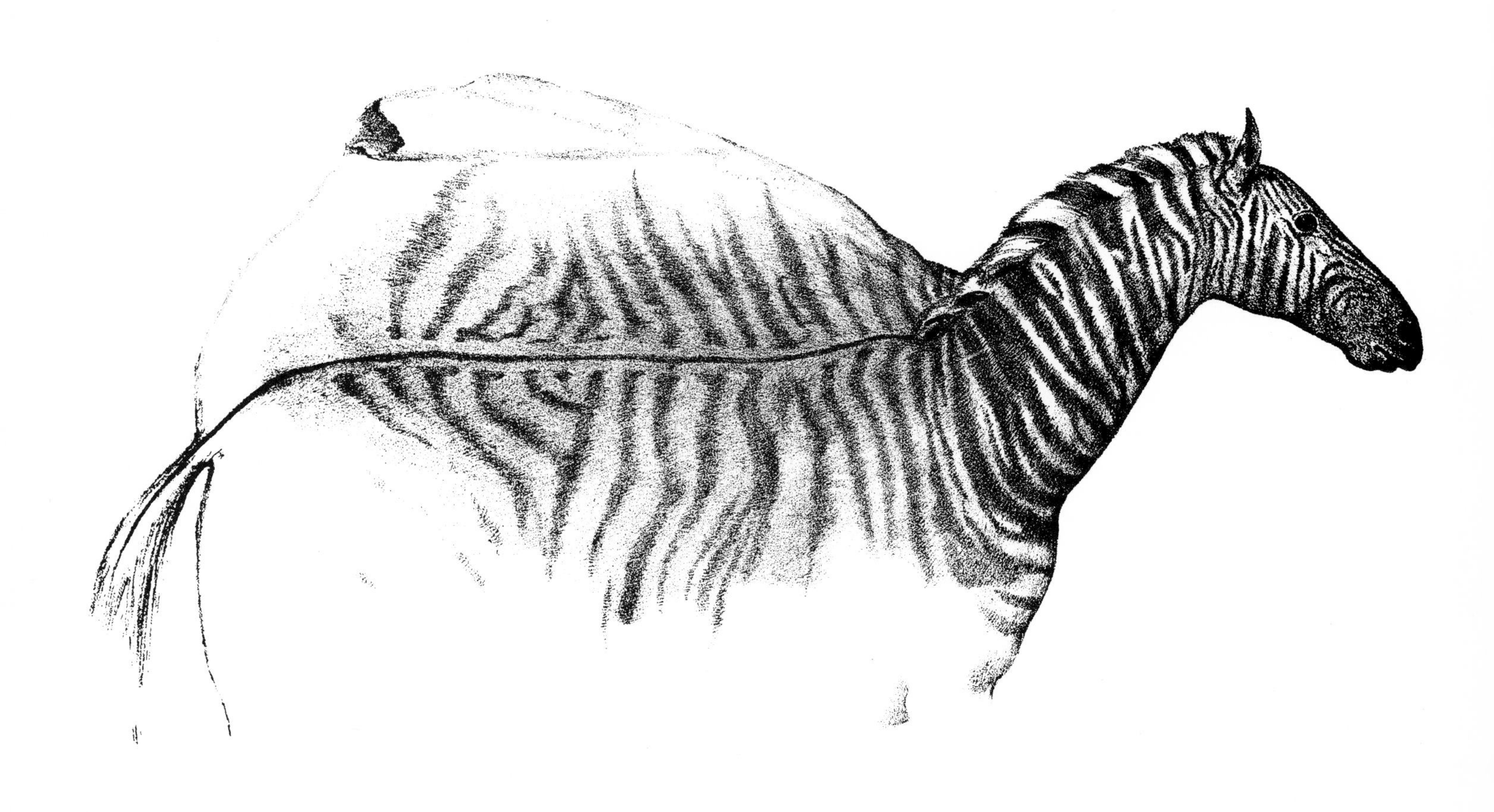

Head and skin of the animal exhibited as a quagga at the Zoological Gardens, Regent's Park

3

Springbok

My home is 'mid the mountain rock
The desert my domain:
The countless springboks form my flock,
Spread o'er the boundless plain.
Song of the Wild Bushman

Amongst the many striking novelties which present themselves to the eye of the traveller in southern Africa, there are perhaps few objects more conspicuous or more beautiful than the dancing herds of graceful springboks which speckle the broad plains of the interior, as well as some of the more remote districts of the Cape Colony. It not infrequently happens indeed, that the wide stretching landscape literally offers no other object to rivet the attention — countless myriads of these interesting ornaments of the desert, which are apparently identical with *tzebi* of the Hebrews being scattered like flocks of sheep over the plains and valleys; abounding, at times, to such an incredible extent, that the whole face of the country, far as the eye can sweep, is absolutely white with their congregated multitudes.

Matchless in the symmetry of its form, the springbok is measurelessly the most elegant and remarkable species of the comprehensive group to which it pertains. The dazzling contrast betwixt the lively cinnamon of its back, and the snowy whiteness of the lower parts, is agreeably heightened by the intensely rich chestnut bands which traverse the flanks — its dark beaming eye with its innocent and lamblike expression of face and the showy folds of gossamer on the haunches — displayed or concealed at the animal's volition — combining to render it one of the most beautiful objects in the animal creation. As the traveller advances over the trackless expanse, hundreds of this delicately formed antelope bound away on either side of his path with meteor-like and sportive velocity, winging their bird-like flight by a quick succession of those singularly elastic leaps, which have given rise to its colonial appellations, and which enable it to surpass as well in swiftness as in grace, almost every other mammaliferous quadruped.

But although frequently found herding by itself, the springbok is more usually detected in the society of gnoos, quaggas, ostriches or blesboks. Fleet as the wind and thoroughly conscious of its own speed, it mingles with their motley herds, sauntering about with an easy careless gait, occasionally with outstretched neck approaching some coquettish doe, and spreading its own glittering white folds so as to effect a sudden and complete metamorphosis of exterior from fawn colour to white. Wariest of the wary, however, the springboks are ever the first to take the alarm, and to lead the retreating column. Pricking their taper ears, and elevating their graceful little heads upon the first appearance of any strange object, a dozen or more trot nimbly off to a distance, and having gazed impatiently for an instant to satisfy themselves of the actual presence of an enemy, putting their white noses to the ground, they begin in colonial phraseology to *pronken* or make a brave show. Unfurling the snowy folds on their haunches so as to display around the elevated scut, a broad white gossamer disk, shaped like the spread tail of a peacock, away they all go with a succession of strange perpendicular bounds, rising with curved loins high into the air, as if they had been struck with battledores, rebounding to the height of ten or twelve feet with the elasticity of corks thrown against a hard floor; vaulting over each other's backs with depressed heads and stiffened limbs, as if engaged in a game at leapfrog; and after appearing for a second as if suspended in the air, clearing at a single spring from ten to fifteen feet of ground without the smallest perceptible exertion — down come all four feet together with a single thump, and nimbly spurning the earth beneath, away they soar again, as if about to take flight, invariably clearing a road or beaten track by a still higher leap than all — as if their natural disposition to regard man as an enemy induced them to mistrust even the ground upon which he had trodden.

The *trek bokken* as the colonists are wont to term the immense migratory swarms of these beautiful antelopes, which to the destruction of every green herb, occasionally inundate the abodes of civilization — not only form one of the most remarkable features in the zoology of southern Africa, but may also be reckoned amongst the most extraordinary examples of the fecundity of animal life. To form any estimate of their numbers on such occasions would be perfectly impossible — the havoc committed in their onward progress falling nothing short of the ravages of a wasting swarm of locusts. Pouring down, like the devastating curse of Egypt, from their native plains in the interior whence they have been driven, after protracted drought, by the failure of the stagnant pools on which they have relied, whole legions of springboks, abandoning the parched soil, throng with one accord to deluge and lay waste the cultivated regions around the Cape; and so effectually does the van of the vast column destroy every vestige of verdure, that the rear is often reduced to positive starvation. The lion has then been seen stalking in the middle of the compressed phalanx, removed little more than a paw's length from his powerless victims; while flocks of sheep have not infrequently been swept away by the living torrent, and no more seen. Ere the morning's dawn, cultivated fields, which the evening before appeared proud of their promising verdure, despite of every precaution that can be taken, are reaped level with the ground; and the grazier, despoiled of his lands, is driven to seek pasture for his flocks elsewhere, until the bountiful thunderclouds reanimating nature, restore vegetation to the burnt up country. Then these unwelcome visitors, whose ranks, during their short but destructive sojourn, have been thinned both by man and beast, retire instinctively to their secluded abodes, to renew their depredation when necessity shall again compel them.

Yet so distinctly has the unerring hand of nature prescribed to each species of antelope the limit of its own cantonment, that whilst those which inhabit the wide and open savannahs, are never known either to wander into the woodlands or climb to higher levels, others, whose locality is restricted to the fen, the forest, or the mountain top, evince no disposition to trespass upon the prairie. Although liberally distributed over every level part of southern Africa, the uninterrupted sandy plains which border upon the equator, may be considered the headquarters of the springbok. In this region of stunted bushes and brackish pools, they increase and multiply to an unlimited extent, and are

III. GAZELLA EUCHORE – THE SPRING BOK.

disturbed by none save by wild beasts, and the yet wilder sons of the desert, who, regarding them as their own flocks, occasionally entrap them in pitfalls, or poison the stagnant waters to which they resort. Like all creatures, however, whose weakness renders them a prey to the more ferocious, their increase bears to their diminution a relative proportion; and though thousands annually fall to glut the prowlers of the waste, their loss is yearly resupplied. Retreating as human society advances, the wilds, the deserts, and the solitude, have still formed their homes. Preferring scorched and open tracts where they are least likely to be assailed with success by any of their numerous enemies, these vigilant and timid animals would appear to select for their haunts, the most bleak and barren heaths — treeless and sometimes shrubless flats, where they browse on the heather and withered herbage, and nibble the bitter succulents which abound in such situations, thriving especially:

O'er the brown Karoo, where the bleating cry
Of the springbok's fawn sounds plaintively.

In common with most gregarious quadrupeds, those of the antilopine tribe more particularly, this species evinces the greatest curiosity at the sight of objects to which it has been unaccustomed — bounding away in the utmost alarm, with a lightness and grace absolutely unrivalled, but suddenly stopping in the midst of its headlong flight, to turn and gaze at the object of its terror. Its usual cry is a feeble bleat, resembling the voice of a lamb, but whilst thus scrutinising strange objects, it utters a sneezing noise, accompanied by an impatient twitching of the head; the taper foot being stamped petulantly on the ground at the same time. The young fawns are easily reared, and in a domesticated state are extremely gentle, playful and confiding; going forth with the flocks to pasture, and constantly forming the cherished pet of the farmer's children, whom they will follow about with the attachment of a dog.

Trusting for their escape to speed alone, in no animal are the senses of sight, of hearing and of smell, found in more exquisite perfection than in the true antelope. Its dark glancing eye, no less than its proverbial symmetry of form, has ever been a theme of poetical enthusiasm; and both have furnished to eastern bards the choicest images wherewith to illustrate perfection in female charms. The most celebrated of our modern poets have employed the same beautiful metaphors; and:

Maidens in whose orient eyes
More than summer sunshine lies

might 'look on those of the gazelle' and envy their long silken fringes and speaking brilliancy. From the increased volume of the auditory cavity, which determines the power of hearing, the ear of the antelope derives great superiority over that of every other ruminating animal; and the powers of scent, as well as the facilities of breathing, are greatly increased by the sack or suborbital pouch, which in different species is found variously developed and more or less capable of contraction and expansion. The antelopes constitute far the largest assemblage in the whole order of ruminants, and although subdivided into numerous small groups or sections, possess in common the distinguishing feature of persistent horns, standing usually above and between the arches of the orbits. Consisting of solid osseous cores externally sheathed over with true horny matter, which increases by the addition of successive layers in proportion to the growth of the internal nucleus, they form part and parcel of the frontal bone, and are consequently never shed like those of the stag. Nothing therefore can be more grating to the ear either of the sportsman or the naturalist, than to hear the antelopes termed deer, not a single species of which tribe exists in southern or central Africa. The horns of all antelopes are simple or unbranched, but whilst some are perfectly smooth, the surface of others, like the lyriform appurtenances of the springbok, are more or less annulated with raised circular rings. Buffon was however mistaken in supposing the age to be indicated by the number of these rings, Pallas having clearly shown that although there is a positive augmentation in their number as the animal advances in age, yet, since the horns themselves increase less and less in volume during each succeeding year of existence, there can subsist no equal relation between the progress of life and the development of the annuli.

Alas! in the Colony of the Cape of Storms, how have the wild sports dwindled from their former prosperity. Those gloomy forests that no longer clothe the base of the cloud capped mountain which frowns over the metropolis were tenanted in ruder times by the noblest as well as by the wisest of the brute creation. But before the strides of civilization, together with the rugged aborigines, have receded also the scarcely more savage quadrupeds; and saving certain diminutive antelopes which will hereafter be noticed as frequenting the sea coast, the springbok now affords the only four-footed game that occurs in any abundance. Man, whether in an uncultivated or civilized state, is ever a hunting animal; *venator* has been his synonym from time immemorial; and this beautiful antelope is consequently slaughtered in vast numbers by the Dutch boers both on account of the pleasant pastime its pursuit affords, and for the sake of the venison, which although lean, is delicate and well tasted. No facilities existing for approach on foot, the sport, as well from necessity as from choice, is universally followed on horseback — a dozen farmers or more, usually assembling for the purpose of *yaking and scutting de wild,* each on his broad shoulder bearing a *roer* or gun, of astounding bore and gigantic dimensions. A large square of ivory which is invariably attached by a stout leathern thong to the muzzle, performs the duty of sight; and,

Plate III: *Gazelle euchore* — springbok of the Cape colonists — *tsepe* of the Kaffirs and Bechuana

Generic Character — Adult male about two feet eight inches high at the shoulder, and two or three inches more at the croup. Extreme length about four feet ten inches. Form characterised by elegance and elasticity. Head small and light; face white; both resembling a lamb's in shape and expression. Horns black, lyrate, robust; twelve or fifteen inches in length, with about twenty complete rings; the tips turned inwards, and generally inclined either forward or backward. A chestnut streak passing from the back of the horns, through the eye, to the nose. General colour of the hair, cinnamon or lively dun above; beneath pure white; the two separated by a broad rich chestnut band passing abruptly along each flank to the shoulder. On the croup are two longitudinal foldings or duplication of the skin, which commence about the middle of the back, and pass over the loins to the tail, bordered by a band of chestnut. The interior of these folds are lined with long silky hair ten or twelve inches in length, of the most dazzling and snowy whiteness, which may be concealed or displayed at pleasure. When the animal is quiescent, a white dorsal stripe only is perceptible, margined with chestnut; but when excited or in motion, the folds are suddenly expanded, so as to form a broad disk spreading over the whole croup, and producing a most singular affect. Legs slender and wiry; white inside only. Nose truly ovine. Lachrymary sinus not remarkably distinct. Ears long, attentuated, and of a dirty white colour. Eyes very full, dark and lustrous, with long dewy lashes. Tail eight inches long, resembling a large white goose quill, bare inside, and terminated by an eccentric tuft of long wavy black hair, posterioriy directed.

Doe similar, but smaller, and of more feminine proportions; with very slender horns, either straight or capriciously bent, exhibiting a few indistinct annuli at their base. Has an udder with two mammae. Still abundant in the colony, and distributed over the arid plains beyond it, in unlimited herds.

it being next to impossible to find a Dutchman who would lend himself to the modern detonating innovations, the apparatus for accomplishing ignition is scarcely less primitive. On a shaggy three-cornered *paard,* whose outward appearance betokens neither acquaintance with the grain bag nor curry comb, sits *Mynheer* Buffel as though ensconced on his easy chair; a *meerschaum* [pipe] of half smoked tobacco, his never failing companion in arms, protruding from the pocket of his greasy waistcoat. He is clad in a jacket, somewhat coarser in the texture than sackcloth; and a pair of tanned sheepskin trousers, commonly called crackers, envelop his nether man. His lower extremities are thrust into pieces of fresh hide, which have accommodated themselves to the shape of his huge feet; and a white felt hat with an ample quaker brim, shades his uncombed head. By his side dangles a magazine of powder, constructed of an entire ox horn of those Brobdignagian dimensions which only Africa can produce; and his loins are girt about with a pouch containing a corresponding supply of two ounce balls. Similar in size and shape of person, similarly arrayed, and similarly equipped, forth ride the boers to the hunting ground, distributing themselves over the plain, and approaching at a slow pace as near as the game will permit. Like most other antelopes the springbok almost invariably runs against the wind when alarmed. By preserving the windward gauge therefore, to use a nautical expression, and galloping on a diagonal course, nothing is easier, upon a tolerable horse, than to intersect their path, and thus compel the whole herd to cross within a few yards of the gun:

In speed
They sprightly put their faith, and roused by fear
Give all their swift aerial forms to flight;
Against the breeze they dart that way the more,
To leave the murderer's lessening cry behind.

As the white rumped bucks sweep past, harlequin-like, by a succession of magic bounds, ricochetting over each other's heads as if struck with a cricket bat, and invariably following every four or five springs by as many strokes of a gallop — the Dutchman, vaulting heavily from the well padded saddle, delivers his shot, first casting the bridle over the head of the perfectly trained horse, which will stand if necessary for hours together without attempting to stir from the spot. Delicate and fragile as the springbok appears, many a choice morsel of its venison nevertheless escapes the spit or the cabob stick, after the successful marksman has counted it his own. What boots the loss of a limb? Every antelope can run better upon three legs than upon four and a heavy bullet may pass through and through the tender form of one of these tough lived little animals without so much as causing its pace to slacken; although, after keeping up the race for some distance with its more fortunate *confréres,* it is destined to sink upon the wide plain and close its bright eye for ever.

The mystic operation of breaking, or in vulgar phraseology, of cutting up the quarry, preparatory to packing it away behind the saddle, immediately follows. The head and offal having first been removed, and either thrown to the vultures, or quarreled for by the Hottentot attendants, whose perquisite they are acknowledged to be, the cavity is stuffed with whatever grass or herbs may be obtainable. A portion of the front skin being left entire, the knee joints are then divided, and the tarsal bones stripped to the fetlock; the bones of the pelvis are also cut through, and the *couteau de chasse* introduced between the two middle vertebrae of the spine to make it ride steady. The carcase, which in an adult buck is fully as heavy as that of the largest sheep, having then with some difficulty been thrown across the horse's crupper, the dangling tarsal bones are twisted under the girths on either side in order to secure it in that position, and Mynheer resumes his saddle and his sport. Of a truth a field of portly boers fully harnessed, pricking their wretched garrons over the plain, and having each a cumbrous carcase bumping at his breech, is a sight passing goodly to behold. Two springboks may even thus be carried without alarming inconvenience to the equestrian; but as the steed cannot of course under such circumstances move beyond a foot's pace, it is usual to bring pack horses into the field — although in default thereof, and as a *dernier ressort,* a third carcase may still be thrown across the saddle. This arrangement is little patronized by the boers, who at best are sorry pedestrians, but it was one to which, in the absence of assistance, I was frequently compelled to have recourse. Having no fear of the *sjambok* before their sullen sunken eyes, the Hottentots of our party greatly preferred shooting on their own account, to assisting me in the toils of the chase, which indeed they rarely condescended to do. The most brilliant exploit of venery claimed by these lazy gentlemen during the whole expedition, was achieved before crossing the colonial boundary, when three of the best shots having wheedled us out of a supply of ammunition to admit of their proving their new *roers* — expended no less than six rounds of it upon a feeble fawn which had recently been dropped under a thorn bush. Failing altogether in their murderous designs, the little wretch was ultimately taken prisoner, only alas to become food for our famished Zoroastian domestic, whose religious antipathies prevented his even tasting the flesh of any animal that wore a bovine expression of face, and who, but for this timely windfall, might peradventure have been starved.

Head of springbok, as preserved by Captain Harris

4

Kokoon

Upon the forehead of the bull, the horns stand close and near,
From out the broad and wrinkled skull, like daggers they appear.
His neck is massy like the trunk of some old knotted tree,
Whereon the monster's shaggy mane, like billows curled ye see.

To solve the mysterious causes that control the apparently capricious distribution of animal forms, has always been considered one of the most difficult problems in the grand scheme of the creation. An Almighty fiat, 'Thus far shalt thou come but no farther, has fixed the unalterable limit to the range of every creature, however insignificant; but the nature of the laws, unconnected either with congenial food or temperature, by which are regulated the phenomena of local dispersion, have hitherto been most effectually concealed from human research. In no quarter of the universe, perhaps, are these phenomena more remarkable than in Africa, and amongst the ten thousand which might be adduced, not the least conspicuous is the sudden appearance to the north of the Orange River, of the subject of the annexed portrait. Instantly after crossing that stream, the kokoon or brindled gnoo, usurps the place of the white tailed species: and although herds of the former may actually be seen grazing on the northern bank, not a single individual has ever been known to pass the barrier. Equally ungainly in point of figure, the animal now delineated differs materially from its brother of the same genus, from which, at the greatest distance, it is readily distinguishable by its black mane and tail, more elevated withers, and clumsier gait. Whilst, however, it possesses neither the spirit, activity nor speed of its absurd congener, it is in many respects fully as whimsical, and exhibits in all its peculiarities, even a still greater predominancy towards the bovine character.

In the kokoon, the forehand bears to the rest of the frame a most remarkable disproportion. The ponderous neck and head are uniformly sunk below the level of the hunch, whilst the forelegs which are slender and crooked at the knee, are thrown so far behind the shoulder as to give the animal the semblance of being ill-balanced and under-limbed — an appearance which is still further augmented by cat-hams and by great obliquity of the crupper. The ludicrously aquiline nose and the small black leering eyes, placed like those of the hippopotamus, almost at the summit of the cranium — together impart to the face an almost idiotic expression. Looming at a little distance even blacker than night, the forehand appears like that of the American Bonassus, to be completely muffled in long shaggy hair; although on closer inspection this is found to be limited to an ample mane and a streaming beard. No third variety of the gnoo occurs in southern Africa and the actual existence thereof is greatly to be questioned. By the Dutch boers the present species is termed the bastaard or blauw wilde beest, i.e. spurious or blue gnoo; throughout the country of the Bechuana as far to the tropic, it is recognised as the kokoon, and the Hottentot tribes designate it the kaop or baas, both of which terms signifying master, refer in all probability to its bold and terrific bearing.

When excited by the appearance of any suspicious object, or aroused by any unusual noise, the kokoon is wont to appear much more grim and ferocious than it actually proves — not infrequently approaching with an air of defiance as if resolved to do battle with the hunter, but decamping upon the very first exhibition of hostility on his part. On being pursued, the herd bring their aquiline noses low between their knees, and flourishing their streaming black tails tear away in long regular files at a furious gallop; wheeling curiously about, at the distance of two or three hundred yards, advancing boldly towards the danger, tossing their shaggy heads in a threatening manner — presently making a sudden stop, presenting an impenetrable front of horns and staring wildly at the object of their mistrust. The slightest demonstration, however, is sufficient to put the whole squadron to flight, when they make a somewhat shorter excursion, again wheeling in a circle, showing a more menacing and imposing front than before and most probably taking up their position within sure rifle range. When engaged in grazing they have an extremely dull and clumsy appearance and at a little distance might often be mistaken for wild buffaloes; but their usual manner is sportive — at one moment standing to gaze at nothing, and at the next scampering over the plain without any apparent object in view, making various grotesque curvets and plunges, with their preposterous Bonassus-looking heads held down between the forelegs. Blustering along at a little distance, the solitary bulls loom even more like the whiskered monarch of the forest, than do their white tailed congeners; the resemblance being not a little enhanced by their possessing, like the furious white Uri, produced in days of yore in the forest of Caledonia, *jubam densam, ac demissam instar leonis,* or as Holinshed has it, 'crisp and curled manes like unto fiers leonis!'

It would be difficult for those who have never visited the interior of southern Africa, to form even a remote conception of the countless herds of this ungainly quadruped, which are occasionally to be met with on the bosom of her broad plains. Lack of water, the curse and the prevailing feature of these savage regions, frequently compels the *ferae naturae* to assemble in countless companies around the last dregs of expiring moisture, without reference either to caste or hereditary animosities; and on such occasions the picture they present to the eye of the sportsman, if one of no common enchantment. Delighting in shade, the brindled gnoo especially resorts to level tracts, thinly sprinkled with the picturesque and feathery mimosa, reclining beneath spreading clumps of which, or scattered over the boundless landscape like 'cattle grazing upon a thousand hills,' they impart to the sylvan scene a truly pastoral effect. At a single *coup d'oeil,* may be seen mixed multitudes of those inseparable friends the kokoon and Burchell's zebra — the Damon and Pythias of the brute creation — interspersed with gaily painted groups of the hartebeest and sassaybe, both seeming to have just escaped from the hands of the sign dauber. Some are quietly cropping the short grass and others are huddled together beneath the shadow cast by some tall umbrella shaped mokaala, the tree that forms the favourite food of the stately giraffe. From the

IV. CATOBLEPAS GORGON.– THE BRINDLED GNOO.

spreading boughs of this magnificent species of acacia, the only approach to a tree which may be seen in these regions, dangle clusters of evergreen mistletoe, sparkling with scarlet berries. And under the deep shadow cast on the sunny landscape by yonder clump, the twisted branches of which literally groan under the weight of the huge haystack-looking nests of the industrious little republican bird [loxia socia; the social gresbeak], stand the sombre and massive figures of a pair of unwieldy elands, indolently defending their sleek, pursy sides from the buzzing persecutions of a host of yellow-bodied cattle flies, or leisurely chewing the cud in the midst of a knot of recumbent gnoos, whose high humps per above their elliptical horns. Mixed squads of kokoons and zebras are practising their wild gambols over the level plain — kicking, frolicking, butting and pursuing each other with untiring perseverance. Here a pair of exasperated combatants are engaged in a deadly joust, in the presence of a group of dames, who, as of old, will bestow their favours on the most valiant. Battering their hard fronts against each other, tossing their curled manes aloft and lashing their swarthy sides with their strength tails, their fierce little round eyes glisten the while, like sparks of fire beneath their shaggy forelocks. Umpire-like on one side of the scene of this gentle passage of arms, behold a few solitary bulls at gaze, posted apparently as sentinels and standing at attention full to the front, their dark eyes glancing wildly from the duellists to the enemy and a deep hollow moan occasionally escaping from their innermost recesses. The human foe still approaches and is observed to be armed with weapons of offence! Up go their taper heels with a sideling flourish, the signal for the cessation of intestine hostilities, and for an indiscriminate retreat. With their high Roman noses almost raking the earth, *sauve qui peut,* away they scour in headlong haste, turning up the sand by bushels-full. Now the sleek variegated coats of a well-drilled troop of Burchell's zebras glisten in the rays of the sun as they charge furiously past in close squadron — at one moment obscured under the gloom of an avenue of spreading mokaala trees — at the next emerging in unbroken files, followed by a smoke-like pillar of dust, which traces their serpentine course long after they have disappeared over the brow of yon gentle eminence. Crack goes the rifle, and the leading gnoo of the next sable section, arrested in full career, cuts three or four perfect somersaults, measures his shaggy length upon the ground, and is trampled underfoot of his thronging companions. Troop upon troop now pour in from every quarter and continue to join each other, until the whole plains seems literally alive; and thousands still bearing down from every point of the compass, a vast extent of country, which presently becomes chequered white and black with their congregated masses, at length presents the appearance of a moving mass of game. The clatter of their hoofs becomes perfectly astounding and can be compared to nothing but a din of a tremendous charge of cavalry, or the rushing of a mighty tempest. Their incredible numbers so impede their onward progress, that the horseman experiences no difficulty in closing with the motley band. As the panic caused by the repeated reports of his rifle increase, the rear ranks pressing tumultuously upon the heels of the leaders of the retreating phalanx, cause indescribable confusion. Dense clouds of dust hover over them and the long necks of troops of ostriches are to be seen, towering above the heads of their less gigantic neighbours and sailing past with astonishing rapidity. Groups of purple sassaybes and brilliant red and yellow hartebeests, charging down from every direction, likewise lend their aid — whilst a host of hungry vultures, which wheeling in airy circles like small specks in the firmament, have been gradually descending and now stoop with the velocity of lightning as each succeeding flash of the deadly tube gives token of prey — serve to complete a picture which must be seen to be understood and which beggars all attempt at description:

Rolling and blackening, swarms succeeding swarms,
With deeper murmurs and more hoarse alarms,
Dusky they spread, in close embodied crowds,
And o'er the vales descend in living clouds.

It was on the banks of the Meritsane, south of the twenty sixth parallel of latitude, that we first witnessed one of these grand and imposing spectacles. Countless herds, which had congregated from every quarter to drink of the stagnant waters of that river, literally covered the wide extended landscape for many miles, nor could the numbers assembled have fallen short of fifteen or twenty thousand. 'You should have seen this ground ten years ago,' is the observation which usually grates on the ear of the disappointed sportsman who visits some boasted hunting grounds in India, only to find it tenantless; and so little game had been seen by our party previous to reaching this river, that we were strongly tempted to treat the accounts that had been given of its abundance, as altogether fabulous. With this noble panorama, however, we opened our campaign against the African fauna. A host of famished savages scoured in our wake, dexterously despatching the wounded animals, as they fell, by a touch on the spine with the point of an assegai — hastily covering up the carcases with thorn branches, to secure them from the voracity of the impatient vultures, which stooped in myriads and seeming utterly heedless of the presence of man, plucked out the eyes of the yet living victims. Never perhaps has there been witnessed such an onslaught since the days:

When Nimrod bold,
That mighty hunter, first made war on beasts,
And stained the woodland green with purple dye.

Although the kokoon instantly disappeared after we had crossed the Likwa on our return to the colony, it was more or less abundant throughout our northern perigrinations. On the grassy

Plate IV: *Catoblepas gorgon* — kokoon or brindled gnoo — *bastaard* or *blauw wilde beest* of the Cape colonists — *kokoon* of the Bechuana — *kaop* or *baas* of the Namaquas and Hottentots

Generic Character — Adult male about four feet six inches high at the shoulders, and nine feet eight inches in extreme length. Head, neck and shoulders, extravagantly thick and powerful. Withers very elevated, forming a positive hump, and carcase very deep. Neck massy, but not arched. Head nearly two feet in length. Nose ridiculously aquiline and covered with extremely coarse black grizzled hair. Muzzle broad, square and flabby; bare, with ample hanging nostrils; the latter furnished internally with a moveable valve. Horns black, placed horizontally on the summit of the forehead, which is prolonged between them; the points turned upwards and then acutely inwards; a few rugosities at the base forming a sort of false burr. A long flowing black mane on the neck, glossy, curled and extending beyond the withers, so as to add considerably to their height and argument the appearance of obliquity in the back. Chin covered with a copious bristly black beard, frizzled and descending along the dewlap to the brisket. Crupper drooping. Tail equine, black, flowing, wavy, nearly three feet in length and reaching to the heels. Ears small and pointed. Eyes small, black and piercing; mounted very high in the head. A large glandulous naked spot of an oblong form below each eye, distilling a white viscous humour. Legs cervine, slender and sinewy: crooked at the knee. Hoofs blue-black, small and pointed. Coat close and silky. General colour dark ashy grey, clouded with sepia and variegated with obscure vertical streaks or brindles. Four or five horizontal stripes on each arm.

Female precisely similar, but on a smaller and more feminine scale. Very gregarious. Never found to the southward of the Orange River. Inhabits the wooded plains of the interior in vast herds.

slopes that form the environs of the Cashan mountains, large herds were constantly to be seen, and from nearly our last encampment on the willow-grown Limpopo [River], only a few miles south of the tropic, a large troop of them — pursued through a valley by an infuriated rhinoceros, which had been worried almost to madness by the peppering of the Hottentots — dashed into a narrow defile leading through the hills. Having reconnoitred the ground not an instant before, I galloped to the only other outlet and stationing myself behind an abutting rock, disposed of two with each barrel, the muzzle of my rifle being only a few yards removed from the dense phalanx, which, still goaded on by the stiff horn of the rhinoceros, rushed at the top of their speed through the opening, as closely packed together as a Manchester mob. Generally speaking it was found requisite to hunt these animals on horseback; but from the screen of the advancing caravan, I repeatedly slew them at long balls, a rifle bullet thrown from a distance of even three or four hundred yards into the middle of a squad, being nearly certain of tripping up somebody. The flesh of the kokoon, like that of the white tailed gnoo, although lean, is tender and palatable, not much unlike beef in grain. It is greatly sought after by the savages, who entrap the animal in a variety of ways hereafter to be described, converting the hides into mantles, by dressing them without removing the shaggy hair of the mane and beard, which prove highly ornamental tippets.

The kokoon is most abundantly found in level grassy tracts, intersected by gentle slopes, where green lawns are shaded by clumps and labyrinths of stately trees, distributed with almost park-like regularity. Among the many species of mimosa which occur in these regions, the *acacia giraffae* is the most remarkable, its spreading umbrella-shaped top casting a delicious umbrage, while the gaudy yellow blossoms shaped like a powder puff, with which they are covered, fill the atmosphere with an aromatic and overpowering perfume. The boughs of many are decorated with green clusters of mistletoe, the bright scarlet berries hanging from which prove highly ornamental; and the huge thatched nests of the *loxia socia* which are piled up amongst the branches of others, attract the attention of the traveller at every step — the little speckle-headed tenants fluttering round their hive like a busy swarm of bees, or assembled in congress upon some old withered branch, where they perch in a long row and gravely discuss the important affairs of the commonwealth. The banks of the Orange River constitute the southern limit to the range of this industrious little architect, which is about the size and has much the appearance of the common house sparrow that, without the smallest variation, pesters mankind in every known part of the globe. To this species of the feathered race are exclusively confined those republican principles which actuate a number of individuals to associate; and clubbing their labour, to build their cities under one common roof. A large and lofty tree having usually been selected, the little community proceed heart and hand to construct the public canopy, in the completion of which all are equally interested; and having piled up a sufficient quantity of coarse grass to serve as a general roof, each pair constructs its own nest beneath, of similar materials — placing them side by side, until the lower surface of the mass exhibits the perforated appearance of a honey-comb. Never frequenting the old nests a second season, but year after year adding a fresh tier to the under part of the old pile, it not infrequently occurs, that although firmly interwoven with the branches of the tree to which it is suspended, and often embracing also within its substance a portion of the stem, the superincumbent weight of the mass at length causes the fall of the support, and with it, the annihilation of the overgrown fabric.

Head of kokoon, as preserved by Captain Harris

5

Burchell's Zebra

Oh yes, there is freedom, and joy, and pride,
Afar in the desert alone to ride!
There is rapture to vault on the champing steed,
And to bound away with the eagle's speed;
With the death-fraught firelock in my hand,
The only law of the desert land.

Intermediate in point of colouring betwixt the common quagga and the true zebra, the brilliant species of the equine genus here portrayed, supplants the first named of its allies to the north of the Orange River, as does the kokoon, its congener the gnoo; and seldom congregating in herds of fewer than eighty or a hundred, it abounds to a great extent in all the districts included between that noble stream and the southern tropic. Occupying the same regions and delighting in the same pastures as the brindled gnoo, rarely is it to be seen unless in the companionship of that fantastic animal, whose presence would appear to be almost indispensable to its happiness. It is singular enough that the members of two families so perfectly foreign to each other, should display so great a predilection for each other's society, uniformly intermixing as they do, and herding together in bonds of the closest friendship. Fierce, strong, fleet and surpassingly beautiful, there is perhaps no quadruped in the creation, not even excepting the mountain zebra, more splendidly attired, or presenting a picture of more singularly attractive beauty, than this free-born of the desert. It would be difficult to convey to the uninitiated a suitable idea of the sparkling effect produced by their vivid and strikingly contrasted convey to the uninitiated a suitable idea of the sparkling effect produced by their vivid and strikingly contrasted colours, when seen pawing in the valley in all the pride of conscious liberty, or flying in compact columns before the equestrian foe; but I shall nevertheless attempt the description of a scene which is one of every day occurrence in the interior wilderness of southern Africa.

Mixed up with the tracks of the kokoon, the prints left by the compact hoofs of a herd of Burchell's zebras are perceived in the naked sand, and presently afterwards a small troop consisting of both species — the vanguard of a vast horde — is observed leisurely grazing in the distance. An extensive plain of glaring red sand exhibits here and there patches of sun burnt herbage, interspersed with tufts of the prickly cactus; the landscape being scantily shaded by occasional clumps of light plume-shaped mimosas, and the view abounded by a trivial ridge of distant blue hills.

Bare are those sands, yet smiling there,
Th' acacia waves her yellow hair,
Lonely and sweet, nor loved the less,
For flowering in the wilderness.

Anon, a dark pillar of dust arises from the plain, and undisturbed by any breath in heaven, mounts upwards to the clear azure sky like a wreath of smoke — three ill omened vultures soaring in circles above it. Nearer and more near, rolls on the thickening column, until several dark living objects are shortly perceived dancing beneath it. Emerging from the obscurity, their glossy and exquisitely variegated coats glittering in the sun's rays, *ventre au terre,* the head of the column of a Burchell's zebras next appears, and instantly afterwards the serried horde sweeps past in gallant array, their hoofs clattering on the hard ground like a regiment of dragoons. Tearing by at racing speed, straining neck and neck with their shaggy and whimsical looking bovine allies, their own striped and proudly curved necks seem as though they were clothed with thunder, and their snowy tails are streaming behind them. Now the troop has wheeled and halted for an instant to survey the foe. A powerful stallion advances a few paces with distended nostrils and stately gait, his mane newly hogged and his ample switching his gaily chequered thighs. Hastily reconnoitring the huntsman, he snorts wildly and instantly gallops back to his cohort. Away they scour again, neighing and tossing their striped heads aloft, switching their light mule-like tails in all the pride of fleetness and freedom. Another halt and another reconnaissance. Her small equine ears laid viciously down, a skittish mare has now fallen out of the ranks, and is in the act of delivering both her active heels plump into the ribs of an admirer, whose wantonness has prompted him to seize a tempting opportunity for inflicting upon her sternum an amorous bite. And now, with a neigh of exultation and a vain glorious toss of her coquettish head, free and unfettered as the wind, away she careers again, still waited upon by her lover, who is nothing daunted by his rebuff — and their forms are finally concealed by the cloud which follows the heels of the again retreating squadron.

Thus moving in compact bodies, this beautiful animal, like its brother already described, may be ridden up to and slain with little difficulty; although — carrying no weight, and being withal passing speedy — it could puzzle the best horse in a single chase. A very short run was sufficient to seal the fate of three stallions out of the first herd I met with. Not having seen a single human being either before or during the chase, I believed myself perfectly alone, but no sooner had I dismounted to secure the game, than a woolly head protruded itself from behind every diminutive bush, and in an instant I was surrounded by upwards of thirty hungry savages, who having, by not to be mistaken signs, expressed their unqualified approbation of my performance, proceeded uninvited to devour the carcases with frightful avidity — greedily drinking the blood, besmearing their bodies with the yellow fat, and not leaving even so much as the entrails for the disappointed birds of prey. A large mixed herd of sassaybes and zebras, alarmed by the sudden appearance of our cavalcade, charged past me on another occasion so close that one of the latter fell to each barrel of my rifle, and was in like manner immediately cut up by the savages, the remnant, which they could not eat, being spitted on their assegais to dry. So voracious and impatient were these gentlemen, that a splendid stallion whose hinder leg I had fractured, and whom I had left alive on the plain with the design of eventually driving him to the wagons to stand for his portrait, was absolutely devoured before I could return to the spot; whilst killing other two out of the herd, the villians had stolen behind him as he sulked, and making a long arm, had slipped an assegai into his heart. The scattered inhabitants of the part of the country

V. EQUUS BURCHELLII.– BURCHELL'S ZEBRA.

in which this occurred, and in which we found the zebra in greatest abundance, are the remnants of various Bechuana tribes, which have been despoiled by the strong arm of the conqueror. Living in small communities, these indigent wretches are utterly destitute of cattle, and depend entirely for subsistence upon locusts, or such game as chance may direct to their pitfalls. Crowds of them, attracted by prey, hovered around us during most of our hunting excursions; and having obtained a supply of meat, with the luxuries of snuff and tobacco, for which they were constantly importuning under the denomination of *lishuena* and *muchuco,* they composed themselves to sleep, appearing to be in the enjoyment of as much happiness as man, in a state of mere animal existence, probably ever attains.

Xenophon, when describing the chase of the wild ass on the plains of Mesopotamia, during the march of the army of the younger Cyrus, declares the flesh of that animal to have been found on trial fully as well flavoured, but even more tender, than that of the red deer! The savage epicures of southern Africa would certainly appear to entertain the same sentiments with respect to that of the zebra, although to us it appeared infinitely more rank, oily and carrion-like, than horse-flesh. Many of our savage associates had their incisorial teeth filed to a point, probably to admit of their more readily separating the tough fibres; and at one time even our own followers affected to prefer zebra's flesh to excellent mutton, which John April, on the part of the fraternity, expressed their inability to eat on account of its fatness. Latterly, however, the lazy rascals became somewhat less dainty; mutton was actually eaten, and the flesh of the zebra rejected, upon the score of a tradition that those who ate long of the latter invariably became striped! The fact of the ostrich and wild ass mixing together with a seeming relish for each other's society, which was also remarked by Xenophon, is likewise observable with reference to Burchell's zebra, the spire-like neck of the gigantic camel-bird being very commonly seen towering in the midst of the richly painted herd.

Beautifully clad by the hand of nature; possessing much of the graceful symmetry of the horse, with great bone and muscular power, united to easy and stylish action — thus combining comeliness of figure with solidity of form. *Equus Burchellii,* if subjugated and domesticated, would assuredly make the best pony in the world. Although it admits of being tamed to a certain extent with considerable facility — a half domesticated specimen with a jockey on its brindled back being occasionally exposed in Cape Town for sale — it has hitherto contrived to evade the yoke of servitude. The love of liberty, which in our own species is extolled to the skies, never fails when found in the animal creation, to bring reproach under the denomination of obstinacy and vice; and those persons who have had the best opportunities of becoming acquainted with the character of this species, pronounce it, even in its most tractable state, as wicked, treacherous, obstinate and fickle. The voice of this free-born of the desert has no analogy to the discordant braying of the ass, but consists of a shrill abrupt neigh, which may be likened to the barking of a dog, as heard by a passer by, from the interior of a house. The senses of sight, hearing and smell, are extremely delicate. The slightest noise or motion, no less than the appearance of any object that is unfamiliar, at once rivets their gaze, and causes them to stop and listen with the utmost attention — any taint in the air, equally attracting their olfactory organs. Instinct having taught these beautiful animals that in union consists their strength, they combine in a compact group when menaced by an attack either from man or beast; and if overtaken by the foe, they unite for mutual defence with their heads together in a close circular band, presenting their heels to the enemy, and dealing out kicks in equal force and abundance. Beset on all sides, or partially crippled, they rear on their hinder legs, fly at the adversary with jaws distended, and use both teeth and heels with the greatest freedom.

The wagons having started betimes one delightful morning towards the Meritsane River, which was to be our next stage, I turned off the road, if so a few wheel ruts may be termed, in pursuit of a troop of brindled gnoos, and presently came upon another, which was joined by a third still larger — then by a vast herd of zebras, and again by more gnoos, with sassaybes and hartebeests, pouring down from every quarter in the manner noticed in the preceding chapter, until the landscape absolutely presented the appearance of a moving mass of game. Closing with their front ranks and riding parallel to the cohort in order to escape the dust and pebbles which were cast up by their hoofs, I dismounted as opportunity offered — firing both barrels of my rifle into the retreating phalanx, and leaving the ground behind me strewed with the slain. 'In all guns there is danger, but in a double gun there is double danger,' was the aphorism of a sporting gentleman of the olden schools, who held second barrels in most salutary dread: and doubtless the ghosts of the slaughtered gnoos could testify to its correctness! Still unsatisfied, I could not resist the temptation of mixing yet again with the fugitives, firing and reloading until my jaded horse suddenly exhibited symptoms of distress, and shortly afterwards was unable to move. Discovering at this moment that I had dropped a pocket compass which I carried in preference to a watch — and being unwilling to lose so valuable an ally — I turned loose my steed to crop the scanty grass, and carefully retraced by steps several miles in search of it without success, the print of my horse's hoofs being at length obliterated in those of the countless herds which had crossed the plain. Completely absorbed in the chase, I had retained a very imperfect idea of my locality, but returning to my horse, I led him in what I believed to be a north-easterly direction, knowing from a sketch of the country which had been given me at Litakoo by our excellent friend Mr Moffat, and which together with drawing materials, I always carried about me, that that course would eventually bring me to the Meritsane. Seating myself under a tree, I repeatedly and deliberately scanned the heavens in order to satisfy myself of the direction, and after dragging my weary horse nearly the whole of the day under a burning sun, my flagging spirits were at length revived by the appearance of several villages. Under other circumstances, I should have avoided intercourse with their inhospitable inmates, but dying with thirst, I eagerly entered each in succession, and to my inexpressible disappointment, found them deserted. Evidence existing to their having been recently inhabited, I shot a hartebeest, in the hope that the smell of meat might attract some straggler to the spot. But no! Though the keen sighted vultures, that were my only attendants, descended in multitudes, not one woolly headed negro appeared to dispute the prey. In many of the trees I observed large

Plate V: *Equus burchellii* — Burchell's zebra — *bonte quagga* of the Cape colonists — *peetsey* of the Matabili and Bechuana

Generic Character — Male measures four feet six inches high at the shoulder, and eight feet six inches from the nose to the point of the tail. Figure sturdy, but graceful. Carcase round. Limbs clean and muscular, rather less robust than those of the quagga. Crest remarkably arched and surmounted by a standing mane, hogged, five inches high and banded black and white alternately. Ears and tail equine; the latter thirty five inches long, white and flowing; muzzle black. Coat short and glossy, general ground colour of the head, neck and body lively sienna, capriciously but harmoniously banded with black and deep brown transverse stripes, imparting a brilliant affect and arranged singly and doubly so as to form various figures, all unconnected with the dorsal line which widens over the croup. Belly and legs pure white. Obscure traces of black transverse markings on the arm. Bare spots above the knees on the inside.

Female similar. Has an udder with four mammae. Inhabits the plain country beyond the Gareep or Orange River, in immense herds, but is never found to the southward of that stream.

thatched houses resembling haystacks; and under the impression that these had been erected in so singular a position by the natives, as a measure of security against the lions, whose recent tracks I could distinguish in every direction. I ascended more than one in the hope of at least finding some vessel containing water. Alas! they proved to be the habitations of large communities of social grosbeaks, those winged republicans already described, but of whose architecture and magnificent edifices, I had until then entertained a very inadequate conception. Faint and bewildered, my prospects began to brighten as the shadows of evening lengthened. Large troops of ostriches running in one direction, plainly indicated that I was approaching water: and immediately afterwards, I struck into a path impressed with the footmarks of women and children, soon arriving at a nearly dry river, which, running east and west, I at once concluded to be that of which I was in search.

Those only who have suffered as I did during that day from prolonged thirst, can form a competent idea of the delight, and I may add, energy, afforded me by the first draught of the putrid waters of the Meritsane. They equally invigorated my exhausted steed, whom I mounted immediately, and cantered up the bank of the river, in order if possible to reach the wagons before dark. The banks are precipitous — the channel deep, broken and rocky: clusters of reeds and long grass indicating those spots which retain the water during the hot months. It was with no small difficulty, after crossing the river, that I forced my way through the broad belt of tangled bushes which margined the edge. The moonless night was fast closing around, and my weary horse again began to droop. The lions, commencing their nightly prowl, were roaring in all directions, and no friendly fire or beacon presenting itself to my view, the only alternative was to bivouac where I was, and to renew my search in the morning. Kindling a fire, I formed a thick bush into a pretty secure hut, by cutting away the middle, and closing the entrance with thorn branches; and having knee-haltered my horse to prevent his straying, I proceeded to dine upon a guinea fowl — whose head I had fortunately knocked off with a rifle ball, as the speckled fowl roosted with many others on the tree overhead — concluding the repast with another draught of impure water. Hoping to descry a beacon fire I again ascended the tallest tree, but my eye ranged round the gloomy horizon in vain. The monarchs of the forest now roared incessantly and so alarmed my horse that I was obliged repeatedly to discharge my rifle in order to give him confidence. It was piercingly cold, and all my fuel being expended, I suffered as much from chill and cramp, as I had done during the day from the scorching heat. About three o'clock however, completely overcome by fatigue, I could keep my eyes open no longer, but commending myself to the protecting care of Providence, fell into a profound sleep.

My first thoughts, on opening my eyes in the morning, were naturally of my horse. Starting from my heathy bed, and extricating myself with some difficulty from the *abattis* behind which I was ensconced, I hastened to the spot where I had last seen him, but his place was empty. I roamed everywhere in search of him, and ascended every tree which offered a good look out, but he was nowhere to be seen. It was more than probable that he had been eaten by lions, but when I had almost given up the search in despair, and was reluctantly resolving to depart without him, to my joy I at length found his footmark and traced him to a deep hollow near the river's brink, where he was quietly grazing. The night's rest, if so it could be called, had so far restored him to strength, that I forthwith pursued my journey along the bank of the river, which I now recrossed opposite to the site of some former scene of strife, marked by numerous human skeletons, bleached by exposure. A little farther on I disturbed a large lion which walked slowly off, occasionally stopping and looking sulkily over his shoulder, as he deliberately ascended the opposite bank. In the course of half an hour, I reached the end of dense jungle, and immediately discovered the wagon road; but as I could detect no recent traces upon it, I turned southward and after riding seven or eight miles in the direction of our last encampment, had the unspeakable satisfaction of perceiving the white wagons drawn up under a spreading tree in the middle of the plain. A volley from my rifle, fired at a little distance from the camp, had already relieved the anxiety of my companion and followers, who, in consequence of the unexpected length of the march, had been compelled when darkness overtook them, to halt in that position. During the whole night they had entertained the most gloomy forebodings on my account — *Coeur de Lion,* my valet, perching himself, pipe in mouth, on his favourite post on the wagon top, and exclaiming with agonised accents every ten minutes 'I don't see master.' Having, however, tasted little nourishment for thirty hours, it will easily be understood why I was not over attentive to his anecdotes — introduced apropos of my adventures, of sundry luckless pilgrims of his acquaintance, who had been torn piecemeal by lions, or toasted upon the assegais of the cannibals!

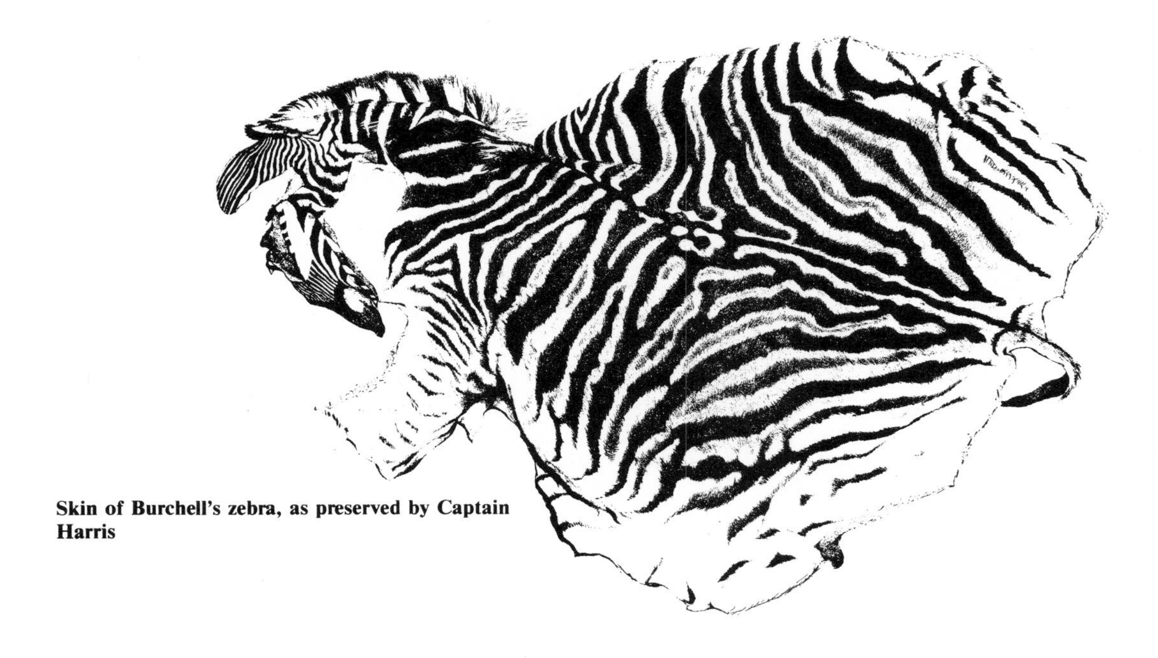

Skin of Burchell's zebra, as preserved by Captain Harris

6

Eland

Then they cast on their gownes of grene,
And took theyr bowes each one;
And the merrye-men away to the grene forrest,
All a shooting forth are gone.
We will kill a fat bucke then said bold Robyn Hoode,
And dress it on the way side here,
Go kill me a bucke, quoth bold Robyn Hoode,
Go slay me a faire fat deere.

Obesity forming one of the exclusive prerogatives of African royalty, it is not surprising that the eland — more lusty, fat and well looking than any other wild quadruped — should assume unto himself an air of princely consequence. 'Lord of an hundred does,' amongst which he moves with all the pomp and self-importance of a nabob in his harem, the stately bull is at once the most corpulent, one of the most ponderous, and certainly the most magnificent of all the ruminants. In shape and general aspect, he resembles a well conditioned Guzerat ox, not infrequently attaining the height of nineteen hands at the withers, and absolutely weighing from fifteen hundred to two thousand pounds! But notwithstanding this enormous bulk of carcase, which is literally enveloped in goodly collops of quaking fat, the head is strictly that of the antelope — light, graceful and bony. It is armed with a pair of elegantly diverging horns, which rising from a mask of bright rufous feathers, incline somewhat below the plane of the face and forming two sides of an isosceles triangle, are encircled by a ponderous spiral ring, the internal nucleus, or bony core of which is nearly of the consistency and weight of ivory. A deep pendulous dewlap fringed with coarse hair, dangles at his knees; and added to a fatty eminence, which approaches to a slight hump, on the withers, together with sundry rolls of brawn about the collar, produces an extraordinary depth of chest and forehand. The colour varies considerably with the age, being in some specimens dun — in others, ashy blue with a tinge of ochre — and in many, sandy grey approaching to white. The female — infinitely less voluminous, and more lady-like in her figure — exhibits all those separating characters which distinguish the sexes of domestic horned cattle. She resembles in general conformation, a red Guernsey cow, and is provided with longer and more attenuated horns than her very apoplectic-looking lord.

The feelings of exultation which attended my first introduction to this noble quadruped on the wooded banks of the Meritsane, will not readily pass from my recollection. My companion and myself had been for some time engaged in the hot pursuit of a motley group of brindled gnoos, quaggas, ostriches, sassaybes and hartebeests — one of those astounding herbivorous assemblages described in a foregoing chapter — the thunder of whose hoofs, like the distant din of war, sounded in our ears.

As if men fought upon the earth,
And fiends in upper air;

A band of hungry harpies following in our track, tripped nimbly up to each victim as it fell, completing by the scientific insertion of the point of an assegai between the vertebrae of the back, the work which our rifle bullets had commenced and instantly covering the carcase with branches to secure it from the voracity of a host of attendant vultures — when two strange figures were suddenly perceived in the distance, monsters of obesity, which we instantly recognised to be elands. Swinging their pendulum-like tails from side to side, and sometimes brushing away the troublesome flies with their moist noses, these mountains of flesh and lard were lazily standing under the shade of one of those immense thatched cities constructed by the loxia in a wide-spreading mokaala, of which tree numbers were distributed with park-like regularity over the level face of the landscape. At the first glimpse of the sleek forms of these animals, the savages became strangely excited. Water trickled from the corners of their capacious mouths, and they impatiently urged us to the pursuit, by running in advance of our horses, pointing energetically with their fingers and exclaiming with eager delight, 'Pooffo! Pooffo' — nor had many seconds elapsed ere we found ourselves pressing our panting steeds to the utmost of their retreating heels. Trusting to escape by mixing with the flying troops of gnoos and quaggas — which continually dashed across our path, or diverged on either side to admit of the passage of the chase — their deep hairy dewlaps vibrated from side to side and their pursy ribs quivered again with the unwonted exertion. Notwithstanding their unwieldy shape, however, they had at first greatly the speed of our jaded and toilworn horses — covering the ground with a celerity truly surprising and making the firm earth ring under their efforts to escape; but on being pushed, they presently exhibited symptoms of distress and turning their beautiful heads, looked repeatedly over their plump shoulders to learn if they had not shaken off their persecutors. Finding us still at their heels, they shortly separated; their sleek coats turned first blue, and then white with froth, and foam fell in bell ropes from their open mouths, grease trickled from their nostrils and the perspiration streamed from their lusty sides. The steeds came up hand over hand and in another moment were abreast of the now labouring fugitives, whose pace gradually slackened till it had dwindled into a clumsy trot, when with their full brilliant eyes turned imploringly towards us — saying almost plainer than words could speak, 'Do pray now leave me alone,' at the end of a mile, unresisting, each was laid low with a single ball.

How little resemblance did any of the portraits that I had seen of this superb animal, bear to the ponderous original now lying at my feet! In place of the plethora for which the eland is remarkable, the cunning artist must have surely striven to portray the features indicative of the last stage of a consumption! I was engaged in making a sketch of one of our noble victims, when the savages coming up, breathless with haste, proceeded with cold-blooded ferocity to stab the unfortunate and dying animal — stirring up the blood, and shouting with barbarous exultation as the tide of life gushed from each newly inflicted wound — regardless alike of our remonstrances, and of the eloquent and piteous appeal expressed in the beautiful clear black eye of the mild and inoffensive eland, whose tears might well have wrung remorse from a far more ruthless disciple of Nimrod than myself and have even caused him to sink the exultation of the sportsman

VI BOSELAPHUS OREAS - THE ELAND.

in the feelings of the moralist. The stoutest of our savage attendants could with difficulty transport the head to the wagons, where one of the Hottentots had just arrived with the carcase of a sassaybe, that he had dragged a considerable distance, with the assistance of some twenty barbarians, who were no sooner made acquainted with the occurrences of the morning, than they set off at speed upon the fresh tracks of our horses, returning about sunset gorged to the throats and groaning under an external load of meat, which they had found it quite impossible to make room for, and had therefore thriftily slung about their necks for a future occasion!

By all classes in Africa, the flesh of the eland is deservedly esteemed over that of any other animal-

Nor finer, nor fatter,
E'er roamed in a forest, or smoked on a platter.

Both in grain and colour it resembles beef, but is far better tasted and more delicate, possessing a pure game flavour and exhibiting the most tempting looking layers of fat and lean — the surprising quantity of the former ingredient with which it is interlarded, exceeding that of any other game quadruped with which I am acquainted. The venison fairly melts in the mouth; and as for the brisket, that is absolutely a cut for a monarch! With what satisfaction would not King Jamie of hunting memory, have drawn his good blade adown the breast of a plump eland, to be rewarded with five full inches of *prime white fat on that ilk,* instead of three, as on the occasion in Greenwich Park, when Nigel assisted his sporting Majesty in the sylvan ceremony. The vast quantity of tallow yielded by the fat bulls, furnished us with constant materials for manufacturing dips in a candle mould with which we were provided; and during the greater part of our journey it was to the flesh of this goodly beast that we principally looked for our daily rations, both on account of its vast superiority over all other wild flesh and from the circumstances of its being obtainable in larger quantities with comparatively less labour. Pursued, the fat sluggards delay their flight as long as possible, but when no longer able to avert the evil hour, they go off at a smart pace, galloping less clumsily, leaping and clearing broken ground with much greater facility than could be expected from their huge proportions. Once blown, however, the unfortunate beast is far more manageable than a Smithfield ox; and after giving the unwieldy old bulls a spurt in order to render them somewhat less frisky, in spite of their repeated attempts to break away — made whenever their wind returned — we were in the constant habit of driving them at a walk before our horses, to the camp, from their pastures several miles distant. No opportunity of levying a tax upon their herds was ever suffered to pass. We invariably selected the fattest and bonniest of the whole lot and after hitting upon this plan of driving them up to the shambles, not only was the trouble of carrying the meat from a distance avoided, but a constant supply of hides obtained for the repair of our traces and wagon gear.

The eland frequents the open prairies and low rocky interspersed with clumps of wood, but is never to be met with in a continuously wooded country. Rejoicing especially in low belts of shaded hillocks and in the isolated groves of *acacia capensis* which, like islands in the ocean, are scattered over many of the stony and gravelly plains of the interior, large herds of them are also to be seen grazing like droves of oxen on the more verdant meadows, though which some silver rivulets winds in rainbow brightness betwixt fringes of sighing bulrushes. Fat and lethargic, groups may be seen scattered up and down the gentle acclivities, some grazing on the hill side, and others lazily basking in the morning-sunbeam. Advancing they appear to move like a regiment of cavalry in single files; the goodliest bulls leading the van: whereas during a retreat, these it is, that uniformly bring up the rear. As the day dawned over the boundless meads of the Vaal River spread with a rich carpet of luxuriant herbage, and enamelled with pastures of brilliant flowers, vast droves of these lordly animals were constantly to be seen moving in solemn procession across the profile of the silent and treeless landscape, portions of which were often covered with long coarse grass, which when dry and waving its white hay-like stalks to the breeze, imparted to the plain, the delusive and alluring appearance of ripe cornfields.

Amongst themselves the males have frequent and desperate battles, many specimens that came under our observation being covered both with scars and green wounds, and humbled also of one horn. This was the case with the largest we killed, which measured nineteen and a half hands at the shoulder, and was armed, unicorn-like, with a single horn, nearly two feet six inches in length. The oldest and stoutest bull not infrequently expels all other males from the herd; and compelling them to flock together, takes the ladies under his own especial charge. It is, however, more usual to see both sexes feeding indiscrimately together and the cows being found in calf all the year round, there can be no determined season for rutting. Although in disposition the eland is so extremely docile that it may be trained without the smallest difficulty, its strength is neither proportioned to its gigantic bulk, nor are its apparently massive shoulders possessed of sufficient solidity to bear the yoke of domesticity, or render it capable of labouring with advantage to the agriculturist. The existence of a second species, the *Boselaphus Canna* of naturalists,

Plate VI: *Boselapus oreas* — eland or impoofo — *eland* of the Dutch colonists. — *t'ganna* of the Hottentots — *impoof* or *poofo* of the Kaffirs and Bechuana

Generic Character — Full grown male about six feet six or eight inches high at the shoulder, and upwards of twelve in extreme length. Head light and bony. Facial line perfectly straight. Muzzle broad. Forehead square; covered with a cluster of strong wiry twisted hair, forming feathers of an intense sienna brown colour, margined on either side by a bright yellow crescent, which commences above the eyes and nearly meets about half way down the face. Eyes large, brilliant and melting. No expression of ferocity in the face. Ears small, white, flexible and pointed. Horns placed on the summits of the frontals; about two feet in length, massy, slightly divergent and nearly straight; but twisted on their own axes and encircled by a ponderous ring which ascends in a spiral direction almost to the tips. A few transverse wrinkles on the more prominent parts. Bony cores approaching to the weight and substance of ivory. Proportions of the body resembling those of a bull. Figure, square and ponderous. Neck very thick, compressed laterally as in the ox; shoulders very deep, withers slightly elevated owing to the length of the spinous processes. Larynx very prominent and larger than an apple. An ample pendulous dewlap, very thin, lax and wrinkled, fringed with long wavy wiry brown hair; and descending to the knees. A crest of bristles from the forehead passing upwards and recurrent along the ridge of the neck, in the position of a mane. Hindquarters extremely heavy. Tail two feet three or four inches long; slender, with a tuft of short and coarse brown hair at the extremity. Hide black. Hair very short and scanty. General colour rufous dun, or ashy grey tinged with ochre. Legs extremely short and bull-like; rufous and buff below the knees. Hoofs large, rounded and black; the succentorial hoofs much developed. Has a muzzle. No suborbital sinus, or lachrymary depression.

Female much smaller and of slighter proportions; with longer and more slender horns, generally diverging more and often capriciously twisted. They are usually about thirty inches in length and have a swelling of the axis between the spiral turns, which forms a knot, above which they incline backwards. She has no dewlap, but a protruding tuft of stiff rufous hair on the larynx. Colour considerably redder than in the male. General appearance not unlike that of a Guernsey cow. Has an udder with four teats. Gregarious in large droves. Formerly common, but now extinct in the Cape Colony and only found in the open or slightly wooded plains of the interior.

called by the Colonists the bastaard eland, is I think, extremely questionable in southern Africa. I could never myself meet with any such variety and all the descriptions given of it answer exactly to the appearance of a growing bull, the horns and colour of which , as in other quadrupeds, are then constantly changing. The word eland, in the Dutch jargon, signifies elk, an animal to which I need hardly say the subject of the annexed portrait bears little resemblance beyond the fact of its being the proprietor of four legs. In days of yore, the species was abundant in the Cape Colony, but it has long since become extinct within the boundary - the value of its flesh and hide, added to its inability to escape from the mounted pursuer, having soon led to its utter extermination. Large parties of boers, however, occasionally proceed across the boundary and return with wagon loads of beef, salted and packed away in the skins. The Griquas, also persecute these noble creatures unceasingly; and even the savages who have no horses, not infrequently race them down on foot and then stab them with their assegais; converting the horns into tobacco pipes, which, from their huge dimensions, admit of the weed being inhaled after the most approved fashion.

Returning one day from hunting the giraffe to the northward of the Cashan mountains, and looking for our wagons which had moved a march in the meantime, we mistook a large herd of elands grazing in a mimosa brake, for our own oxen, and were literally amongst them before we had discovered the truth. But by far the largest herd seen during the expedition was on the plain of the gurgling Chonapas, shortly after moving to the southward of the Cashan mountains, on our way towards the Vaal River. It may probably have consisted of three hundred head or more and in appearance could only be compared to a vast drove of stall-fed oxen. Ignorant of the nature of the country in advance, we had determined to obtain a supply of tongues and briskets for salting, lest our provisions should run short from the failure of game. Lighter bodied and more active than their ponderous chiefs, the dun coloured cows jumped nimbly over each other's heads as if they had been all their lives accustomed to the use of the skipping rope; but the apoplectic old bulls puffed and laboured in the rear, shaking the firm earth with their heavy tramp — their colloped sides quivering again with fat and embossed with froth and foam. At intervals, we crossed solid natural pavements of granite, which ringing to the tramp of their hard hoofs, gave forth a clangor as from a blacksmith's forge. Two minutes sufficied to reduce the whole cavalcade to a painful trot. We dashed into the middle of the herd and although some few of the toiling victims turned in desperation with the design of impaling their persecutors on their marline spike looking horns, the giants of obesity were so easily disposed of, that every individual might have been incontinently massacred. The weapon I carried was a double-barrelled rifle, gauged eighteen balls to the pound; and upon coming up hand over hand with the spent *quarree* — reeling, covered with foam, and steaming with sweat, its nostrils expanding as it gasped for breath — a single shot delivered pistol fashion at arms length, into any part of the soft and sinewless frame, invariably brought the unwieldy beast to the ground, like a lasso'd bull, with a force that made the earth tremble again — the impetus acquired in the sturdy animal's progress causing it to plough the soil a considerable distance on its knees and horns.

We had terminated the chase, and strolling over the scene of carnage were filling in the list of casualties, when one of the largest bulls, which had been knocked over by Richardson about the beginning of the skirmish and left under a thorn tree, to all appearance in a dying state, was remarked to be missing. After a laborious search, his twisted horns were at length observed protruding from a pit, barely large enough to contain his vast bulk; and on being approached he set off again as if nothing had happened, and gave a better run than at first. Leading my own horse, laden with *spolia,* I was walking slowly along, witnessing this singular scene, when an enormous bull rose leisurely from a tuft of grass, and seeing the horns of some of his beheaded comrades peering above my saddle bow, approached with cautious step to scrutinise them. Although I had stayed my hand from slaughter, I was not proof against this temptation. Casting the ponderous trophies on the earth I vaulted again into the saddle and presently took the conceit out of the burly fellow, accounting also for another, equally large, by which he was joined during the chase. Leaving the carcase a banquet for the vultures, we loaded our meagre steeds with the choicest morsels and rejoined the cafila in the afternoon. The camp had been formed on the sedgy banks of the deep Chonapas, the murmuring waters of which seemed with difficulty to force their way through the reeds which choked the channel. Not a single twig could be obtained for fuel in the whole neighbourhood, but after breaking up some useless wagon boxes, the feasting became general; nor can I better describe the proceedings of this day of carnage, than by drawing again upon the Water Poet, who in his work entitled the *Pennylesse Pilgrimage,* has favoured us with the following graphic description of the finale of a great hunt celebrated by the Earl of Marr in 1618, at which he had the good fortune to be present. 'In the space of two hours,' says he, 'fourscore fat buckes were slaine, which after were disposed of, some one way and some another; more than enough being left for us to make merrey withall at our rendezvous; and being come to our lodgings there was such baking, boyling, rosting and stewing as if cook Ruffian himself had been there to have scalded the deyvill in his feathers.'

Heads of elands, as preserved by Captain Harris. Male left and female right

7

Caama Or Hartebeest

Will Scarlett he did kill a bucke,
And Midge he killed a doe,
But Little John killed a Harte of Greece,
Five hundred foot him fro.
Joy on that heart, said Robyn Hoode,
Shot such a shot for me,
I'll ride my horse a hundred miles,
To find a match for thee.

Africa was looked upon by the ancients as the land of zoological prodigies. It is not possible to open the works of those amongst them who have treated of the natural productions of the country, without finding some passage, in unison with the general opinion of the time, that in this wild quarter of the globe, nature sported even to prodigality and was profuse of monsters in her chartered libertinism.

The subject of the annexed portrait, which is undeniably entitled to a very distinguished place in the catalogue of animal eccentricities, throughout the more southern regions of the continent represents the Bubalis of northern Africa, which was known by that title to Aristotle, Oppian and Pliny and is styled by the Arabs the *Bukr el Wash,* or cattle of the forest. In size and character the two species very closely resemble each other, the principal distinctions being, that the black daubing on the legs is wanting in the latter and that the flexures of its horns are less strongly pronounced than in the Hartebeest. Both animals are alike found in small flocks, headed by three or four stout males, which, adopting the law of *detur fortiori,* expel the less powerful adults of their own sex and oblige them to form a society of their own. Their single combats are frequently fierce and bloody. Dropping down on their knees to fight and placing the forehead parallel with the ground by bringing the nose between the forelegs, brow to brow like rams, they batter each other's skulls with the greatest fury — their gnarled and angular horns rattling together with a great noise and not infrequently becoming so fast locked in each other as to be disengaged with difficulty — the wounds inflicted during these sanguinary tournaments being jagged and often of a very extensive nature.

Beest, in the language of the Hollanders, bearing exactly the same signification as beast with the English grazier, the colonial nomenclature bestowed upon this animal may correctly be rendered the ox stag or cervine cattle. The hartebeest was formerly common in all parts of the Cape, but persecution has gradually reduced the strength of the species to a single herd, the surviving remnant having now been taken, like the bontiboks at Swellendam under the special protection of Government — no more being suffered to compass their destruction. This species is liable to the fatal distemper already noticed as originating in a kind of *bots,* probably the larvae of an *Aestrus,* which force their way into the nostrils and consume many of the larger African game quadrupeds. The head of the hartebeest is literally crammed with these queen-ant-looking maggots, numbers of which are constantly expelled by the process of snorting. The calves, which are produced singly in April and September, are tractable and readily domesticated; and so distinctly are all the peculiarities in the horns of the Bubalis marked on those of certain ox-like animals which are represented in antique Egyptian sculpture as harnessed to a chariot, that it has become a question whether that animal was not formerly used by the people of that country as a beast of draught. In their paintings the wild ox is often too much made to resemble a common ox; but it is nevertheless sufficiently evident that the artist had in view the Bubalis, or Barbary cow; and the Theban sculptors, who had a better opportunity of becoming acquainted with that animal, have succeeded in delineating its character far more satisfactorily than the painters of Beni Hassan.

William Twici, grand huntsman to King Edward the Second and author of a skillful treatise upon the gentle art of venery, would unquestionably have included the hartebeest among his 'beasts of sweete flight.' Although the great elevation of the withers, and the singular obliquity of the back towards the crupper, give the animal a grotesque and somewhat awkward appearance when galloping, its paces — long, oily and beautiful — form the very *beau ideal* of racing action. Moving at a smooth and swinging canter, throwing the hind quarters well under the body, brandishing the glossy black tail and carrying the huge beamy head in the most stylish manner, its beetling brows surmounted by a lozenge-shaped coronet of embossed horn and its brilliant orange hues eccentrically variegated with abrupt black markings, all sparkling in the sun, the Caama — notwithstanding its three-cornered build — cuts a very majestic appearance. Followed, it frequently stops; and turning proudly towards the foe with a most sapient look, sneezes with great violence — an overt act of folly, which was noticed drolly enough by Bewick who, in speaking of this animal, says 'when it has once got ahead of its pursuers, it is very apt to turn round and stare them full in the face.'

Wild through their red and sable hair,
Look out their eyes with savage start;

and in a thinly wooded country, destitute of brushwood, they would really almost appear to be playing a game at hide-and-seek with the hunter — ever peeping at him from behind the trees, so that they may be easily killed from horseback, although they generally contrive to keep out of the range of the pedestrian marksman. The longest shot that I recollect to have made during our expedition, sealed the death warrant of the magnificent male specimen here portrayed, part of whose splendid robe had assumed the deepest crimson dye. Stupidly sticking himself up as a target at four hundred and twenty yards, he converted his heart into the bull's eye; and the caravan passing presently afterwards, we slung the carcase behind one of the wagons and brought it on to the bivouac. But although remarkably dark coloured and venison-like in appearance, the flesh of this species was nevertheless invariably lean, dry and tasteless and on no occasion proved worth the trouble of carrying.

In the course of my sylvan rambles, I not infrequently came upon the fresh and sometimes even reeking remains of the hartebeest, in the very scene where it had been surprised and rent

VII. ACRONOTUS CAAMA:- THE HARTEBEEST.

by some beast of prey - the many bleaching skulls and worm-eaten horns, which are to be seen strewed over the plain, in regions nearly, if not totally, depopulated, fully attesting the success that has attended the carnivorous prowler, the lion and the *hyaena venatica* more especially. Like the wild dogs of India, these dogs of the African desert, which are called by the colonists the *wilde honden,* take the field in large organised packs, seldom failing by their perseverance to weary out the swiftest antelope, whilst the confederacy enables them to subdue the strongest, with which, single handed, their slender form would render them incapable of coping. Nor does King Leo, as affirmed, restrict himself to game that he has killed himself. I one morning shot a noble bull hartebeest out of a large herd that had been capering before me for some distance — their red and yellow painted bodies glittering in the sun, in one of the green glades at the foot of the Cashan mountains; and having cut off his great hammer head, the hooked and knotted horns of which were splintered from age and hard thumps received in many a well fought *duello,* concealed it in a bush and continued my sport. Meeting one of our Matabili guides shortly afterwards strolling about by himself, seeking for something to eat, I directed him to the place and requested that when he had finished his dinner, he would be so obliging as to take the head to the wagon. Passing the spot on my return, I was surprised to perceive my friend perched on the summit of a mimosa tree, making signs towards a neighbouring bush; the half devoured carcase — of which the forequarters only remained — together with the heavy footprints of a lion stamped around the spot, rendering the real state of the case at once intelligible. Having however, fortunately taken the rough edge off the royal appetite, his shaggy majesty did not deem it worth his while to interfere with the removal of my humble share of the spoils — although, since the truth must be spoken, I confess to having afforded him the briefest time that might be, to ponder over the subject, before taking my departure.

The annexed scene lies in the immediate environs of the Cashan mountains, where the hartebeest occurred in the greatest abundance — the herds often containing so many as two or three hundred individuals. Gambolling and luxuriating over the grassy downs, they revel in the shady recesses of the odoriferous mimosa groves which abound in those unfrequented solitudes — their gaudy colours presenting a most brilliant contrast to the foliage of the 'green-wood-tree', against the stem of which they are constantly raking their rough horns, until they have acquired a complete coating of bark.

In South African scenery, the nests of the pismire form a very singular feature; some, arising from the solitary plains in the form of a pile of gigantic sugar loaves, or reminding the spectator of a Christmas cake — whilst others, shaped like the humble cabins of the Bushman tribe, resemble a native kraal or village. The country over which we passed, was usually covered with these latter dome-shaped mounds of clay, from two to four feet in height, which were almost invariably scooped out, either by the long nails of the ant-eater, or by savages, so as to resemble a baker's oven. In wet weather especially, or during a dearth of fuel, these ant hills were our stoutest allies; but, on the other hand, the Hottentots not infrequently put the strength of our wagons to the test, by driving carelessly over them, the structure, although honey-combed being often sufficiently hard to resist the pressure of the wheel, and thus throw the vehicle off its equilibrium. The kitchen fire having one rainy night been kindled with great difficulty in one of these friendly mounds, and the tea kettle placed over an artificial chimney therein, the light, which could not be produced by any other means, served as a beacon to one of the Hottentots, who having gone in advance to reconnoitre, had contrived to lose his way. A lady at the Cape, looking at the annexed drawing, inquired with great simplicity, 'whether that', placing her fair finger on the ant hill, 'was not the house in which the hartebeest resided?' Some one had the ill manners to laugh, whereupon she rejoined, 'beavers build houses, pray why should not the poor hartebeest also?'

Two distinct animals are found in this part of the country, that alike burrow in the ground and appear to subsist entirely upon ants and termites, uprooting the laboured works constructed by those minute and industrious insects and leaving upon every habitation unequivocal marks of their desolating visits. Of these, the earth-hog, or aardevark — [*orycter opus capensis*] of the Colonists, is the most common; it is from six to seven feet in extreme length, scantily covered with coarse brown hair and furnished with a slimy flexible tongue, capable of being protruded to the extent of eighteen or twenty inches beyond the attentuated nose. It possesses the snout and ear of a hog and withal, a pig-like expression of face. The forefeet are provided with four robust nails, which , forming a complete rake, enable the animal to dig into the bowels of the mount; its taper tongue covered with a glutinous secretion, being always in readiness to seize the swarming inmates as fast as they issue from their beleaguered abode. Never moving abroad during the day, this animal is rarely seen; and any attempt to unearth it usually proves unsuccessful - the beast continuing to burrow deeper during the operation and digging out the soil with its long toe nails, much faster than can his two footed enemies, even when armed with an iron spade.

Differing greatly in external appearance, the equipments as well as the habits of the second species are yet essentially the same. Seen from a distance, the pangolin, or *manis* [*manis Temminckii*], might easily be mistaken for a small alligator, the neck being totally confounded with the head and body. The upper parts are clad in a complete panoply of flexible armour, consisting of numerous stout horny triangular scales, of a cockle-shell shape, overlapping each other like the tiles of a house and presenting an appearance precisely similar to the bark of the brab tree. Slow,

Plate VII: *Acronotus caama* — caama or hartebeest — *hartebeest* of the Cape colonists — *intoosel* of the Matabili — *caama* of the Bechuana and Kaffirs

Generic Character — Adult male about five feet high at the withers, and nine in extreme length. Crupper very drooping; shoulder very elevated; carcase robust; head remarkably narrow, heavy and long. The whole animal made up of triangles. Horns seated upon the summit of a beetling ridge above the frontals; very close together, and almost touching at the base; robust, divergent and again approximating, so as to describe an imperfect lozenge, with double flexures strongly pronounced, turned obtusely forwards and again acutely backwards, thus forming a zigzag of two angles; the points directed horizontally to the rear, and the whole embossed with five or six prominent knots on the anterior surface only. Coat — short, close and glossy. General colour bright orange sienna, with a deep red and crimson cast, abruptly streaked and painted as follows. A black spot at the base of the horns above the forehead, continued behind and terminating in front of the ear. A black streak down the nose, commencing below the eyes and terminating at the nostrils. Chin black. A narrow black list stripe down the ridge of the neck. A black streak down the front of each foreleg, commencing about mid-shoulder and gradually diminishing in width; another down each hind leg, commencing about the middle of the buttock — all terminating in an angular band above the fetlock. A triangular spot of white immediately above the black on each buttock and a yellow spot above each eye. Tail reaching to the hocks, covered with posteriorly directed glossy black hair. Legs slender, with taper hoofs. Ears whitish, long, pointed and flexible. A half muzzle. No suborbital sinus, but a constant mucous discharge of a waxy nature. Eyes wild, high in the head and of a fiery colour.

Female precisely similar but on a slighter scale, with more slender horns; fainter in colour and of a hue approaching to yellow and cinnamon. Mammae two. Almost extinct within the limits of the colony. Inhabits the open plains of the interior, beyond the Orange River, in considerable herds.

gentle and inoffensive the pangolin lives in holes, burrows and fissures in the rocks, seldom wandering far from its lonely retreat; and although calculated neither by appetite nor by disposition for a life of predatory warfare, it can deride the attack of every beast of prey — possessing, in addition to its coat of mail, the power of rolling itself, like the hedgehog, into a ball — by which faculty this otherwise defenceless animal is rendered perfectly invulnerable to the assaults of its foes.

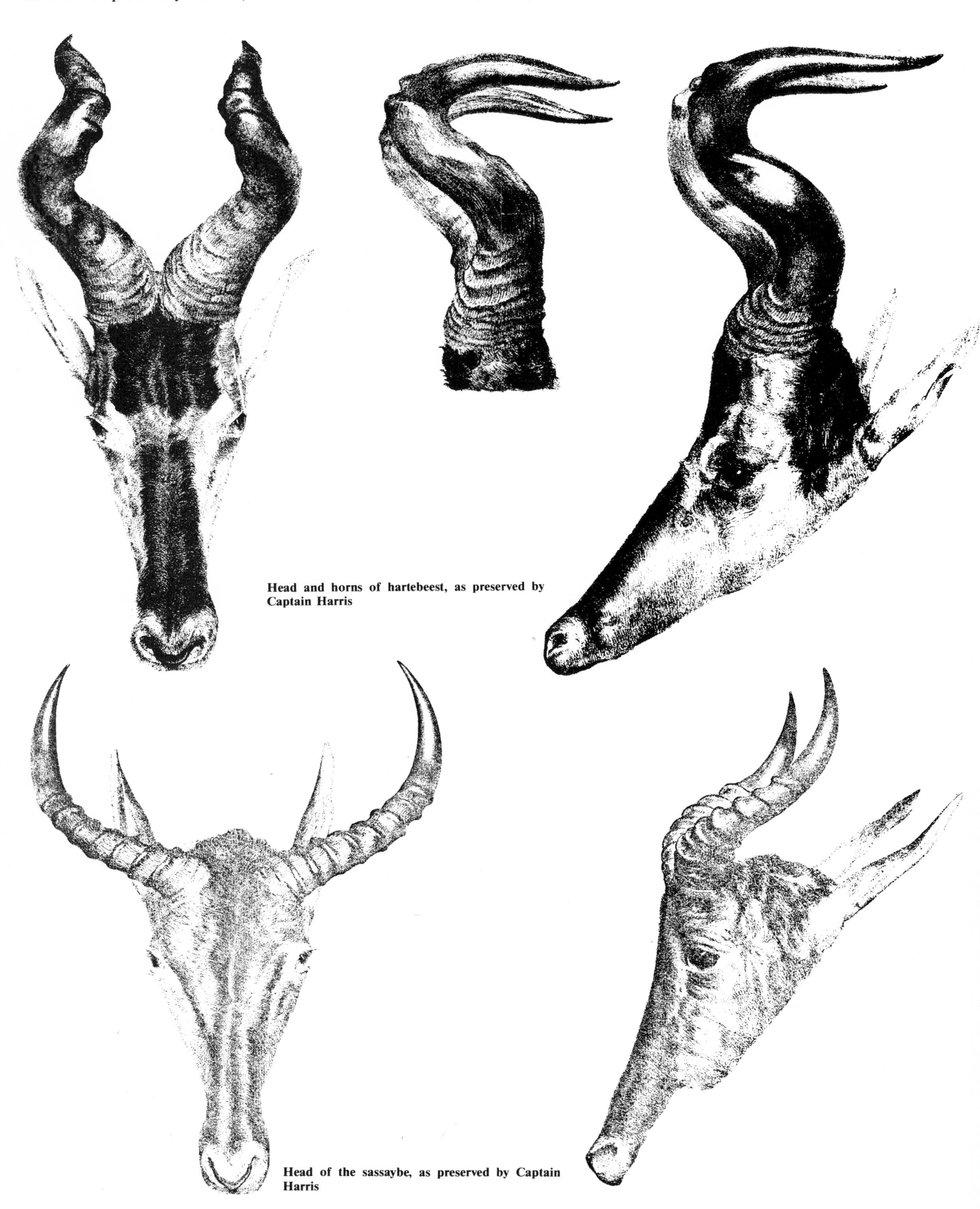

Head and horns of hartebeest, as preserved by Captain Harris

Head of the sassaybe, as preserved by Captain Harris

8

Sassaybe

Spread out below, in sun and shade,
The shaggy glen lies full display'd,
Its shelter'd nooks, and sylvan bowers,
And meadows, flush'd with purple flowers.
The sultry summer noon is past,
And mellow evening comes at last,
With a low and languid breeze,
Fanning the mimosa trees,
Which cluster o'er the tangled vale,
And oft perfume the panting gale,
With fragrance faint — that seems to tell,
Of primrose tufts, in Scottish dell.

A member of the same subgenus as the hartebeest and generally appearing with it, the sassaybe is neither less singularly coloured than its gaudy congener, nor less remarkable for its elevated withers, drooping hind quarters and triangular form. The brush of the sign painter too, has evidently been busy with the robe of this whimsical animal and would seem equally to have left the goodly work unfinished. Seen under different lights, the hues of the body vary and shift from purple violet, to puce, pompadour, lilac pink and a deep blackish purple brown — the daubings on the hams and forearms being of a slate colour or iron grey. Nothing can surpass the beauty of the paces of this animal, which are characterised throughout by the same speed and oily smoothness as those of the hartebeest — the colours above described forming a curious contrast to the bright orange and red tints of its brother, whether quietly consorting in mixed herds, or racing past, neck and neck, as if contesting the gold cup! Like the hartebeest, the sassaybe also frequently turns to reconnoitre the pursuing foe — its long, wise looking noddle and fiery red eyes, giving it a most sinister appearance. Whilst engaged in taking off the hairy spoils of a brindled gnoo shot near the Mariqua River where the present species was particularly abundant, a large male advanced to the distance of two hundred yards and taking up his position in the shade of an umbrella-topped tree, quietly scanned our operations. The first ball from my rifle struck the stem of the mimosa close above his head, though it merely caused him to shift his position to the other side; but the second bullet told upon the point of his shoulder with a crack that could not be mistaken. Retiring to a small bush and quietly subdsiding, he was gathered unto his fathers and it was from his remains, the finest of many dozens killed during the expedition, that the annexed portrait was made.

The sassaybe, like its congener, delight in the neighbourhood of hills, frequenting the open country with island-looking mimosa groves, as well as the patches of scraggy forest that skirt the foot of many of the superior mountain ranges, which, however, neither species ever ascends. Amongst the parks of mokaala trees and about the Cashan and Kurichane mountains, the bases of which are fringed with stately trees, from whose boughs depend clusters of moss and festoons of various parasitic plants, we constantly saw them. In such situations the ground is often broken and stony, abounding in parts with deep holes. When in the act of killing a sassaybe, my horse put his feet into one of these and coming down with frightful violence, broke his own nose, cut my knee and elbows to the bone and what was a far greater misfortune and one that I had long anticipated, fractured the stock of my only and especially favourite rifle. Would tears have availed anything, I would have wept over the fragments. A strip of the sassaybe's hide, however, rectified the damage for the time, until a second fall ultimately obliged me to open a blacksmith's forge, in order to put the weapon into an efficient state of repair.

In the thinly peopled regions of southern Africa, where the indigent inhabitants, unacquainted with firearms, subsist almost entirely by the chase, artificial fences, stretching over a great extent of country, are commonly employed to assist in gathering and conducting the wild beasts to particular spots, where the pitfall, the spear and the club, await them, to their destruction. The game from far and wide having been collected and driven onward by a host of marshalled savages, is forced by the gradual contraction of the line to some central spot, where hundreds are promiscuously slaughtered. These princely *battues* are especially carried to a great extent in Moselekatse's territories — that mighty potentate, who has long ceased to lead his victorious armies to battle, still condescending to honour with his presence the great hunting expeditions which frequently take place. On these occasions, the remnants of the conquered nations being expressly assembled, he is attended by a retinue of several thousand vassals, who, extending themselves in a circle, enclose many square miles of country and gradually converge so as to bring incredible numbers of wild animals within a small focus. Still advancing, the ring at length becomes a thick and continuous line of men, hemming in the game on all sides, which in desperate efforts to escape, display the most daring and dangerous exhibition of sport that can be conceived. As the scene closes, the spears of the warriors deal death around them, affording a picture, thrilling to the sportsman and striking in the extreme.

No haunt unsearched, they drive,
From every covert and from every den,
The lurking savage. Deep in his gloomy lair,
The lion starts, and morsels yet unchewed,
Drop from his trembling jaws. The shouts,
Of eager hosts through all the circling line,
And the wild howlings of the beasts within,
Rend wide the welkin. Pressed on,
At length within the narrow plain confined,
A listed field marked out for bloody deeds,
An amphitheatre more glorious far,
Than ancient Rome could boast, they crowd in heaps,
Dismayed and quite appalled. Flights of arrows,
winged With death, and javelins launched from every arm,
Gall sore the brutal band, with many a wound
Gored through and through. Prostrate on the ground
The grinning monsters lie, and their foul gore
Defiles the verdant plain. With pointed spears men pierce
Through their tough hides, or at their gaping mouths
An easier passage find. The King of brutes,
In broken roarings breathes his last.

W. C. Harris del.

VIII. ACRONOTUS LUNATA:- THE SASSAYBE.

Through beasts of every kind,
A strange promiscuous carnage drenched in blood,
And heaps on heaps amassed, grim Slaughter strides along,
Glutting her greedy jaws.

Pitfalls of various kinds are also constantly employed to entrap game, and throughout the Matabili country they were of almost daily occurrence. The first we saw were at Chooi, to the north of the great salt pan, to which, and similar reservoirs, the wild animals resort in great numbers. Excepting a belt of crisp and sour grass, by which it is encircled, the country around is destitute of verdure, a few brown stunted bushes being the only covering to the gravelly soil. A tract of low ground is occupied by a vast sheet of fine dry crystallized salt, of brilliant whiteness, resembling a frozen lake; and the saline efflorescence receiving the impress of the foot in the same manner as hoar frost, was covered with the slot of every species of animal. From fifty to a hundred pits were dug at suitable openings left in a high thorn fence which extended in the form of a crescent a mile or more on either side, in such a manner that gnoos, quaggas, hartebeests, sassaybes and other heavy game, might readily be driven into them. These pits, which are called *keisi* by the savages, are generally arranged in a treble row and close together, the dimensions in length and depth being nearly the same, by about one half in breadth at the top, but gradually contracting like a wedge toward the bottom — an arrangement by which the prisoner becomes jammed and perfectly incapable of exertion, the circumscribed dimensions rendering escape impossible. The mouth of the aperture is carefully covered over with grass, leaves or twigs, the mound of mould taken from the excavation being in a little time so grown over as not to excite suspicion. To impale the more formidable animals, such as the rhinoceros and hippopotamus, a sharp stake is sometimes fixed at the bottom and heaps of whitened bones bear ample testimony to the destruction they have occasioned.

In those parts of the country that are infested by the Bushman hordes, every paltry pool of water is surrounded by a chain of sunken pits for entrapping game, which, when overgrown with reeds and sedge, not infrequently prove fatal to the straying cattle of a traveller. Others, which are often constructed in the gorge of two converging ranges of hills and have no fence to give warnings of their existence, are even more dangerous. Whilst riding down a sassaybe, whose leg I had broken, I once narrowly escaped being engulfed in one which had a stake at the bottom — the wounded animal falling into another just in time to admit of my perceiving the danger and putting the horse over what must otherwise have proved his grave.

The painted skins of both the hartebeest and sassaybe, but especially of the latter, are in great request amongst the savages for *kobos* or leathern mantles — as well on account of their brilliant colours, as from the extreme suppleness of their nature. The shining black tail, being opened and squeezed flat, depends from the back of the neck like queue, the universal admiration in which this elegant appendage is held, rendering it the subject of many a quarrel. Ignorant of the process of tanning by the use of bark and astringent lyes, the wretched savages, whose time is quite valueless, cure these skins by dint of continual rubbing, stretching and scraping, for which purpose they are constantly carried about and referred to as an amusement in moments of leisure. The process of converting larger hides into leather, however, is one of greater difficulty, requiring the united efforts of ten or a dozen hands, who knead in concert, pushing and distending the skin by various evolutions, until the object is at length accomplished. This operation, which, to an indolent savage especially, is one of great manual labour, is rendered less tedious by the constant addition of grease and ochre and somewhat less irksome by certain savage howlings and gruntings of a nature highly complementary to the pigs and doubtless intended to pass current for singing, though in fact much more resembling the music of curs contending over a bone.

The kobo or kaross, which in addition to the scanty leathern girdle and apron worn by both sexes, forms the aboriginal dress of all the Bechuana and pastoral tribes inhabiting the regions we visited, who can afford so extravagant a luxury, is neither more or less than the Roman toga in its rudest and most primitive form; and being simply fastened across the breast, may be readily thrown off and resumed according to the caprice of the wearer. In common with the filthy body of the owner, these cloaks are so besmeared with a pigment of red ochre and grease, as to contaminate everything they touch and even the sides and poles of our wagons, against which they frequently rubbed themselves, were indelibly stained with red, like the fleece of an English sheep after having been shorn. A more expensive and very beautiful description of fur mantle is manufactured of the skins of smaller animals, such as the jackal, the weasel and the wild cat, from fifty to a hundred of which are curiously sewn together with the animal's sinews and the skin of the head and muzzle left entire in the upper row, so as to form a scalloped border. All perforations and flaws are elaborately patched and repaired, the inner side of the garment being finally strengthened with a neat leathern edging, stitched with a praiseworthy exactness, that is rendered perfectly wonderful by the rudeness of the implements with which it is achieved. The operation of sewing is not confined to the ladies, but performed by the gentlemen also, through the agency of a huge skewer or awl, of the most unworkmanlike manufacture and which upon occasion would serve to truss a fillet of veal. A hole having been bored with this weapon, a thread is introduced, in texture resembling a fine fiddle string; a large bundle of the dorsal sinews of the antelope, from which this article is principally manufactured, being usually slung at the girdle, to be converted into thread and employed also in the important service of stringing beads and buttons, as well as to suspend about the neck, knives, whistles, snuff boxes and other essentials, which by more civilised beings would be lodged in the waistcoat pocket.

Plate VIII: *Acronotus lunata* — sassaybe or bastard hartebeest — *bastard hartebeest* of the Cape colonists — *sassaybe* of the Bechuana and Matabili

Generic Character — Adult male four feet six inches high at the shoulder; four feet at the croup. Eight feet two or three inches in extreme length. Horns robust, about twelve inches long, turning outwards and then sweeping inwards with a regular curve, so as to form two segments of a circle, with a general inclination backwards — the whole when seen from the front, forming a complete crescent. They are marked with from twelve to fifteen incomplete annuli, occupying about half their length; the rest smooth. Neck short. Body rather bulky. Legs slender. Hoofs black and tapering. Withers very elevated. Back remarkably sloping and crupper very drooping. Head long, narrow and shapeless; wearing a bubaline appearance. Facial line straight. A dark soot-coloured streak extending in a lozenge shape from between the horns to the nose, widest below the eyes. Ears fawn colour, nine inches long. Hair of the body close, silky and glossy. General colour, deep blackish purple brown above, forming a pompadour as it descends; beneath fulvous and tawny. A dab of slate colour extends from the middle of the shoulder to the knee; and another from the middle of the flank to the hock outside. An abrupt transverse band of the same colour passes diagonally across the inside both of fore and hind legs, upon a fulvous ground. Lower part of the legs deep fulvous. Tail twenty two inches long, descending to the hocks, rufous and covered below with posteriorly directed wavy black hair. Rump fawn colour. Eyes high in the cranium and fiery red. A semi-muzzle separating the nostrils and a very indistinct lachrymary perforation.

Female precisely similar, but smaller and less robust, with more slender horns. Mammae two. Gregarious. Inhabits the country of the Bechuana and as far as the Tropic, in considerable herds — generally associating with the hartebeest.

9

Oryx

From his steed's shoulder, loin, and breast,
Silk housings swept the ground,
With Scotland's arms device, and crest,
Embroider'd round and round.
The double treasure might you see,
First by Achaius borne,
The thistle, and the fleur-de-lis,
And gallant unicorn.

Romance, aiding the skillful hand of nature with her brightest drapery, has succeeded in investing the group to which the oryx belongs, with a degree of interest that few other quadrupeds can claim. The figure of the renowned unicorn can be traced in all the ancient carvings, coins, and Latin heraldic insignia, to someone of the members of the Orygine family; and from our earliest childhood, the form of that fabled animal has been made to ocuppy so prominent a place in our juvenile imaginations, the fictions of the nursery having first indelibly engraven its outlines upon the tablet of our minds, that arriving at years of discretion, we are still almost tempted to regard it as a creature having actual existence. Of all the whimsies of antiquity, whether emanating from the unbridled and fertile fancies of the people of Egypt and Persia, or devised by the more chaste and classic taste which distinguished Greece and Rome, the unicorn — unquestionably the most celebrated — is the chimera which has in modern ages engrossed the largest portion of attention from the curious. Like the sphinxes of Egyptian sculpture, or the centaurs of Grecian fable, the animal, as it is figured at the present day, can exist solely in imagination; but philosophers and zoologists, directing their energies and talents to the subject, and seeking amongst the actual works of the creation for the form which could first have suggested so strange a fiction, have selected as its most probable basis, the group to which the subject of the annexed portrait belongs. The rhinoceros is supposed to be the animal so often alluded to in Scripture under the name of reem or unicorn; yet the combination presented in the oryx of the antelopine and equine characters — the horns and cloven hoof of the one, blended with the erect mane, general contour and long switch tail of the other — corresponds in all essential particulars with the extant delineations and descriptions of the heraldic unicorn, which is universally represented to have been possessed of a straight slender horn, ringed at the base and to have the hoof divided; to have worn a mane, reversed, a black flowing tail and a turkey-like tuft on the larynx — whilst both the size and ground colour were said to be those of the ass, with the addition of sundry black markings imparting to the face and forehead, a piebald appearance.

The alterations required to reduce the African oryx to the standard of this model, are slight and simple; nor can it be doubted that they have been gradually introduced by successive copyists, the idea of the single horn having been derived in the first instance from profile representations of that animal given in bas-relief on the sculptured monuments of ancient Egypt and Nubia. Excepting in the position and forward inclination of the horn, the *cartazonon* of the ancient Persians, figured on the monuments of Persepolis, and described by Aelian, tallies in every respect so exactly with the Algazel, or north African oryx, as the latter would appear en profile, with the straight and almost parallel horns precisely covering each other, that little question can exist as to that animal having furnished the original of the design. Accident may indeed have contributed still further to strengthen the opinion, once conceived, of the existence of a monocerine species, for it is well known that among the savage tribes of Africa, the art of twirling, carving and otherwise adorning the horns of their domestic animals, was carried to a singular extent — the most fanciful forms being imparted and the two even sometimes twisted together. It is, however, unnecessary to look beyond the ignorance of the limner and the credulity of the describer, satisfactorily to trace the progress of the whole delusion. Unacquainted with the science of perspective, the sculptor could contrive nothing beyond a rude representation — exhibiting a single horn and often also a single leg only, before and behind; and his clumsy designs being, by Ctesias, Herodotus and other writers, handed down as the matter of fact delineations of realities, a general belief in the existence of one horned asses became rapidly disseminated. Both the oryx and the wild ass inhabit the same regions and possess in common the essential attributes of figure, colour and carriage; nor is it at all unlikely that the mutilation of individuals of the first named species, by the fracture of a horn, may afterwards have tended to strengthen the belief derived in the first instance from these imperfect representations. A pair of oryxes thus partially humbled, were seen by Belon at Mecca: and the fierce and frequent encounters in which the males engage during the rutting season, cannot fail to multiply the number of specimens continually. Having once caught the idea, the classical fancies of the Greeks soon added the details and modified the figure of the unicorn so as to suit their *beau ideal* of its attributes; its beauty, strength and agility, being readily perfected by reducing the voluminous proportions of the body and elongating the limbs; arching the neck at the same time, to bring it to a hostile attitude and shifting the long slender horn to the centre of the forehead. Such would appear to have been the origin and progress of the fable of the unicorn, from its foundation in ancient Persia, to its diffusion over the whole of western Europe; and such, at the present day, is the figure of the fictitious animal forming the sinister supporter of the Royal Achievement of England.

That the Romans saw the oryx in their games, is attested by Martial; and the straight horned species would even appear to have been known to English Heraldry at the close of the fourteenth century, the earliest indication of this kind being among the cognizances of the Plantagenet branches, issuing from King Edward III. The antelope was a symbol of honour held by the house of Lancaster. John of Lancaster, the great Duke of Bedford, bore his arms supported by this animal. Amongst various embellishments which are painted in the Bruges style of the period, in a prayer book once the property of that prince, are found his armorial devices, with the antelope black; the straight spiral horns of which, although placed almost at right-angles with the head, are evidently designed from those of the oryx. The animal is adorned with gilded tusks, but in other respects is not ill drawn. It is conjectured that this book was illuminated on the marriage of the Duke of Bedford with Anne, Princess of Burgundy; but in no case can it be later than the period of his death in the year 1435, which fact would almost prove, that the straight horned oryx must have been known anterior to the Portuguese voyage round the Cape of Good Hope; and Mr Pennant was probably well informed when he asserted an oryx to exist in Egypt; for the figure of the animal is found among the ancient hieroglyphical representations in the tombs of its kings. The office of *Antelope Pursuivant* was instituted in the time of King Henry IV, and continued to the end of the Lancastrian branch. Whether heralds had an obscure knowledge of the animal through their intercourse with the crusaders, cannot now be ascertained; but the name itself appearing nowhere in classical Greek or Roman writers, seems derived, according to the learned researches of Baron Cuvier, from a book used by Eustathius, Bishop of Antioch, who wrote during the reign of Constantine.

The oryxes, of which no less than four distinct species are recognized, are disposed over an immense extent of territory, inhabiting the more desert and thinly peopled districts from Moultan and even the borders of China, through southern Persia, and Arabia, over the deserts of northern and central Africa, to Senegal and south to the Cape of Good Hope. Their great strength, swiftness and power of endurance, added to their ability to subsist upon the most scanty vegetation, including acrid succulents and thorny shrubs, are facts which sufficiently account for the vastness of their native regions; as they are thus enabled to pass rapidly over a great extent of country and to shift their position as reasons or circumstances may dictate. Although possessed of the graceful and symmetrical proportions which characterize the genus antelope, there is yet in their aspect a certain bovine expression, which generally has obtained for them a nomenclature having reference to that class. The Arabs, indeed, and other natives of the climates which these animals inhabit, never consider them as antelopes, but as species of the buffalo, an idea which they extend also to the bubalis and other species of that genus. The Chinese Nicu Kyo Fo, or flying cow, with one horn only, remarkable for its swiftness and love of salt, if not the *Leucoryx,* or the *Kemas,* is probably an oryx. The white antelope, with lyrate annulated horns, rode by the goddess Chandra in Hindu Mythology, and which appears to be the Ruru of the *Institutes of Menu,* must likewise be referred to this class. The Dutch colonists of the Cape alone have fancied some resemblance between their oryx and the chamois of Europe and have therefore named it gemsbok.

The South African oryx very nearly corresponds with the algazel of the northern regions of that vast continent, and with the Beiza of Abyssinia. It is a most wild and warlike looking animal, not less remarkable for beauty, speed and vigour, than famed for the excellence of its venison, which is everywhere held in the highest estimation. Although usually found in pairs on the Karoo and unfrequented stony districts, which form its invariable habitation — the males sometimes possess two females, constituting, with their young, a family of five or six individuals. The calves, which are born of a reddish cream colour, become whiter as they increase in bulk, and are easily domesticated; but their uncertain temper renders it difficult at any time to pronounce them tame. Their horns, at first blunt and round at the tips, are soon ground to a fine needle-like point, by dint of raking and whetting them against rough stemmed trees — thus becoming most formidable weapons, whether for offence or defence. The horns of the females are much longer and more bodkinish in appearance than those of the males, who never meet during the rutting season without desperate battles, their courage and quarrelsome disposition frequently rendering their duels fatal, one of the combatants often being run slap through the body by a lunge from the long rapier-resembling weapons of his antagonist. The natives of southern Africa occasionally arm their spears with the horns of the oryx; and the Hollanders of the Cape have them polished and headed with silver, to serve as walking sticks for which purpose they are frequently too long! Strong, active and vigorous, the gemsbok boldly defends itself, when pressed by the hunter, using its horns with amazing energy and address, by striking right and left at its assailants with prodigious violence. Oppian, the modern Arabs of the desert and the Hottentots, are all agreed in describing the danger of approaching these animals before they are totally disabled. It is said that even the lion dreads the encounter, and never ventures upon an attack unless irresistibly compelled by the cravings of hunger, when his temerity often costs him his life. To prove this, it is stated that the skeleton of the oryx has not infrequently been found locked in that of the king of beasts, the assailant having been transfixed by the formidable horns of the quarry in a conflict which has proved fatal to both. Of the truth of this somewhat improbable story, however, I do not pretend to offer an opinion — merely hinting, that a single blow from the heavy paw of Leo, falling with the force of a sledge-hammer, will deprive the largest ox of life more effectually than the pole-axe of a Smithfield butcher.

Although rather common in Namaqualand, the gemsbok was of sufficiently rare occurrence throughout the regions we traversed, to render it an object of the greatest interest. The first specimens we met with were on plains that skirt the northern bank of the Molopo, a spot which had been previously indicated to me at Grahamstown, by a trader named David Hume, as one in which the animal was to be seen. That wild country, dotted over with isolated groves of the *acacia capensis,* and clothed with a species of wild basil, yielding an aromatic scent when crushed beneath the foot, afforded the subject of the plate annexed — the river, which constitutes the western boundary of Moselekatse's territories, having a broad shallow bed, covered with turf and traversed by a deep *cunette,* forming a stream about ten yards wide, completely overgrown with high reeds. We had taken the field about daybreak to look for the promised unicorns, and were admiring the long slender horns of a bleaching skull on the ground, when one of the Hottentots pointed out a distant figure *statant gardant,* among a group of hartebeests. The magnifying powers of a pocket telescope presently corroborated the assertion of the discoverer, that this was a *bona fide* gemsbok. There he stood, clad in half mourning, looming as large as a donkey and scanning our party most attentively — his long taper toasting-fork horns, like a pair of walking sticks, standing out in bold relief against the blue horizon and his black bushy tail whisking over his piebald sides. '*L'on comprend,*' observes M le Comte de Buffon, in speaking of this superb animal, '*que ce bizarre assemblage de couleurs, offre un coup-d'oeil trés frappant,*' — and never were words more truly spoken. I was mounted on my favourite horse, who, before he came into my possession, by virtue of a disbursement of one hundred and fifty rix dollars, had carried off several stakes on the Cape turf; and the infallible Hottentots being unanimously of opinion with myself, that: 'Beslar could catch de bok', my companion made a circuit to intercept him from the jungles, whilst I cantered slowly towards him, looking, of course, in the opposite direction, affecting most profound ignorance of his princely presence, but treating myself, as I drew nearer and more near, to an occasional peep from under my cap.

On my arriving within eighty or a hundred yards, the beast uttered a shrill cry and dropping his wild head, which looked exactly as if encased in a black patent leather head-stall with nose-band and chin-strap complete, wheeled to the right about and scoured off with amazing swiftness, leaving the hartebeests in the rear to pursue their own devices and making straight as an arrow for the densest jungle. Here, however, the appearance of the party fortunately turned him, and as he crossed ahead of me, luffing up in the wind, I obtained a beautiful lay in. Unable to

IX. ORYX CAPENSIS:- THE GEMSBOK.

shake me off, his object now appeared to be to gain a gorge, formed by a conical tumulus which stood in advance of a low range of hills. Thus far, the ground in parts covered with detached patches of long, white, hay-like grass, was a perfect bowling green; but a few seconds brought us to the end of it, and after threading a narrow strip of *acacia detinens,* the hooked thorns of which shrub have obtained for it the title of *wagt een bityes* or wait-a-little, we dashed through the gorge together — the quarry leading by ten yards. The chase now lay over undulating stony ground, the vegetation of which had recently been cleared off by fire — the white slabs that were bared around, strongly contrasting with the black charred bushes which grew amongst the crevices. In order to burn off the withered grass, a considerable tract of country had been set on fire a few weeks before, and the bountiful thunderclouds having caused the young green blades to make their appearance, large herds of game had been attracted to the spot. Without gaining or losing a single inch upon each other, on we clattered, the strait antennae-looking horns of the fugitive laid back along his magpie flanks — his belly almost touching the ground at every stride and his ample tail sweeping behind him. Now the dust raised by a retreating herd of zebras and ostriches, whose feet rattled over the hard soil, caused a momentary diversion in his favour; and now, regaining my lost ground, we passed together under the sneering noses of three statue-resembling rhinoceroses, who had literally not time to make up their minds what was to be done, before, meteor-like, both pursuer and pursued were far beyond their reach.

Rapidly was the peach-blossom coat of the gemsbok growing darker with sweat and charcoal and fast were the fleshless sides and bleeding flanks of my exhausted steed, getting whiter with froth, as we continued to leave the ground behind us, clearing stones, ravines and bushes, without swerving one inch from our arrow-like course. At length the tongue of the quarry was lolling out, and his tail drooping between his tired legs; but although his black list stripe was almost under my bows, he was far fresher than my blowing horse, and I perceived, beyond the shadow of doubt, that another hundred yards would see me planted. Taking a strong pull upon the bridle, therefore, and cramming in the rowels, I gained a few strides upon the quarry, and throwing myself from the saddle, let fly both barrels of my rifle. The first bullet knocked up the dust behind his heels, as it glanced off the stony ground at a tangent — whizzed through the vacuum with the music of a humming-top, and finally fell harmless to the earth. To my inexpressible delight, however, the second discharge was responded by a dull heavy pat, which was instantly followed by the dangling of a hind leg. Hurrah for the hard earned spoils!

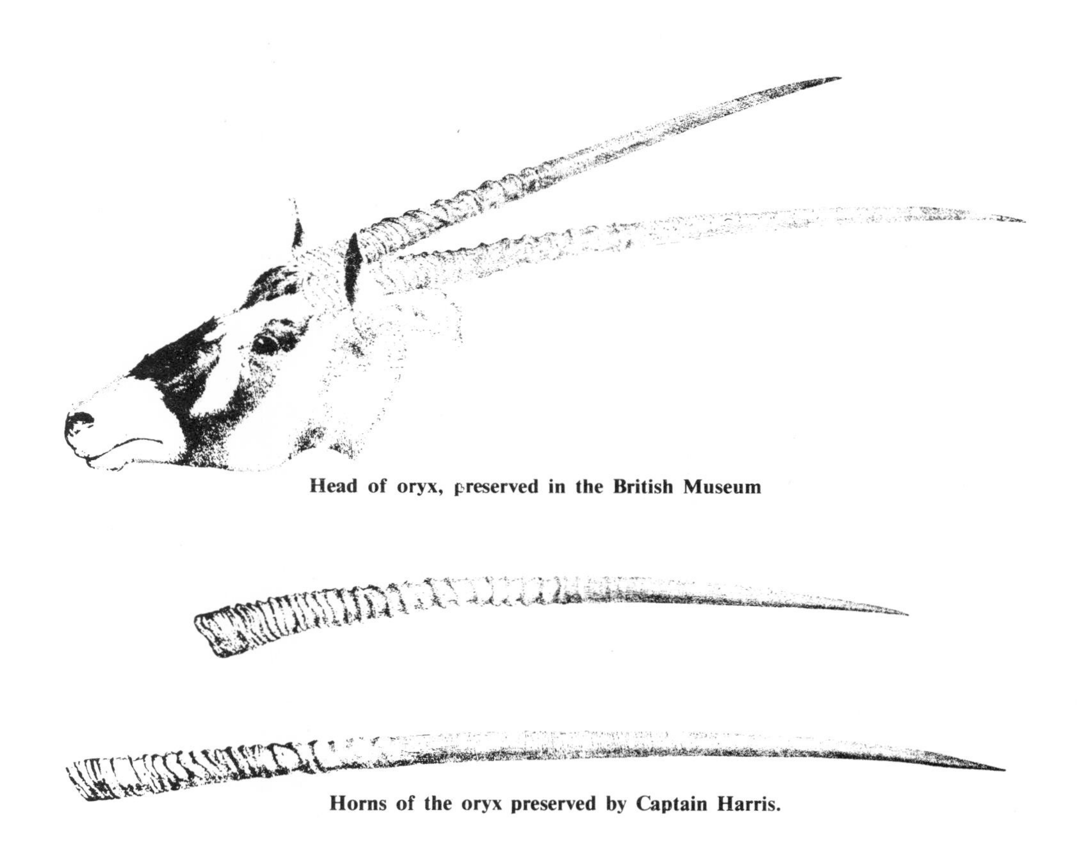

Head of oryx, preserved in the British Museum

Horns of the oryx preserved by Captain Harris.

Plate IX: *Oryx capensis — gemsbok, or South African oryx — gemsbok* of the Cape colonists — *kookaam* of the Matabili and Bechuana

Generic Character — Adult male three feet ten inches high at the shoulder; ten feet in extreme length. Figure equine and carriage majestic. Horns upwards of three feet long; placed near the summit of the frontals upon the prolongation of the plane of the face; straight, or very slightly bent; round, divergent and tapering to the points; sharp, black and shining, the lower part annulated with from twenty five to thirty rings, which usually occupy about one half the horn. In old specimens, the base is widened like the mouth of a clarionet. Eyes full, dark and prominent; high in the head. A black space between the base of the horns, descending in a streak down the forehead and chaffron; another passing through the eyes to the corner of the mouth, connected by a third which runs round the head, over the nose; a fourth passes like a chin-strap from the base of the ears under the throat, completing the appearance of a head-stall: the rest of the head white. Ears round and white, with black edgings. General colour of the coat, vinous buff, or bloom colour; soft, sleek and glossy. The breast, belly and extremities white. A tuft of bristly black hair, like that on the breast of a turkey, upon the larynx, which is also edged with black. A mane reversed: and a black list stripe of reversed hair from the nape of the neck along the back, widening angularly over the croup and terminating in a bushy black cow-like tail, three feet long, which sweeps the ground. A broad black bar across the elbow, embracing the arm, passing along the flank and ending in a wide angular space on the thigh, above the hocks. A black spot upon each leg between the knee and fetlock, leaving the rest of the extremities pure white. Limbs wiry and of exquisite proportions. Hoofs pointed and shining black. Nose ovine. No suborbital sinus.

Female similar, but slighter, with longer and more slender horns, less distinctly ringed and sometimes slightly bent. An udder with two mammae. Occasionally gregarious, but more usually found in pairs on the Karoo, or on the open plains of Namaqualand.

10

Ostrich

Gavest thou the goodly wings unto the peacocks?
or wings and feathers unto the ostrich?
Which leaveth her eggs in the earth,
and warmeth them in the dust,
And forgetteth that the foot may crush them,
or that the wild beast may break them.
She is hardened against her young ones, as though
they were not hers:
Her labour is in vain without fear.
Because God hath deprived her of wisdom, neither hath
he imparted to her understanding.
What time she lifteth up herself on high, she scorneth
the horse and his rider.

Famous from the most remote antiquity, and constituting in the chain of being, the link between the *aves* and the *mammalia,* the ostrich — largest and least bird-like of all the feathered race — is distributed over the whole of Africa, from Egypt and Barbary to the Cape; wandering also through those portions of Asia which border upon that vast continent, and setting up the staff of habitual sojourn in the sandy deserts of Arabia. Herding in troops which consist of thirty, forty or more individuals of both sexes, these giant birds inhabit the most sterile and desolate regions, commonly associating with the quagga, or with Burchell's zebra, their fellow tenants of the waste, for whose society it has already been remarked that they evince a singular predilection; and uniformly frequenting the widest and most naked plains, where their towering heads are so far elevated above their four-footed companions, and above the surrounding country, as to admit of their discovering objects at a distance which renders them secure against the stealthy invasion of man, their hereditary foe. Prudent and circumspect, the ostrich — in southern Africa at least — betrays none of that stupidity with which the species has been taxed by naturalists; and, if decreed to remain upon the earth by being denied the faculty which is the eminent prerogative of its class — it has nevertheless received in compensation, a fleetness of foot, imparting that force and rapidity in the race, which enables it to outstrip with ease, every other animal in the creation.

Aristotle pronounced the ostrich to be of a equivocal nature, 'part bird, part quadruped', and, as well in external character as in internal structure, it undoubtedly presents numerous peculiarities by which it closely approximates to the beasts. Viewed as a member of the feathered creation, its dimensions are perfectly astounding — the cock not infrequently attaining the enormous height of nine feet at the crown of the head, and actually weighing from one to three hundred pounds — whilst the muscular thigh alone, is superior in point of size to the largest leg of mutton. Unlike other birds, its tongue is short, and moulded in the form of a horseshoe; the sternum, instead of being shaped in the usual manner like the keel of a vessel, rather resembling a broad cuirass. This callous breastplate, covered with an extremely thick skin, forms no contemptible defensive armour, and is particularly favourable to the motions of the bird, in all its uprisings and down-sittings, these manoeuvres being performed much after the fashion of the dromedary, to which animal, the length of the bird's legs, as well as of its neck, combined with its singular habits, have caused it to be aptly compared. The *Strouthos* of the Greeks, as well as the *Struthio Camelus* of the Latins, have both been derived from this analogy of feature, which has even given rise amongst the people of Persia and Arabia, to a vulgar belief that the *Shutur-moorg* [Angl. — camel-bird] is produced by the union of a camel with a bird!

So easily is the ostrich satisfied in regard to water, that it is constantly to be found in arid and desolate tracts, which have been long abandoned both by antelopes and beasts of prey — a circumstance which has given rise to another absurd tradition amongst the Arabs and Hottentots that it never drinks at all, but even avoids those places in which water is to be found. Inhabiting parched and burning climes, which are seldom refreshed by rain — vast deserts of naked sand, equal in extent to the entire dominions of European sovereigns, but affording neither 'green herb nor limpid stream' — this bird, like its prototype the camel, may, in its wild state, frequently pass several days without drinking; yet in refutation of the charge of hydrophobia, it is well known to have no difficulty, when domesticated, in disposing of a gallon of liquid daily. Naturally herbivorous, it feeds principally on the tops of heather and of various shrubby plants, which even the most barren parts of Africa produce in sufficient abundance, but which would not appear to contain more moisture than an old worn out broom. So voracious is this bird, however, and so obtuse are its senses of taste and smell, that, although vegetable matter constitutes the basis of its diet, it will devour animal and mineral substances indiscriminately, until its enormous stomach can absolutely hold no more. Without any choice, and merely, as it were, to serve for ballast, it swallows in succession, stones, wood, glass, iron, copper, gold, leather, quicklime or any substance in fact which comes in its way, however hard, indigestible, and usually deleterious it may be. Hence the showman's story that the running ostrich feeds entirely upon iron; for pieces of this metal have actually been found in its stomach, greatly worn down by trituration with other hard bodies, and even eaten into, in parts, by the gastric fluid. Nevertheless the digestive powers are confined to matter of an alimentary character; nails not infrequently piercing the coats and membranes of the stomach; and copper, far from being converted into nutriment, acting upon it like poison. Nearly a pound weight of stone, metals and coins, half worn down, were discovered by M Cuvier in the body of an individual that died in the French menagerie, which during its captivity had preferred barley to any other aliment, disposing of four pounds daily, with a pound of bread and sundry heads of lettuce.

Those of the Dutch colonists who resided on the borders of the Karoo and other remote districts of the Cape, formerly made the chase of the *Volstrüys* one of their principal and most profitable occupations. As they destroyed them at all times of the year, however, without any regard to the breeding season, their numbers are now greatly brought down and in a few years the race will probably be altogether extirpated within the boundaries.

From the earliest times this noble bird has been held up to derision as the emblem of stupidity, and amongst many other ill-natured jokes cut at his expense, it has been maliciously asserted of him, that when he has hidden his own head in the sand, he foolishly believes himself to be screened from the gaze of his ruthless pursuers. Although, to withdraw itself from danger, the ostrich has uniformly recourse to flight, yet when reluctantly forced to defend itself, it will break a man's arm or leg with a single kick, striking violently also with its bill and the spinous appendages of the wings. The sound produced by a blow of the scaly foot against a board, is not less than would be produced by a horse's hoof, or by a hammer; and Pliny even went so far as to declare that the bird possessed the faculty of casting large stones behind it as its pursuers!

In southern Africa the voice of this bird, which by the sacred writers has been compared to the bellowing of a bull, is seldom heard, except during the season of incubation, when the *brommel* — as the grumbling sound emitted by the cock is termed by the Hottentots — although less prolonged, might almost be mistaken for the roar of the lion; when brought to bay, however, the bird does little more than hiss like a gander. Notwithstanding the decided predilection of the ostrich for liberty, adults taken alive are easily tamed and will suffer themselves to be parked up in flocks. If captured young, they become extremely docile and may even be left at liberty to go out of the farmyard at pleasure, in search of food; but their voracity is greatly complained of, as they frequently evince an ogre-like inclination for swallowing your chickens alive, after having demolished the hens by trampling them underfoot.

Many will suffer themselves to be ridden and might doubtless be brought to carry burdens and rendered otherwise serviceable to mankind; but although its vigour is said by authors to be so surprising that when mounted by two negroes it will run faster than the best English horse, no attempt has yet been made to apply such wonderful speed and strength to any purpose of practical utility. The exercise of bestriding the ostrich at speed is represented by the same authorities to be so distressing that the rider must be habituated to it by degrees in order to prevent its producing suffocation.

If cloudless skies and continual sunshine be favourable to human happiness, the wretched people of southern Africa might be supposed to enjoy it in a high degree of perfection. For days together, rarely does it happen that the azure field above is blotted of blemished by even the smallest speck; or that a single cloud is visible in the spacious vault of heaven. Certain tracts, of which these strange birds are the undisputed lords — unlike the sandy deserts of Arabia, consist of a hard gravelly soil of indurated clay, much impregnated with saltpetre and sprinkled over with heath and with black sickly looking shrubs. Extensive sterile plains of a brownish yellow hue, displaying neither eminence nor hollow, are on all sides expanded to the view, so that without any great effort of imagination, the spectator might fancy himself standing in the very centre of the universe. No object meets the straining eye but a solitary vulture soaring with motionless pinions in the blue firmament, or an ostrich standing out in bold relief against the distant horizon — either mounted on its stilts and pecking the tops of stunted and sun-scorched shrubs, or striding at a racing pace over boundless flats, variegated in parts with tufts of grass, whiter than mown hay.

Occasionally the sameness of the scene may be varied by a wide — stretching, surge — like undulation — hill following hill, and hollow succeeding hollow with the same regularity as the billows of the ocean, for whole miles together; and at last, peradventure, a range of blue mountains, hazy and indistinct, starts up to bound the prospect; but still, over the wide desolation of the stony waste, not a tree can be descried, and the only impression left upon the mind is, that of utter and hopeless sterility.

'Tis
A region of emptiness, howling and drear,
Which man hath abandoned from famine and fear;
Which the ostrich and lizard inhabit alone,
With the twilight bat from the old hollow stone;
Where grass, nor herb, nor shrub take root,
Save poisonous thorns that pierce the foot;
And the bitter melon for food and drink,
Is the pilgrim's fare by the salt-lake's brink!
A region of drought where no river glides,
Nor rippling brook with osier'd sides —
With no reedy pool nor mossy fountain,
Nor shady tree, nor cloud-capp'd mountain.

In my own imagination, the idea of sterility is quite inseparable from the abode of the ostrich; yet no African landscape can be considered complete without a group of these birds, and they are frequently to be seen in the greenest parts of the country. Observing them for the first time, pasturing after the fashion of a flock of geese, the stranger might easily believe that he beheld a herd of white or black cattle, according as the tails or heads were turned towards him. Many a time have I seen a solitary coal-black cock, looming as large as an ox, standing phlegmatically by himself, in the most exposed situation — the sun's rays pouring perpendicularly upon his bald pate, but he appearing most enviably regardless of the heat, drought and desolation that surround him. I have already elsewhere remarked, that amidst the vast assemblage of wild beasts frequently found congregated in the vicinity of water, a knot of stately ostriches bedizened with their showy plumes, sometimes enact the part of general officers and staff with such grave propriety, as almost to impress the spectator with a belief that he is witnessing a review on Hounslow Heath. But of the many wild scenes exhibited by Dame Nature on her African theatre, there is none wilder — no, not one more engrossing, than a fleet of these giant birds crowding all sail, their towering masts raking gallantly, with every stitch of canvas bellying to the breeze, as, like ships on the desert, they are bearing down for some particular point in the ocean-like expanse, that has been previously determined by their sailing orders and from which nothing can induce them to swerve.

The man who seeks to improve his acquaintance with the desert-loving ostrich, will presently discover why it was that she was created with a long neck. Like many other wary animals, she will often suffer a wagon to approach very close before taking the alarm, and will sometimes even feign lameness to lure the hunter from her nest; but generally speaking, her great range of vision: renders approach within moderate shot impossible, otherwise than upon horseback. Riding down an ostrich dead on end, however, is a thing not to be mentioned, or even thought of — for without distress this bird can perform its three miles in rather less time than Flying Childers, and might put its tongue in its cheek at the *tyro* who essayed to catch it in a stern chase. 'What time,' says the inspired writer, 'she lifteth up herself on high, she scorneth the horse and its rider.' Yet even miserably mounted as we were, we could generally obtain a running shot at duelling distance whenever a steed could be afforded — the enormous bulk of the object rendering the odds rather against its escaping at such close quarters. Reader, suffer me to present yonder group of more than a dozen, of which you instantly make up your mind to despoil the largest, even though the doing so should cost you a favourite horse. They have already been peering over their shoulders at you for a considerable time past, and having apprehended your design, now raise their white plumed wings above their backs, and working them like paddles with a motion corresponding to that of the legs, are getting gently under way. No sooner do they

X. STRUTHIO CAMELUS. - THE OSTRICH.

perceive by your increased pace that you are really in earnest, then letting on the steam, they begin to travel at a rate that beggars all description — moving their pillar-like legs with a rapidity that might make you believe they were skimming above the ground, did not their great heavy toes, make the dust and pebbles fly behind them and create as much clatter as a horse in trotting. With their long, straight, slender necks reared high above the withered shrubs, like knobbed stakes in a hedgerow, and their delicate white plumes fluttering in the rude breeze of the desert — those snowy plumes which are destined perhaps some day to wave in Regal palaces above the marble brow of beauty — with long, hasty strides, oars and paddles going, here come 'the running ostriches', and in ten more seconds will cross the very path upon which from another direction, you are urging your panting courser to meet them. A noble cock is leading, in stature some yard or so loftier than yourself, and clad in a suit of deep mourning, his sable shroud surmounted by three bunches of nodding plumes, *argent*. Now you are nearly across his bows. Halt, as he luffs up in the wind to pass you — abandon your blowing steed, who, by the by, is not very likely to run away from you, hold your breath tight — and as the gigantic bird thunders past within a few dozen yards, let drive at his swarthy ribs. Kicking his huge heels like a fallen camel, and striking his bill into the barren earth in his agony, there lies the noble fellow prostrate; whilst, without so much as casting one tender glance behind to ascertain what ails their lord, yon dusky ladies of his seraglio are fast vanishing in the distance. Resuming his stilts and shaking his drooping wings, he makes one strong effort to follow them — ah no! brave bird, that fleet foot is tied for ever and will obey thy call no longer. With neck reined back and ample crop dilated, swelling and boiling like a turkey-cock, he still raises himself with stately mien, hissing and agitating his white pinions; but though he fain would do you the honour of fracturing your thigh bone, you prudently prefer discharging the contents of your second barrel at his broad cuirass, which terminating his reign on earth, stretches him upon the sun-baked plain, in all his piebald majesty of rumpled feathers!

From the earliest periods, whether amongst rude or civilized nations, the downy plumes of the ostrich have been in such universal request, that the value of the spoils more than compensating the labour of the pursuit, this swift-footed bird has held out to the hunter the greatest possible temptations. The Roman soldier often wore ostrich plumes on his helmet, and they still continue to form an ornament for the head of the warrior. The whole defensive armour of the Nasamones, inhabitants of Libya, was manufactured of the bird's thick skin, which even at the present day is used as a cuirass by some of the Arab troops. In Turkey, the Janissay who signalized himself in arms had the privilege of empluming his turban; and in the kingdom of Congo the feathers mixed with those of the peacock are employed as the ensigns of war and victory. Amongst the ancient Egyptians a religious veneration for the long white feathers, as symbols of truth, so enhanced their value, that, together with the eggs, which were regarded as the emblems of watchfulness, they formed a part of the tribute imposed by the kings on the conquered countries wherein the bird abounded — the nobles of the land invariably adorning the rich trappings of their horses, as well as their own persons, with a profusion of the choicest.

Lo! white-plumed steeds, and riders bold
Throng in their rich and proud array;
And countless banner-staves unfold
Their glimmering sheen of burnished gold,
Before the torches' ray.

The purpose to which the eggs were applied is not so well understood; but from the religious prejudice which exists in their favour among the Christians of Egypt, it may be inferred that some superstition was formerly connected with them, and that they were suspended in the temples of the ancient Egyptians as they still are in the Churches of the Copts. Vast numbers of entire skins are sold by the Ethiopians to the merchants of Alexandria, for exportation to Europe, where they occupy so high a place in female estimation; those feathers being more valued by the fair, that have been plucked from the wing of the living bird, than any which are obtained from the defunct subject, the latter being lighter and more liable from their dryness to the attacks of worms.

Extremely elegant parasols are manufactured by the Bechuana, who fix the larger plumes around a circular piece of leather, through the centre of which a long stick is thrust; and it is a pleasant sight to behold a savage, whose skin, somewhat coarser than the hide of a rhinoceros, might vie in point of colour with a boot, protecting his complexion by the inter position of such an umbrella. The small black feathers of the body, being strung on a strip of leather and so twisted around a long staff as to resemble the nodding plumes of a hearse, often render most important service to the owner; the implement, if flourished before the eyes of a charging beast, and then planted in the ground, usually betraying him, half blinded with fury, to vent his rage upon it instead of upon the hunter.

We more than once fell in with a large party of Corannas engaged in an attempt to tire out an ostrich on foot, a feat which they are said sometimes to achieve, knocking him off his legs by *squaling* with a club of rhinoceros horn, fashioned like a hockey stick. Disguised in the complete spoils of the dead bird, and mimicking all the motions of the live one, by pecking at the tops of bushes and occasionally rubbing its head against its body to brush away the flies, the puny Bushman experiences no difficulty in mixing with a troop of wild animals, and can even deceive the species whose spoils he has borrowed. At the twang of his tiny bow, which rather resembles a child's toy than a mortal weapon, away scours the stricken victim with the herd, in dire consternation; and infinitely more alarmed than all, off scuds the unsuspected impostor with them, again propelling a poisoned shaft as soon as the first panic has subsided. Incredible is the destruction committed in this manner — a slender reed, only slightly barbed with a portion of the leg bone of an ostrich, embued with a subtle poison and launched with unerring dexterity, being sufficient to effect the death of the most powerful animal.

Plate X: *Struthio camelus* — ostrich — *Volstrüys* of the Cape colonists — *neechey* of the Matabili and Bechuana

Generic Character — Largest of all known birds. From seven to nine feet high at the crown of the head, and upwards of eight feet long. Body large and ponderous. Back angularly pitched, like the roof of a house. Wings short, unfit for flight, but covered with loose flexible feathers which form elegant bunches and aid the animal's progress while running. Head small and flat. Bill sub-conic, depressed horizontally, of a horn colour and blunted at the end. Nostrils oval: surrounded by bristles. Eyes large and brilliant; irides hazel; lids fringed with lashes. Greater part of the head and neck nearly bald; of a dull flesh colour, wrinkled, with a few scattered hairs, Feathers of the body lax, jet black, decomposite; the webs on each side of the shaft equal. Quill and tail feathers snowy white, long, waved and downy; the edges here and there margined with black. Chest callous and shaped like a buckler. Thighs and flanks perfectly naked. Legs very elevated and robust. Tarsi scaly. Feet strong and heavy; of a grey flesh colour. Toes two on each, connected at the base; the inner about eight inches long, the outer not more than four. Unarmed. Internally furnished with an enormous crop.

Female slighter; of a dirty umber brown complexion; otherwise similar. Gregarious, though often ranging in pairs. Still found in many parts of the Cape Colony. Extremely common throughout the interior, resorting chiefly to the Karoo's and arid plains.

Strabo relates that a somewhat similar stratagem was practised in days of yore by the inhabitants of a part of Abyssinia, who from the circumstance of their subsisting almost exclusively upon the flesh of the ostrich were denominated *Struthophagi,* and who, covering themselves with the skin, and passing the right hand into the neck, so as to import to it the motions exhibited by that bird, scattered grain with the left in order to allure the quarry into the snares which had been set for them. Oppian likewise mentions the employment of snares into which ostriches were driven *en masse,* by a brisk pursuit with horses and dogs; but for a great length of time the Arabs have used horses alone in the chase, following it with the greatest success when the birds unite in vast numbers and traverse the desert like an army of cavalry. Never putting them to their speed, but driving the troop as much as possible against the wind, and repeatedly intersecting its course by judicious riding, the hunters harass them incessantly; and having fairly wearied them down, rush in and knock them over with cudgels, to avoid sullying the lustre of the feathers. In this manner some are not infrequently taken alive and having been bereft of their costly plumes, are restored to liberty. When slain, the throat is opened, and a ligature being passed below the incision, several of the hunters raise the bird by the head and feet and shake and drag him about until they obtain from the aperture nearly twenty pounds of a substance of mingled blood and fat, of the consistence of coagulated oil, which, under the denomination of *manteque,* is employed in the preparation of dishes and the cure of various maladies. In an old subject especially, the flesh is excessively coarse and stringy, of a very dark colour, resembling beef in grain and flavour.

During the breeding season, the South African ostrich associates himself with several females, which deposit their huge eggs in one common nest, if we may so term a shallow cavity, simply scooped in the sand, of such dimensions, that it may be conveniently covered by each mamma in rotation. No attempt at concealment is made, nor is the smallest particle of any kind of material employed, the eggs being nevertheless surrounded by a shallow embankment, and thus prevented from rolling away. In the middle of the day, when the heat of the sun is sufficient to preserve them at a proper temperature, the nest is abandoned; and during the night, when marauding visits are to be anticipated from beasts of prey, the male is said to relieve his mates of the responsible office of incubation — those cocks whose feathers have been draggled by this piece of gallantry, being named *nest birds* by the Hottentots, who, be it known, are no despicable *connoisseurs* in ostrich plumes, and wear them on all occasions when desirous of making a conquest. The ground colour of the egg is pure white, marbled with clear yellow, and the number found in one place has been known to exceed sixty, the hens continuing to lay during the whole period of incubation, which extends to about forty days, and depositing surplus eggs outside, to serve, it is pretended, as nourishment for the young birds, until they shall be capable of digesting the hard and acrid food upon which the adults subsist.

The discovery of an ostrich's nest was an incident of very frequent occurrence, and any change in the monotony of an unvaried bread-and-meat diet proving highly agreeable, we always considered fresh eggs to be a prize worth carrying away. The old birds are said to kick them to pieces, should even the print of a human foot be discovered, but our followers were so unable to endure the idea of leaving a single one behind, that they never failed to render this trouble superfluous. The number being often far greater than could be conveniently dealt with, the expedient by which the removal was effected proved highly diverting. Taking off their leathern inexpressibles, which by the way, were more frequently carried on the muzzles of their guns than upon their own nether extremities, the Hottentots tied the lower ends, so as to form a double sack, and cramming them full, and placing them either across the saddle or on their own backs. Few exhibitions can be conceived more grotesque and diverting than the appearance of a procession of the bandy-legged gentlemen *en chemise,* their baboonish physiognomies protruding betwixt the straddling legs of such a load, and each diligently smoking a clay pipe as he advanced.

The Bechuana females frequently wear girdles curiously composed of circular pieces of the eggshell, about the size of a crown piece, which are so strung together as to convey the appearance of a solid zone of ivory. All the savage tribes of southern Africa use the shells for drinking cups, and in the inventory of the effects of a defunct Bushman especially, they must form a prominent item. The women of that Lilliputian race, much less shy than their husbands, often followed upon the tracks of our wagons many miles, in order to barter new laid eggs, for which they were exorbitantly paid in tobacco, the grand circulating medium of the country. The sounds uttered by the frail daughters of the desert, although serving to express their meaning, could hardly be termed a language, being, in fact, little more than a succession of clucks and claps of the tongue, such as are employed by a wagoner to urge on a jaded horse. Not easily I shall forget the appearance of one decrepit old hag, who, with an infant slung at her back, was in the daily habit of undertaking a journey of five miles from her wretched abode, for the sole purpose of filling two eggshells with water from a dirty pool at which we were encamped. Wild and withered, the beldam reminded the beholder of one of Macbeth's weird sisters — her emaciated and famine-worn frame presenting the appearance of a human skeleton enveloped in a wet leathern shroud — the shrivelled sapless limbs and protruding joints positively resembling dry knotted sticks. Her odour tainted the atmosphere; and whilst treating the little half inanimate miniature of herself to *bon-bons* obtained from the greasy folds of her scanty attire, she explained to us that she had seen me ride past her den in the morning in pursuit of the ostrich. Certain cluckings, like those of an old hen, accompanied by animated gestures, which ill befitted such a mummy — the see-saw motion of the attenuated arm corresponding with the pursing of the parchment lips, together rendering such a correct imitation of the galloping of a horse, and the retreat of the bird, that no one could mistake it — and the exhibition was immediately followed up by a learned lecture from *Coeur de Lion,* touching the imminent risk incurred by the man who should wend his solitary way through a country, infested by so imperceptible a population of pygmy.

Head of an ostrich, exhibiting at the Surrey Zoological Gardens

11

Giraffe

Magnificent creature! to reach thee I strain,
Through forest and glen, over mountain and plain,
Yet now thou art fallen, thy fate I deplore,
And lament that the reign of thy greatness is o'er.
Thine heart's blood is streaming, thy vigour gone by,
Thy fleet foot is palsied, and glazed in thine eye,
Now the last hard convulsion of death has come o'er thee,
Magnificent creature! who would not deplore thee?

During three centuries and a half, the accounts given of this extraordinary animal were deemed entirely fabulous. Its apparent disproportions and colossal height had classed it with the unicorns, and sphynxes, the satyrs, and the cynocephali of the ancients; and had induced a belief that so singular a form belonged rather to the group of chimeras with which the regions of imagination are tenanted, than existed amongst the actual works of the creation.

Loftiest of all the *mammiferes,* and isolated among the ruminating creation, whether in family, in genus or in species, the animal now before us is one so extraordinary in form, and so stupendous in stature, that even the stuffed spoils, the almost shapeless representative of the living creature, produce upon the eye of the beholder a mixed effect of astonishment and awe. Involuntarily is his imagination led back to the early epochs of the world, when colossal beings peopled the earth and were the undisputed possessors of every region. He fancies himself at once in the presence of one of the survivors of the great diluvian catastrophe, when the mastodon, the Megatherium, and perhaps its own congeners, were swept away, leaving the *camelopardalis* to attest, amongst a few others, what were the forms of a primitive animated nature!

The first of this noble species ever seen in Europe is said by Pliny to have been exhibited at Rome, during the dictatorship of Julius Caesar. Several of the emperors subsequently displayed others in the games of the circus, or in their triumphal processions; and Gordian III is said to have possessed no fewer than ten living examples at the same time. It was displayed by Aurelian amongst other remarkable animals, in his triumph over Queen Zenobia, on the conquest of Palmyra; and it is represented both in its grazing and browsing attitudes on the Proenestine mosaic pavement. In that part of the mosaic which designates the cataracts of the Nile, a larger animal is likewise represented with shorter horns. Since the southern regions of Africa were a *terra incognita* to the Romans, these specimens must have been obtained via Egypt, from the northern, or north eastern line of that vast continent. Nevertheless the animal was at no time a native of Egypt, and in the ancient sculptures is introduced only in subjects which relate to Ethiopia, whence it was brought with apes, rare woods and other native productions, as part of the tribute annually paid to the Pharaohs.

Amongst the earlier writers, Pliny, Aelian and Strabo, have all noticed the *camelopardalis,* but the first satisfactory description is to be found in the *Aethiopica* of Heliodorus, Bishop of Tricca. 'The ambassadors,' he says, 'of the Axeomitae [Abyssinia] brought presents to Hydaspes, and among other things there was an animal of a strange and wonderful species, about the size of a camel, which had its skin marked with florid spots; the hinder parts from the loins being low, like those of a lion, but the shoulders, forefeet and breast, elevated above proportion to the other parts; the neck was small and lengthened out from its large body, like that of a swan; the head in form resembled a camel's, but was in size about twice that of a Libyan ostrich, and it rolled its eyes, which had a film over them, very frightfully. It differed in gait from every other land or water animal, and waddled in a remarkable fashion; each leg did not move alternately, but those on the right side moved together, independently of the other, and those on the left in the same manner, so that each side was alternately elevated. This animal was so tractable as to be led by a small string fastened to the head, and the keeper could conduct it whithersoever he pleased, as if with the strongest chain. When it appeared, it struck the whole multitude with terror, and it took its name from the principal parts of its body, being called by the people, extempore, cameloparadalis.'

The terms of exaggeration in which the old travellers have mentioned the camelopard, were naturally derived from the distorted reports of Africans. It was 'a beast not often seene, yet very tame, and of a strange composition, mixed of a libard [leopard], harte, buffe and camel; and by reason of his long legges before, and shorter behind, not able to graze without difficulty.' Again, he was 'so huge, that a man on horseback may passe uprighte under him, feeding on leaves from the tops of trees, and formed like a camel.' In a very curious old Spanish book, however, which describes the second embassy from Henry III of Castile to Tamerlane the Great, in 1403, there is the following minute, and in many respects, accurate account of the animal: 'The ambassadors sent by the king of Castile, Henri III, to the Great Tamerlane, arrived at a town called Hoy, now Khoy, on the confines of Armenia, here the Persian empire commences. At that town they fell in with an ambassador whom the Sultan of Babylon had sent to Tamerlane. He had with him as many as twenty horsemen, and fifteen camels laden with presents, which the Sultan sent to Tamerlane. Besides these there were six ostriches, and an animal called *jornufa* which animal was formed in the following manner: In body it was the size of a horse, with the neck very long and the forelegs much taller than the hind ones: the hoof was cloven like that of the ox. From the hoof of the foreleg to the top of the shoulder, it was sixteen hands [palmos]; and from the shoulder to the head sixteen hands more; and when it raised its neck, it lifted its head so high as to be a wonder to all. The neck was like that of the stag; and so great was the disproportion of the length of the hinder legs to that of the forelegs, that one who was not acquainted with it would think it was sitting, although it was actually standing. It had the haunches slanting like the buffalo and a white belly. The skin was of a golden hue and marked with large round white spots. In the lower part of the face it resembled the deer, on the forehead it had a high and pointed prominence; very large and round eyes, and the ears like those of a horse; near the ears, two small round horns, the greater part covered with hair, resembling the horns of a deer on their first appearance. Such was the length of the

XI. CAMELOPARDALIS GIRAFFA: - THE GIRAFFE.

neck, and the animal raised its head so high when he chose, that he could eat with facility from the top of a lofty wall; and from the top of a high tree it could reach to eat the leaves of which it devoured great quantities. So that altogether it was a marvellous sight to one who had never seen such an animal before.'

Prior to the arrival, in 1827, of two living specimens, sent by command of the Pacha of Egypt to the Courts of England and France, none had been seen in Europe since the end of the fifteenth century, when the Soldan of Egypt sent one to Lorenzo di Medici. This individual was represented in the frescoes of Poggio Acajano, near Florence, with the inhabitants of which city it was very familiar — being accustomed to walk at perfect liberty about the streets, stretching its long neck to the balconies, to implore apples and other fruits, whereupon it delighted to feed. To modern naturalists the species has been known only since its discovery in southern Africa — no very precise account being obtained of its figure and habits, until within these last fifty years; and for these the world were principally indebted to the amusing and enthusiastic M Le Vaillant, whose assertions, like those of many other travellers, were nevertheless originally received as pure fabrications. So early as the year 1774, a rude design, made from a specimen killed in an expedition two hundred leagues to the north of the Cape of Good Hope, was transmitted by Governor Tulbagh to the Academy of Sciences, and this drawing, together with the ill-stuffed skin of a young one, presented at the same time, first proved that the species was not confined to Ethiopia as originally surmised; though it served also, by its incorrectness, to confirm the common error, into which even Buffon had been betrayed, of describing the forelegs to be twice as long as the hind, 'so that the rump seems brought down to the ground, and the beast, when it sits on its crupper, appears to be entirely on end.'

'I saw,' says Belon, 'at the castle of Cairo, an animal commonly called Zurnapa. It was anciently styled by the Latins, camelopardalis, a name compounded of leopard and camel for it is sprinkled and variegated with the spots of a leopard, and has a long neck like the camel. It is a most beautiful creature, as gentle in its disposition as a sheep, and more amiable than any other wild beast. The legs are long and slender, and those behind are so low, that the animal seems to stand on end.' Such blunders as these have been long exploded; but even the improved delineations of the present day, having been all derived from half grown and stunted prisoners, limited to an enclosure which they could traverse from end to end in a few dozens of their ogre-like strides, are very far from being faithful portraits of the princely *Zerapha,* as he appeared to me in his native deserts.

Where is the man who could behold the soil he treads upon, impressed with the recent footprints of this colossal quadruped, and not experience emotions of the deepest interest? Who is he amongst the votaries of the chaste goddess, that shall hear tell of riding familiarly by the side of a troop, ranging unfettered in their own wild abodes, and not feel the spirit stirred within him? The recollection of a spectacle so marvellous and so animating, awakens in my own breast a tingling renewal of past impressions, more lively than any written description can render intelligible. The chord once touched — I have already in fancy's wanderings left the haunts of men and dived anew into pathless wastes, traversed only by the brute creation — into wide savannahs where the grim lion prowls, and where the gaunt hyaenas and the wild dogs fearlessly pursue their prey. Though the glories of the African wilderness may have closed for ever on my view, so long as memory lasts they can never fade from my recollection. Intensely delightful is it to look back upon the sunny scenes that are past, and especially dear to my remembrance are the thrilling passages of which I am now to treat; but abler pens than mine, dipped even in the brightest ink, would fail to represent the reality, and leave much to be supplied by the imagination.

Well do I recall the avidity with which, in the days of my boyhood, I devoured M Le Vaillant's picturesque and eloquent account of his first success in the chase of the giraffe, at a period when men had long doubted of its existence; and many a time has my own bosom since leapt to the very emotions he describes. The appearance of a troop of those antediluvian figures, gliding majestically amid the wild magnificence of an African landscape, never failed to transport me beyond myself. Methinks I see them now — in yonder 'field, spacious and delightful by the shade of many stately and aged trees' — the white chintz-pattern garments of the ladylike cows contrasting vividly with the chocolate coloured robe of that mighty bull. Aye, there they stand, grouped tranquilly in graceful and dignified attitudes, elevating their stately crests to the clouds, some craning over the tops of the smaller trees, whilst others — burying their light heads among the reticulated boughs and darting out their long black tongues like the chameleon, are busily drawing in the tender sprigs.

It was on the morning after our departure from the residence of his Amazooloo Majesty, that I first actually saw the giraffe. Although I had been for weeks on the tiptoe of expectation, we had hitherto succeeded in finding the gigantic footsteps only of the tallest of all the quadrupeds upon the earth; but at dawn of that day, a large party of hungry savages, with four of the Hottentots on horseback, having accompanied us across the Mariqua in search of elands, which were reported to be numerous in the neighbourhood, we formed a long line, and having drawn a great extent of country blank, divided into two parties, Richardson keeping to the right, and myself to the left. Beginning at length to despair of success, I had shot a hartebeest for the savages, when an object which had repeatedly attracted my eye — but which I had as often persuaded myself was nothing more than the branchless stump of some withered tree, suddenly shifted its position, and the next moment I distinctly perceived that singular form, of which the apparition had ofttimes visited my slumbers — but upon whose reality I now gazed for the first time. Gliding rapidly among the trees, above the topmost branches of many of which its graceful head nodded like some lofty pine, all doubt was in another moment at an end - it was the stately, and long-sought giraffe. Putting spurs to my horse and directing the Hottentots to follow, I presently found myself half choked with excitement, rattling at the heels of an animal which to me had been a stranger even in its captive state, and which thus to

Plate XI: *Camelopardalis giraffe* — camelopard or giraffe — *kameel* of the Cape colonists — *naip* of the Hottentots — *intootla* of the Bechuana and Matabili

Generic Character — In stature the tallest of mammiferous animals. Adult male, twelve feet high at the shoulder and eighteen at the crown of the head. Twenty feet in extreme length. Legs slender and very long. Feet terminating in a divided hoof, shaped like a parellelogram, with rounded heel and pointed toe. No succentorial hoofs. Body short. Withers very elevated, a scanty upright rufous mane extending along the whole neck. Back very oblique. Tail thirty four inches long, terminating in a tuft of bristly black hair about the same length, which reaches to the hocks. Head light and tapering, thirty four inches long; provided with osseous peduncles (common to both sexes), eight inches long, covered with a hairy skin and terminating in a pencilled tuft of black hair. A tuberculum on the chaffron. No muzzle. Upper lip entire; hairy and pointed. Eyes large and melting, with long lashes. No lachrymary sinus. Ears pure white and ample. Callosities on the breast and knees. Tongue very long, pointed and flexible. General colour, deep sienna, with large angular ferruginous spots, variously disposed over the whole; each spot darker in the centre. Belly and cheeks white, with dark blotches.

Female, sixteen or seventeen feet in height at the crown, of a dirty white colour, with pale ferruginous spots as in the male. An udder with four teats. Gregarious in small troops. Inhabits the great wooded plains of the interior.

meet, free on its native plains, has fallen to the lot of but few of the votaries of the chase. Sailing before me with incredible velocity, his long swan-like neck keeping time to the eccentric motion of his stilt-like legs — his ample black tail curled above his back, and whisking in ludicrous concert with the rocking of his disproportioned frame, he glided gallantly along 'like some tall ship upon the ocean's bosom,' and seemed to leave whole leagues behind him at each stride. The ground was of the most treacherous description — a rotten black soil overgrown with long coarse grass, which concealed from view innumerable gaping fissures that momentarily threatened to bring down my horse. For the first five minutes I rather lost than gained ground, and despairing, over such a country, of ever diminishing the distance, or improving my acquaintance with this ogre in seven league boots, I dismounted, and the mottled carcase presenting a fair and inviting mark, I had the satisfaction of hearing two balls tell roundly upon his plank-like stern. But as well might I have fired at a wall; he neither swerved from his course, nor slackened his pace, and pushed on so far ahead during the time I was reloading, that after remounting, I had some difficulty in even keeping sight of him amongst the trees. Closing again, however, I repeated the dose on the other quarter, and spurred my horse along, even and anon sinking to his fetlock — the giraffe now flagging at each stride — until, as I was coming up hand over hand and success seemed certain, the cup was suddenly dashed from my lips and down I came headlong — my horse having fallen into a pit and lodged me close to an ostrich's nest, near which two of the old birds were sitting.

Happily there were no bones broken, but the violence of the shock had caused the lashings of my previously broken rifle to give way and had doubled the stock in half — the barrels only now hanging to the wood by the trigger guard. Nothing dismayed, however, by this heavy calamity, I remounted my jaded beast, and one more effort brought me ahead of my wearied victim, which stood still and allowed me to approach. In vain did I now attempt to bind my fractured rifle with a pocket handkerchief, in order to admit of my administering the *coup de grace* — the guard was so contracted, that as in the tantalizing fantasies of a nightmare, the hammer could not by any means be brought down upon the nipple. In vain I looked around for a stone, and sought in every pocket for my knife, with which either to strike the copper cap and bring about ignition, or hamstring the colossal but harmless animal, by whose towering side I appeared the veriest pygmy in the creation — alas, I had lent it to the Hottentots to cut off the head of the hartebeest, and after a hopeless search in the remotest corners, each hand was withdrawn empty. Vainly did I then wait for the tardy and rebellious villains to come to my assistance, making the welkin ring and my throat tingle, with reiterated shouts — not a soul appeared — and, in a few minutes, the giraffe having recovered his wind, and being only slightly wounded in the hind quarters, shuffled his long legs — twisted his bushy tail over his back — walked a few steps — then broke into a gallop, and diving into the mazes of the forest presently disappeared from my sight. Disappointed and annoyed at my discomfiture, I returned towards the wagons, now eight miles distant, and on my way overtook the Hottentots, who, pipe in mouth, were leisurely strolling home with an air of total indifference as to my proceedings, having come to the conclusion that, 'Sir could not fung de kameel' [Angl. Catch the camelopard] for which reason they did not think it worth while to follow as I had directed.

Two days after this catastrophe, having advanced to the Tolaan River, we again took the field, accompanied by the whole of the male inhabitants of three large kraals, in addition to those that had accompanied us from the last encampment. The country had now become undulating, extensive mimosa groves occupying all the valleys, as well as the banks of the Tolaan, winding amongst them on its way to join the Mariqua. Before we had proceeded many hundred yards, our progress was opposed by a rhinoceros, who looked defiance, but quickly took the hints we gave him to get out of the way. Two fat elands had been pointed out at the edge of the copse the moment before, one of which Richardson disposed of with little difficulty, the other leading me through all the intricacies of the labyrinth to a wide plain on the opposite side — on entering which I found the fugitive was prostrate at my feet in the middle of a troop of giraffes, who stooped their long necks, astounded at the intrusion — then consulted a moment how they should best escape the impending danger — and in another, were sailing away at their utmost speed. To have followed upon my then jaded horse would have been absurd, and I was afterwards unable to recover any trace of them.

Several hours' diligent search the following day, brought us within telescopic range of twelve, whose carpet robes flickered amid glare and vapour, by which their lower parts were quite obscured. Pursuing them a considerable distance, over an extensive plain, where mokaala trees grew among thistles and mat-rushes, we repeatedly wounded the largest male, a gigantic dark coloured fellow, probably eighteen feet in height; but he merely acknowledged the receipt of each bullet as it whacked against his stern-posts and bulwarks, by wincing a little as if stung by a gnat — and then, tying an extra knot in his tail, increased his pace. Our famished horses falling repeatedly into the numerous buffalo holes with which the ground was covered, we at length relinquished the chase, convinced of the impossibility of humbling the lofty head of the giraffe, until our steeds should have improved in condition upon the fine pasturage which now abounded. A range of blue mountains which we visited some weeks afterwards with better success, bounded the wide prospect to the north eastward, and the face of the country being covered with large herds of elands, we vented our spleen upon them — the great host of savages by whom we were attended, quickly clearing away the carcases of those we slew and even quarreling for the entrails.

Many days elapsed before we again beheld the tall giraffe, nor were our eyes gladdened with his sight until after we had crossed the Cashan Mountains to the country of the Baquaina, for the express purpose of seeking for him. After the many *contretemps,* how shall I describe the sensations I experienced, as on a cool November morning, after rapidly following some fresh traces in profound silence for several miles, I at length counted from the back of *Breslar,* my most trusty steed, no fewer than thirty two of various sizes, industriously stretching their peacock necks to crop the tiny leaves that fluttered above their heads, in a flowering mimosa grove which beautified the scenery. My heart leapt within me, and the blood coursed like quicksilver through my veins, for, with a firm wooded plain before me, I knew that they were mine; but although they stood within a hundred yards of me, having previously determined to try the *boarding* system, I reserved my fire. Notwithstanding that I had taken the field expressly to look for giraffes, and in consequence of several of the remarkable *spoors* of those animals having been seen the evening before, had taken four mounted Hottentots in my suite, all excepting Piet had as usual slipped off unperceived in pursuit of a troop of koodoos. Our stealthy approach was soon opposed by an ill- tempered rhinoceros, which with her ugly old fashioned calf stood directly in the path; and the twinkling of her bright little eyes, accompanied by a restless rolling of the body, giving earnest of her mischievous intentions, I directed Piet to salute her with a broadside, at the same moment putting my spurs to my horse. At the report of the gun and the sudden clattering of hoofs, away bounded the herd in grotesque confusion — clearing the ground by a succession of frog-like hops, and soon leaving me far in their rear. Twice were their towering forms concealed from view by a park of trees, which we entered almost at the same instant; and twice on emerging from the labyrinth, did I perceive them tilting over an eminence far in advance, their sloping backs reddening in the sunshine, as with giant port they topped the ridges in right gallant style. A white turban, that I wore round my hunting cap, being dragged off by a projecting bough, was instantly charged and trampled under foot by three rhinoceroses; and long afterwards looking over my shoulder, I could see the ungainly brutes in the rear fagging themselves to overtake me. In the course of five minutes, the fugitives arrived at a small river, the treacherous sands of which receiving their spider legs, their flight was greatly retarded; and by the time they had floundered to the opposite side and scrambled to the top of the bank, I could perceive that their race was run. Patting the steaming neck of my good steed, I urged him again to his utmost, and instantly found myself by the side of the herd. The lordly chief, being readily distinguishable from the rest by his dark chestnut robe and superior stature, I applied the muzzle of my rifle behind his dappled shoulder with the right hand and drew both triggers; but he still continued to shuffle along, and being afraid of losing him, should I dismount among the extensive mimosa groves, with which the landscape was now obscured, I sat in my saddle, loading and firing behind the elbow, and then placing myself across his path to obstruct his progress. Mute, dignified and majestic, stood the unfortunate victim, occasionally stooping his elastic neck towards her persecutor, the tears trickling down the lashes of his dark humid eye, as broadside after broadside was poured into her brawny front.

His drooping head sinks gradually low,
And through his side, the last drops ebbing slow
From the red gash, fall heavy, one by one,
Like the first of a thunder shower.

Presently a convulsive shivering seized his limbs — his coat stood on end — his lofty frame began to totter — and at the seventeenth discharge from the deadly grooved bore, like a falling minaret, bowing his graceful head from the skies, his proud form was prostrate in the dust. Never shall I forget the intoxicating excitement of that moment! At last, then, the summit of my hunting ambition was actually attained, and the towering giraffe laid low. Tossing my turbanless cap into the air — alone, in the wild wood, I hurraed with bursting exultation, and unsaddling my steed, sank exhausted with delight beside the noble prize that I had won.

When I leisurely contemplated the massive frame before me, seeming as though it had been cast in a mould of brass and wrapped in a hide an inch and a half in thickness, it was no longer a matter of astonishment that a bullet, discharged from a distance of eighty or ninety yards, should have been attended with little effect upon such amazing strength. 'Did stature alone constitute precedency, observes M Le Vaillant, the giraffe would undoubtedly claim the highest rank among quadrupeds.' From the crown of the elegantly moulded head to the sole of the hoof of this magnificent animal, the extreme height was eighteen feet; the whole being equally divided into neck, body and leg. Two hours were passed in completing a drawing; and Piet still not making his appearance, I cut off the ample tail, which exceeded five feet in length and was measurelessly the most estimable trophy I had ever gained; but on proceeding to saddle my horse, which I had left quietly grazing by the side of a running brook, my chagrin may be conceived, when I discovered that he had taken advantage of my occupation to free himself from his halter and abscond. Being ten miles from the wagons and in a perfectly strange country, I felt convinced that the only chance of saving my pet from the clutches of the lion, was to follow his trail, whilst doing which with infinite difficulty, the ground scarcely deigning to receive a footprint, I had the satisfaction of meeting Piet and Mohanycom, who had fortunately seen and recaptured the truant. Returning to the giraffe, we all feasted heartily upon the flesh, which, although at this season highly scented with the rank Mokaala blossoms, was far from despicable, and losing our way, in consequence of the twin-like resemblance of two scarped hills, we did not finally regain the wagons until after the setting sunbeams had ceased to play upon the trembling leaves of the light acacias, and the golden splendour which was sleeping upon the plain, had gradually passed away.

The spell was now broken and the secret of *camelopard* hunting discovered. The next day Richardson and myself killed three; one, a female, slipping upon muddy ground and falling with great violence, before she had been wounded, was despatched by a shot in the head as she lay floundering like a tommy-long-legs. From this time we could reckon confidently upon two out of each troop that we were fortunate enough to find, by always approaching as near as possible, in order to ensure a good start, galloping into the middle of them, *boarding* the largest and riding with him until he subsided. A few only, struck in a vital part, fell at once in a mighty crash and arose up no more. The rapidity with which these awkwardly formed animals can move, is beyond all things surprising, our best horses being unable to close with them under two miles. Their gallop is a succession of jumping strides, the fore and hind legs on the same side moving together, instead of diagonally, as in most other quadrupeds, the former being kept close to each other, and the latter wide apart like a pair of oars, so that in riding by the animal's side, the hind hoof extends behind and beyond the horse, momentarily threatening to overthrow him. The motion arises less from the roof-like slope of the back, than from the total absence of channel, the stern appearing exactly as if it had been plastered. Perhaps the complicated sawing progress of this strange animal might be aptly compared to that of a horse whose fore feet were shackled; but altogether it reminded me rather of the pitching of a ship, or the rolling of a rocking horse, than of anything living; and the remarkable gait is rendered still more automaton-like, by the switching, at regular intervals, of the long black tail, which is invariably curled above the back, and by the corresponding action of the neck, swinging as it does like a pendulum and literally giving the creature the appearance of a piece of machinery in motion.

The ordinary pace, although more stately and dignified, is also rapid, by reason of the great length of the legs; and owing to the condensation of the carcase, the hinder feet instead of covering the fore, as in most other quadrupeds, are still invariably placed in advance of them, considerably on the outside. The cloven hoof measures from ten to twelve inches in length, and being parallelogrammatic, with a rounded heel and pointed toe, resembles a pair of slippers placed side by side. Be the giraffe running or walking, the lofty neck is invariably protruded and carried in the prolongation of the slope of the back, without forming any angle with the withers, in the manner usually represented; and possessing only seven joints, it appears, although beautifully flexible, to move on a pivot, instead of being curved, like that of the swan or peacock. Numerous folds of loose skin betwixt the forelegs enable it to straddle wide, but the operation of bringing the head to the ground is still one of extreme awkwardness, and from the browsing habits of the animal can be rarely necessary — the leaves, tender shoots and blossoms of that singular species of mimosa, called by the colonists, *kameel doorn* [giraffe thorn], and found chiefly on the dry plains or sandy deserts, forming its ordinary food. The size of this tree, together with its thick and spreading top, shaped like an umbrella, distinguish it at once from all others of the country — the Namaquas terming it the *kanaap*, whilst by all the Bechuana nations it is recognized as the *mokaala*. Both in flower and foliage it closely resembles the common Cape acacia, but the pod is an oval husk, filled with a solid mealy substance, and the stem is covered with stout thorns. The wood, excessively hard and heavy and of a dark red colour, with a black heart, is much used by the Africans in the manufacture of spoons and other domestic utensils, many of which are ingeniously fashioned after the model of the giraffe.

So far as came under my observation both sexes are mute, and utter no cry whatever. The male, whose maximum stature appears to be about eighteen feet, increases in depth of colour with his years — the patriarchs becoming well nigh black; but the cows, whilst they seldom attain the height of seventeen feet, are uniformly of a fainter hue, bordering upon straw colour. Both sexes have crisp flaky coats, similarly marked with a rhomboidal or pentaganol carpet pattern, somewhat symmetrically disposed — and they possess in common, obtuse horns, or rather peduncles, about six or eight inches in length, covered with hair like the footstalk of a stag's antlers, but terminating in a black pencilled tuft. On the chaffron also is a remarkable prominence, which increases with age and in the young females is scarcely perceptible. The senses of sight, hearing and smell are acute and delicate; the full humid eye, fringed with dark silken lashes, eclipsing those of the oft sung gazelle of the East. Beaming with the mildest and most intelligent expression, they are so arranged that the animal can see both before and behind without turning its graceful head. Nor is the construction of the tongue less remarkable — its mobility being such as to enable it to perform in miniature the office of the elephant's proboscis, by coiling round the twigs of lofty trees, and assisting, like the nose of the tapir, in drawing the tender sprouts betwixt the flexible lips.

Amongst the Griquas or Bastaards, as the Mulatto Hottentots residing beyond the border are termed by the colonists, large parties are annually formed for the purpose of hunting the eland and kameel, the flesh of both being held in equal estimation, and the thick robe of the latter considered the *ne plus ultra* for sandal soles. Many of the wretched wigwams of these people are thatched with an entire hide. During our sojourn at Chooi, we had an interview with a party returning from the Molopo, freighted with the spoils of not fewer than thirty three, in obtaining which they had expended the whole of their ammunition and worn their wretched horses to skin and bone. A trader whom I met in the Cape Colony, assured me before I visited the interior, that he had himself counted so many as eight hundred kameels in a single day, and during his extensive travels had ridden down hundreds. But on our return, after a little cross-examination, the number destroyed gradually dwindled down to *one;* which solitary individual appeared upon further investigation to have been entrapped in a pitfall! They are sometimes taken in this manner by the savages, who can never speak of the lofty *intootla* without rising on tiptoe and stretching their black necks to the utmost. A full grown female, heavy in foal, was one night slaughtered by a lion whilst in the act of drinking at no great distance from our wagons; and in the morning, an inspection of the scene of the noisy conflict, proved that the giant strength of the victim had been paralyzed in a moment by the grip of its tawny foe. Indeed, notwithstanding the amazing power of the animal, I should be disposed to doubt its ability to maintain a race under the merciless jockeyship of the 'great destroyer' — who, clinging with teeth and talons, is said, or rather fabled, to be carried fifteen or twenty miles before the quarry sinks under him, and not unusually to be hurled off at last without effecting his purpose.

Heedless at the ambushed brink
The tall giraffe stoops down to drink:
Upon him straight the savage springs
With cruel joy! The desert rings
With clanging sound of desperate strife —
For the prey is strong and strives for life;
Now plunging tries with frantic bound
To shake the tyrant to the ground;
Then bursts like whirlwind through the waste,
In hope to 'scape by headlong haste:
While the destroyer on his prize
Rides proudly, tearing as he flies.
For life the victim's utmost speed
Is mustered in this hour of need;
For life, for life, his giant might
He strains, and pours his soul in flight,
And, mad with terror, thirst, and pain,
Spurns with wild hoof the thundering plain.

An inhabitant of Nubia and Abyssinia, as well as of the adjacent regions east of the Great Desert, the princely Zerapha occurs southward over central Africa, toward the settlement at the Cape, but is now to be found lower than the twenty fourth parallel of latitude. Of sequestered habits, it seeks the most secluded deserts, and even at its headquarters is by no means a common animal. Whilst we seldom saw one without having followed the trail, we never found more than five and thirty in the same day; and the range of its habitat, although so extensive, is exclusively confined to solitary regions, in which the *kameel doorn* is abundant. It was delightful to witness the courage evinced by our horses, in the pursuit of game, and even when brought into actual contact with this almost unearthly quadruped, they evinced no symptom of fear — a circumstance which, I confess, we felt sometimes disposed to ascribe rather to their meagre diet, than to the virtue of their training. Not indeed that there existed any real cause for alarm; for naturally gentle, timid and peaceable, the beautiful colossus has no means of protecting itself but with its heels; and although jammed into a corner, rarely even resorted to kicking as a mode of defence. Meek and resigned, it trusted to its speed alone, and having learned to its cost that 'the race is not always to the swift,' wept such bitter tears, when vanquished, that but for its fleetness and rarity, the expression of its dove-like eyes might almost have disarmed me.

Head of giraffe from North Africa, exhibiting in the Zoological Gardens, Regent's Park

12

Hippopotamus

Behold now Behemoth, which I made with thee; he eateth grass as an ox.
Lo now, his strength is in his loins, and his force is in the navel of his belly.
His bones are as strong pieces of brass, his ribs are like bars of iron.
Surely the mountains bring him forth food, where all the beasts of the field play.
He lieth under the shady trees, in the covert of the reed and fens.
The shady trees cover him with their shadow, the willows of the brook compass him about.

Modern commentators are nearly all agreed in identifying *Behemoth* of the Sacred writings with the hippopotamus — as well as in pronouncing the scaly crocodile, to be *leviathan,* created 'hugest of beasts that swim the ocean stream'. Alike amphibious and inhabiting the same waters, these aquatic monsters were uniformly associated together by the ancients, who were wont to describe them both as being possessed of the most marvellous powers; and when the changes are considered which time and civilisation have wrought in the relative position of man and the wild beasts, the poetical descriptions given in the Book of Job will be found throughout so characteristic of the habits of each, as to leave little doubt upon the mind that these must have been the animals implied; for in arriving at our conclusions upon a subject so remote, it should be borne in mind that creatures which in the earlier history of our own species, were 'words of fear', have gradually been rendered more timid and less formidable, in the ratio of the encroachments of man upon their wild haunts, armed with more efficient weapons for their destruction. But of all the mammalia, whose portraits, drawn from exaggerated descriptions or mutilated specimens, have been foisted upon the world, poor Behemoth has doubtless been the most shamefully traduced and the most ludicrously misrepresented. Although celebrated from the most remote antiquity, engraven both on Egyptian obelisks and on Roman medals, sacrificed in combats of the arena, and exhibited with other rare and singular animals in triumphal processions, his history was nevertheless so imperfectly understood by the ancients, that both Aristotle and Herodotus awarded him the voice and mane of a horse, the hoofs of an ox and the tail and tusks of a wild boar — the whole tastefully combined with the fair proportions of an ass! Pliny did not fail to add handsomely to this catalogue of blunders; and yet, according to his own account, the citizens of Rome were treated by Scaurus during his edileship, to the sight of a live hippopotamus, which, together with four crocodiles, was exhibited in a temporary lake prepared for the occasion.

And a deformed sort of monsters came
Which by their shape we might sea-horses name.

Augustus next producing one of the prodigies as an appropriate emblem of conquered Egypt, on his triumph over Cleopatra. The paintings at Herculaneum, which are delineative of Egyptian scenery, represent the might river-horse browsing upon the herbage of an island while the crocodile is basking amid flags and bulrushes. In the famous mosaic pavement at Praeneste, also, which exhibits the plants and animals of Egypt, the two figures are given in the same group upon the Nile. But although, after that date, the figure of the hippopotamus appeared on various medals of the Roman emperors, it was not until many ages afterwards that any authentic history of the animal could be obtained.

About the middle of the sixteenth century, Belon saw at Constantinople a living hippopotamus, of which nevertheless he gives but an imperfect representation — the two figures with which he has illustrated his description not having been drawn from the animal he saw, but copied from the reverse of Adrian's medal, and from the Egyptian colossus at Rome. Hence the era of any exact knowledge of this animal must be brought down to the beginning of the seventeenth century, when Frederico Zerenghi, a surgeon of Narni in Italy, published at Naples the history of two hippopotami which he had taken alive near Damietta, in a great ditch dug for the purpose in the neighbourhood of the Nile. 'With a view,' says the Doctor, 'of obtaining an hippopotamus, I stationed men upon the Nile, who, having seen two of these animals go out of the river, made a large ditch in the way through which they passed, and covered it over with thin planks, earth and herbage. In the evening, when returning to the river, they both fell into the ditch. I was immediately informed of the event and having hastened to the place with my Janizary, we killed both the animals by pouring three shots into each of their heads from a large arquebuse. They almost instantly expired, after uttering a cry which bore greater resemblance to the bellowing of a buffalo than the neighing of a horse. This exploit was performed on the 20th day of July 1600. The following day they were drawn out of the ditch and carefully flayed. They proved male and female, and I caused their skins to be salted and stuffed with the leaves of the sugar cane, in order to transport them to Cairo, where they were salted a second time with greater attention and convenience, each skin requiring four hundred pounds weight of salt. On my return from Egypt in 1601, I brought them to Venice and from thence to Rome, and showed them to several intelligent physicians. Doctor Jerome Aquapendente and the celebrated Aldrovandus, were the only persons who recognised them to be the spoils of the hippopotamus; and as the latter's work was then printing, I allowed him to draw a figure from the skin of the female, which he inserted in his book.'

The aquatic habits of the species, no less than the secluded nature of its haunts, are of course greatly opposed to an intimate acquaintance with its manner of living; but one thing is certain, that modern hippopotami have retained little of the dexterity or the cunning of their ancestors, whom Pliny represents to have been in the constant habit of walking backwards in order to deceive their pursuers — the more simple plan of getting their shoes reversed, as King Robert Bruce did those of his horse, having not perhaps occurred to them. The mode in which the animal, when wounded, contrived to moor himself by the teeth to the roots of water-trees; and his method of performing venesection,

XII. HIPPOPOTAMUS AMPHIBIUS. – THE HIPPOPOTAMUS.

when he found himself so shamefully *embonpoint,* as to be in danger of apoplexy, were even more ingenious. 'The hippopotamus,' says Pére Labat, 'being of a very sanguiferous temperament, knows well how to let blood of himself. For this purpose, he searches for a sharp pointed rock, and rubs himself against it, till he makes a sufficient aperture for the blood to flow. To promote the flux, he then agitates his body, and when he thinks he has lost a sufficient quantity, he rolls in the mud in order to shut up the wound.' 'I have known,' says Captain Covent, in a letter to Dampier, 'the hippopotamus to open his mouth, and set one tooth on the gunnel of a boat, and another on the second strake from the keel (which was more than four feet distant), and there bit a hole through the plank, and sink the boat; and after he had done, he went away shaking his ears. His strength is incredibly great, for I have seen him in the wash of the shore, when the sea has tossed in a Dutchman's boat with fourteen hogsheads of water in her, upon the said beast, and left it high and dry on its back, and another sea came, and fetched the boat off and the beast was not hurt, in as far as I could perceive. We made several shots at him, but to no purpose, for they would glance off him as from a wall. It is the custom of the natives when he comes near their canoes, to throw him fish and then he passeth away, and will not meddle with their fishing craft. They call him *Kittimpungo.* He doth most mischief when he can stand on the ground; but when afloat hath only power to bite. As our boat once lay near the shore, I saw him go under her, and with his back lift her out of the water and overset her with six men aboard, but as it happened did them no harm. Whilst we lay in the road, we had three of them which did trouble the bay every full and change, and two or three days after. The natives say they go together, two males and one female, and their noise is much like the bellowing of a large calf.' The males are said to contest each other's right to the females and the attack of two such powerful animals, as may naturally be imagined, is terrible. The earth shakes beneath them — the water trembles — their blood flows in torrents, and the masses of flesh torn out by their mighty grasp of teeth, lie scattered upon the blood-stained scene of conflict. Sometimes, the weaker, perceiving his efforts ineffectual, leaves his antagonist master of the field, but this does not often happen, for it is seldom that one or both of them does not perish on the spot.

Onesicritus and other old authors, assert that the hippopotamus inhabited Asia, and abounded in the River Indus, but Alexander's letter to Aristotle, which forms the only foundation for such an opinion, is so far from being conclusive, that it seems probable the range of its habitat has always been limited to the lakes and rivers of Africa, more especially to those of her southern and eastern regions. Common in Egypt in days of yore, ere modern weapons had taught it to fear man as an enemy before whom it must retire, it divided with the mail-clad crocodile the empire of the Nile and its delta — that noble stream, over whose source mystery had cast a veil, and whose waters whilst spreading the blessings of seed time and harvest throughout a country where millions greeted their overflow, teemed at the same time with productions monstrous and terrific, against which neither the spear nor the arrow availed but little. The hippopotamus was consequently well known to the Israelites of old, and with the Egyptians the chase of him formed a favourite amusement. Although not so hostile to man as the voracious crocodile, he was yet looked upon as an enemy, on account of his extensive nocturnal depredations, and the value attached to his spoils, of which were manufactured whips, shields, javelins and helmets created an additional incitement to his destruction. Their mode of attach would appear, from the sculptures of Thebes, to have been very similar to that practised at the present day about Sennaar, where the hunters prefer badgering the animal in the river, to an open combat on shore, and employ the harpoon as in whaling. 'It is chased,' says Diodorus Siculus, who describes the hippopotamus more correctly than any other ancient author, 'by many persons armed with iron javelins. No sooner does it make its appearance at the surface of the water, than they surround it with boats and closing in on all sides, strike it with blades furnished with iron barbs, and having hempen ropes fastened to them, in order that when wounded they may be let out until its strength fails from struggling and loss of blood.' Authors inform us, that after the species had become nearly extinct in Nubia, the accidental descent of a luckless straggler along the river, occasioned scarcely less astonishment to the people who witnessed the intrusion, than to the bewildered animal itself. As usual on such occasion, the unintentional trespasser upon ground where it had ceased to be an object of terror, was punished with a promptitude which would hardly have been displayed in places where it was really obnoxious — every Turks or peasant who could muster a weapon, being fired with the same proud desire of destroying the intruder, and evincing the same chivalrous feeling which is usually called forth against an imprudent porpoise that may have ventured to pass the bridges of the English metropolis.

Dr Edward Rüppell, who partook of the sport of harpooning the hippopotamus in Dongola, gives the most appalling description of the death of the largest he met with. 'One of those which we killed,' he writes, 'was a very old fellow, and of an enormous size, measuring thirteen and a half French feet, from the nose to the extremity of the tail. His incisor teeth were twenty six French inches long, measured from the root to the point, along the outer bending. We fought him for a good four hours at night and were very near losing our large boat and probably our lives too, owing to the fury of the animal. As soon as he spied the huntsmen in the large canoe, whose business it was to fasten the long rope to the float, he dashed at them with all his might, dragged the canoe with him under the water, and smashed it to pieces. The two huntsmen with difficulty escaped. Of twenty five musket balls aimed at the head from a distance of about five feet, only one pierced the skin and the bones of the nose. At each snorting the animal sprouted out large streams of blood on the boat. The rest of the balls stuck in the thick hide. At last we availed

Plate XII: *Hippopotamus amphibius* — hippopotamus or sea-cow — *zeekoe* of the Cape colonists — *imfoobo* of the Kaffirs and Bechuana

Generic Character — Between four and five feet high at the shoulders, and from eleven to twelve in extreme length. Figure particularly massive and heavy. Body ponderous and shapeless with fat. Neck brawny as in a stall-fed bull, short, voluminous and rounded, with a colloped crest formed by a continuation of the arch of the back. Head thick and square. Muzzle broad, truncated and furnished with a few detached pencils of split bristly hair. Gape wide. Lips full and bulging, so turned up towards the angles of the mouth as to impart to the face a quaint and waggish expression, enhanced both by the very elevated position of the diminutive eyes, which are seated in a pulpy prominence, and by the singular appearance of the rounded ears, which are approximated, and would seem to have been unsparingly cropped. Lower incisors long and placed horizontally. Canine teeth greatly developed; those in the lower jaw forming tusks, which, when the mouth is closed, are nevertheless completely concealed by the overhanging lips. Legs so extremely short that the belly almost touches the ground. Feet disproportionably small, and terminating in four detached anterior toes, armed with hoofs. Tail twelve inches, flabby like that of a tortoise and beset with bristles towards the extremity. Skin rough, hard and remarkably thick; entirely destitute of hair. General colour dirty pinkish brown, waxing lighter on the belly and flanks, where the skin is clouded and freckled with a darker tint upon a blush or flesh coloured ground.

Female differing little in point of appearance, but smaller than the male. Has an udder with two teats. Amphibious. Inhabits the rivers and lakes of the interior and was once common within the colony.

ourselves of a swivel, but it was not until we had discharged five balls from it at the distance of a few feet, and had done most terrible damage to the head and body that the colossus yielded up the ghost. The darkness of the night increased the danger of the contest, for this gigantic animal tossed our boat about in the stream at his pleasure; and it was at a fortunate moment indeed for us that he gave up the struggle, as he had carried us into a complete labyrinth of rocks, which, in the midst of the confusion, none of our crew had observed.'

But the most usual, as well as the most effectual method of disposing of the hippopotamus, is by the aid of pitfalls, which, when cunningly excavated on the river bank, and daily covered with fresh grass, so that no withered appearance may excite the animal's suspicion, not only prove fatal to the river-horse, during his excursions on shore, but frequently also to the rambling cattle of the traveller. In the paths trodden by hippopotami, boards armed with sharp teeth like a harrow, are also sometimes concealed, and the heavy beasts striking the spikes into their feet, are rendered so incapable of exertion, as to become in the morning the victims of a horde of assailants. Hasselquist has, however, recorded a still more ingenious plan by which the Egyptians were wont to relieve themselves in some degree from this destructive animal. 'They remark the places,' he says, 'which they frequent most, and there lay a large quantity of peas. When the beast comes ashore, hungry and voracious he falls to eating what is nearest him, and filling his belly with the peas, they occasion an insupportable thirst. He then returns immediately into the river, and drinks upon these dry peas large draughts of water, which suddenly cause his death; for the peas soon begin to swell with the water, and bursting his belly, the Egyptians not long after find him dead on the shore, blown up as killed by the strongest poison.'

Shortly after the establishment of the Dutch colony at the Cape, Governor Plettenberg transmitted to His Highness the Prince of Orange, the spoils of a hippopotamus which had been shot near the Mountains of Snow, by a peasant of French extraction, named Charles Marais. This man stated, that in consequence of the great speed of the animal on land, the hunters durst fire at him nowhere but in the water; for which reason it is usual to lie in wait for him about sunset, when the animal being in the habit of raising his head above the water, his small ears are kept in perpetual agitation in order to hear if any danger is near. While he is listening in this manner and floating on the surface of the water, they shoot him in the head; and when he feels that he is wounded, he plunges below the water and walks or swims about till he loses both motion and life. Then, by means of about twenty oxen, he is dragged on shore and dissected. 'An adult hippopotamus,' adds Dr Klockner of Amsterdam, 'usually yields about two thousand pounds of fat or lard, which when salted and sent to the Cape, sells very dear, as in relish it excels all others. Besides his usual cry, the animal when asleep, makes a kind of snoring noise which betrays him at a distance. To counteract the danger arising from this peculiarity, he generally lies among the reeds that grow upon marshy ground, which it is difficult to approach. He is extremely tenacious of life, and the hunters therefore endeavour to break his legs by large blunderbusses charged with iron wedges; and whenever they succeed in this, they are fully masters of his person.'

All the large rivers of the Cape were once teeming with hippopotami, but the terror inspired by the Dutch invasion of their hereditary domains, and by the introduction of gunpowder, soon operated to clear the streams of the small remnant that escaped the bullets of the colonists. The great value attached to the fat as a dainty relish — to the thick hide for the manufacture of whips, and to the teeth as an article of trade — have combined to render the brawny animal an object so coveted by the hunter, that at the present day scarcely a single individual exists in any of the colonial rivers, or even in those lying within a moderate distance of the border. The only surviving specimens, two in number, are females and reside in the Berg River under the special protection of the Government. One remaining male was shot by some evil disposed poacher, a few years ago, in spite of the edict prohibiting their destruction. In regions more exempted from the white man's intrusions, however, they occur in the greatest abundance; and there, living in a state of comparative security, they are still generally prepared to welcome with curiosity the trespasser upon their wild haunts — exhibiting themselves with the same familiarity that they probably did some two centuries ago, towards the southern extremity of the continent. Swarming in all the rivers in our route, from the Likwa to the Tropic of Capricorn, the unwieldy monsters divided the aquatic sovereignty with their amphibious and scaly neighbours and might often be heard snorting and blowing during their uncouth gambols, within pistol shot of our encampment — the banks of every stream being deeply stamped with their singular footprints and strewed with huge cylindrical masses of comminuted grass which they had voided. Occasionally, a shapeless fellow might be seen basking in the sun, or wallowing near the shore amid ooze and mud — not less to elude the teasing attentions of the hunting population common to warm humid regions, than to free himself from the ticks and other parasitic vermin infesting the cavities of his ears, as well as the softer parts of his rank hide. But within inhabited districts especially, the ungainly beasts pass the greater portion of the day in the water, rising frequently to the surface — protruding the whole of their broad heads, blowing and bellowing so lustily, that they may be heard at a great distance. Their diet is entirely confined to coarse vegetable matter — the roots and bark of water trees, together with the succulent stems of aquatic plants, furnishing them with employment during the day. Grass, however, constitutes their chief food — and night the season of their activity. As evening draws on, quitting their watery retreats and reed-grown coverts, they sally forth to graze — retiring with the approach of dawn, and never wandering to any great distance from the river, their place of refuge, and the stronghold to which they betake themselves on the smallest alarm, where plunging to the bottom, they remain perfectly secure from the assaults of their foes. During the bright moonlight nights we not infrequently detected the ugly monsters in the very act of making a sortie, their sleek slimy hides glistening like the back of a fish, as they emerged, dripping, under pale Cynthia's beams, and waddled clumsily up the river bank. Devouring at a single meal as much or more than a team of oxen, several bushels of chewed vegetable matter were usually found, on a *post mortem* examination, in the cavity of the stomach; whence it may reasonably be inferred, that the whole night is barely sufficient to admit of their laying in the supply requisite to keep up their ungainly obesity.

The hippopotamus not infrequently resorts to the ocean and to the mouths of those of her tributaries which are influenced by the tides; but he is more usually an inhabitant of muddy inland lakes, of reedy marshes and of fresh-water rivers, whose:

Cavern'd banks, by the tenacious roots
Of hoary willows arched —

are overshadowed by impenetrable forests. Few of the rivers that we visited, possessed sufficient depth of water in all parts of the channel, to conceal so voluminous a beast. They more usually consisted of a chain of deep pools, termed by the Hottentots *Zeekoe gatten,* or sea-cow's holes, from their having been gradually hollowed out by the trampling of the bulky tenants that they harbour; and whilst travelling from one to another of these, a huge back was often quite exposed, or so slightly covered by the water, that the eye could follow the progress of the corpulent owner, as he shuffled along the bottom. Notwithstanding this ability to walk with ease along the bed of the deepest river, or even in the sea, the animal cannot long remain without rising to the surface — squirting, grampus-like, a stream of water out of the truncated nose, whenever it is protruded; but the eyes, ears and nostrils being placed nearly on the same plane, it is necessary to expose a very small portion only of the face, in order to accomplish respiration. The great size of the colloped belly renders the specific gravity of the carcase nearly equal to that of water; and being built without any angles, it slips glibly through the stream and floats as cleverly as an old tub, or as a life buoy, which latter in general contour it closely resembles.

The hippopotamus, amid the flood
Flexile and active as the smallest swimmer
Though on the bank ill balanced and infirm,

is vulnerable only behind the ear, or in the eye, which latter organ is placed in a pulpy prominence, so as to resemble the garret window of a Dutch house. He therefore requires the perfection of rifle practice, and after a few shots, performs the movements necessary for respiration, with extreme caution and sagacity — exhibiting his square muzzle only and as instantly withdrawing it. If slain, the ponderous body rises incontinently to the surface; but it often happened after a severe day's ball practice, that the noisome and unseemly corpse of some hapless fellow, that, despite of his skill in surgery, had contrived to die of his wounds, was seen drifting down with the current — the blue swollen carcase and disgustingly freckled belly, inflated almost to bursting, serving as a raft to voracious alligators, as they luxuriated on the dainty blubber among buzzing myriads of bluebottle flies.

Yielding the firmest and hardest of ivory, which never changes colour from exposure, the teeth of the hippopotamus are extremely valuable. The dental formation is very singular, being equally adapted for uprooting, cutting and bruising; the tusks, which are three-sided and usually weigh from three to four pounds, crossing each other like a pair of shears. They are said to strike fire with steel — a circumstance which may possibly have given rise to the assertion of writers of antiquity, that the animal vomited forth flames! In the hide, however, is found the principal source of profit; since it furnishes some five hundred strips, three feet in length, each of which, when rounded to the size of a man's finger and tapered towards the point form a *sjambok* a most indispensable piece of furniture to every boer proceeding either through his grounds, or on a journey. But setting aside the value of all these *spolia,* no occupation could be devised more perfectly in unison with the indolent habits of the sporting Hottentot, than the lying in wait for the hippopotamus. Whilst blockading a pit which the beasts are known to infest, the pleasures of the pipe are interrupted only to fire an occasional shot from an overloaded musket, when, as our friend Andries had it, '*De Zeekoes stick up dere snouts to blow demselves.*' Nevertheless, our people generally managed to expend their ammunition in vain. Their balls whizzed about at random — cutting ducks and drakes as they ricochetted along the glassy surface of the stream; and if, accidentally, they did strike the object at which they had been projected, the huge animal, more frightened than hurt, simply dived its ugly head, resolved to afford the ambushing marksman no opportunity of repeating the salute. In short, the performance of these very ordinary marksmen, always reminded me of Sparrmann's graphic account, which had previously afforded me many a hearty laugh. 'On my journey homewards,' he writes, 'many of these animals, thrusting their queer heads up above the water, blowed themselves in broad daylight; and one of them in particular, which had been wounded by an ill-directed shot in the nose, neighed from anger and resentment!'

No scenery could surpass in beauty that of the wood clothed borders of the larger rivers, that form towards the Tropic, the chief haunts of the hippopotami. An unbroken tier of weeping willows, clad in a soothing robe of vernal freshness, lean their fragile and trembling forms over the placid stream, as it rolls majestically along, and dipping their slender pendant branches into the water, are reflected back from the limpid mirror. Here the wreck of some stately tree rears its dilapidated head — a mouldering monument to the resistless violence of the flood, by which, during some vast inundation, it has been up-torn from its rock of ages:

There the Chaldee willow weeps
Drooping o'er the dangerous steeps,
Where the torrent in his wrath
Has rifted out a rugged path
Like fissures cleft by earthquake's shock
Through mead and jungle, mound and rock.

Beyond, clumps of airy acacias, with a countless multitude of stems, form vistas and mazes, overshadowing grassy banks, which, under a fervid and cloudless sky, are doubly refreshing to the eye. Gay flowers deck the path of the hunter, as he wanders down the shady labyrinth of these delightful groves — greeted at one moment by the noisy cackling of a troop of loquacious guinea fowls — at the next, by the recent footprints of the lion, the rhinoceros or the stately water-buck. Winding on amongst the grass grown ravines, his progress is presently obstructed by a chain of yawning sepulchres, especially constructed for the empalement of the mighty river-horse, and surrounded, perhaps, by the bleaching bones of some unwary victim that has recently been entrapped and eaten. That shapeless skull, despoiled of its ivory armament, resembles a huge mass of rock — and those picked thigh bones, are like the trunks of trees, newly stripped of their bark. Emerging with a snort and a splash from beneath yon belt of Bablylonian willows that fringe the opposite shore, behold Behemoth suddenly cast his unwieldy circumference into the flood. Next see him warily lifting out his visual organs, to steal a glance at the intruder — and then, crack! he is treated to two ounces of hard lead through his attic store. Blowing and floundering, down he pops his tiny ears again, sending a thousand bubbling circlets eddying round the spot where his funny snout has disappeared — while the outposts and headquarters of an encampment of clamorous baboons, are heard to challenge all down their line, as the vibrations of the echo prolong the report of the rifle along that chain of mountains which flank the river. A few seconds more and bursting bubbles, dyed with a crimson tide, rising rapidly to the surface of the stream, attest the accuracy of the aim and tell of the giant's death struggles. They are presently followed by the enormously fat carcase, slimy and cylindrical, which having been towed and floated to the bank and hauled ashore with considerable difficulty, appears perfectly black — the colour gradually waxing fainter as it becomes dry. Now the cutting up has commenced — every knife and assegai is at work and the barely flexible hide, fully an inch and a half in thickness, is being dragged in long strips from off the ribs, like the planks from a ship's side. Beneath them appears a deep layer of fat, known to the epicures in the colony by the appellation of *zeekoe spek,* [sea-cow's pork] and esteemed so great a rarity, that to obtain it, the utmost influence is exerted with the traders and border colonists. As this delicacy would at once be turned into oil by exposure to the sun, it can only be preserved by salting; for which purpose a vat having been formed of the immoderately thick hide, the choicest morsels are laid in pickle; a number of self-invited guests by whom the death of such a beast is esteemed the greatest of jubilees, then proceeding to help themselves liberally from the mountain of fat and lean. Like a flesh market, banks and bushes are presently garnished with flaps and fids of meat, nor is anything to be seen, but hacking, carving, slicing and gnawing — whole hordes of indigent and starving wanderers removing their domicile to the shambles, in order to admit of their feasting more entirely at leisure. Resembling the finest pork in flavour, the flesh is so surpassingly delicious that none who have once partaken of a steak, can fail to unite with Burchell in recommending the English lovers of good eating not to rest, until they shall have caused 'fine lively hippopotamus' to be an article of regular importation.

Our wild camp on the Molopo was one dark night thrown into the greatest consternation by an obtrusive visit from a river-horse, whose heavy footsteps caused the vigilant *Coeur de Lion* to scramble up to the top of the baggage wagon, and there scream for assistance; whereupon, each Hottentot, springing from his slumbers, instantly discharged his loaded piece in any direction that the muzzle might happen to have assumed! In the course of one afternoon, five goodly carcases were hauled out of a small pool near the source of the osier-fringed Limpopo, to be stripped of their tough panoply; and had we not been weary of the occupation, the list of casualties might have been doubled without difficulty. So abundant was the species in the Likwa, that when we reached its banks on our return from the Cashan mountains, more than forty of the amphibious monsters, like demons of the river, protruded their waggish countenances at the same moment, blowing aloft a tremendous spout of muddy water, as if in honour of our arrival. Well might the savage loneliness of that spot have constituted it the metropolis of *ferae,* and the panorama that there presented itself have called to mind the inconsistent medleys of a dream. Two shaggy lions had been seen to enter a ravine, hard by only the moment before, yet the thoughtless Hottentots, without unyoking the oxen, left the wagons standing on the very brink of a perilous precipice, and all scampered like schoolboys to the water's edge to 'kek to de Zeekoes'. One gigantic bull was making directly for the shore by a succession of plunges — his broad snout appearing nearer and more near every time he rose, puffing, to the surface. Creeping towards him, I was in the act of projecting a leaden sphere through one of his garret windows, when my eye was attracted by the tail of a couchant lioness, thumping angrily within a few yards of my foot. To Piet she was nearer than to myself, but I silently drew him back by the arm, and her ladyship's attention being completely engrossed by the oxen, she fortunately did not condescend to notice us, and was retiring — when Cobus, like a blockhead as he always was, discharging his rotten old musket at her, she galloped back, roaring, through the middle of our party and being joined by her mate, vanished amid the bushes.

Although, to us, the disposition of the hippopotamus appeared indolent and peaceable enough, the animal is doubtless quite capable of being bullied into a rage, and then his strength and bulk could not fail to render him a formidable antagonist in the water. If wounded on land, he is said to charge with reckless fury, and the females are reported occasionally to display great ferocity in the defence of their young. Will not an old village cow do the same, if people either torment her calf, or persist in firing leaden bullets into herself. The few specimens that were slain by our party on *terra firma,* being unfortunately killed outright from behind the ambush of a willow grove, by a single shot below the ear, we found no opportunity of taking evidence touching the behaviour of the species when worried. In the unwieldy obesity and swinish outline of the defunct subject, in vain was it that I sought for that colossal head, or for those cavern-like jaws, garnished with a double row of elephantine tusks, with which, after tearing off the keel of a vessel, Behemoth wantonly cuts in twain the bodies of her crew. Fruitlessly did I search, too, for those ponderous feet, under which the 'formidable and ferocious quadruped' is prone, during his nocturnal forays, 'to trample down whole fields of corn during a single night!' Defenceless and inoffensive, his awkward, bloated and shapeless trunk, is but feebly supported upon clumsy and disproportioned legs; and his cylindrical barrel almost trailing upon the ground, whilst he might not inaptly be likened unto an overgrown prize pig, a still more befitting similitude would probably be found in a tun of blubber, hoisted upon a wooden rack. Though the bulls may often weigh about three tons, the largest of many goodly specimens of obesity that were hauled on shore during our campaign, measured less than five feet at the shoulder; and the reality falling thus lamentably short of the monstrous conception that I had formed of the mighty river-horse. His Corpulence proved the first, and indeed the only, South African game quadruped, in which I felt disappointed.

Skull of hippopotamus in the British Museum. Old and supposed to be female. Teeth preserved by Captain Harris

13
African Buffalo

Mightiest of all the beasts of chase,
That roam in woody Caledon,
Crashing the forest in his race,
The Mountain Bull comes thundering on.

Although confessedly inferior to the 'carnivorous and blue eyed wild bulls' that were vanquished by the heroes of antiquity, and with whose shaggy spoils the vestibule of the temple of Hercules was adorned by Philip of Macedon, the genus *Bos* does not, at the present day, include an animal more formidable in character, or more malignant in disposition, than the Cape buffalo; neither do 'Afric's desert hills', throughout their prolific wildernesses, produce a quarry more difficult to be subdued. Yielding little in point of bulk to an ordinary size hippopotamus, and wrapped in a tough mantle of hide, which is in parts impenetrable to a ball of unadulterated lead — more especially if propelled from a smooth bore — the dark brow of the Kaffrarian bull is overshadowed by a rugous mass of horn, spreading like a helmet horizontally over the summit of his head, and forming a bullet-proof casque, beneath which a pair of piercing, black, downcast eyes, look gloomily forth with a mischievous and sinister twinkle. Neither are appearances, often so deceitful, in this instance belied — the sullen, forbidding and malevolent aspect of the species, being strongly indicative of its fierce and treacherous nature; whilst the ponderous and powerful frame — bony and gaunt — is encased in ribs of such extraordinary breadth as almost to unite with each other, and is supported upon stout muscular limbs of truly prodigious strength.

Short are his legs, his hams are thick, his hoofs are black as night,
Like a strong flail, he holds his tail, in fierceness of his might.

The males average from sixteen and a half to seventeen hands at the shoulder, their height being nevertheless greatly disproportioned to the general bulk and chiefly made up of the enormous substance and depth of forehand, unaided either by length of leg, or by any hunch or excrescence upon the wither; whence specimens in the prime of years have been found to weigh so heavy as two hundred stone. Unless among the dense forests and jungle skirting the sea coast of the eastern districts, in which a few surviving elephants also still find a precarious shelter, the *buffel* is now totally extirpated throughout the Cape Colony, where so many local names testify to its former presence. Lead and gunpowder have done their deadly work and the perpetual warfare waged by the advancing white population, has so effectually cleared every preserve, that the hunter now seeks in vain for a solitary specimen, in scenes which one formed the headquarters of the largest herds. So far, however, as the country has yet been explored, this noble beast is extremely abundant, in all the eastern portions of southern extra-tropical Africa — troops, led by the largest and fiercest bulls, holding their haunts amid all the mountain forests and wooded valleys, whence they make wide incursions upon the open plains. Resorting also at seasons to the deep verdure of rivers, swamps and stagnant pools, in the muddy waters of which they delight to wallow, they sink their giant forms so deep in the stream, as to be effectually screened from the poisonous flies of the tropical forest. Thus surrounded by tall grass and reeds, which afford both concealment and shade, the herd will lie for hours together, the nostrils and gloomy downcast eyes alone protruded, appearing in the enjoyment of perfect ecstacy — certain clod-like lumps, which have scarcely attracted the attention of the passerby, springing suddenly into life; when some dozens of grim looking customers emerging with a general splash and forming up to gaze for an instant with menacing front at the intruder, turn tumultuously about and plunge into the nearest covert.

All writers are agreed as to the hazard of invading the haunts of this savage animal, whose skulking habits, no less than his tremendous strength, render him an object to be greatly dreaded. Although neither exasperated by wounds, nor driven to extremity in the chase, he is described to be of so irascible a disposition, that he will even attack his great enemy, man, without the smallest provocation — darting upon the ill-fated object of his vengeance with blind fury, and with a swiftness and activity which could ill be expected from so awkward and lumbering a figure. And should he succeed in destroying his victim, it is his wont to stand over the inanimate corpse for a considerable time, goring and tossing it in vindictive fury with his formidable horns, trampling it under his feet, crushing and mangling it with his knees, and stripping off the skin with his rough and prickly tongue; desisting occasionally, but to return again with renewed appetite, as though his revenge might never be glutted! Yet these wanton acts of aggression, could they be properly sifted, would in all probability be found to constitute the exception, rather than the rule, of the animal's ordinary habits. If left to itself, the natural instinct is to retire from before the presence of the lord of the creation, instead of provoking his hostility; and any instance to the contrary which may have come under observation, are doubtless to be laid at the door of some solitary outcast from the herd, ejected at the point of the horn by a stronger rival, and left to prowl about the forest in a state of sullen irritation, with every inclination to molest, and to be mischievous.

In the season of love, when the passions of the males are at their height, fierce and terrible are the single combats in which they engage. The *mechans* eyes of the contending rivals sparkle with fury, as, glaring one upon the other, and shaking their huge heads they emit a deep roar and paw up the earth in defiance, preparatory to placing themselves in the posture of attack. Then, with foreheads depressed and tails which indicate by their whirling motion the determination and vigour of the owners — like champion knights in the lists, they tilt forward at full speed, bringing their protruding brows together with a mighty crash and making the glades to ring again with their wild joust, which is thus continued until one of them is worsted.

Onward they rush, and from alternate blows
Down their gored sides the purple current flows;
Front clashed on front their battering horns rebound,
Olympus bellows and the woods resound.

XIII. BUBALUS CAFFER. - THE AFRICAN BUFFALO.

The combat o'er, insatiate rage remains,
The vanquished exile roams o'er distant plains;
Mourns o'er his shame and each ignoble scar,
That marks th' insulting victor's might in war;
Mourns, in far lands unknown, that forced to rove,
In battle unavenged, and lost to love,
He leaves, oft turning ere he quit the plain,
The native honours of his proud domain.

Excepting the ancient and lethargic bulls, which often wander about singly, these wild denizens of the waste roam usually in herds, the fiercest and stoutest males leading a large seraglio of cows, and even defying the attack of the tawny lion himself. In the open savannahs, rarely disturbed by human presence, which we traversed, vast droves were frequently congregated; and long strings might be seen as the day dawned, filing in formidable procession along the level profile of the silent landscape. Huddled together and galloping, when hard pressed by the pursuer, in dense masses, they formed a most imposing spectacle and raised in their headlong course, a cloud of dust, which completely obscured the rear of their sable column.

Like most of the other large African quadrupeds, this animal is frequently entrapped in pitfalls by the savages, the more warlike tribes of whom follow the hazardous chase armed only with a sheaf of assageis, trusting to their agility for escape among the intricacies of the forest, should the infuriated beast 'turn again to rend them'. In the woods of Kaffraria especially, where the species is very abundant, they are thus constantly hunted by the Zooloos on foot; but the victory is often to the quadruped:

He tramples on earth and tosses on high
The foremost who rush on his strength but to die

and many a stout warrior has been expended without a record, in his bold endeavours to carry to his royal master a tufted tail in token of his prowess.

It was at Mimori, a few miles south of the then flourishing valley of Mosega, since laid waste by the emigrant farmers, that we first encountered the wild buffalo. Unyoking late one afternoon, a chain of lakes to the left of our camp was observed to harbour a sluggish herd, whose formidable heads, resembling rough masses of rock, protruded from the water amid waving sedges — the bodies of the greater number being totally submerged. We contrived to wound one from the top of the wagons and observing that he was unable to keep pace with his flying comrades, I attempted to ride him down; but the numerous sharp-pointed flints with which the ground was studded, cutting the shoeless feet of my horse to pieces, I not only failed in my design, but brought back my steed to the wagons dead lame. Our object, whilst outward bound, being to husband our resources as much as possible against our return march, we did not fail from our next camp at Mosega, to revisit Mimori with the intention of obtaining a supply of beef for our numerous followers. Passing through a gorge in the hills behind the American Mission houses, we entered upon a succession of plains, intersected by low stony eminences, scattered over with clumps of acacia; and the old herbage and wiry grass having recently been cleared off by fire, we presently foregathered with the same lordly herd, grazing upon the young and tender blades, and looming, in so open a spot, as voluminous as elephants.

On being pursued, they made straight for the lakes, at a heavy gallop, and dashed pell-mell among the flags, into which we followed them, the water reaching to the horses' girths, and the reeds far above our own heads. We could hear the monstrous beasts forcing their way through the shaking bulrushes immediately in advance, but after several hours' severe labour in the overgrown swamp — where it now appears wonderful to me that we were not repeatedly charged — our party could only succeed in driving out a single cow, which, breaking at the opposite side of one piece of water, had contrived to gain another before we could overtake her. Then commenced a general skirmish — some of the more foolhardy of our followers wading to their middles, whilst others kept up a running fire from the banks whenever a glimpse of anything black could be obtained. Half the random balls either fell harmlessly, or rattled against the impervious mass of horn which shielded the bluff foreheads of the badgered herd; others however took effect, and Piet, in attempting to despatch a wounded cow whose leg he had broken, was charged and knocked over by a bull from behind. Capless and disarmed we could see the poor fellow through a telescope, lying beneath a shady karree tree, which reared its venerable head in the middle of the lake, holding his hands to his stomach as if he were mortally wounded — his coal black adversary drooping sternly near him, and seeming half disposed to renew the combat, although the blood fast trickling from its nostrils, showed that the moment of dissolution was approaching. A broad deep stream, tangled over with sedge, which encircled this spot on three sides, defying approach either on horseback or on foot, without incurring the certainty of drowning, compelled us to ride some three miles round before we could arrive to the rescue. By that time the buffalo was in its last struggles; and the sufferer appearing to be more frightened than hurt, we soused him with water, and having removed his leathern doublet, which was much torn by the animal's horns, ascertained that there were no serious holes in his own skin. A laborious search among the prostrate reeds around the scene of recent strife, at length brought the bruised Nimrod's cap and gun to light, and the savages having borne him out of the swamp, he was placed groaning upon a pack horse and reconducted to our camp, where, having enjoyed the advantage of Dr Wilson's professional aid, he consented, after a little bleeding and coaxing, to forego his often expressed determination of closing at Mosega his mortal career.

The pursuit of the wild buffalo was some months afterwards productive of a still more serious accident to this same unfortunate man, of whom I will aver so much, that he was by far the staunchest sportsman of our whole Hottentot retinue. Wending our journey homeward on the southern side of the Cashan Mountains, the route — hitherto untrodden by white foot — lay

Plate XIII: *Bubalus caffer* — African buffalo — *buffel* of the Cape colonists — *qu'araho* of the Hottentots — *'neaat* and *bokolokolo* of the Matabili — *naari* of the Bechuana

Generic Character — Adult male about five feet six or eight inches high at the shoulder, and upwards of twelve in extreme length. Structure extremely powerful, but low in proportion to its bulk. Body ponderous. Neck short, very thick and indicative of amazing strength. Breast and shoulder deep and slightly dewlapped. Back straight and hunchless. Limbs short and solid, terminating in a divided hoof, which is nearly circular. Spurious hoofs, pendent and much elongated. Tail three feet long, slender and terminating in a swish of coarse black hair, which reaches below the hocks. Head short and small in proportion to the general bulk. Ears funnel-shaped and flaccid. Eyes small and sinister, overshadowed by rough and ponderous dark-coloured horns, nearly in contact at the base, but divided by a narrow channel or furrow. Spreading horizontally, they completely shield the forehead, sweeping downwards and then turning upwards and inwards at the tips, which measure from four to five feet between. Hide blueish purple-black, and, with exception of a few distichous bristles chiefly along the ridge of the spine, naked. Muzzle bovine, square and moist slightly bearded at the chin.

Female similar, but smaller, with smaller and more vertically disposed horns. An udder with four speens. Still exists within the colony. Inhabits the wooden valleys, plains and forests of the interior in large droves.

across a belt of green wooded hillocks, intersected by formidable ravines, and constituting, as it were, the suburbs of the mountain range. Over these knolls our unwieldy and heavily freighted wagons toiled with infinite difficulty — their snail-like progress being frequently arrested altogether by the snapping of one of the tow ropes — some of the strands of this important portion of our harness having recently been gnawed through by alligators, which, assisted by the half starved dogs of the savages, ate up everything that fell in their way, not even excepting the untanned leather shoes of our followers. We were splicing the rotten *trek touw* for the third time, when a stately herd of Buffaloes

Crook knee'd and dewlap'd, like Thessalian bulls,

were perceived at a little distance in the open plain. They were throwing out signs of defiance, in consequence, it was conjectured by a wag, of the warlike appearance of poor *Coeur de Lion,* whose *caput* was as usual decorated with a woollen night cap of that crimson hue, to which the bovine class are proverbially averse! Mounting our lead horses, my companion and myself ascended the ridge immediately above the herd, and firing a volley at their broad backs, brought a splendid bull to bay, and had despatched him in less than five minutes. Whilst several of the delighted followers were employed in flaying the carcase, and appropriating the tit bits, we cantered after the wagons and sent back Andries with a pack horse for the hide which, being as much as any two men could lift, promised to become in due time a right serviceable *trek touw.* In the course of a few minutes, however, the worthy squire returned at speed, pale and speechless, stammering forth at length, in reply to our interrogations of what the matter was, '*Sieur, Piet shot him.*' Having already had experience of the fellow's disposition to claim first blood, Richardson refuted this bold assertion, by the assurance that we had ourselves slain the bull; but it was sometime ere we learned from an interpreter, who proved better conversant than ourselves with Andries' application of 'our maternale Englysshe tongue', that Piet had been badly wounded in the leg by the accidental discharge of Claas' detonating gun. 'Lingap also presently arrived and after pointing with breathless dismay to a round hole drilled by the same agent through his own ox-hide target, proceeded to a minute practical illustration of the circumstances which led to the catastrophe, by placing Andries' clumsy elephant gun against a pliant tree in such a manner that it also fell down and was discharged — though fortunately without fracturing any more legs. The unhappy Piet being shortly afterwards brought in upon a litter, our nervous anxiety respecting him was not a little relieved by an inspection of the damaged limb, which, though dreadfully burnt and lacerated, was providentially unbroken. The ball having glanced round the shin bone had perforated 'Lingap's buckler, as already described, and passing through the carcase of the defunct bull, upon which some dozen savages were busily feasting, had finally winged its wanton flight into the wide world!

During the time that we were encamped near the source of the Limpopo, we could from the wagons, frequently perceive wild buffaloes grazing quietly, and unsuspicious of danger, among verdant valleys within half a mile of our position. Through their wandering and restless disposition, these favourite haunts are traversed by numerous well worn footpaths, along which they saunter morning and evening, retiring during the sultry period of the day, to ruminate in the mountain shade on the brink of some tranquil stream,

in which the willows dip
their pendant boughs, stooping as if to drink.

Herein they lave their bare hides at will, and swimming stoutly, cross the broadest rivers without any hesitation. A noble bull, weighing not less than a ton and a half, was shot whilst in the act of thus navigating the dark silent channel of the placid Limpopo, across which the Hottentots, stripped to their skins, had twice waded and swum in pursuit of him. Under a volley of well directed balls, the huge carcase turning suddenly on its side, floated away with the blood-stained current, against which the gallant beast with all its remaining strength, had been struggling to gain the opposite shore.

Riding one morning before it was well light, up a narrow defile flanked by steep banks, in order to attain the summit of an eminence, a strong bovine taint suddenly assailed my nose, and I found myself most unexpectedly confronted with the van of a vast troop ascending from the opposite side — their malevolent grey eyes scowling beneath a threatening brow. Unable to turn, the formidable brutes must inevitably have charged over me, had not my horse dexterously contrived, under a severe application of the rowels, to scramble up the bank, from the top of which I fired both barrels into the leader, a ponderous bull, whose venerable appearance stamped him father of the herd. Falling on his knees, the grey patriarch was instantly trampled under foot of his reckless followers, as they dashed, bellowing, down the declivity which I had so recently occupied — moving in close squadron with the fury of a passing whirlwind, and making the woods re-echo to the clatter of their wild hoofs.

On the afternoon of the same day, another noble troop was observed filing sluggishly through the scraggy forest which flanked our bivouac, led by a stately bull, whose slow and funereal pace called to mind the creeping progress of some enormous reptile. Although the sight is clouded by an overhanging brow, the sense of smelling in this species is exquisite. Seizing our weapons, we glided against the wind therefore, and creeping on all fours to a strong position in advance of the course that they were taking, squatted in close ambush behind the leafy screen. The tramp of their heavy feet drew nearer and more near, until the branches began to move and crackle, and their odour became quite overpowering. One passed, and then another — flapping lazily their long pendulous ears, which were slit and torn by the brambles — and carrying their short noses so horizontally that the horns were thrown back along the swarthy shoulders. Twice was the fatal aim taken, and twice were the rifles lowered from the shoulder — both had proved to be cows, and their sex befriended them. Next with lordly tread came on the great master bull. The hoary villain fancying that he had heard a sound to which he was unaccustomed, was casting many suspicious glances around — stooping occasionally, and narrowly scrutinizing every object. There was a momentary pause — another second and two balls whizzing through the air, had entered his brawny shoulder close behind the elbow, bringing him heavily upon his knees, whilst a crimson tide gushed from his distended nostrils. '*Daar lay de bull*', chuckled Andries from his concealment; and the herd, cocking their long tails and snuffing at the prostrate figure of their humbled chief, snorted, tossed their wild heads aloft, threw up their mighty heels with a flourish that cast the dirt some dozen feet high — and then dashed headlong through the trees, with a terrific crash, goring, overturning and trampling under foot every object that opposed their progress!

Dat euntibus ingens
Silva locum, et magno cedunt virgulta fragore.

The finest bull buffalo slain by our little party, measured at the shoulder seventeen and a half hands — his wide spreading beams being split and completely worn away at the point from constantly raking and tearing up the ground. Whilst in pursuit of a herd of roan antelopes, I had remarked his dark form stationed, statuelike, in a narrow passage at the water's edge, these rugged horns overshadowing his small grey sinister eyes, and imparting to his countenance the most cunning, gloomy and vindictive expression. An ill-timed shot fired by one of the Hottentots, putting every creature to flight, he thundered past me on his retreat to the hills; and my first barrel fortunately fracturing his hind leg as he was in the act of topping an eminence, I jumped upon my horse and closed with him immediately. Plunging, roaring and rendered desperately furious, no less by the smarting of his wounds than by the triumphal shouts of savage merriment that his maimed condition elicited from various mouths — groaning as he pawed up the earth — the bleeding and reeling quarry ran wildly round upon three legs, as though in pursuit of his own tail. The shattered bones of the fourth, which protruded through the skin, ground together as it dangled; and whilst his bloodshot eye-balls, starting from their sockets, flashed with portentous fury, the white foam churned round his chaps, and the earth flew in showers from his heels. Missiles and assegais poured in upon the victim from every side and not less than twenty shots had struck him ere he was totally subdued. Full of strength and fury — his nose lowered betwixt his forelegs and his tail brandishing in the air, twice did the maddened and baited animal rush gallantly to the charge — receiving, during the last, a brace of balls in his broad chest which closed an exhibition that could not fail to call to mind the barbarous though soul-stirring spectacles of the circus and of the Moors and Spaniards of olden time.

From the summit of a hill which commanded an extensive prospect over a straggling forest, I shortly afterwards descried, through a telescope, a large herd, to which this champion belonged, quietly chewing the cud beneath an umbrageous tree. Creeping close upon them from leeward, and resting the rifle against a forked tree, I dropped a bull with a single ball behind his elbow. The confused echo reverberating amid the mountains, caused the survivors, about fifty in number, to dash from their concealment, panic-stricken and in ignorance whence the sound proceeded; and everything yielding before their giant strength, I narrowly escaped being trampled under foot in their tumultuous course. Moving ground in the afternoon to the eastward, we stopped to take up the head of the bull first vanquished, a trophy which the brawny arm of Andries could with difficulty lift upon the trap of the wagon. Myriads of vultures, and the dense clouds of smoke which arose from the fires of the savages, directed us to the scene of the humiliation of this noblest of the herd. It was the fifth day of November, and in commemoration I presume, of the exploits of Guy Fawkes, they had kindled a bonfire which bid fair to destroy all the grass in the country, the crackling flames, fanned by the wind already beginning to ascend the mountain side. Nothing can be conceived more horribly disgusting than the appearance presented by the savages, who, crammed to the throat, and liberally besmeared with blood, grease and filth from the entrails, sat nodding torpidly around the residue of the carcase, sucking marrow from the bones — their lean and famished curs regaling themselves meanwhile upon the garbage. Every bough was bending under collops of flesh and every man had turned beef-butcher — numerous swollen vultures still eyeing the sylvan shambles from the adjacent trees, whilst others, yet ungorged, were inhaling with keen nostrils the odours that arose.

Proceeding betimes the next morning into the hills, again to beat up the quarters of the fugitives, we entered a deep wooded defile, which, having been spared by the conflagration, was literally crammed with game that had retired before the flames. The scorched and blackened sides of the lofty mountains — in many parts thickly wooded — were scattered over with huge masses of pointed rock, frowning in 'craggy nakedness sublime', and completing all that can be conceived spirit-stirring or magnificent in wild and desert scenery. A rhinoceros was presently laid low; and ere we had reloaded our rifles a noble herd of nearly one hundred and fifty buffaloes showed itself on a slope overhanging a sedgy stream beneath us. Having crept under the cover of a grey cliff, to within five and twenty yards of them, we pinked off two bulls before the alarm was spread. Crushing through the forest and overturning decayed trees in their route, they swept in fearful confusion along the brow of the opposite hill, squeezed together in a compact phalanx — blindly following the leader — whisking their tasselled tails aloft — and raising an incredible cloud of dust to mark their progress. We quickly mounted our horses; and after sticking and floundering some minutes in the treacherous mud of the rush-grown rivulet, gained the opposite bank. Pouring in a broadside, we there brought two more to bay, which fell after several charges, to rise up no more — the heavy carcase of one, that for some time had balanced itself with outstretched legs on the very verge of the precipice, rolling at last like an avalanche over the bank, preceded by a huge fragment of earth that its weight had brought away, with which it splashed, ere life had become extinct, into a deep pool at the bottom.

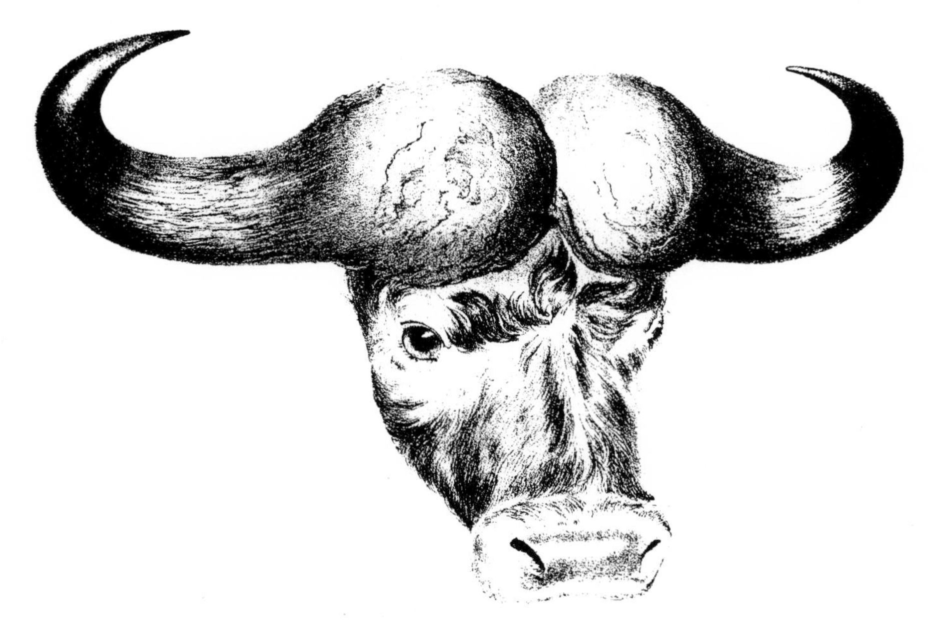

Head of buffalo, as preserved by Captain Harris

14

Water-Buck

The antler'd monarch of the waste,
Sprung from his heathery couch in haste.
but ere his fleet career he took,
The dew drops from his flanks he shook;
Like crested leader, proud and high,
Tossed his beamed frontal to the sky;
A moment gazed adown the dale,
A moment snuffed the tainted gale.

It is not possible for the Indian deer stalker to contemplate the splendid figure of the rare and majestic antelope now depicted, without finding himself forcibly reminded of the sambur, or Rusa stag of the sunny jungles which have so often echoed to the merry crack of his tried and trusty rifle. Whether in size, in carriage, or in general aspect, the *ellipsiprymnus,* notwithstanding that he is the proprietor of a pair of persistent horns, in lieu of branched and deciduous antlers, yet preserves the closest resemblance to *cervus aristotelis* in the 'vaward of his youth', ere his brawny neck has been bowed by a superincumbent load of ponderous attire. Many a time, when the stately fellow, apeing the style of the 'antlered monarch of the waste', has sprung from his solitary lair in the deep recesses of the grove — erected his towering front, and tossing his proud head, has waved his great horns to the right and to the left — ay, many a good time, as he nobly shook his shaggy and redundant mane, have I fancied myself transported from the wilds of southern Africa, back to the aromatic forests which embosom the cloud-capped mountains of Aboo, [a famous hunting ground in western India] and believed myself again in the lordly presence of a *bona fide* member of the cervine group.

Nowhere to the southward of the Mariqua is the water-buck to be met with, nor is he ever found at any great distance from the banks of tropical rivers — abounding chiefly along the margin of the willow-grown Limpopo and her tributaries, in the rippling waters of which he delights to lave his grizzled sides — immersing himself to the chin during the heat of the day and rolling in his favourite soiling pool for hours together. This addiction to cold bathing and decided predilection for the vicinage of water, has suggested the appropriate colonial appellation; his specific nomenclature having been derived from the singular and perfect ellipse of milk-white hair, which, like a band of snowy ribbon, encircling the tasselled tail as it dangles from the superior focus, stamps the animal among a thousand. Like the *sambur,* the hair of both sexes is throughout of so coarse and harsh a texture as to resemble the scraping of whalebone; that along the throat and back of the neck being chiefly reversed and of sufficient length to form a complete wiry ruff, which adds, in the male subject especially, not a little to the importance of the *tout ensemble.* The colour and stature are those of the largest ass but measuring from the hoof to the summit of the attire, the front exceeds seven feet in height, and the lofty tiara of white horn standing almost perpendicularly over such wild brilliant eyes, imparts a presence so commanding, that on first introduction, the animal cannot fail to strike the beholder with admiration.

Without much fear of contradiction, I believe I may affirm myself to be the only European that with his own hand has ever slain a water-buck. It was towards the source of the Limpopo as indicated to me by Dr Smith, that the species occurred in the greatest abundance, and in that favoured spot, so well adapted to woodcraft, I have in the course of a morning's ramble, often met, besides solitary bucks, with so many as five or six herds, consisting each of a dozen of both sexes; some having been even seen swimming across the river within shot of the wagons. Who is disposed to follow me down the green banks of the lone Limpopo, where the mournful willows, stretching their long arms over the leaf-stained stream, form the most agreeable of canopies? Through those shady labyrinths of sweet smelling mimosas, 'ringing with wood notes wild' — whose fairy recesses, traversed by paths worn under the nocturnal tramp of hippopotami, are bedizened with golden blossoms and festooned with purple pods? From the branches of yonder tree which borders the stream, observe, suspended like a ripening gourd, the basket nest of the pensile grosbeak [*loxia pensilus*], one of the little winged architects sitting snugly below in the porch of its 'tree-rocked cradle', which with no less industry than ingenuity it has woven of stout threads of the wiregrass.

Mark it well, within, without!
No tool had he that wrought, no knife to cut,
No nail to fix, no bodkin to insert,
No glue to join; his little beak was all:
And yet how neatly finished! What nice hand,
With every implement and means of art,
Could compass such another?

Now from behind the stems of that airy clump of mimosa, is thrust the long red and yellow phiz of an inquisitive hartebeest, who has presently satisfied his suspicions, and cocking his black scut, is sweeping away with the easy motion of a rocking horse. Ever and anon, as he scours through the grove, there issues from beneath the shelter of some mouldering trunk of driftwood — cast long since by the boiling flood upon the strand, and now matted over with clustering creepers, which hide the decay that works beneath — a troop of pearled Guinea pintados, whose cracked music resembles the grating of a hundred old doors upon their rusty hinges. And see, what strange trail is this? 'Tis the recent and hurried tread of the gallant water-buck broad and rounded at the point — the footsteps left by the ladies of his seraglio, being at once distinguishable from his own by their taper toe, and more feminine proportions. Shy and solitary, the herd nine in number, must have taken the note of alarm from the hoarse cackle of those querulous birds, and are doubtless hurrying towards the river- brink — their sober colours enabling them to traverse the grove from end to end, without so much as a glimpse of their grey form being obtained. Ay, here is the harbour on which they have been lying for hours undisturbed — it is warm, and by their droppings absolutely tainted like a sheep fold.

Advancing on the tracks, a more extended view of the river has opened upon us, and in that thorny vista, flapping his large round ears and snuffing restlessly about with wide distended nostrils, behold the wild desert-looking master buck, *in propria persona*, exhibiting all the self importance of the grand Sultan in his harem. What a picturesque and noble beast it is! One of loftier mien, or more stately and gallant bearing, has never ranged the greenwood; and what a towering pair of horns too! 'Aha,' he would seem to say, 'I told you so — here's the man with a gun' — whereupon, suiting the action to the word, he places himself like a great leader as he is, at the head of his confiding band. Obedient to the signal, they rush gallantly forward, sweep along the glade in glorious array, dash furiously down the steep bank and plunge at once right into the flashing waters of the Oori. Hark! how their hard hoofs clatter over the pebbly channel, as the bright ripples spread and the white spray flies behind them! Already beyond their depth, they are stoutly breasting the current, their wet backs alternately rising on the surface and again sinking beneath it, as the bubbling waters curl before their slim, but shaggy necks. Again they have found their footing and one after the other, their stately forms are emerging to view. With that last brave bound, they have each gained the opposite bank, where, facing about for a second, at the verge of the mimosa copse, and shaking the pearly drops from their dripping flanks, they stand majestically at gaze. Now for a steady hand and a true aim — another moment's pause, and, bang! The leaden sphere has spun from the deadly tube:

Hark what loud shouts
Re-echo through the groves.

The master buck has fallen with his bleeding nose betwixt his knees, and is ploughing up the yellow sand with his great horns — the savages, yelling with delight, are hurrying assegai in hand, to despatch the struggling victim — whilst his bereaved and affrighted does, closely packed, are pressing forward, reeking and steaming, towards the nearest covert!

After crossing the Mariqua, I had been daily looking, with disappointed impatience, for the first glimpse of a water-buck until late one evening, that we halted on the banks of the Bagobone River in a lone meadow, under a secondary range of the Cashan Mountains. Our route had for some hours lain through a forest of ancient trees, some standing stately and dark in their foliage, others riven and blasted by the storm, which had extended their bare arms across the path. But around our solitary bivouac, the scenery was of a wilder and even still more romantic character. On either hand the mountain rose in bold majestic forms, clothed in parts with luxuriant verdure, whilst in others their steep rocky sides were only sparingly besprinkled with light bushes, serving to enliven the rich and varied tints of the broken crags. Rugged cliffs, which margined the gurgling river, shut in the lower prospect and the great range of the Cashan Mountains towering above them in the distance, exhibited their spiry blue crests to eyes which had for months, over the ocean-like surface of the plain, beheld nothing larger than an ant hill and seemed almost to rival the Alps in grandeur. Our larder being quite empty, I left the Hottentots engaged in the construction of the usual thorn pound, for the better security of the cattle; and taking my rifle, dived into the unfrequented recesses of the nearest grove, for the purpose of obtaining a supply of wild flesh. Ere I had proceeded many yards, a stately figure, which I at once recognised to belong to the water-buck, emerging with slow and measured pace, placed itself directly across my path, and having received a ball through the point of the broad shoulder, sank quietly down upon its haunches and staggering a few yards, rolled back lifeless into a dry ravine. A lion and his consort, disturbed by the near report of the rifle, bounced meanwhile out of a neighbouring bush and with an indignant roar, slunk instantly into the jungle. Covering up the much prized carcase of the defunct quarry with thorn branches, I hastily retraced my steps to the wagons, intending to send out some of the people by torch-light to procure rations; but Piet, who had also narrowly escaped stumbling over a lion couchant in long grass, had already returned, laden with an abundant supply of the flesh of a brindled gnoo, upon which until a late hour, our followers made merry to the music of roaring *felinae* engaged on their nocturnal patrol.

At early dawn I proceeded with 'Lingap to the carcase, with the determination of adding the head to my daily increasing collection of trophies; and although the hyaenas had been lustily tugging at the branches, they had fortunately not succeeded in obtaining their supper in that quarter. 'Lingap, with an eye to his own interests, proceeding forthwith to cut out the dorsal sinews, which are in great demand for the manufacture of thread, the *mauvaise odeur* that followed the insertion of his assegai almost drove me from the spot. Far from keeping pace with the game exterior, the flesh of this singular species, is uniformly coarse, carrion-like and ill-savoured, that even savages are unable to devour it.

As we advanced towards the Tropic of Capricorn, the species waxed more abundant. During several successive days that we hunted over the green valleys which skirt the principal mountain chain, the long white-ringed horns of the bucks were frequently to be seen through the telescope, raking above ruined stone walls of great extent, the crumbling memorials of 'cities long gone by'. Ere the devastating wars of the ruthless Chaka, followed by those of his successful rival Moselekatse, had laid waste this lovely country, these enclosures served to confine the countless cattle of prosperous Bechuana tribes, the peaceful proprietors of the soil — now:

whilst they droop without one arm to save,
Their country blooms a garden and a grave;

and in place of the once busy throng, we found the deserted areas strewed with mouldering human relics and overrun with flowering weeds, interspersed with plants of uncultivated tobacco. I had here a ridiculous pedestrian chase after a magnificent buck, that suffered himself to be detected within a dilapidated amphitheatre, under cover of which having approached, I suddenly exhibited myself, and as he rushed by like the wind, lodged a bullet betwixt his ribs. For half an hour, in vain efforts to elude my untiring pursuit, the poor beast scoured over the broken knolls, dodged among ruins and threaded the intricacies of decaying habitations — his entrails trailing behind him upon the ground; nor was it until I had fairly worn the sole off one of my rude mocassins, that with the assistance of Andries, I at last contrived to secure the fugitive, walking finally barefooted above three miles, to overtake the advancing cafila.

But it is at the source of the Limpopo, as I have already said, that the *ellipsiprymnus* would appear to have established its headquarters. Arriving there one drizzling morning, a little after the gloomy day had dawned and almost before it was sufficiently light to observe the sight of a rifle, the booming of one of the Hottentot's overloaded muskets, was followed by a prolonged shout from the successful marksman: *'Here lay de vater bok.'* Hurrying to the spot, we found Mr Claas exulting over the prostrate carcase of a young buck in the last agonies; but to his disgust the spoils of his accidental victim being declared not worth the having, we continued our course down the vistas of blossoming mimosas that with other fragrant trees lined the banks of the rapidly widening river. Presently a dark and stately figure was perceived on the opposite shore standing at gaze under the shade of a clump of umbrella-topped acacias — his redundant mane erect, and his beetling brows garnished with a pair of sweeping horns. 'Daar staan een mooi groot bul,' whispered Piet, jogging my elbow and cautiously pointing at the same time with his finger. Whilst the noble beast, uncertain what to do, was yet

XIV. AIGOCERUS ELLIPSIPRYMNUS:- THE WATER BUCK.

staring at us, dropping upon one knee, I laid my rifle on the rest and quickly touched the hair trigger; a dull heavy pat followed the report and the quarry was instantly rolling, hoofs uppermost, on his back, kicking and struggling with all his might. The smoke, curling from the muzzle in thick white wreaths, was kept down by the moist hazy atmosphere; and ere it had floated past, the rascal had resumed three of his legs and was making off at score, with the fourth swinging from side to side like a pendulum at his shoulder. A full minute had elapsed before Claas, who was behind in a reverie, holding the bridle of my dumpy grey mare, could be aroused by the impatient waving of our caps, accompanied by sundry complementary *viva voce* summonses. That minute appeared to me an hour. Running towards him and springing upon the back of the mare, I dashed, at the broadest and most shallow part of the river, holding the reloaded rifle high above my head in order to keep it dry; and after much scrambling and floundering, contrived to gain the opposite bank, at the very spot where the quarry, in his struggles, had left a pool of wet blood on the newly disturbed soil. Following the stain, and gazing impatiently down the avenue before me, the drooping form of the wounded buck soon caught my eye, limping painfully through the grove. In went the rowels, and away for dear life, again scampered the three-legged fugitive — long maintaining his place most stoutly in advance of the dappled mare, whose tortoise-like paces were but little accelerated even by the smarting of her gore-stained sides. At length, after excessive toiling and labouring, by a most desperate effort I closed with the tottering victim. Overtaken, he reeled to one side, and stopping under a bush, made a faint effort to charge as I shuffled past, but being met by a bullet in the chest, stumbled a few paces and then sank to rise no more.

Right furiously did it pour during the whole operation of divesting the humbled game of its thick robe, which — in many parts quite destitute of hair — shone with a polish falling little short of Warren's jet blacking. Returning, thoroughly drenched, with the spoils packed upon the sluggish pony, I regained the bank of the Limpopo just in time to detect another noble fellow in the very act of taking *soyle.* Holding his gallant muzzle high in the air, and throwing forward his legs, while he glided stoutly through the current, he was curling the water before his slim neck as from the beak of an ancient galley, and snorting at each breath with his aquatic exertions. Despite of the rain, the first lucky bullet reached his heart, and as he turned over on the surface a lifeless corpse, the warm blood welled from the wound, and dyed the ripples round for many a foot. Wheeling in the eddies, and jostling against each abutting rock, the carcase was carried rapidly along with the swelling current, until at length — being brought up by a projecting angle where the mountain, to afford a passage to the stream, divides like the cleft hoof of an antelope — it was dragged on to the shore, and the head having been severed from the body, was thrown across the back of the mare and with its gory companion, borne into the camp in triumph.

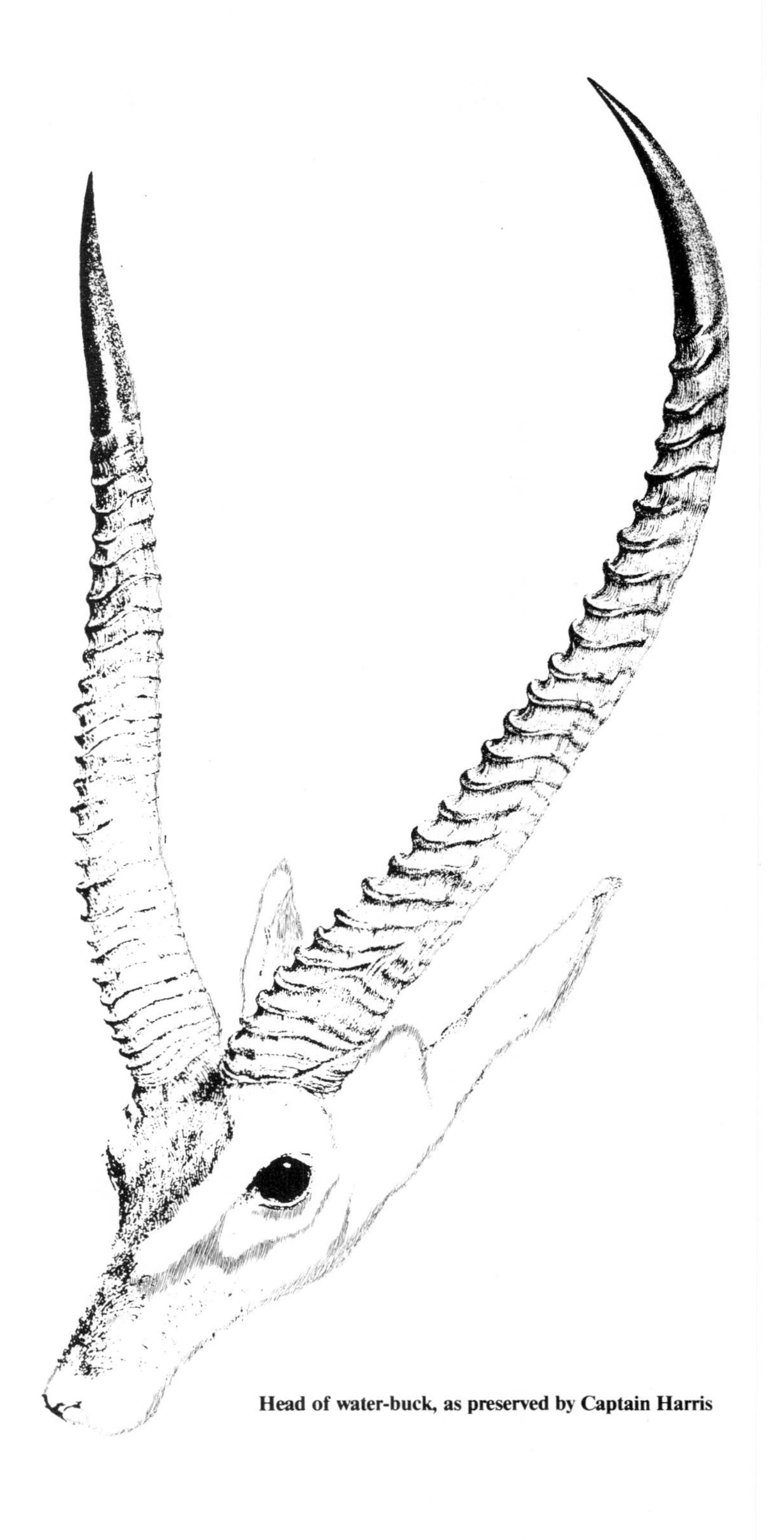

Head of water-buck, as preserved by Captain Harris

Plate XIV: *Aigocerus ellipsipyrmnus* — water buck — *water-bok* of the Hollanders — *phitomok* of the Matabili

Generic Character — Adult male four feet six inches high at the withers; nearly nine feet in extreme length. Carriage particularly stately. Figure cervine. Back straight. Neck raking. Horns upwards of thirty inches long, placed almost perpendicularly on the cranium; ponderous, curved forwards and sometimes rather inwards at the tips, but always diverging from the base; of a whitish green colour; the first third slightly compressed, the other two thirds nearly cylindrical; very strongly and closely annulated along the front and outside, to within six inches of the points, which are jet black. Chaffron intense sepia brown. Forehead, base of horns and behind the eyes, rufous. A white patch on the throat. Under lip and muzzle white. A white streak before each eye, and a white eliptical band strongly defined, encircling the tail in its upper focus, by passing over the croup, down the posterior face of each hip, and uniting between the thighs. Ears cervine, rounded and ample — white inside, sepia without. Hide black and in many parts visible through the hair, the general colour of which is greyish sepia brown, in texture coarse, crisped and resembling split whalebone; scantier on the body, but on the neck long, white and reversed, wearing the semblance of a mane. Legs dark brown, muscular and cervine in appearance. Tail slender, brown and tasselled at the end like that of the lion — reaching not quite to the hocks. A muzzle. No suborbital indent.

Female precisely similar, but hornless, hind-like and very feminine. Mammae two. Gregarious in small herds and families. Found only on, or near, the banks of rivers towards the Tropic, the Limpopo and Mariqua especially.

15

Pallah And Duiker

And now along the grassy meads
Where the skipping rooye-bok feeds
Let me through the mazes rove
Of the light acacia grove;
Now while yet the honey bee
Hums around yon blossomed tree,
And the pearled pintado calls
With grating cry at intervals;
And the duiker at my tread
Sudden lifts his startled head,
Then dives affrighted in the brake
Like wild duck in the reedy lake.

Standing at the head of the true antelopes, a model at once of elegance and vigour, the rare and graceful pallah first gladdens the sight of the traveller in southern Africa upon the elevated tracts to the northward of Litakoo. After plodding our most uninteresting way for several hundred miles through the barren wastes which lie beyond the colonial boundary, and gaining at length this more cheerful region, we advance through the wooded slopes and valleys that environ the mountain ranges of Kurrichane and Cashan. There, and especially under the latter, the species is observed amongst a thousand other novelties, in daily increasing abundance; but still, amid the mimosa groves which trace the serpentine course of the principal rivers, or in some sequestered and thinly wooded vale in their vicinity, only is it to be seen. Rarely do the families consist of more than a dozen or twenty individuals of both sexes, the number of bucks found among the largest groups being usually limited to three or four. Shy, capricious and secluded in its habits, I can recall few objects more picturesque than the graceful figures of a wanton herd, dancing and bounding through the thousand stems of the airy acacia grove, in all the poetry of motion. Whilst the delicate finish of their limbs is absolutely unrivalled, their soft radiant eyes, fringed like those of a Persian beauty, with long silken lashes, sparkle with animation. In the exercise of their acute faculties of hearing and smell, they will stop at every whisper, erect their slender necks — toss their light heads — and stamping their taper feet upon the ground, seem ready to catch the faintest and most distant sound. Some are quietly ruminating or grazing in the shade — and the young fawns are tripping sportively at the tufted heels of their dams. Yonder buck with his amorously curled upper lip and his long knotted horns reaching almost to his dun flanks, is darting like a meteor through the wood by a series of untiring circles, in an abortive attempt to overcome the coquetry of a retreating doe; whilst that knot of active ladies, amusing themselves with the exercise of the skipping rope, are lifting all four feet from the ground at the same time, and occasionally, like the springbok rebounding playfully over each other's backs.

Of the habits of this elegant and retired antelope, few particulars have hitherto been obtained, and naturalists, I think, have most erroneously stated it to be an inhabitant of the open plain. Although in the course of our wanderings, we visited its headquarters, not one single specimen was observed throughout the champaign country, to which had it even occasionally resorted, it would surely not have escaped the notice of men, whose eyes, from morning till eve, were on the stretch for game. Along the sides of the Cashan Mountains, and among the wooded valleys of the Limpopo, in all the favourite haunts of the stately waterbuck, its red figure was the most frequently observed — several large herds being there resident, out of which no fewer than four bucks were more than once brought in during a single day. The flesh, like that of the tribe generally to which it belongs, although dry, is tender and palatable, and being much patronized by our faithful Zoroastrian domestic, we never let slip the opportunity of realising a leg for his private consumption. By the Bechuana nations, to whose country it would seem to be entirely restricted, the species is universally recognised under the title of paala; whilst the Griquas and Bastaards, who occasionally pursue their hunting avocations to the northward of the Kamhanni Mountains, have dubbed it the rooye-bok [red buck], in allusion to its prevailing complexion. Professor Lichtenstein, who was the first to notice the animal, conferred the specific nomenclature of *melampus,* from the singular tufted cushions of dark mealy hair with which the hinder fetlocks are decorated. These occur in no other antelope, and in the pallah, remind the spectator of the heels of Mercury, a similitude which its nimble motions are well calculated to sustain. In both sexes the succentorial hoofs are wanting — a brown dot supplying their usual place — and the horns occur in the males only. Gnarled and eccentrically inflected, these are not less remarkable for their angular construction than in their dimensions, and although slender enough, can boast of at least double the length to which, from its delicate and feminine proportions, the wearer would appear to be entitled. The scut, which as a head ornament is greatly esteemed by the savages, tapers gradually to a point, and instead of being adorned with a terminal tuft, is decorated with a broad streak down its centre, corresponding with a parallel brown stripe on either buttock; whilst the abrupt gradation of colour on the body, descending from rusty red to the purest white, never failed to remind me of the tinted examples given in books which profess to illustrate the art of drawing in water colours.

The smaller antelope delineated in the annexed plate, is a denizen of the same locale as the pallah; and although claiming from its diminutive stature an extremely limited portion of attention, was yet never neglected when accident placed it in our way. The pair which furnished the originals of this portrait, were on my own shoulders borne three miles to the wagons from one of the central steppes of the Cashan Mountains, whither having gone out alone, I killed the buck as he sat on a projecting ledge — knocking over his disconsolate relict with the second barrel as she stood gazing in mute amazement at her mate's death struggles. The pasterns of this robust and sturdy little animal, which are singularly rigid, have the appearance of being encased in Bluchers or ankle boots, two other of its most remarkable features being the long suborbital slit that traverses the whole length of its Roman features, and the pencilled toupet of bright fulvous hair arising from the forehead, neither of which occur in any other of the antelopes. Writers have noticed three distinct species of the duiker, but the peculiarities in the horns that have led to this division are so trivial, that I should rather feel disposed to place them to the score of age, disease or accident, few specimens being exactly alike. The animal is extremely common in many parts of the Cape Colony, and on the outskirts of the deep forests which border the sea coast especially — wherein on my return from the interior I killed several — it is even more abundant than beyond the boundary. Occurring either singly or in pairs, the little dwarf is usually found crouching amid the shelter of bushy localities, and the dexterity with which it seeks to foil its pursuers among the intricacies of these, has gained for it the Dutch sobriquet in which it rejoices. Aroused from its snug form, the artful dodger clears with one vigorous and elastic bound the nearest bush and diving low on the other side among the heather and brushwood, continues alternately leaping and plunging whilst it flies straight as a dart to the nearest thicket — before seeking an asylum in which, and not infrequently also during its retreat, it rises like the hare upon its hinder legs, and having thus reconnoitred the foe above the intervening vegetation, wheels with an impatient sneeze to the right about, and proceeds ducking and bounding as before.

The approved colonial mode of hunting the duiker-bok is with dogs — and whilst thus topping the covert, or darting from one copse to another, the little wretch, despite of all its dodging and artifice, is easily slain with a hat-full of buck shot discharged from a piece of ordnance of such calibre, that four fingers might be introduced without much squeezing! Like the rest of the Cape venison, the flesh is utterly destitute of fat, a deficiency which the thrifty Dutch housewife seeks to remedy with her usual skill by calling in the aid of a sheep's tail. The animal is often to be seen running tame about the farm houses, but it never ceases, even in a domestic state, to take the note of alarm from the least sound to which it has been unaccustomed — thunder invariably causing it to fly to the nearest shelter in order to hide itself away.

Broadly characteristic is the singular scenery here portrayed of all those African rivers along whose wooded banks the pallah most delights to roam — and of the Mariqua in particular, where the first herd was observed by our party. It was early in the afternoon when we reached the banks of this long sighed for stream, some thirty miles below the point where it issues from the mountains of Kurrichane. Emerging unexpectedly from an extensive wood of venerable thorn trees we descended by a winding path to a lawn spread with a thick and verdant carpet of the greenest turf. This was succeeded by a belt of drifted sand hillocks bordered, in their turn, by a grove of the many stemmed acacia, which on either hand margined the river as far as the eye could reach. Robed in a rich scarf of yellow blossoms, they diffused around the most grateful of odours; and the whole effect was heightened by detached clumps of slender mimosas, hung with fragrant festoons of flowering creepers, under the screen of which, troops of clamorous pintados and bands of graceful pallahs were hurrying from our approach. Whilst threading these mazes, a peep of the river itself was suddenly obtained. A deep and shady channel, about twenty yards in width and flanked with reeds, was lined next to the water with an unbroken tier of weeping willows. Leaning 'in pensive guise' over the little stream, their drooping branches would positively have embraced but for the force of the crystal current which, as it foamed and bubbled over the pebbly bottom, swayed them with it. Swarms of new and interesting forms here hold their accustomed retreat; and the grass in the neighbourhood having that very morning been set on fire, the conflagration had caused every straggler in the vicinity to flock to this sanctuary, on the borders of which we accordingly set up our staff.

Silvery and bright peeps Aurora over the scathed and blackened mountain top, moving with her refreshing breath the light leaves of the scented acacias, whose graceful forms, scattered in careless confusion by the hand of nature, are still glistening with the falling dew drops. The long lines of mimosas resound with the incessant *ceuk ceuk* of the restless pintado, accompanied by the chirrupping of a host of smaller birds which are hopping among the fairy foliage, as its tiny leaves quiver to the zephyrs.

Wide waving groves a chequered scene display
And part admit, and part exclude the day;
Fit dwelling for the feathered throng,
Who pay their quit-rent with a song.

Softness and beauty characterize the whole landscape. Each tree admitting through its foliage as much of sun as it casts shadow, there is even in the depth of the grove an airiness of colouring not less graceful than remarkable. Throughout the endless vista of stems scarcely one solitary trunk is to be seen. From every hillock of sand arise a dozen or more slender stems, supporting a canopy of minute leaves, interspersed with golden blossoms — some of the lower branches already in the 'sear and yellow leaf' of age, having snapped spontaneously in the middle, and dropped their withered heads upon the ground. Ever and anon, as we wind among the more sacred glades, a duiker springs from the brake, and clearing with a bound the tops of the waving grass, pygmy-like vanishes amid the gloom of an adjacent thicket. Then a flock of slate-coloured pintados may be descried through an opening avenue, busily raking up the earth, and striving by weltering in the dust, to free themselves from a host of parasitic tormentors. Flocks of forty or fifty of the screaming fowls gather as we advance, and precipitately abscond before our path. Elevating their crested head, they shuffle along in laughable confusion shaking, their hunched backs, and uttering that far from melodious cry with which the ears of all are familiar. Now in their onward progress they have aroused a shy herd of ruminating pallahs, of which the dun leader comes skipping gallantly to the front, where, with:

Airy step and glorious eye,

he begs leave to inquire, on behalf of a large parcel of mincing females, what may be the cause of this alarm. A crack of the rifle, which lays him sprawling on the red sand, proves the instantaneous reply. Freedom in their looks and independence in their tufted heels, away go the survivors, scampering and galloping amid their native groves. In two seconds more they are both out of danger and out of sight, the mortal remains of their fallen leader being in the meantime, unceremoniously strapped upon the back of a pack horse, there to keep company with a duiker, three brace of guinea-fowl and a pair of leathern trousers — which latter, having been vacated by the bandy legs of Frederick Dangler — are now crammed full as they can hold of the gigantic eggs of the ostrich.

Africa must be considered the great nursery of the *Numida Meleagris.* Her western shores have always formed the peculiar habitat of the species, which there unite in even much more extensive flocks than we met with in the interior of the continent — flying in large bands, and resorting at stated hours to the neighbouring springs or rivulets, whence at sunset they retire to the woods and perch upon the loftiest trees. The title by which they were generally known to the ancients would render it probable that the specimens first imported into Europe, were brought from Nubia, though the testimony of Varro proves them to have been sufficiently rare before the African coast was visited by Europeans. During the zenith of the Roman Empire, the bird was held in the highest estimation, and considered a delicacy at the banquets of the great; but with her decline it became lost altogether in Europe until eventually restored by the Spanish navigators. To the Dutch colonists of the Cape, the guinea-fowl is known by the facetious appellation of *Jan Tarentaal,* and in many of the

W. C. Harris del.

Cephalopus mergens.—The Duiker.

XV. ANTILOPE MELAMPUS:— THE PALLAH.

more remote districts, where it is still common, considerable troops are to be found lying among long grass and undergrowth along the dry beds of rivers. Flushed by the farmer's dog, they ascend, whirring like pheasants, high above the tops of the stunted trees; and when weary, not infrequently perch upon the branches. On our way to Graaff Reinet, we were first treated on Mynheer de Klerck's estate near Somerset, to the, to us, then novel sport, but subsequently, towards the tropic, a day seldom passed without our seeing them around our bivouac in abundance. The pintado in its wild state exhibits the fleshy caruncles on the cheeks, and the callous crest on the cranium, rather less developed than in our domestic bird; but it possesses the same lively, restless and clamorous disposition; the monotonous cry which has aptly been compared to the creaking of rusty hinges, being often incessant for hours together. Morning and evening the wary troops emerge into the green glades to feed, and about roosting time their wretched noise becomes so perfectly stunning as uniformly to betray the position on which they design to pass the night. Under many of the isolated trees which grow along the river banks in the interior, the ground is absolutely white with their ordure; and although usually difficult to be approached during the day, we could frequently about dusk perceive them flying up in the manner of tame fowls, one after another to their perch, until the loaded branches had become such a positive poultry house that the larder might easily be replenished with any number.

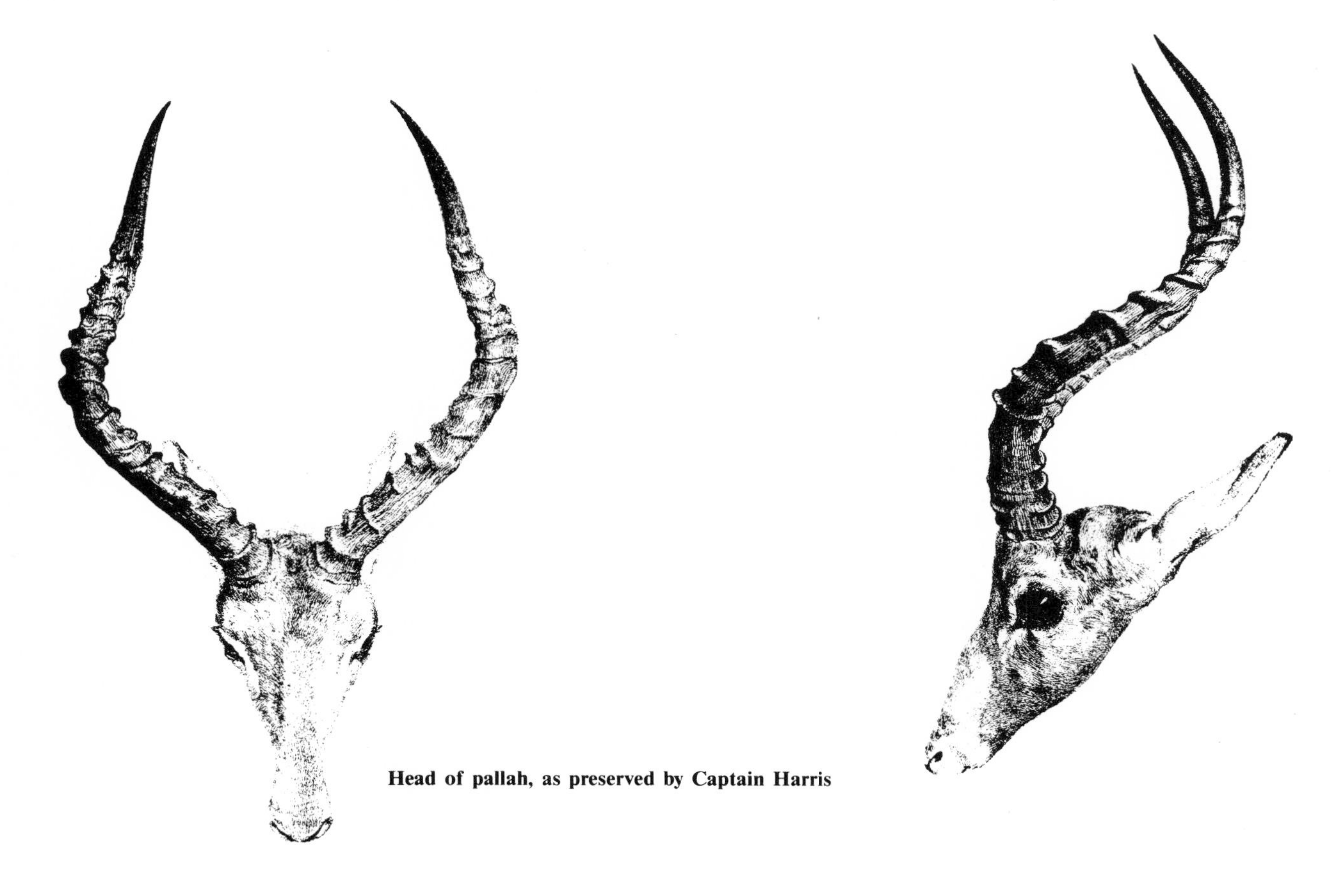

Head of pallah, as preserved by Captain Harris

Plate XV (1): *Antilope melampus* — pallah — *rooye-bok* of the Cape colonists — *paala* of the Matabili and Bechuana

Generic character — Adult male about three feet four inches high at the shoulder and six in extreme length. Very light and high on the legs. Horns about twenty inches long, of a angular lyrate tendency; ascending obliquely upwards, outwards and backwards; and midway at an obtuse angle, obliquely inwards and forwards; brown, coarsely annulated and striated between for about two thirds of their length; the rings often splitting in two and forming prominent nobs on the front only, whilst they become partially and sometimes altogether obliterated on the sides; the tips smooth and polished. Ears round, seven inches long, tipped with black. Tail thirteen inches long pointed, white, with a dark brown streak down the middle. Colour of the head, neck and upper part of the body, deep fulvous or rust colour. Sides and hinder parts yellow dun. Belly white. A dark brown streak down each buttock. A dark spot in place of the spurious hoofs, which do not occur in this species. A large cushion of brown hair between the hock and fetlock. A white spot before each eye. A dark spot between the horns. No trace of a suborbital sinus. Small bare space for a muzzle.

Female similar but hornless. Eye very large, soft and full. Mammae two. Gregarious in small families or herds. Inhabits the thinly wooded banks of rivers in the Bechuana country.

Plate XV (2): *Cephalopus mergens* — duiker — *duiker-bok* of the Cape colonists — *impoon* of the Matabili

Generic Character — Adult male about two feet high at the shoulder, and three feet eight inches in extreme length. Limbs solid. Horns four inches long, approximated, nearly parallel, standing a little outwards, with a longitudinal ridge on the front, traversing four or five annuli on the middle, but not traversing the wrinkles of the base. Forehead covered with a patch of long bright fulvous hair, terminating in a pencil. A dark streak down the chaffron. Three dark striae inside each ear. A dark streak down the front of the legs, terminating in a black fetlock as if booted. Colour various; usually cinerous olive above and white beneath. Tail eight inches long; black, tipped with white. Pasterns rigid. Spurious hoofs scarcely developed. A long suborbital slit traced down the side of the face, but no external opening visible. A small naked muzzle.

Female similar with very tiny horns, almost concealed beneath the long rufous hair. The females of the cephalopine group are represented to be universally hornless; but every female specimen of the duiker that I have seen, possesses short horns, nearly if not totally obscured by the rufous tuft. Mammae four. Solitary or monogamous. Common throughout the colony, and especially so towards the sea-coast among bushes and brushwood.

16

African Rhinoceros

The devilish iron engine wrought
In deepest hell, and framed by furie's skill,
With windy nitre and quick sulphur fraught,
And rammed with bullets round, ordained to kill.
Spenser's Faery Queene.

'If you draw your beast in an emblem,' observes Peacham quaintly enough, 'show a landscape of the country natural to the beast.' In accordance with which sound and excellent counsel, although not directly dealing in emblems, I have striven to display annexed the scenery natural to the smaller, and more common of the two species of rhinoceros that infest southern Africa. He is a swinish, cross-grained, ill-favoured, wallowing brute, with a hide like a rasp, an impudent cock of the chin, a roguish leer from out the corner of his eye, a mud-begrimed exterior and a necklace of ticks and horse flies! Nineteen times out of twenty shall you see the crusty old fellow standing listlessly in the society of gnoos, quaggas and hartebeests, upon a plain bounded by a low range of azure hills, and dotted over with mokaala trees, distributed with park-like regularity. In imitation of the pendulum of a Dutch clock, his tail is swinging mechanically from side to side — and the odds are fifty to one that, having eaten his fill, he is at that very moment in the enjoyment of perfect idleness, under the shade cast by one of the many thatched cities of the loxia which are within the scope of vision. Indolent and slovenly, he would appear, notwithstanding his enormous bulk, to be a slow and dainty feeder, tasting few of the many shrubs which he approaches, or has even touched with his tortoise-like nose, as though designing to browse thereon, and whilst exclusively subsisting upon brushwood and the smaller branches of dwarf trees — he is to be found in none but wooded districts, his traces become there abundantly apparent, from his accumulated heaps of ordure wherein he delights to roll, from his singular trefoil-shaped *spoor,* and from the extensive mutilations of his favourite bushes.

Whether from a limited sphere of vision, arising from the extraordinary minuteness of the eyes, which resembling a pig's in expression, are placed nearer to the nose than in most other animals — or whether from an overweening confidence in its own powers — the rhinoceros will generally suffer itself to be approached within even a few yards, before condescending to take the smallest heed of the foe who is diligently plotting its destruction. At length, pricking its pointed ears at some unusual sound, it listens with a ludicrous assumption of shrewdness — its elevated snout, armed with a double plough shear, imparting an inimitable expression of contempt. In an instant the dull and vacant physiognomy has become lighted up with the essence of all that is spiteful and malevolent. Twinkling its hoggish eyes, and turning its shapeless head enquiringly from side to side — elevating its double chin, and restlessly rolling its bemired carcase from side to side — it trots forward a few paces with the vivacity and mincing gait of a French dancing master — wheeling presently to the right about to reconnoitre the enemy. Then uttering a great blast or snort of defiance, and lowering its armed muzzle almost to the ground, grunting and trumpeting, on comes the villain with reckless impetuosity, displaying a degree of activity but ill according with such unwieldy proportions. Once roused from his apparent lethargy, throwing down the gauntlet, he charges with blind fury to the onslaught, aided no less by the length of his stride than by the propelling impetus of his body. Yet his rush is invariably a straight one, and his awkward structure preventing him from turning with facility, it is only necessary to step on one side to be perfectly secure — a bullet, hardened either with tin or quicksilver, and thrown in behind the elbow at the proper moment, being almost sure to prove fatal, after a race of three or four hundred yards. But though, glorying not in panoply of plate armour which encases the ribs of his Asiatic brother, the stupid and vicious beast is nevertheless enveloped in a suit of mail which will successfully repel any ordinary bullet — one of unadulterated lead, far from penetrating, most frequently flattened from his hide.

When the Dutch first established themselves at the Cape of *Bon Esperance* — now nearly two centuries ago, the *zwart rhinoster* existed in considerable numbers on the present site of Cape Town, along the base of Table Mountain; but within the Colony the species has long ceased to exist, the remnant having instinctively fled before the destructive cannonade to which it was subjected. Gregarious in fives and sixes, they are extremely abundant in the wilds of the interior and I have, during a single day, counted upwards of sixty. The Hottentots, ever gasconading of their skill in hunting them, had long kept us on the *qui vive,* but it was not until we had reached the sedgy Molopo, that the animal's dusky form actually appeared to me. Whilst the teams were being unyoked, I had gone out on horseback with the design of ministering to the inordinate appetites of a party of savages who had joined us on the road; and was busied in the pursuit of a troop of hartebeests, when two colossal figures which my friends at once pronounced to be *borili,* were descried, motionless as statues, in the middle of the level and treeless expanse. I at first endeavoured to approach, frog-fashion, upon all fours, under cover of the grass, but with a strong wind setting towards them, they went off at a heavy trot, and as it was getting dark, I remounted my horse and galloping within seventy or eighty yards — the nearest I felt disposed to venture on so short an acquaintance — treated the more bulky to a brace of rifle balls. Carrying his snout close to the ground, he did but run the faster and by the time I had repeated the dose without any better effect, it had become so dark that I was compelled to abstain from further hostilities.

The next apparition was even more shadowy. Accompanied by a band of natives who volunteered to show me a giraffe, I had ridden so far in advance of the wagons — them plodding at a funeral pace through the heavy forest that envelopes the food of Kurrichane — that night overtaking me, I began to feel apprehensive of having to bivouac in the bush. My companions evidently contemplated a similar contingency and evinced a vast longing to rejoin four of their number who had wisely tarried behind with the carcase of a sassaybe that I had inconsiderately shot. Giving by signs to understand that I disapproved of the measure, we pushed on briskly towards the halting ground that had previously been agreed upon. A contumacious rhinoceros was stationed directly in our path, and although repeatedly hailed, most peremptorily refused to make way. There was just twilight sufficient to admit of my discharging both barrels of my rifle into his unwieldy form from behind a strong breastwork of thorn bushes. Sneezing violently and wheezing, he ran off in the direction that we were taking, but presently subsided heavily in the path. We approached him with caution, and were well pleased to find that he was extinct — a volley of musketry at the same moment in reply to my rifle, together with a bright beacon fire which suddenly blazed forth towards heaven, directing our benighted steps to the encampment. Arriving at the Mariqua several days after this occurrence, we had formed the camp on a verdant spot on the river bank near to an extensive Matabili kraal — the captain of which, at the head of some ten of his clan, being clamorous for victuals, I willingly placed myself under his guidance, and dived into the heart of the extensive groves, where, although the sun was shining brightly, a dry cutting wind rendered the cold scarcely endurable, even under the defence of a duffel jacket. After running a few hundred yards, the savages, halting, pointed to a huge shapeless mass, which bore so strong a resemblance to a sleeping rhinoceros, that without asking any questions, I poured through the trees at his indistinct outline a broadside, which from treble the same distance, would have more than satisfied any other animal in the creation. But notwithstanding that the beast was mortally wounded, he twice contrived to cross the river, and I had no alternative — a cold one though it proved — but to wade after him through water which reached to my middle, following the bloody trail among the intricacies of the grove, until from single drops the traces became splashes of frothy crimson. Still striving to force his tottering frame through the tangled covert, the dying monster at length sank upon his knees, when another bullet behind the shoulder terminated his giant struggles, as he was tearing up the earth with his ponderous horn.

A flash like fire within his eyes
Blazed as he bent no more to rise;
And then eternal darkness sunk
Through all the palpitating trunk —
Nought of life left save a shivering
Where his limbs were slightly quivering.

My companion the next morning achieved a 'gentle passage of arms' with the very duplicate of this gentleman; but his antagonist could not be prevailed upon to surrender to superior weapons, until it had considerably disfigured with the point of its horn the stock of the rifle employed in its reduction. Aroused from a siesta in a thick bush by the smarting of a gunshot wound, the exasperated beast pursued its human assailant so closely, that Richardson was fain, in self defence, to discharge the second barrel down its open throat! On our way to the Ooli River, a few days subsequently, having left the wagons to proceed by the direct route, I took a circuitous line to the left, and was ascending a stony eminence, when sundry discharges of musketry accompanied by loud shouts and clamour, were followed by the sudden appearance of an infuriated female. Streaming with gore, she rushed over the brow of the hill with snorts and grunts, looming like a colossal sow — and was actually within pistol shot ere a soul was aware of her advent. No bush presenting itself behind which to hide, I threw my hunting cap to divert her attention, 'Lingap meanwhile striking his shield, and shouting with stentorian lungs until the brute turned off, when I saluted her fat buttocks with the contents of both my barrels, and she was immediately afterwards overturned by a running fire from the Hottentots.

As we advanced, the species became daily more and more abundant, and I shall hardly gain credence when I assert, that in the valley of Limpopo specimens were so numerous, that on arriving in the afternoon at our new ground, it was no uncommon thing to perceive a dozen horned snouts protruded at once from bushes in the immediate vicinity. No sooner were the teams unyoked, than the whole party in the regular routine of business, having assumed their weapons, proceeded to dislodge the enemy, and right stoutly often was the field contested. But where is the quadruped that can stand before the grooved rifle? It will take the conceit out of the most contumacious, and like a sedative, will calm his ruffled temper in a minute. Every individual came in for a share of cold lead and quick silver; and the stubborn brute that would not quietly withdraw, satisfied with the mercurial dose he had received, was ultimately badgered to death as a matter of course. Daily almost, two or three were thus annihilated within view of the camp; and not only during our hunting excursions was the path constantly disputed by some rebellious rascal, who refused to move on one side until the smarting of his wounds compelled him — but when on the point of drawing the trigger at some object that I coveted, a scoundrel has frequently leapt with a grunt out of a bush not many yards removed from my elbow. I have elsewhere related, that on the occasion of my first humbling a giraffe, my advance towards the herd was opposed by a spiteful old vixen, that twinkled her wicked eyes, and with her antiquated little calf, seemed so bent upon interference, that I had no alternative but to direct Piet van Roy to salute her with a broadside; a white turban that during the chase was torn by a projecting bough from around my hunting cap, being afterwards charged and trampled under foot by no fewer than three ungainly beasts in concert, whom I could long perceive snorting and wheezing in an abortive attempt to overtake me.

During the time that we were encamped in the valley of the Limpopo, a huge male came sauntering down one evening after we had all returned tired from hunting, and proceeded coolly to take up his position under a spreading tree, not three hundred yards from our wagons. A general move was made towards the guns, which had been slung in their accustomed places within the awning; and Andries, contriving to obtain his *roer* the first, pompously announced his intention of giving the party a lesson *gratis* in the art of rhinoceros shooting. '*Ja,*, said he confidently, '*Daar in the veld ik zaal de schelm dood maaken.*' [Angl. 'Aye, I shall smash the rogue on that very spot!'] Impelled by this bold determination, he crept with suitable caution against the wind, taking special care ever to keep the trunk of a tree interposed betwixt himself and the object for whose life he thirsted; and deliberately seating himself at last upon the ground within thirty paces of the unconscious target, he levelled a full minute over a branch and drew the trigger. The clattering together of the heavy flint and steel was the only response, and the rhinoceros, quite in the dark as to the cause of the sound so unusual, pricked its sharp ears, elevated its snout, and, having sniffed about a little, trotted quietly on to the next tree. The foiled preceptor nimbly advanced to the position that it had vacated, and another minute's aim produced a flash in the pan. Again the beast trotted on, and wheeling about, fronted the adversary and commenced winking its little eyes in a most ominous manner. Still resolved to learn how a rhinoceros ought to be slain, not a man interfered, and Andries having leisurely cleared the ample touch-hole of his blunderbuss with an acacia thorn, and then by the aid thereof inserted a suitable modicum of powder, obtained with some difficulty from his gigantic ox-horn magazine — which complex operation occupied another two minutes and a half — levelled for the third time. On this occasion the bullet did leave the tube, and away thundered the irritated animal — the sanguinary sportsman offering large bets that death would overtake his victim ere it had travelled a hundred yards! But from the top of an eminence we gazed at the dusky figure as it waned smaller and smaller to the perception, now trotting, now galloping over the

XVI. RHINOCEROS AFRICANUS: – THE AFRICAN RHINOCEROS.

plain below, until at length it stood stock still, and began browsing upon the bushes; whereupon the preceptor, covered with infamy, having tossed his empty gun over his brawny shoulder, cocked his only optic at his jeering mess mates and acquainted them that the failure of his experiment was solely to be attributed to the infamous quality of the *kruid* [Angl. Gunpowder].

Our friend on the other hand, received upon a subsequent occasion rather an awkward lesson in the process by which the rhinoceros conducts the war against the human species. We were leading the hot trail of a herd of elephants, and whilst passing a little green knoll, an old lady was perceived sunning herself under the walls of a deserted stone kraal which crowned the summit. Andries had that morning drawn the dappled mare in the lottery, and being in an unusually crusty humour thereat, was resolved to mar the sport to the utmost of his poor ability. Dismounting without saying a syllable, and making fast the bridle to a tree, he boldly advanced towards the quarry — which for once in a way appeared to be most peaceably disposed — and cocking his long gun with an air of singular success, truimphantly fired a four-to-the-pound ball into the animal's ribs. Forth she came, brandishing her plough shear in a towering passion — and whilst not an object appeared in the whole landscape behind which to seek refuge, the mare, having broken her bridle, was trotting quietly away. A pair of tight leathern inexpressibles, which from their fashionable cut had long formed his boast, so impeded his downward progress, that he was overtaken in a trice, and the rent inflicted in their nether portion by a thrust of the animal's sharp horn, sufficiently proved how nearly we had been bereft for ever of the valuable services of our now crestfallen hero.

One stormy morning, when hunting was altogether out of the question, our little party was on its way to cut out the teeth of sundry elephants that had been slain the preceding day. The road lay under a ruined cattle enclosure, whence a vicious rhinoceros, the only tenant, perceiving the difficulty with which we extricated our feet from the deep black mud — of which several pounds attached themselves at every step — resolved to take us at a disadvantage. With a grunt and a whistle, out he sallied accordingly, fully bent upon mischief; and the dampness of the atmosphere causing no less than three out of our four guns to missfire, the assassin was actually in the middle of us, when a ball from my second barrel fortunately piercing his eye, he fell dead at our feet. Ere many days had elapsed, however, I took my revenge for this act of unprovoked aggression upon an unhappy member of the fraternity that I detected asleep in another of these stone enclosures. The walls, which were extremely extensive, had only one outlet, before which having drawn a stiff thorn branch and taken post outside, I aroused the slumberer by a shot under the left ear. Never shall I forget his amazement. Starting upon his legs, he ran with closed eyes full butt against the opposite wall, and finding the masonry harder than his ugly head, made divers uncouth attempts to scramble over, pawing down the loose stones, and in his bursting rage, kicking them backwards and forwards among the wild tobacco plants. A brisk fire from the gateway deterred him from following up any decided attempt in that quarter, although as he raved round and round the enclosure, and flew from one compartment to another, he eyed it perpetually. Bullet after bullet whacked against his devoted ribs, and it being next to impossible to take any aim, no less than twenty seven had stuck the miserable fellow before he finally gave in — his riddled carcase, as well as the foam which had churned around his chops, having by that time assumed a die of crimson. Fearful indeed was the uproar that attended the division of his mutilated remains — a large party of famished Baquaina females, whose wardrobes were even more remarkably slender than usual, rushing forth like so many weird witches, and leaving in the course of a few hours nothing to attest the slaughter, saving a pool of blood!

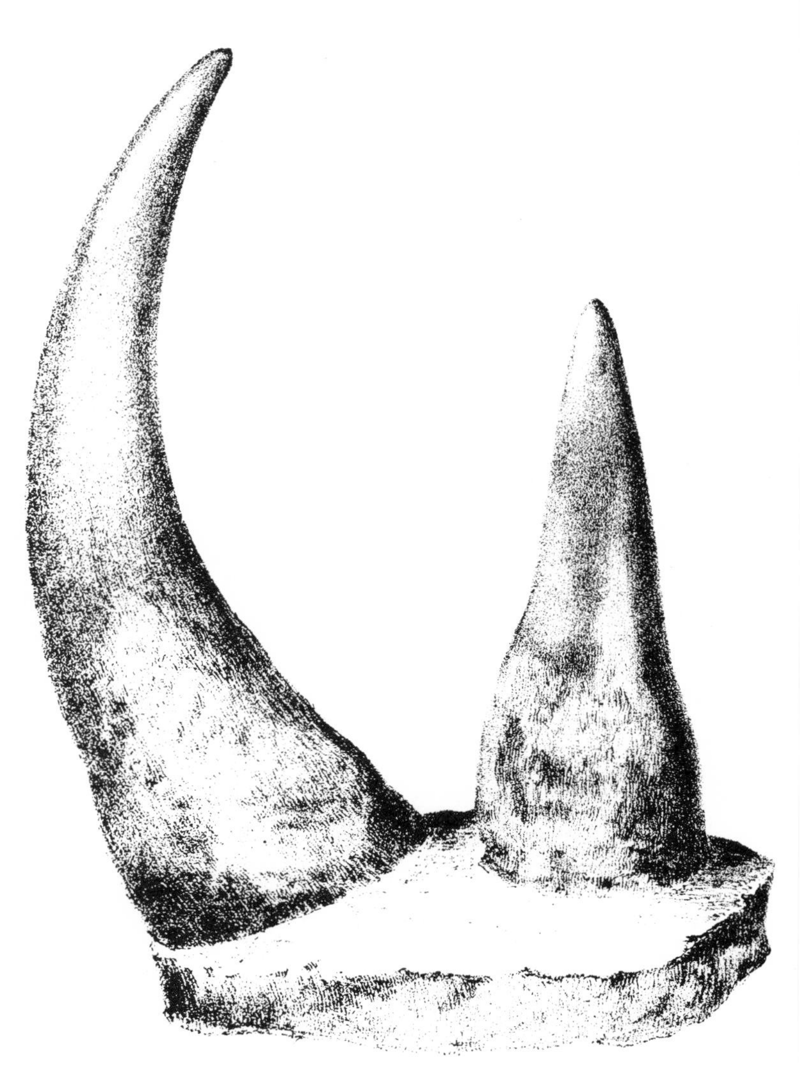

Horns of rhinoceros Africanus, as preserved by Captain Harris

Plate XVI: *Rhinoceros Africanus* — African rhinoceros — *rhinoster* of the Cape colonists — *borili* of the Bechuana — *chukuroo* of the Matabili

Generic Character — Often six feet high at the shoulder and about thirteen in extreme length. General contour that of gigantic swine. Body very robust, clumsy and underlimbed; feet very small in proportion and furnished with three toes; the hocks unnaturally prominent, as though spavined. Head shapeless. Eyes lateral and extremely small; encircled by a series of deeply furrowed wrinkles, extending over a great portion of the face. Muzzle hooked and resembling that of a tortoise; armed with two horns on the snout, placed one behind the other, over an arch formed by the nasal bones; they are solid, fibrous, consisting of an agglutination of hair, and attached to the skin only; variously fashioned; usually rough at the base and highly polished above; the anterior from one to two feet long, the posterior generally much smaller, but capricious, attaining in some specimens the same or nearly the same length. In no two specimens of this animal which came under my observation were the horns built exactly upon the same model. Disease or accident had not infrequently rendered the anterior horn the shorter of the two. Ears pointed, small, approximated and fringed with a few bristles. Hide naked, very thick, rugous and knotty, but destitute of plaits or folds, a few loose wrinkles about the neck excepted. Usual colour olive brown, approaching sometimes to that of clay mire. Tail about two feet long, laterally compressed at the end and furnished with a few terminal bristles.

Female similar, but smaller. Mammae two. Very common in the interior, and frequently gregarious in small groups not exceeding five or six. Inhabits variously, but is most usually met with on thinly wooded plains.

17

Bontebok

Lo! where in triumph o'er his boundless plain,
The free born chief of Libya loves to reign;
With fires proportion'd to his native sky,
Strength in his arm, and lightning in his eye —
Scours with wild feet his sun-illumin'd zone,
The spear, the wild buck, and the woods his own.

Upon the ocean-like and untrodden prairies of the interior — those especially lying south of the Vaal River, of which large tracts are strongly impregnated with saline particles — the incredible numbers of the pied antelope here depicted, and of its still gayer congener the blesbok, that are frequently congregated in the vicinity of the salt flats of the few stagnant pools of brackish water, would seem almost to realize fable. There is in these brilliant herbivorous assemblages something peculiarly wild and striking, and one feels amid such scenes, as though wandering over a new planet. The sky is without a speck — the vast landscape without an undulation. All around bears the original impress of nature untouched by human hand since its first formation. One boundless expanse spread out on every side until it meets the horizon, here and there only is broken by solitary clumps of stately mokaalas, flourishing near some scanty reservoir — the countless variety of wild flowers which blossom spontaneously over tracts of land, otherwise bare and barren, affording in their rich colours, a singular contrast to the uniform sterility of the soil from which they have been called up, as by a touch of the magician's wand.

Advance, and for whole days together the traveller shall see no man, neither he hear aught save the strange notes of desert-loving animals — the aboriginal, and often the only inhabitants of the soil. At each step the elegant korhaan popping its black top-knot above the grass, rises with hoarse raven-like croaks before the horse's feet, and squeaking forth its monotonous *kirra-kirr-kac,* again alights a few yards beyond. Vast herds of quaint looking antelopes, the offspring as it were of a second creation, are everywhere exhibiting their gaudy coats in endless variety of shade and hue. Hundreds are licking up the crystallised efflorescence, over which dances the dazzling and treacherous mirage, whilst large troops in the performance of their complicated manoeuvres are absolutely, forming by their incessant tramp, roads which resemble so many well-travelled highways!

Through flowery champaigns roam these joyous creatures
Of many a colour, size and shape — all graceful
In every look, step, attitude, prepared
Even at the shadow of a cloud to vanish,
And leave a solitude where thousands stood
With heads declined, and nibbling eagerly;
As locusts when they light on some new soil
And move no more till they have shorn it bare.

Until we had reached the headquarters of the bontebok, in the heart of these great unexplored plains, whereon thousands upon thousands were seen, and numbers daily slain — one small troop near Kapain, and half a dozen stragglers at the foot of the Cashan range, were all that occurred after the first specimens which we met with on the Chooi desert. These latter appeared to have been attracted by an oasis, containing the only moisture that we were fortunate enough to discover on that region of emptiness, after a weary search of six and thirty hours, the greater number of which had been passed by the oxen in the yoke. Throughout, the features of this waste and howling wilderness, were those of a land accursed:

Like burnish'd steel
Glowing, it lay beneath the eye of noon,

exhibiting one dreary expanse which seemed as if it had been for ages consecrated to drought, desolation and sterility. Bare stony ridges, glaring worse than the heated hills of Pandemonium crossed the forbidding landscape at long intervals, and the parched earth rent and seamed with gaping fissures, was devoid of even a single spot of verdure, its scanty vegetation being scorched to one uniform brown. Not a solitary tree raised its sickly head to diminish the aspect of barrenness, and the sun, like a ball of metal at a white heat, blazed over the nakedness.

A journey of twenty miles first brought us to Loharon, at which there was said to exist a fair prospect of obtaining water, when that in the bottle, like Hagar's, should be spent; but alas! the only tank in the whole country was completely exhausted, and we dug in the sun-cracked bed to no purpose. The small supply that we had brought in the wagons was barely drinkable even in coffee, yet what were our sufferings compared with those of the unhappy oxen. Although tired to death with so long and sultry a march, they ran frantically in every direction in quest of some pool at which they might slake their burning thirst, making the air resound with their mournful lowings. No alternative presented itself but to travel night and day in search of this necessary of life, and as the sun went down for the second time, and the gloomy night again closed around us without even one hour's moon to guide our path, the prospect was indeed most disheartening. At length some horses that we had obtained from our enthusiastic friend Sutton — and which having recently crossed the desert, were fortunately well acquainted with the locale — by a singular instinct, suddenly separating themselves from the party, galloped off the road — when, following in the direction they had taken, the screaming of water-fowl sounded like music in our ears, and we had the gratification of finding a small pond of mephitic water. Of this cheering discovery both man and beast appeared to be simultaneously apprised. Water was the universal cry. Rushing to the brink, and throwing themselves on their faces, the Hottentots swallowed large gulps of the impure liquid, indifferent to the crowd of oxen, horses and sheep, which pressed close upon their heels — whilst the teams in the wagons were with the utmost difficulty restrained until the yokes had been removed, when impatient of their burning thirst, they dashed headlong into the now muddy pool. A dense fog ushered in the following morning, and as it rolled tardily away, disclosed some fifty bonteboks standing at the water's edge within pistol shot of our camp, but in utter ignorance of our proximity. As the herd scampered off, a volley was sent after it without effect, nor were their numbers sufficient to admit of our way-worn and famished horses overtaking them.

The country through which we travelled, being chiefly characterized by open plains or straggling forests, the Indian deer-stalker will readily comprehend why wood-craft availed little in the destruction of game. Many of the wild animals that occur in southern Africa are by nature slow and heavy; the gregarious habits of the fleeter — of which, notwithstanding its clumsy proportions, the bontebok is one — rendering them so easy of approach *á cheval,* that from the mighty elephant down to the most diminutive antelope, almost every species may be successfully pursued and shot from the saddle. The usually level character of the ground, moreover, is highly favourable to this mode of proceeding, and after galloping to the head of a closely jammed column of bonteboks, for example, there is ample time to dismount, fire, load and fire again, before the glittering army has passed — a fine heavy fellow usually falling to each crack of the rifle. Who shall attempt to describe the sense of buoyancy and exultation that glows within our bosom whilst thus flying at the heels of retreating thousands! Free are we as themselves, and as the winds that blow over the broad plains that we traverse!

It is sufficiently obvious, then, that the success of a campaign directed against the wild denizens of such a region, must mainly depend upon the number and condition of the horses; but neither is the safety of the party in event of an attack from savage tribes, hanging less upon the same contingency. Scarcely a day elapses, either during which some of the steeds are not pressed into the service for the recovery of straying cattle, and owing to some peculiarity in the Hottentot conformation that ill adapts him for equestrian exercises, in lieu of being:

Incorps'd and demi-natur'd,
With the brave beast,

whilst 'witching the world with noble horsemanship' he rolls and bumps in the saddle like a sack of peas, and never fails to bring home the palfrey with a galled back. Instead of our sixteen half starved shoeless garrons, with nothing more solid than grass to eat, and not so much even as a cloth to protect their bare ribs from the cold and wet during a long succession of inclement nights, we could therefore have found ample employment for forty, with ten wagon-loads of grain and at least a hundred weight of shoes! But whilst none of our many trading advisers, who had doubtless in their time experienced the difficulty of destroying on foot sufficient game for the subsistence of their followers, had suggested our going provided with a better stud, they had unfortunately succeeded in dissuading us from our intention of carrying a supply of the two latter essentials, of which we never ceased to deplore the absence. The anxiety may be estimated, wherewith, as each succeeding day drew near its close, we watched the condition of our meagre hunters after this hard day's work — received the report of one or more of the favourites being away and likely to prove food for lions — or, during the construction of the pound designed for the security of the rest, strove to free them from the clusters of bursting ticks, which having been contracted among the bushes, sought to rob them of the little blood that they possessed. What would we not have given for a tough little stall-fed Arabian, with abundance of hard flesh upon his ribs? To men circumstanced as we were, the sorriest scrub that was ever ridden in the East, would well have been worth his weight in the purest gold! Nevertheless it is only justice to the manifold merits of the Cape horses to declare, that ragged and rawboned though they be, they do but require feeding to render them the most useful allies during an African foray. Hardy, docile and enduring, any number may be driven along the line of march by a single Hottentot and whilst, like camels, they can subsist for weeks together upon the tops of sapless and sun-scorched bushes, they are readily habituated to graze unattended within sight of the wagons, wherever grass is to be found — the more restless being simply knee haltered, or shackled like a gypsy's donkey, to limit their rambles. In the chase, the most formidable looking animals inspire them not with the slightest alarm, and the bridle being thrown over their heads, although sometimes guilty of playing the truant, they will generally remain standing in the wilderness for hours together, without attempting to stir from the spot. Anon it shall be shown that in point of shape and contour; the bontebok and the blesbok bear to each other the closest resemblance, being equally robust, hunch-backed and broad-nosed, and rejoicing in the same whimsical and fine venerable old goatish expression of countenance. But the species here delineated, is both more soberly clad, and more remarkably skewbald than that which will be hereafter portrayed, the legs being perfectly white from the knee downwards instead of along their inner sides only, and the crupper moreover being marked with a white disc or gusset. The lyrated horns, which are alike placed vertically on the summit of the cranium, are in the bontebok jet black whereas they are light brown in the blesbok; but the two animals possess in common an abrupt snowy blaze down the face, a white belly, a hoary glazed back, as it wore a saddle and fiery red eyes. Rarely intermixing, the habits of the species are yet precisely similar. They resort to the same localities, are equally addicted to the use of salt, and excepting in certain embarrassed situations, invariably scour against the wind, holding their square noses close to the ground, as though they were running scent.

The bontebok, or *painted goat* — largest of all the gazelles — has long ceased to exist within the colonial limits in those enormous multitudes that are described by early travellers as spreading over the wide plain like a flock of springboks; but a few are still preserved in the district of Zwellendam, through the potent influence of a penalty of rix-dollars five hundred, which has been attached to the destruction of a specimen without especial license from Government. Anxious on my return from the Tropic, to ascertain whether the animal thus rigorously protected, differed in any respect from that found in the interior, as pretended by the colonists, I obtained, through the kindness of Sir Benjamin D'Urban, a formal warrant, duly signed, sealed and delivered, affecting the lives of some four individuals. Armed with this instrument, we proceeded through *Zoëtendal's Vley,* on our way from Zwellendam to the metropolis, and after having been grossly insulted by a surly Dutch boer named De Toit, than whom no savage could more closely resemble a wild beast, set up our headquarters near the hospitable mansion of Mynheer Oëdendal. Lower down the valley towards Cape L' Agulhas — that melancholy scene of so many appalling shipwrecks — lay the extensive estate of Field Commandant Laurens, the merriest old sportsmen and most warm-hearted Hollander I have ever met. My writ being duly produced, leave was readily accorded to shoot over these lands, on which were several herds, comprising in all about three hundred head; but they proved the wildest of the wild, and after I had ridden all my horses to a stand, I was fain to confess that to obtain permission to slay a bontebok, was a far easier business than to turn that permission to account. The following day, however, old Laurens obligingly came to my assistance and first exacted a solemn promise that I would not inform against him for becoming an accomplice in the murder without a government license, harnessed a team of frisky young horses to his long travelling wagon, which, besides myself, carried no fewer than four inside and two outside passengers, armed each with a species of swivel. No sooner was a herd perceived making for a particular point — their broad white muzzles raking close to the ground like a pack of fox hounds — than the Field Commandant standing on the coach box, cracked his long whip with an astounding report, and set off a Dover-mail-pace across

XVII. GAZELLA PYGARGA: - THE BONTEBOK.

the flats to intercept them, taking in his orbit, ploughed fields, dykes, ditches and embankments, with the most reckless indifference to the probable consequences. As might reasonably have been anticipated, one of the many ginjals exploded, carrying with its contents one half of the brim of a hat, and a very considerable portion of the canvas awning above our heads; but in spite of this untoward disaster and the subsequent fracture of a trace or two, our forces were so judiciously dropped behind convenient cover, as opportunity served, that the herd, from being puzzled in a corner, became at last fairly checkmated. Running in a ring, in an attempt to extricate themselves from this unpleasant dilemma, the *capias* was presently served upon the bodies of three out of the four individuals; and these proved amply sufficient to satisfy not only my curiosity, but my inclination for such sport, so immediately following upon the glorious scenes of the interior where:

Sorrow it were, and shame, to tell,
The butcher's work that oft befel.

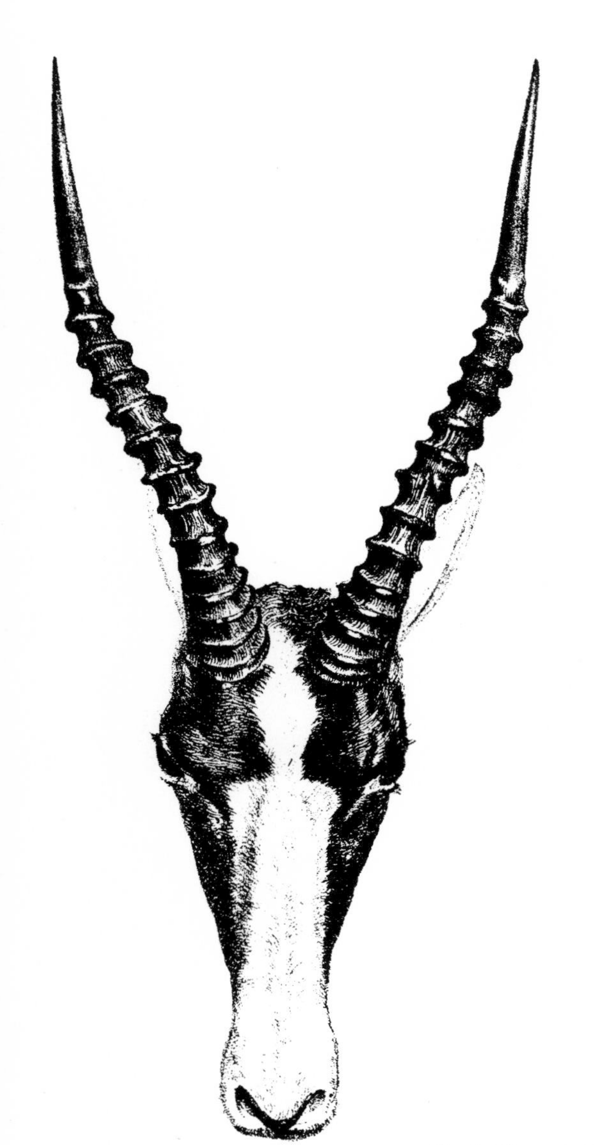

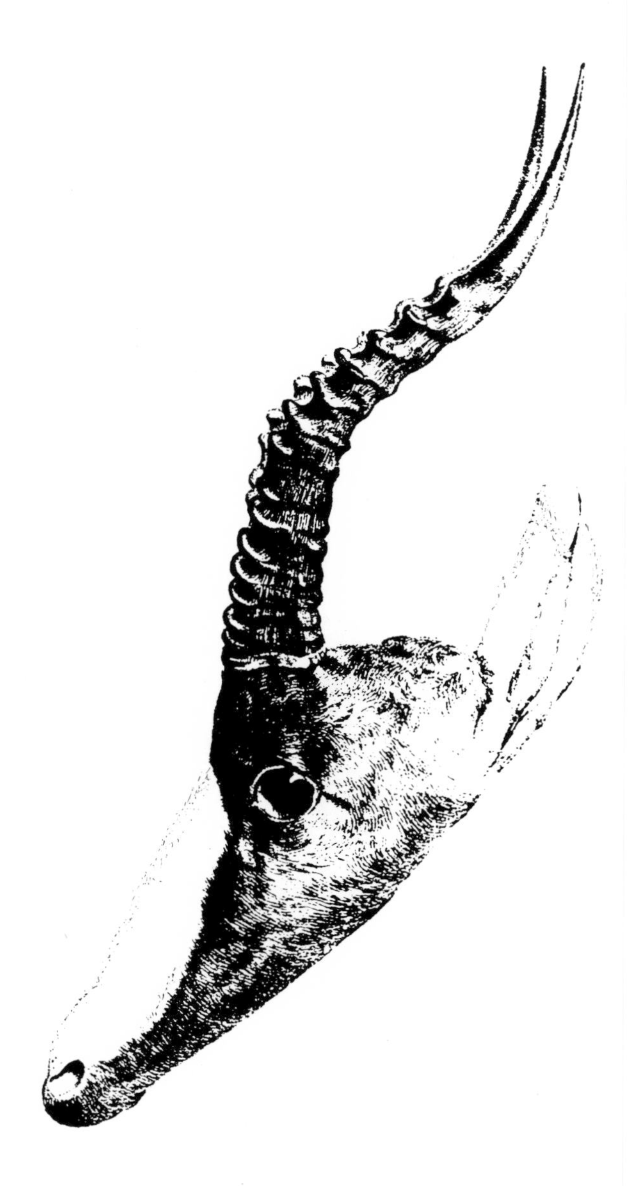

Head of bontebok, as preserved by Captain Harris

Plate XVII: *Gazella pygarga* — bontebok or pied antelope — *bontebok* of the Dutch colonists

Generic Character — Adult male about three feet ten inches high at the shoulder, and nearly six and a half feet in extreme length. Head long, narrow and shapeless, with a remarkably broad muzzle. Horns fifteen inches long; black, lyrate, divergent, erect; placed on the summit of the cranium, very robust at their base, with ten or twelve incomplete annuli, broken in the middle, and striated between. A patch of deep chocolate coloured hair at the base of the horns is divided by a narrow white streak, which suddenly widens between the eyes to the whole breadth of the face, down which it passes to the nose. Ears long and reddish. Sides of the head and the neck and flanks, deep purple brown, with a reflected cast of crimson. Back marked with a saddle of blueish lilac, highly glazed. Legs from the knee and hock downwards, pure white. Belly and inside of thighs white, and a large white triangular patch on the croup. Tail reaching to the hocks; above white with a terminal tuft of posteriorly-directed black hairs. A small detached lachrymary perforation. Linear nostrils. Very indistinct muzzle.

Female precisely similar, but on a slighter scale, with more slender horns. Mammae two; gregarious. Common in the interior and still found in Zoétendal's Valley near Cape L' Agulhas.

18

Roan Antelope

So far was heard the might knell
The stag sprung up on Cheviót's Fell,
Spread his broad nostrils to the wind,
Listed before, aside, behind,
Then couched him down beside the hind,
And quaked amid the mountain fern
To hear that sound so dull and stern.

Hark! along the blue mountain's furrowed side the boom of a rifle rolls in prolonged echoes, until at last it has died away in the north like distant thunder! Undisturbed heretofore even by the voice of man, these silent solitudes have reverberated from the first time to the report of his death-dealing engine. Again the stillness of ages has sunk upon the wilderness. The lengthening shadows cast by a few straggling trees have proclaimed the near approach of evening. The sun already painting those distant hill-tops with his parting rays, is flinging his last golden beams over the plain beneath, where the face of nature:

Untouched as yet by any meaner hand
Than His who made it,

is clad in a broad carpet of green, and enamelled with clusters of brilliant wild flowers, that scent the pure air with their varied perfume.

Reader, thou art standing on the elevated downs near the source of the willowed Limpopo, and art looking up one of those lone glades that stretch along the base of the mountains of Cashan.

It is a barren scene and wild,
Where naked cliffs are rudely piled;
But ever and anon between
Lay velvet tufts of loveliest green.

Yon solitary hunter, bronzed and bearded, is advancing with noiseless tread up the shadowed side of that verdant knoll — his body crouched almost to the ground, and his trusty rifle trailing at his side. He has sunk on his hands and knees, and having removed his cap, is stealing upon all fours, and raising his eyes inch by inch above the crest of the ridge. To him nothing is yet visible on the other side, save the scimitar-shaped horns belonging to that sturdy rose-coloured buck, which, shaking, its great piebald head, is idly lying in the grass, flapping its long asinine ears, and whisking its tail to drive away the flies. Ever and anon, however, the glorious fellow looks up as though he suspected treachery, and sniffing about him with expanded nostrils, seems searching for some taint in the atmosphere. Presently a herd of females — his hitherto concealed companions — emerging from a broad ravine, draw closer together, and having gazed around in evident mistrust, begin to put themselves in motion. Springing suddenly upon his feet, and tossing his pied head in defiance, their desert-loving lord canters heavily to the brow of the opposite eminence, and facing quickly about, erects himself to his full and towering proportions; whilst his seraglio, also crowning the hill, and wheeling their ranks behind the flag of their proud leader, stand with curious gaze — their shadowy forms looming like sculptured monuments on the blue skyline.

The opportunity is favourable to the hunter. Quickly laying his trusty weapon in the crotch of a wooden rest which has hitherto served him as a staff, and setting cautiously the hair-trigger, he directs the heavy barrels at the fair and inviting mark offered by the point of the bull gemsbok's shoulder. Crash flies the bullet through the hard bone, and away it spins from out of the opposite flank. Many an aged rock around is still ringing to the clangour, as the affrighted herd go racing over the naked slope, forcing with them their crippled chief, who, frequently catching his punctured side — now fast changing from *couleur de rose* to crimson — first pauses a moment in the hollow, then hangs his sick head and follows mournfully in their rear. Reloading, and advancing rapidly upon the blood drops with which the ground is freely bespattered, with fluttering heart the hunter now pauses on the summit of the knoll, and having examined the extent of the damage through a telescope, returns it depondingly to his pocket and sighs for another hour of daylight. He is far from his wild bivouac — already is the sun below the western horizon — evening is closing fast — the stars are beginning to peep out; and whilst the dusky mountains are each moment looming larger and larger in the gloom, the first melancholy shriek of a solitary jackal has been quickly responded from the dim valley by the protracted and dreary yell of hundreds. Although the drooping quarry is frequently turning to gaze at its shattered shoulder and bleeding flank, there is no steed at hand; and the herd keeping a constant eye upon their enemy, to obtain another shot before dark is utterly hopeless. Noting well the spot, and repeatedly looking back in recognition of the various landmarks, the disappointed sportsman at last returns to the foot of the knoll, resumes a bundle of trophies which he has there deposited, shoulders his heavy ordnance, and with a still heavier heart retraces his solitary steps towards his wagons, to the position of which he is guided by a wreath of ascending smoke.

It is morning; and the dawn has scarcely peeped, ere the hunter, elated with new hope, is again wending his way towards the scene of his last evening's vexation. Accompanied by a party of savages and Hottentots, he is leading his horse over the same grassy slopes which form a succession of deep valleys, bounded at last by mountains rising in shadowy perspective. Stretched beneath him also in sombre obscurity, lies the wood-clothed river — a grey mist floating over the tops of the trees; and the party, as they advance, brushing off the dew drops which sparkle like gems on the herbage and flowers, are leaving a broad track behind them. The sun, as he again arises, lighting up in succession each mountain summit which had lately slept in shade, is tinging with prismatic hues the condensed vapours which now hang in white wreaths upon their steep and broken sides; but long after the grey gleam of the river has become apparent, the deep valley through which it winds is reposing under a calm blue shadow. At a little distance from the spot where the gemsbok was last seen, the party hold a brief consultation over a pool of clotted blood and hair, marking the bed on which the wounded beast has passed a restless night; but the blood is already congealed, and he from whose side it trickled has been gone an hour. Now is the lark rising merrily from the dewy earth, and with a prolonged whistle again lowering herself upon motionless pinions; the azure sky is spotless and beautiful; and every object around wears the most cheerful aspect of liberty and light. Passing over a spur of the mountains which for some time has closed the prospect in advance, the party has entered upon a spacious upland terrace, whereon all animated nature would seem to reign unmolested. The signal being quickly given that man the destroyer is approaching, beasts of various complexions, assembling with snorts and bounds, are flying in every direction; but the eye of the hunter is riveted upon the trail of the one quarry that he covets, and he heeded them not. Slowly, but with certainty, the party advances over the drying sward scoring out each footprint in succession; and their doubts, occasioned by the crossing and confusion of hoofs, being relieved at intervals by drops of fresh blood, they are guided at length to a solitary bush in the plain, from beneath the shelter of which the wounded and watchful quarry is disturbed — a disappointed jackal sneaking off in the meantime from beneath an adjacent stone. Crack goes the rifle once more against the roan ribs of the fugitive! In the twinkling of an eye the hunter is in his saddle — another instant and he has closed with the flying victim — and the next, he is gloating over his prostrate prize.

Not less from its singular beauty, than from its extreme rarity, there were few game animals in the whole African catalogue that I more eagerly sought for than the roan antelope — my hankerings after its gay spoils being moreover greatly increased by the difficulties that I at first experienced in obtaining possession of them. According to indications given by my kind friend Dr Smith, in whose cabinet I had seen this noble and imposing antelope, it was on an elevated tract of rocky table-land forming a terrace on the mountains between Danielskuil and Kramersfontein, that I first disturbed a herd whilst wandering alone in search of them along the rigging of the hills. The thin covering of earth supported only a scant and faded vegetation, together with a few scrubby trees and bushes which grew from the fissures of the rock. Surmounted by a pair of jagged ibex-looking horns, the magpie head of a sturdy old bull protruded above a thin copse of brushwood through which I was riding, was not to be mistaken. I sprang from my horse, and as the whole bloom-coloured herd rose to make its rush, sent a bullet spinning betwixt the ribs of their gallant leader. But although tantalised by an occasional glimpse of his silvery form, I followed the bloody trail over hill and through dale for eleven long hours, desisting only when the sun had gone down and daylight would serve me no longer, I was finally doomed to disappointment through lack of assistance. Not another specimen was seen until we had reach the Limpopo, the elevated tracts lying between which river and the Likwa, divide the principal waters of southern Africa, and form the peculiar habitat of the *equina*. Even there, it invariably resides in limited families, which seldom contain more than one old bull — a dozen or more of the younger males usually herding by themselves. Equal in stature to the largest Arab horse, the whole structure — remarkably powerful and muscular — is especially adapted for traversing the rugged regions that it frequents. Not less vigilant than active, its wary troops were ever most difficult to approach — the bare mountains crowned with wooded terraces that form the stronghold upon which, when disturbed, they invariably sought an asylum, proving alike impracticable to the sportsman, whether equipped in pedestrian or in equestrian order; and some time had elapsed before I accidentally ascertained the species to be so utterly destitute of foot — that if detected in the open glades, or among the slightly wooded downs, to which morning and evening they resort, the bulls especially may be ridden down upon an inferior horse in a quarter of a mile! For this singular fact I was the less prepared, from having previously ascertained the speed and bottom of the true gemsbok — an animal which is scarcely less heavily built — to be unrivalled among the larger antelopes.

On the day of our first arrival in the valley of the Limpopo, being myself busily engaged in the wagons with the head of a hartebeest, there arose among the Hottentots, a sudden cry of *'Daar lope een bastard gemsbok'* [Angl. There goes a Roan antelope] and looking forth, I could perceive the cunning fellow's broad roan back gleaming in the evening sunbeams, as he ran through the grazing herd of oxen, and clambered up the steep acclivity. But although I lost not a single moment, he contrived to beat me to a deep chasm, wherein having failed to redeem the trail, the honour of slaying him was reserved for Frederick Dangler, the laziest, but most successful pot-shooter amongst our followers. As this worthy was watching our little flock early the next morning from behind the ambush of an old grey stone lying at the foot of the mountains, the identical individual — easily recognized by a broken horn — reversing the order of things, paid the shepherd a visit, and underwent the penalty of its singular rashness. During the greater part of our journey, it was unfortunately requisite to furnish the Hottentots with ammunition for their self-protection whilst herding the cattle, and their incessant firing, which no remonstrance could control, soon disturbing the whole of the game in our neighbourhood, we generally found it useless to sojourn more than one day at the same place.

Although said to be very expert in carrying the tracks of wild animals, our people proved themselves far less skillful than Asiatics; but I was happily quite independent of their assistance, having from the commencement of the campaign made it a rule to preserve a cast of the footprint of every species destroyed. In the secrets of woodcraft, Piet was far better versed than any of his more pretending *confreres,* and besides, being possessed of infinitely more nerve, was the only one of the whole clique upon whom I could depend for the least assistance in the field. The rest were always ready enough to go out, that they might obtain a supply of ammunition without the trouble of stealing it, and gain, besides, a plausible pretext for evading their ordinary duties; but their natural indolence extending itself even to their recreations, they never hesitated to abandon me at their convenience, either to solace themselves with a pipe, or to pursue the common description of game which could be circumvented with little exertion.

In all subjects connected with tracking, the savages proved far more quick and discerning, but unhappily they never accompanied us beyond the carcase of the first large quadruped slain, whereupon having gorged themselves to repletion, they fell fast asleep over the fire. Notwithstanding that the footmarks of many wild beasts so closely resemble each other that few European eyes would detect the difference, the African savage when fasting especially, can distinguish them with unerring certainty — poring over all ambiguous impressions until the doubt has been solved to his own satisfaction, and from his intimate acquaintance with every, the most minute, circumstance connected with the habits of each race, rarely failing to estimate with the greatest exactness the length of time that has elapsed since the animal's transit.

Fifteen noble bucks composed the largest herd of equinas seen during our expedition, and after following them several hours on foot, without once obtaining a shot, I ascended a lofty hill near the source of the Umpeban, and thence marked then into a shallow ravine carpeted with turf and threading a sequestered valley. Rightly concluding that they proposed to tarry there during the heat of the day, I went back for my horse, and sending a party of savages to urge them gently down the glen, intercepted the whole in a narrow outlet, and as they galloped heavily past in single file, brought down a buck to each barrel. In that beautiful part of the country lying due south of the Cashan Mountains —

XVIII. AIGOCERUS EQUINA.- THE ROAN ANTELOPE.

Where trees stand singly on the grass
With no low coppice interlaced,

the species was extremely abundant, and scarcely a day elapsed without several herds being seen. Late one evening, whilst the camp was forming, Richardson who without taking a gun had strolled to a little distance from the wagons, beckoning me to bring my rifle pointed out a huge blush-coloured bull rolling the pebbles before him as he trotted down a stony descent. A severe flesh wound was inflicted *sur le champ,* but night overtaking me, I was compelled to abandon the trail, resuming it betimes the next morning, only to have the mortification of finding the bones clean picked by vultures and jackals. That same afternoon I set out in the opposite direction, accompanied, at their own request, by some of the Hottentots, who proposed laying in a supply of wild flesh for private consumption; when outside the ruins of an old kraal, which crowned a little stony tumulus in the middle of a rugged plain, behold! another splendid fellow, the very duplicate of yesterday's. To approach him unobserved, was not of course practicable; but being well mounted, and resolving to essay his wind, I contrived, whilst pretending to hold another course, to encroach upon him sufficiently to turn his flank!

Suspicious of my design, the wily quarry presently descended on the opposite side, the same from which I had first observed him. But this was exactly the thing I wanted; and no sooner had his horns disappeared below the brow, than dashing up the eminence, I had the satisfaction of perceiving him — now within three hundred yards — leisurely cantering down to the more level ground. Upon hearing the clatter of hoofs behind him, understanding at once the advantage that I had gained, without turning his head, he laid out over the loose stones, which, whilst he thundered down the broken declivity, flew around his heels as from a catapult. But it was in vain! I had so greatly the foot of the unhappy fugitive, that at every stride the distance between us had visibly diminished, and we had scarcely reached the bottom of the hill, ere his tail was betwixt his legs, his furred tongue lolling out of his open mouth, and his breathing hard and husky. Finding escape impossible, he wheeled with a vicious scream to the charge, his hogged mane seeming even stiffer than usual, and the saliva hanging in white bell-ropes from his muzzle. Now his red eyes glare as, lowering his great horns, and flourishing his tasselled tail, he prepares him for the fight.

But a brace of balls in the chest, while they cooled this impetuosity, so completely disabled the poor beast, that with his strawberry flanks, heaving like a pair of bellows, he stood at bay, unable either to advance or to retreat — nor could I prevail upon myself to administer the *coup de grace* until after I had well admired him. Marked with the figure of a head-stall sable and standing fully as large as the steed that I bestrode, I think I never beheld an object more eccentric or picturesque! Taking my seat upon a bed of wild peppermint which margined a little rill, I there completed a colour portrait whilst the original was yet living; and no Hottentot still arriving to my assistance, proceeded straightway to decapitate the victim, and making fast the horns on either side of the saddle-bow, I regained the wagons on foot, as the round red sun was setting.

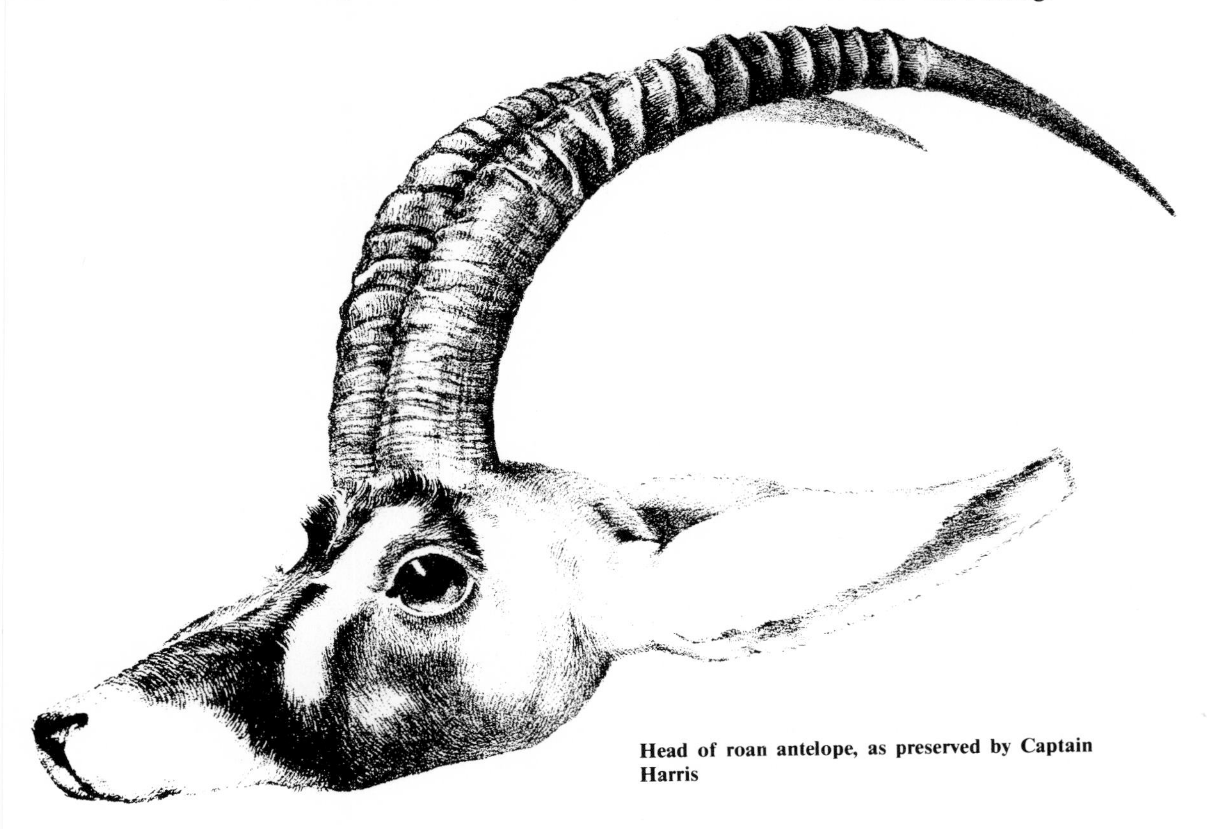

Head of roan antelope, as preserved by Captain Harris

Plate XVIII: *Aigocerus equina* — roan antelope or bastard gemsbok — *bastard gemsbok* of the Cape colonists — *etak* of the Matabili

Generic Character — Adult male about five feet high at the shoulder, and nine in extreme length. General contour exceedingly stout and muscular. Horns very robust, above two feet in length, strongly bent back scimitar-wise, rounded and nearly parallel; with from twenty five to thirty prominent rings, more remote as they recede from the orbits, and extending to within about four inches of the points. Face and head hoary black, with a large white streak before and behind each eye, formed of a pencil of long hairs. A white spot between the horns, and a white mouth and muzzle. Ears of asinine dimensions, full fourteen inches in length, pointed, and the tips bent back very eccentrically; of a grey dun colour tipped with black. Tail descending to the hocks; slender, black and tufted. Hide black. Hair coarse, loose, scant and undulating; mixed red and white, forming a roan or strawberry. Beneath the throat and neck longer and whiter, and towards the flanks often flea-bitten and clouded with sienna, which colour extends more or less over the lower portions of the legs. Neck furnished with a stiff upright mane, terminating at the withers. Head large and heavy; nose abrupt; mouth extremely wide. A half muzzle. No suborbital sinus.

Female similar, but hornless. Mammae two. Gregarious in small herds or families, but rare. Inhabits chiefly the elevated ridges about the source of the Vaal and Limpopo Rivers.

19

White Rhinoceros

The desert gave him visions wild,
Such as might suit the spectre's child.
When with black cliffs the torrents toil,
He watched the wheeling eddies boil,
Till from their foam his dazzled eyes,
Beheld the river demon rise;
The mountain mist took form and limb
Of noontide hag or goblin grim.

Although, during the middle ages, when the western world was immersed in darkness, the remembrance of the rhinoceros, in common with that of many other quadrupeds familiar to the ancients, had altogether passed away, the records of antiquity established beyond a doubt that one at least of the double-horned African species of this animal must have been well known to the Romans, and even swelled the pomp of truimphal processions and the tide of blood that flowed in the murderous arena Not many years have elapsed since the ultra-grotesque figure now introduced — long dead to science — was enrolled by the indefatigable Burchell in the catalogue of extant *mammalia.* Forming in many respects a ridiculous caricature upon the half reasoning elephant and ranking second only to him in point of size among the gigantic pachydermes,

Forma praestanti, et cornibus ingens,

it will hardly fail to be considered a seemly companion for the monsters of Pliny, and might even take its place among the most preposterous creations of heraldry, or the crudest offspring of a distempered fancy. But unnatural and absurd though its proportions may appear to those unacquainted with the ungainly original, we stake our credit as an artist upon the scrupulous fidelity of the portrait. Many a warm and unstiffened corse was measured with tape and two foot rule, as *Snip* would overhaul the dimensions of a schoolboy that needed a suit of holiday garments; whilst the likeness received its finishing touches from a living subject that, as if with the express design of standing for a full length, politely presented its courtly figure within fifty paces of the wagon.

No quadruped with which naturalists are acquainted would appear to correspond more nearly than the white rhinoceros with the stubborn *reem* or unicorn of Holy Writ. Attaining the height of nearly seven feet at the shoulder, and carrying a cranium not very dissimilar to a nine gallon cask; he flourishes upon the extremity of his square and truncated snout, a formidable weapon some three and a half feet long, fashioned after the approved model of a cobbler's awl, and capable, when wielded by a warrior so unquestionable in pith and renown, of being made to force its way through any opposition — its companion, although certainly a horn, being nevertheless such a mere excrescence, that at the distance even of a few yards it is barely perceptible. Superadding to the almost impenetrable folds of shagreen wherein nature hath encased his ribs, a goodly outer coat acquired by constant wallowings in swamps and stagnant pools, the gentleman is but rarely to be viewed under his true complexion, which if not quite so blond as the prefix to his cognomen might indicate, is yet much fairer than that of his swarthy congener, and often approaches to cream colour. Notwithstanding that he is one of the bulkiest land animals in the creation, the cavity which should contain the brain is not nearly so capacious as in the human species; but in removing the horn with an axe, the brain or something very like it, was found seated in a receptacle beneath — a phenomenon in idiosyncrasy which may possibly account as well for the want of intelligence and piggish obstinacy, as for the extraordinary acuteness of the olfactory endowments.

By what means I know not, the subject of the present chapter has contrived to secure unto himself the reputation of being less bellicose than him whose portrait has already appeared. Never extremely wild, it was yet prudently careful of its person, and entertaining a very becoming respect for firearms, was usually ready enough to retire before the bombarding and platoon firing to which it was exposed; but being subject to the same paroxysms of reckless and unprovoked fury, we often found it fully as troublesome as its sable relative. Dull, slow and wallowing in its ordinary state; daring, swift and persevering when excited, it was wont to rush forth with loud snorts and whistles as though it had been the sole object of hostilities, whereas in reality no soul had done more than ken of its presence. Neither, like the black rhinoceros, did it hesitate upon occasion to defend a pass with determined obstinacy, or to pursue our horses with ludicrous and fruitless industry, evincing a spitfire disposition almost peculiar to the class of which it is no unworthy member. Old Chaucer in his *Nonne's Preeste's Tale* has truly enough observed:

For naturely a beest desireth flee
Fro' his contrarie if he may it see;

and it is certain that even the most ferocious and blood-thirsty of the prone and mute creation when disturbed in the native haunts, unless sore pressed by hunger, are much more frequently disposed to make way for man than to oppose him. The savage natives of Africa who regard neither species with much dread, wage a successful war against them with the assegai; and pitfalls containing pointed stakes, constructed purposely for the accommodation of the unwieldy beasts were of very frequent occurrence. Strewed with huge skulls and bones, they differed from those excavated for the smaller quadrupeds in being dug singly, instead of in groups — of increased dimensions — at the extremity of a narrow path cleared through the bushes and stoutly fenced on either side with thorns; a sharp turn leading so directly upon the hidden sepulchre, that the clumsy monster, if driven furiously down the avenue, can have little chance of evading it:

But, by the wily African betray'd
Heedless of fate within its gaping jaws,
Expires indignant.

In no region of the globe does there exist so vast a variety of herbivorous quadrupeds, and of such gigantic dimensions as in the southern regions of Africa — the poor and scanty vegetation afforded by her wide plains, rendering it a matter of some astonishment how such a goodly host can find subsistence. Notwithstanding that the growth of herbage is there surprisingly rapid, and that animals of the greatest bulk undoubtedly wander over a large extent of country in quest of their daily food, one cannot help surmising that a foraging party comprising a dozen monsters such as this eating grass like an ox, would in less than a week devour every blade of which the continent south of the Tropic can boast! Gregarious in small groups, so many as six or seven might frequently be seen herding together; and in the vicinage of the Cashan Mountains especially, where on our first arrival the country absolutely presented the appearance of a zoological garden, or a travelling menagerie turned loose, an abstract of the host that daily exhibited themselves would almost exceed belief. Eighty were on one occasion seen during the day's march, and on my way from our encampment in the valley of the Limpopo to a hill only half a mile distant, no fewer than twenty two were counted, of which we were compelled in self defence to slaughter four.

It was shortly after we had crossed the Mariqua, that the first white rhinoceros seen by our party was numbered with the dead. Numerous savages had followed in our train with the design of obtaining a supply of dried flesh, and being already tolerably well laden with prime joints from the quagga and sassaybe, amongst a large mixed herd of which animals great havoc had just been committed, it is scarcely possible to comprehend the unqualified delight with which they discovered this new mountain of carrion standing stupidly under the shade of a spreading acacia — its dull heavy eye riveted upon the earth as in a brown study. Pointing eagerly towards it, their suppressed exclamations of *'Chickore! Chickore!'* were accompanied by an epicurean smacking of the lips, and by many telegraphic anticipations of the further work which awaited their already swollen abdomens. Before commencing the attack, I had approached unperceived to within thirty yards of the enemy, and being securely ensconced behind an extremely thick bush overhanging the brink of a precipitous ravine that formed a gulf betwixt us, leisurely planted a two ounce bullet behind his armpit. But this assault had no other immediate effect than to bring my antagonist square to the front, in which position he stood eyeing my place of concealment, and practising various absurd contortions of the features, until, having reloaded, I bestowed two ounces more. Snorting, groaning and bleeding, away he then scoured — his nose close to the ground, and the whole meat-laden mob at his heels; but it was not until he had made four clumsy charges, and received as many more shots behind the shoulder, besides four times that number of assegais in his crupper and haunches, that he thought proper to deliver up the ghost. In the chase, as in war, is it that the energies of the savage are displayed to the greatest advantage — the metamorphosis from his usual apathy and listless indifference being never more complete or more sudden. At one moment might their shadowy forms be perceived stealing amid the bushes with noiseless tread; and at the next, uttering a yell of savage exultation, and bounding forward with the elasticity of a tiger, they had sheathed their slender weapons in the tough hide of the tortured quarry, and were dexterously retreating before its reckless charge.

At the close of a long and sultry march, we halted late one afternoon upon the steep bank of the Simalakate, near to where the grey arms of a clump of moss-grown mimosas, entwining, admitted through their loose tresses the last long-dancing gleams of departing sunshine. Beneath, the pensive willows laving their silvery garlands in the blue stream, over a bed of tall flowering reeds that sighed and rustled at their feet, forming the most inviting of canopies; and our two surviving dogs half blind with thirst, running heedlessly down to the water's edge, one of them was unexpectedly arrested by the gaping jaws of a basking alligator. The other instantly returned with his tail betwixt his legs in dreadful consternation. Then a splash was heard, and bubbles of blood rising a moment afterwards to the rippling surface of the stream, too truly told what had been the fate of his less fortunate companion. The sun was now setting, and whilst we were bewailing in no very amiable humour the loss of our valued four footed ally, an unwieldy white rhinoceros:

Sheathed in his iron panoply,

came sauntering towards the wagons, evidently bent upon no friendly designs. It being considered necessary that prompt counter measures should be adopted, and neither bush nor hollow favouring my advance, I crawled towards the conspirator under cover of the long grass, and arriving within forty yards, discharged a brace of balls into his brawny shoulder. He started, sought wildly around for some object on which to wreak its vengeance, and — his mouth streaming with blood — actually charged to within a few arms length of my concealment:

His eyeball glared, deep breath with hollow tone
Heaved his long flanks and burst with frequent groan;

but by crouching low, I was so fortunate as to elude his observation and his fury, and after he had trotted some hundred yards beyond my ambuscade, I had the satisfaction of seeing him drop suddenly down dead of his wounds.

During the time that we halted on the Tolaan, our little camp was one dark night thrown into considerable confusion by the visit of an inquisitive fellow that actually stood some time betwixt the wagons ere their sleeping inmates were aroused by the bellowing and tumult among the cattle. On this occasion, the obscurity befriending him, he had it all his own way, and got clear of the scrape without the smallest personal injury; but the following evening, as the sun was sinking below the horizon, rendered bolder by escape, he again imprudently appeared on the opposite bank of the river, within pistol shot of our position, and five bullets being immediately lodged under his short ribs, he retreated in the greatest disorder, and was picked up at no great distance the following morning.

Being one day on the hot trail of a wounded bull elephant, whose warm life-blood was welling from fifty gaping wounds, we were tracking through a heavy forest, in momentary expectation of closing with the game, when an ill-tempered brute dashed with an astounding grunt out of a bush into the middle of our party, divers of whom were overthrown in their efforts to afford him a wide berth, although fortunately not one was injured. On another occasion, the line of march along the base of the Cashan Mountains, leading through a field of tall reed grass, that waved high above the horns of the oxen, a vicious rascal, starting from his slumbers therein, at once made furiously at the leading team, crushing the dry flags before him, and terrifying the cattle by his loud snorting and hostile demonstrations. A well-directed volley cooling his courage, he retired to a suitable bush, and was there finally gathered unto his fathers. Not half an hour afterwards, whilst sitting at breakfast on the river bank, an old lady, accompanied by her calf, three quarters grown, was perceived to be in undisputed possession of a deserted stone kraal, some two hundred yards distant from our bivouac; and these, as well as another that opposed our progress towards that night's halting ground, were duly added to the list of casualties. With this last, our friend Claas — at best but a bungling sportsman — had a very unpleasant *rencountre,* and withal, a most hair-breadth escape — his little bandy legs encased in a pair of unyielding leathern trousers, only barely contriving to carry his diminutive person out of reach of divers most vigorous thrusts and lunges.

A huge monster having one morning come down to drink at

XIX. RHINOCEROS SIMUS. - THE SQUARE NOSED OR WHITE RHINOCEROS.

a pool hard by our encampment; I advanced behind the screen of a tree at the edge of the bank, and whilst his snout was still immersed in the water, wounded him severely from a distance not exceeding fifty yards. Feeling confident that the ball had pierced the tucks of his elbow, and that his minutes were consequently numbered, I followed the retreating shamrock-shaped *spoor,* in the full expectation of finding him dead. Certain dark objects attracting observation in a thick bush, Piet and myself peeped in, and beheld no fewer than three snoring giants huddled together like so many pigs in a stye, we could not resist the temptation (who could indeed?) of treating them to a salvo, which produced one of the most alarming rushes that I have ever witnessed. Galloping heavily to a little distance, the insulted trio wheeled about with an air of consummate defiance, and perceiving their despicable assailants standing near the bush, charged impetuously back in concert, compelling us to seek refuge in the den whence they had themselves so recently been expelled, and which in their turn they now closely invested. Piet nimbly ascended a tree which arose through the middle of it, and I, making myself as small as I could, stowed away into the snuggest corner of the lair, the besiegers standing round about, grunting and charging with a vigour that I shall not easily forget, in their repeated efforts to carry our stronghold at the point of the bayonet. Our artillery being, however, at length reloaded, we proceeded to batter the most forward and audacious, when his uncouth capers had the desired effect of drawing off his associates — one of them nevertheless twice returning, and with lance in rest, tilting furiously at the bush, as if with the determination, at all risks, of forcing his way in. Heartily rejoiced indeed was I at length to find that they were satisfied, and that we were suffered to effect our escape in a sound skin — a piece of good fortune which at one period of the siege, I confess I saw little grounds to anticipate.

A meddling officious marplot, perpetually in the way, and always prepared for mischief, wheresoever the rhinoceros was not required, there was he sure to be. But the pair that succeeded in giving me the greatest annoyance during all my wars with the wild beasts, were posted in a defile in the Cashan Mountains, by which it was requisite that I should descend, in order to arrive within rifle range of a herd of roan antelopes, then a great novelty, that were grazing in a dell beneath. With this anecdote I must close my account of the obnoxious tribe. Owing to the impossibility of discharging a gun without disturbing the gemsbok, it is with no little difficulty that I escaped from the tormenting attentions of the ugly couple, who ran grunting round our party, returning continually, and trotting daintily up in the most bullying manner to within forty or fifty paces, although pelted and abused whenever they displayed their saucy snouts. For so unprovoked an outrage on the part of himself and partner, we had, however, the satisfaction of calling the belligerent gentleman to a serious account the following morning, when, having afforded us a gratuitous interview in a deep wooded glen, to which he had been driven by a conflagration that had laid bare the greater portion of the mountainside, he thought proper to repeat his attentions, and to his surprise and consternation was received with a general broadside! The simultaneous whizzing of seven tin bullets was followed instantly by cries and squeaks of distress. His side perforated like a cullender, the crest-fallen bravo straightway sounded his retreat, making the loose pebbles spin behind him as his heavy feet clattered less and less audibly over the stony ground. But, alas! the conviction of inferiority had arrived too late. An ominous black vulture swept in all her grand expanse of pinion from the cloudless sky, and wheeling thrice in a diminishing circlet, perched like the genius of desolation upon the bare branch of an aged tree, that extended its scorched and blackened arms over the outlet of the glen. That sign was not to be mistaken. Arriving in the pass, we found the huge bird gloating over the mortal remains of our humbled foe, who, as we had anticipated, was seated stone dead upon his knees and hams, according to the singular fashion in which, when mortally wounded, the rhinoceros almost invariably makes his exit. Arrested by the clammy hand of death, the unwieldy monster doubles his stumpy legs under his voluminous carcase, something in the position assumed by an elephant that is about to receive the howdah and subsiding suddenly in full career:

His glazed eye droops, each flaccid flank extends
And prone to earth, his ponderous neck descends.

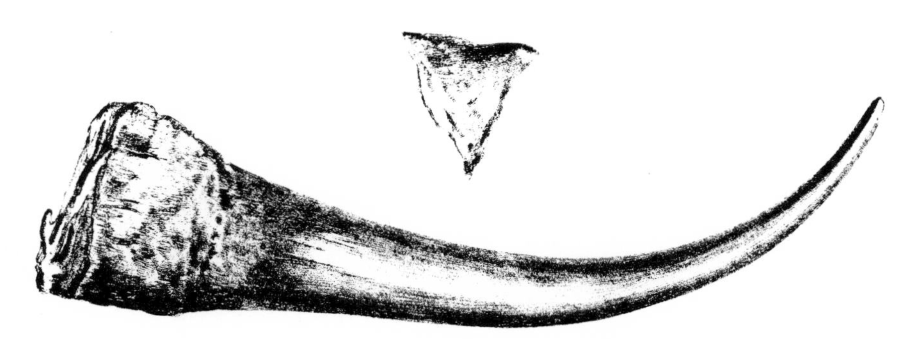

The horns of white rhinoceros, as preserved by Captain Harris

Plate XIX: *Rhinoceros simus* — square-nosed or white rhinoceros — *witte rhinoster* of the Cape colonists — *chickore* and *mohoohoo* of the Bechuana and Matabili

Generic Character — Six feet six or eight inches high at the shoulder and above fourteen in extreme length. General contour somewhat elephantine. Body massive and ponderous. Head shapeless and more than three feet long. Muzzle truncated upwards of eighteen inches in breadth; furnished with two horns placed one behind the other upon the vaulted dome of the nose; the anterior robust and ringed at the base, tapering to a sharp point, and curved to the form of a cock's spur, generally exceeding three feet in length; the upper portion highly polished, and the base often so beset with bristles as to resemble a worn out brush. Posterior horn a mere excrescence from four to six inches long, sometimes ringed at the base. Ears pointed and approximated, their edges fringed with bristles. A square massive hump rising from the neck. Eye very diminutive and lateral. Legs short and terminating in three toes. Tail about two feet long, compressed and bristled at the extremity. Hide rough, naked and knotty; extremely thick, arranged in folds and plaits about the neck, and deeply cut with wrinkles over the face. Colour varying, usually dirty brownish white.

Female similar, but smaller. Mammae two. Very numerous in the interior after passing Kurrichane and usually gregarious in small parties. Inhabits variously, being found in equal abundance on open grassy plains, and in hilly or thinly wooded regions.

20

Koodoo

There the speck boom spreads its bowers,
Of light green leaves and lilac flowers.
And the bright aloe rears its crest,
Like stately queen of gala drest;
And gorgeous erethrina shakes
Her coral tufts above the brakes;
Brilliant as the glancing plumes
Of sugar birds among its blooms.

Did empire belong to beauty, the princely koodoo would experience little difficulty in establishing his right and title to the sovereignty of all the antelopes. Upon not one of this numerous and highly favoured race has Dame Nature showered her costly gifts with more lavish prodigality — in none other has she combined such dignity of aspect, such nobleness of demeanour, and such splendour of attire. Alike majestic in carriage and brilliant in hue, all that marks distinction, or can command our admiration in the wild denizen of the waste, would seem to be in him combined and concentrated. Other antelopes may be stately, elegant or curious, but the solitude seeking koodoo is absolutely regal!

The appointments of an officer of the Surrey Yeomanry, and eke of our Bombay Cavalry, are invariably recalled to my recollection by the colour of this singular looking quadruped. A lively French grey; approaching to sky blue, which forms the basis of his splendid uniform, is faced and turned up with white, and regularly laced with transverse silver ribbons, issuing from a narrow dorsal stripe — a dark horsehair mane of considerable length decorating the brawny neck and shoulder, whilst both chest and dewlap are ticked out in an elaborate tricoloured tippet, answering to the embroidered pouch-belt. Thus accoutred, the chaffron and bearded chin, adorned in their turn with silver scales and crescent, the gallant fellow maintains a passing goodly exterior; but his glory is in his cork-screw horns. Ponderous yet symmetrical, they not infrequently attain the surprising length of four feet; and are boldly convoluted into a wide sweeping spiral, forming, with a prominent wreath that entwines them two complete turns, of which the worm if so unerring, that a spear might be thrust down its axis into the temples. These elegant but cumbrous appendages seeming almost as ill-adapted to the cranium of a quarry that loves the thicket, as the chaco to the brow of the equestrian soldier, are thrown dexterously back along the embroidered flanks, as the lordly wearer dashes, with protruded muzzle, through the mazes of the tangled coppice, or chamois-like, ascends with nimble foot the steep and stony mountainside. Death invariably dims the lustre of his brilliant garb and converting the silvered hues into a dirty rufous brown, has doubtless given rise to the fictitious colouring, invariably adopted in portraits which have been obtained from dried or stuffed originals.

Although still existing in the jungle districts immediately bordering upon the eastern frontier, and even in many portions also of the Cape Colony, where his retired habits have in some measure shielded him from deadly persecution, the koodoo was not once seen by our party until after we had gained the prolific environs of the Cashan Mountains. There:

in the depths of solitary woods
By human foot untrod.

the noble animal occurs in such every day abundance, that many a gory trophy was realised; but his great sagacity, wildness and self possession demanding the most skillful generalship to outmanoeuver him, the pursuit necessarily differs altogether from the usual stamp of African hunting, and involves no inconsiderable acquaintance with the subtleties of woodcraft. We have here no dashing among countless herds, no helter-skelter riding by the side of a closely packed phalanx; yet have we a quarry well worth the hardest day's fag on foot to triumph over. Shunning both the open plain and the society of the multitude, the crafty fellow never ventures from his almost inaccessible fastness, unless during the morning and evening; and even then must he be sought *au pied* amid the dark upland dells which usually form his solitary abode. With all his wits about him, the lordly bull, active and powerful, may now and then be detected browsing at grey dawn upon some rugged hill summit, or ranging some grassy slope, either alone, or escorted by a small troop of skittish dames, all seeming alike his sentinels; but taking the note of alarm from the slightest noise, he stamps his brave foot upon the ground, tosses his spiral frontlet to the blue sky, and once fairly in motion, never stops to look behind until he has gained the threshold of his sanctuary. There, in some deep chasm which the sunbeam rarely penetrates, among tangled ravines and hollows densely clothed with trees and brushwood, he lazily reclines during the solar heat, beside some fern-clad stone, and leisurely turns the cud until the cool breezes of eventide once more invite him from his snug retreat.

Scarcely has the day broke, ere his enemy the hunter, dismounting from a ragged pony, and placing the rudely patched bridle in the hand of a naked attendant, brings a heavy rifle to the trail and followed at the distance of a few paces by a single savage, prepares to ascent the outskirts of that huge pile of mountains which heave up their shadowy crests around. Those towering peaks in the distance, are faint almost as the sky they seem to emulate; but after toiling some time up the first acclivity, he has gained one of the lower steppes of table land, along which he shapes his silent course, alternately casting a keen glance on every side and scrutinising the moist ground, as a book whose pages can reveal the history he seeks to learn. A lone valley stretching away beneath him, discloses at its nearest extremity the white canvas tops of the wagons that he has just quitted, standing out in bold relief against a dark background of trees, before which ascends towards the clear firmament, a column of grey smoke. The verdant meadows upon which he thus looks down like the eagle from her eyrie, are gracefully sprinkled over with yellow clumps of thorny mimosas and evergreen olives, while through their mazes, like some monstrous mythological dragon, winds the tortuous river, now deriving its colour from, the minute leaves of the dishevelled willows that overhang the flood and now emerging at a right angle into silvery or rainbow brightness.

Liberated by the hills, the vale occasionally spreads away to a considerable breadth, and is then embellished with scattered herds of various wild animals, pasturing in undisturbed quietude, and adding life and beauty to the lonely landscape; again contracting, it is straightened betwixt yon wooded heights which frown on either side — ridge surmounting ridge, and summit rising above summit, until at last the gradually converging range, steep and sterile has shut in upon the prospect altogether, and formed one unbroken amphitheatre of mountains.

Ere the sun has yet cleared the horizon, the hunter, peeping cautiously round the angle of an abutting rock, has descried upon the opposite bank of a deep ravine, a small troop of the beautiful objects for which he seeks, decked out in all their blue and silver and browsing unsuspicious of danger on the bare hillside. Their outward slot being apparent in the pass whereon he is now standing, he feels so well assured that they will return by the same track, that taking up his own position behind a natural buttress, whence, unseen, he can both command the path and watch the success of his scheme, he at once despatches his attendant by a circuitous route to disturb the quarry from the opposite quarter. And now, with a slow and measured step, the wary herd, are in motion. At times either partially or wholly concealed — at other emerging slowly to view — they wind leisurely down between the huge masses of impending rock, putting into motion sundry loose pebbles which course each other, bounding from steep to steep, until their last fall is heard on the hard stony bottom. Whilst three or four females in the van are scrutinising the glen beneath, the rear are first gazing intently behind them, and then, as if suspicious of danger, trotting forward to close up their files. One after the other, the whole twelve have at length disappeared under the spreading trees which choke the hollow, but the faint sound of their footfall, accompanied by an occasional rustling of the foliage, fails not to apprize the hunter, whose heart is momentarily beating still higher and higher with nervous anticipation, that his plot is well laid, and that his victims, now picking their way obliquely up the rocky ridge, will shortly reappear within certain range of his ambush.

Twenty minutes have thus been passed in almost breathless suspense; an interval of total silence has twice dashed the sportsman's hopes to the ground, and twice have they been resuscitated by the renewing of these thrilling sounds — at each renewal more audible than before — when at last the points of the leader's corkscrew horns, slowly protruded above the skyline, are succeeded by the stately wearer himself, carrying his armorial devices *argent* upon a field azure; and one by one his shy followers next begin to crown the summit of the hill! Forward they march deliberately and cautiously in single file, examining each object in succession, and stopping at intervals to listen to the echo of the pebbles which are still tumbling over the crags. Halting finally upon a projecting ridge, swelling and proudly jutting out his frilled bosom, the amorous leader now turns to muster his forces. It is a moment of deep and absorbing interest, and the blood of the Nimrod is at a gallop. The bull's broadside is towards the rifle, but his forehand is completely masked by one of the nearest females. Now the lady has obligingly moved on a step, and his dark outline is presented clear against the heavens. Resting the rifle over a projecting stone, the fine drawn sight is brought to bear upon the victim's shoulder. The sharp ping of the explosion returned back from the opposite hills makes the wild valley rattle again, and the ragged bullet having sped truly to its mark, has told upon the hard blade bone with a smack that is never to be mistaken. Hurrah! there must be death in that shot — the stricken quarry having sprung a dozen feet or more into the air, is prostrate for ever upon his grey haunches. Alas! no, he is up again, and as if nothing had happened, is scouring along the height with the rest of the herd; yet see, the blood is pouring from his wound in a stream as thick as one's finger — his race cannot fail to be a short one. Already has he begun to falter, as his timid companions are fast leaving him in the lurch. Sending a wistful look after them, he makes one strong effort to advance, but it may not be. His head is swimming, and by the extension of his forelegs alone can he preserve his equilibrium. Now his knees are tottering together — his crowned head begins alternately to fall and rise; blood gushes from his distended nostrils, his whole frame quivers, and involuntarily staggering back a step or two, down at last he sinks upon the earth, stiff and lifeless.

Abandoning his concealment, the successful stalker is presently by the side of the humbled quarry, where being rejoined by his sable accomplice, they hastily drag over the cerulean carcase a strong abattis of thorns, and silently follow the sinuosities of the glen in exactly the same order as before. Along the bottom of the deep chasm winds the broad bed of the river, here and there encumbered by huge blocks of granite that have been launched from the cliff, and worn smooth as a marble pavement by the sweep of the torrent floods. The lofty candelabra-shaped *euphorbia* towers by the side of the gorgeous *corallodendron,* the latter clothed in one dazzling profusion of the brightest scarlet blossoms. As a contrast to their gaudy brilliancy, the scented *queurboom* next:

> *Spreads in beauty's softest blooms*
> *Her purple glories through the glooms;*

while the snake-like creepers of the monkey's ladder, coiling around the rough trunks of the elegantly shaped mimosas, stretch their lank arms from tree to tree among the golden blossoms like the cordage of a ship, and fling into the air a wild web of tangled vegetation.

A sequestered dell, broken up into rocky nooks half choked with dwarf timber and copsewood, now discloses to the hunter at intervals, grey moss-grown stones partially concealed by the trailing ivy geranium, and backed by cliffs of the deepest red. Here a solitary bull koodoo is lazily reclining in his woodland palace, among bluebells growing at the head of a babbling spring, which, gently issuing from a cavity of the rock, trickles onward beneath an overhanging bower of the *speckboom.* His quick ears having already detected the rustling of a leaf, he has sprung nimbly upon his feet, and as the first bullet spins harmlessly over his striped back and flattens against the rocks behind, he flings up his wild head in derision. Now unharboured:

> *Like deer, that, rousing from their lair,*
> *Just shake the dewdrops from their hair,*
> *And toss their armed crests aloft,*

he shakes his azure flanks, which are but indistinctly visible through the gloom of the thicket, and throwing back his twisted horns, dashes headlong through the flowery copse as it bends under his burly weight. Mounting the naked side of that steep bank by a narrow ledge, impracticable to any animal less surefooted than himself, he exhibits his proud form for one instant only on its verge, and that instant has proved sufficient to place the seal upon his doom. Unhappy fellow! but for this mistake thou hadst escaped scatheless — the second ball has pierced thy laced side! Stung by the wound he rushes forward with meteor-like velocity, but has not fled five hundred yards ere he is fain to pause for breath beneath a friendly knoll; when the nature of the hurt having been ascertained through a telescope by the anxious sportsman, he hastily reloads, advancing at the same time with as much celerity and caution as the nature of the ground will admit. Arriving breathless and streaming with perspiration, within long rifle range of the spot, he betakes himself to his hands and knees but in spite of this quadramanous progress, the bleeding quarry is again off at score before a shot can be obtained. Thrice

W.C. Harris del.

XX. STREPSICEROS CAPENSIS.- THE KOODOO.

is he thus lost, but thrice redeemed by a view of his all-glorious horns, which are protruding above the coppice, his slot having each time been long and patiently traced through strips of fire-disfigured forest, wherein he has vainly sought to conceal his noble figure. The open face both of hill and valley having here been charred by a still inextinguished conflagration, either kindled by design or accident, his track from one scrub to another is easily carried over the bare soil. Four bullets have struck him, and although not in the right place, he has gradually waxed fainter from loss of blood. Again the pursuer is at fault, and on the very verge of an impenetrable forest, is casting earnestly about for the trail, when a violent floundering draws his attention to the ravine below — the exhausted animal in striving to descend has slidden from the bank, and ere he can recover his balance, receiving the *coup de grace,* lies weltering in a flood of purple gore.

Laden with the choicest *spolia,* the weary, but well-requited hunter, has already been some hours at his wild camp, when night, casting her murky shroud over the face of the landscape, gradually reveals a scene which for solemnity or magnificence could hardly be exceeded. The flames which during the stillness of day had made but slow and partial progress over the theatre of his morning ramble, have now by a strong wind been driven into one general conflagration, which is leaping wildly over the country in tumultuous billows, and leaving all behind it scorched and desolate. Ten million burning flakes whirling off like a host of meteors through the pitchy sky, the whole mountainside has presently become enveloped in a sheet of living fire — dense volumes of smoke which roll upwards and hover over its summit imparting the appearance of a burning volcano.

Seizes the trunks, amid the branches soars,
Sweeps through the blazing leaves, and fiercely roars;
From bough to bough the insulting victor spreads,
Pursues his conquest o'er the topmost heads,
Sheets the whole wood in flame, and upwards driven,
Rolls in thick clouds that dim the copse of heaven.

As the night wears on, the crash of falling branches, and occasionally the thundering echo of some prostrated trunk, is heard amid the awful stillness that pervades the air, and which, with the dark clouds that continue to gather in the horizon, portend a coming crisis in the atmosphere. Hark! the thunder of heaven's artillery begins now to roll among the mountains. The flames, as if aware that a mightier Hand were about to arrest their progress, no longer whirl in the uncertain current of their own eddies, but blaze brightly and steadily upwards — the more distant lines appearing like streams of burning lava. The piles of smoke, too, which float above the valley begin to ascend and streaks of vivid lightning come dancing through the black clouds that hang about the hills. Suddenly the storm has burst above the scene. The wind which has hitherto been increasing, is instantly hushed. A death-like stillness succeeds to the crackling of the flames, and every spark of the conflagration being extinguished in an instant by the deluge that descends, the Egyptian-like darkness of the night is unbroken even by a solitary star!

Head of koodoo, as preserved by Captain Harris

Plate XX: *Strepsiceros capensis* — koodoo of the Cape colonists — *eechlongole* of the Matabili

Generic Character — Adult male upward of five feet high at the shoulder, and above nine in extreme length. Horns bulky and compressed; having a prominent anterior ridge or wreath, which forms, with them, two complete spiral circles diverging from each other in their ascent; the points turned outwards and forwards. Length from three to four feet, colour pale brown, the tips black, with a white point; base marked for some distance upwards with slight wrinkles, but not annulated; their bony nucleus of the consistency of ivory. Chaffron straight. Muzzle very broad and square. Ears oblique and slouching as in the ox; of a light brown colour outside, whitish within; very large and broad, but pointed at the tips. Frame very muscular and powerful. Neck thick. Withers elevated into a false hump. Dewlap anteriorly square. Legs robust. Pasterns rigid and hoofs compact. Face brown, becoming almost black on the forehead; a white line passing from the base of the horns over the orbits, unites on the chaffron in the form of a crescent; three white spots on either cheek below the eye. Chin white bearded. A long loose fringe of hair variegated black, white and dun, depending from the dewlap, and a coarse standing brown mane extending loosely from the crown of the head almost to the tail. General colour of the coat, a silvery buff grey, or sky blue, marked with a white line along the spine beneath the mane, and intersected by five or six transverse white ribbons running downwards from it to the belly, and four more over the croup. Buttocks, posterior portion of the abdomen, and part of the inside of thighs white. Legs rufous dun below the knees and hocks. A black and white spot on the posterior side of each forearm. Tail rufous, two feet long, edged with white, tapering to a point and tipped with sable. No suborbital sinus. An entire moist muzzle.

Female slighter, hornless and with fewer and fainter white ribbons. Has udder with four mammae. Gregarious in small families and still found within the colony, though rare. Inhabits thickets and wooded uplands, as well as the banks of rivers, but is never to be found in the open plain.

21

Blesbok

Mong the wild deere, such an archere
As men say that ye be,
We may not fail of good vitail
Where is so great plentie.
And water clere to the rivere
Shall be full sweete to me,
With which right hele I shall right wele
Endure as ye shall see.

The Bontebok Flats, which furnish the subject of this singular landscape, would appear indebted for their nomenclature to the double fact of possessing within their wide limits neither a solitary antelope of the species referred to, nor one single square root of level land! Lying in the country of the Tambookies, immediately beyond the eastern frontier of Albany, and peopled by wild animals alone, this elevated region forms an inexhaustible hunting ground, frequented alike by parties from the colony, and by numerous of the kaffir tribes, whose assegais and throwing clubs have left within their own inhabited districts not even a sparrow alive. In place of the usual flat features of South African scenery, a boundless billowy succession of surge-like sward undulations are clothed throughout with a layer of bright green close browsed by the wild herds that it supports. Everywhere is the sward illuminated by a dwarf flora, endless in variety as in profusion — the daisy, the buttercup and the dandelion, claiming, amid hundreds of strange faces, now first introduced by Dame Nature, the privilege of old acquaintance:

Like some enchantress with her magic wand
In treasures new she decks the smiling land,

and the whole acres positively derive their complexion from the beds of blossoming bulbs by which they are completely covered. Alternate patches of green, yellow, purple or crimson — here bathed in bright golden sunshine, there partially shrouded by silvery mist — impart to the country the appearance of being spread with a carpet of gigantic pattern; but over the whole tract not a solitary tree, no not even a bush of so much as a foot in height, is anywhere to be seen, and owing to the total absence of fuel thus entailed, the Bontebok Flats are equally without one permanent inhabitant.

On our way back to the Colony from the interior, I resolved to pay a flying visit to this boasted preserve, the inaccessible nature of which compelled us to adopt the usual plan of hiring from a farmer residing at the foot of the mountains, teams better inured than our own to so difficult an ascent. Both wagons having been freighted with firewood, we commenced the arduous undertaking early one Saturday morning, but the united strength of fifteen pairs of oxen to each vehicle, failing to carry them more than midway to the summit, we passed the first night on the slope, lying over like ships under a gale of wind. Renewing the attempt with the return of dawn, the omnibus was overthrown through the clumsiness of the boers, who, being pleased to attribute our disaster to the fact of its being the Seventh day, made the matter worse by superstitiously declining to assist in putting together the scattered fragments. It was then determined to advance with pack horses under the guidance of a friend who had joined our expedition from Fort Armstrong and was well acquainted with the flats. Four of the sorriest steeds were accordingly laden with fuel, and after we had watched the sliding descent of the tottering vehicles, which, with all four wheels locked, vibrated from side to side in the most frightful manner, our little party of six set forward, carrying each his rifle across his shoulder, and his bedding beneath his saddle. Crossing the crystal stream of the Klipplaats River, brawling over its shallow and pebbly bottom, we arrived late in the evening at our wild bivouac, roasted a *carbonaadtje,* and spreading every man his sheepskin mantle before the smouldering embers of the niggard fire:

Our curtain see — the starry sky,
Our couch — the green earth's dewy breast.

Wreaths of white mist ascending from the vale, had for some time been twirling and flickering over the mountainside; and not long after we had laid us down, a heavy dew began to fall, which rapidly increased to sleet, and assumed at last the consistency of positive rain. My companion's ample tarpaulin, serving to cover us both, was presently steeped in standing pools; and so bleak and unsheltered was our position, that but for a certain pocket ally, which was snugly stowed away beneath his head, and referred to every tenth minute at least, I believe we might actually have perished. My own bones ached again with the cramp, nor do I ever recollect to have passed a more comfortless night. The moon, that rode on the hurrying rack like a frail bark on the stormy ocean — now lifted on the crest of some curling wave — now lost in the whelming hollow, at intervals peeped down upon us with a pale and ghastly light, but was a moment afterwards utterly blotted out. Most anxiously indeed did we bend our eyes to that point in the heavens where the first glimmering of dawn was to appear, and slowly enough it came, but to exhibit the whole face of nature smothered like a great wash-house under the reeking vapour. A heavy grey canopy sailing above the ground, and fed by cloud driving along after cloud, still for some time rendered it impossible to see a yard before one's nose; and only now and then did it favour us with even a glimpse of the wet soil on which we sat. At last, however, a broad white light expanding in the heavens, discovered the path of the glorious sun as he waded upwards, struggling with his lazy foe — when, impatient of further detention, we mounted our dripping steeds and cantered over the summit of the nearest swell towards the centre of the flats.

In every direction was this singular prospect bounded by undulating downs and hillocks, upon whose verdant slopes as Sol assumed greater sway, and flowerets and diamond dewdrops glistened beneath the dispersing vapour, like a constellation of gems:

The velvet grass seemed carpet meet,
For the light fairies' lively feet.
Yon tufted knoll with daisies strown,
Might make proud Oberon a throne.

Nevertheless, of living objects such as we sought, few indeed were to be seen. The wind unfortunately setting stoutly from the eastward, the great body of game had deserted our neighbourhood to travel towards the *Wind vogel berg,* a square mountain which reared its blue crest under the expanding luminary; and a large party of Dutchmen, whose random firing had been audible since objects became less dim and dubious, having scoured the flats for several preceding days, we returned empty handed and with jaded steeds to our gypsy camp, after many an hour of fruitless toil. Here was a contingency that had never once entered into the philosophy of our program; and, provided as we were with rations for no more than a single day, certain unpleasant apprehension of famine began to present themselves, in addition to the coming discomforts of another foggy night. Nor were these fears a little augmented the following morning, whilst the sunbeams were chasing away the misty wreaths, by the far from opportune arrival of a hungry party of insolent Amakosa. Riding familiarly up to our station, grasping in one hand a light sheaf of assegais, and in the other a rude sheepskin bridle, eleven elastic savages flung themselves carelessly upon the ground; and having cast off their ample togas, and hobbled their bare-backed garrons, proceeded straightway to make themselves at home, assisting uninvited in the discussion of the scanty residue of our edibles, and ungratefully expressing no very qualified discontent at our improvident commissariat. Leaving with our Hottentot attendants a sufficient supply of the munitions of war, to deter these free and easy visitors from any attempt upon the baggage, we again took the field, and being most fortunately rewarded with a brace of bounding blesboks, we were conveying their comely carcases to the spit when we had the gratification of perceiving the group of equestrian blackguards in the act of prosecuting their marauding journey over the flats, as empty bellied as they came.

The third night proved far more clement than its predecessors, but the reduced stock of fuel not affording the luxury of a fire, our dreams were repeatedly disturbed by the prowling visits of a laughing hyena, one of the showman's real indomitable fellows, whose keen olfactory organs had naturally enough been tickled by the savour of our venison. A prolonged whoop, which sounded close to my ear, causing me for the fourth time to start from my slumbers, and the miscreant's apparition being presented in strong nocturnal relief upon the brow of the nearest rise, I took advantage of the moon's light to indulge myself with a quiet pot shot from under the blanket. A dismal howl replied to the report of my rifle and the limping gait of the obtruder, as he fled wailing over the hilltop, with the whole Hottentot hue-and-cry at his heels, afforded the most gratifying evidence that my spherical messenger had so cleverly performed its errand, that we need entertain little apprehension of any further disturbance from that quarter. The next day was to be our last upon the flats, and the wind having by great good fortune shifted during the night, every height in succession was at peep of day crowned with gnoos and blesboks. Numbers of the latter were now slaughtered, and as one troop after the other was set in motion by our equestrian pursuit, each individual arrayed in his coat of many colours — the scene, although falling very short indeed of what I had previously witnessed in regions more remote, might not inaptly be compared to the rout of a goodly army — its retreating masses, lost at one moment in the hollow, at the next reappearing on the opposite brow, again to sink from the sight — whilst at certain intervals the tips only of the bayonets were perceptible, as scores upon scores scoured in extended file along the opposite side of some intervening ridge:

Now low they vanish from the aching eye,
Now mount in air and seem to touch the sky;
No pause, no rest, where'er they sweep the ground
Dust in thick whirlwinds darkens all around.

My first introduction to this splendid antelope took place on the great plains of the Vaal River, where the pursuit of thronging legions led to a solitary pilgrimage, which was conjectured both by my comrade and by our followers, to have terminated in my arrival at that 'bourne whence no traveller returns'. Christmas eve and the greater portion of the day that preceded it, had been passed in a vain search for water, during which we had chanced upon the first faint traces of a wagon road that had been seen for many months. Having resolved to follow this guide, as leading, in all probability to the element of which we were in quest, we arrived as the next morning dawned, upon the summit of a gentle acclivity that had for some miles disturbed the monotony of the previously level landscape. Boundless was the prospect that then presented itself to the gaze, and deeply are its lines engraven upon the tablet of my recollection! Like a huge pineapple in the centre of a flower-decked prairie which spread away to the far horizon, stood one isolated tumulus of conical figure, whilst in the distance, three rectangular table-topped mountains of singularly uniform appearance, reminded the spectator of terraced barrack-rooms — shooting-boxes, perhaps, erected by the giants of olden time. A shower of land tortoises excepted, not a living animal had been seen during the whole of the preceding day; now the welcome appearance of grazing troops of quaggas, ostriches and springboks, with squads of hairbrained gnoos careering madly over the plain amid vast herds of blesboks:

On whose empurpled breast
Glowed the deep hue by bloodstained hand impressed,

proved the welcome harbingers of water; and to our delight a sedge-grown fountain was presently descried, at which, after twenty eight hours of total abstinence, the dying teams were enabled to slake their terrible thirst.

The absence of fuel shortly obliged us to continue our march over a succession of salt-pans, upon which numerous great herds of blesboks were busily licking the crystallised efflorescence. Alarmed at the approach of our cavalcade, vast troops of them were continually sweeping past against the wind, carrying their broad white noses close to the ground like a pack of harriers in full cry. Having never obtained any specimens of this species, and our stock of provisions moreover grievously requiring to be recruited, I mounted *Breslar,* my favourite Rosinante, and little heeding whither I sped, dashed into the very thick of them. The pineapple hill bearing east about five miles, must, I concluded, prove a never failing landmark to direct my return to the road, which, however faint it had become, could still readily be distinguished by a practised eye. Dealing death around, I thus continued to scour the ensanguined plain, and to use my pleasure with the herd before me, which had in the meantime increased from hundreds to thousands — reinforcements still pouring in from all directions, when, crying 'hold, enough' I stayed my hand from slaughter:

Be that it drew to the aware of none
Ane hondrith fat buckes ded ther lay,

of which having divested some of the primest of their brilliant party-coloured robes, I packed the *spolia* on my horse, and well satisfied with my performance, set out to rejoin the wagons. But ah! vainly was it that I sought for them. Cantering to and fro between the string of frosted salt-pans, and the little hill, which, floating in the sea of mirage that environed it, seemed as though poised in the sky, again and again I strained my eyes for the road. The monotony of the landscape baffled all attempts at recognition, and my search proved utterly fruitless. Every feature of the cone was precisely the same — the table mountains were completely obscured by the midday haze — and in the constant

XXI. GAZELLA ALBIFRONS.—THE BLESBOK OR WHITE FACED ANTELOPE.

recurrence of similar forms, I lost the points of the compass, and at last became totally bewildered.

To retrace my steps over plains so trampled by innumerable herds, was clearly impossible. At one moment, as if in mockery, a solitary quagga, magnified ten thousand times by the treacherous mirage, loomed like the white tilt of a wagon; but my joy at the supposed discovery was followed by the bitterest disappointment. Again a group of pygmy Bushwomen walking unnoticed among a herd of blesboks, and seen through the same deceptive medium, personated our followers with the cattle. Alas! these, too, fled at my approach and jabbered like baboons when I had overtaken them. Several hours had thus passed in idle search, and hour after hour the prospect was still the same. Spent by fatigue and anxiety, my parched tongue rattling like a board against the palate of my mouth, I wandered on over flowery wastes still lengthening as I advanced. Dry tanks surrounded by a garden of pinks and marigolds, but yielding forth the croaking of no friendly frog, served only to increase my sufferings. Flights of pin-tailed grouse, rising noiselessly from each sun-cracked hollow, winged their whirring flight in gyrations through the quivering atmosphere — but neither fount, nor pool, nor running stream, greeted my straining gaze. At length, the refraction dissipating with the declining day, the three table-topped mountains became once more visible in the hitherto blank horizon. With the consoling reflection that I was now, at all events, advancing in the same direction as the caravan, I hastened forward, with renewed hope, and before dusk found myself not a little revived by a deep draught of the clearest water, from a serpentine river flowing to the westward, of which the banks were trimmed with reeds and dwarf willows, whilst portions of the sandy bed were imprinted with the heavy footsteps of a troop of lions.

The mind ever becomes more readily reconciled to hardship and suffering than the body. Everything around me was now vague and conjectural, and wore an aspect calculated to inspire deep despondency; yet my heart was light and my spirit buoyant, and no sooner had I become convinced that I was actually astray in the midst of a howling wilderness, inhabited, if at all, by barbarous and hostile tribes, then I felt fully prepared to meet the emergency. The setting sun having given me the bearing of the table mountains considerably to the westward of south, it was evident that I had, without being aware of it crossed the road, and ridden too far to the eastward. In the hope of, yet retrieving my error, therefore, I hurried down the river bank as fast as possible, but night closing in, I was fain to prepare for a bivouac among its bushes. The stars were completely concealed behind a clouded sky, and repeated flashes of lightning were accompanied by the rumbling of distant thunder. All my preparations completed, I was listening with breathless attention for the cracking of a whip, or the signal-guns which I knew would be fired from the wagons, when to my inexpressible delight a joyous beacon fire shone suddenly forth near the river. Upon consideration I felt somewhat puzzled to account for its appearance in a spot which I had so recently passed, but concluding that the wagons must subsequently have arrived there, I 'laid the flattering unction to my soul' and groped my way towards the light. My disappointment and disgust may better be imagined than described, when, flitting like troubled spirits around the unfriendly blaze, I discovered a gang of Lilliputian Bushmen, with their imp-like squaws, carousing over a carcase!

Whilst slinking silently back to my sylvan den, fully impressed with the necessity of remaining perfectly quiet, I scarcely ventured to indulge hope, that the good nag upon whom my sole dependence now rested, would be so fortunate as to escape the prying observation of these lynx-eyed vagabonds. His uneasy snorting, accompanied by constant efforts to get loose, soon apprized me to the presence likewise of lions at no great distance to windward; but the fear of attracting my two-legged enemies to the spot, whilst it prevented my kindling a fire for his protection, denied me also the means of dressing a *korhaan* wherewith I had taken care to provide myself. Dying with hunger, and having my *girdle of famine* tightened to the last hole, I felt strongly tempted to follow the example of the savages and devour my Christmas repast uncooked. About midnight, however, having prepared a deep oven in the ground, I ventured to light a small fire, and the fowl being duly baked and disposed of, I presently betook myself to sleep.

The following morning set in with tremendous rain. Cold, drenched and cramped, I rose from my aquatic bed, and at once perceived that all hope of recovering the trail of the wagons was at an end. The soil consisting chiefly of a red loamy earth, from which the faintly marked tracks were easily obliterated, I resolved to follow the course of the river several miles farther to the westward and should I there unfortunately fail in discovering the camp, to cross the country in a direct line to the conical hill, still a conspicuous landmark — thus certainly intersecting the road, if indeed any vestige of it remained, of which I began to be doubtful. To this program I rigorously adhered, walking the greater part of the day to save my harassed steed, upon whose back I contemplated the probability of having to seek my way alone to the Colony — a probability which was mightily increased about sunset, when I found myself preparing to perfect my acquaintance with the pineapple, by roosting on its summit:

In a deep cave, dug by no mortal hand.

During the second day's weary pilgrimage, scorched by the ardent and reflected rays of a summer sun, I arrived at an extensive pond covered with water lilies, and bordered by a broad belt of flags and rushes. Hastily approaching the margin, I became suddenly engulfed in a pitfall, six feet in depth, filled with mire

Plate XXI: *Gazella Albifrons* — blesbok or white-faced antelope — *blesbok* of the Cape colonists — *nunni* of the Bechuana

Generic Character — Adult male three feet eight inches high at the shoulder, and six feet three or four in extreme length. Head long and narrow, terminating in a broad and bluff muzzle. Horns from twelve to fifteen inches long, greenish white, very robust at the base; divergent, erect on the summit of the cranium, with ten or twelve knobs or semi-annuli on the anterior edge. The colours throughout are so singularly disposed and contrasted, that the animal conveys the appearance of having been artificially painted with divers hues laid on in separate masses. The sides of the head, cheeks and whole of the neck, are of an intense purple chocolate, or venous blood-colour. The horns are divided at their base by a diamond-shaped stripe of the purest white, which, suddenly expanding between the orbits to the whole breadth of the face, passes down the nose to the muzzle, thus forming a perfect blaze. The back and shoulders hoary blueish white, thickly overlaid as if with a glazed or japanned saddle. A cast of rose colour upon the spine. A broad brown band passes from the forearm along the flanks; thence extending over the crupper and haunches, as well as down the whole outside of the hind, and very nearly the whole outside of the forelegs. The inner side of all the legs snowy white, with a cross-band of brown. Belly and buttocks white. A white patch covering each elbow, and one above the tail, either surrounded by a border of bright rufous or sienna. A shade of the latter colour along the chest before each arm. Ears long, taper and white. Tail seventeen inches in length, reaching almost to the hocks, with much posteriorly directed wavy brown and grey hair. Long linear nostrils; very indistinct muzzle. Small circular lachrymary perforations.

Female precisely similar, but slighter, less vividly coloured and possessing more slender horns. Mammae two. Very gregarious. Inhabits the elevated tracts to the eastward of the colony known as the Bontebok Flats; and is found on the great plains south of the Vaal River in astounding herds.

and water, from which I extricated myself with inconceivable difficulty. On recovering my lost shoes out of the stiff blue clay at the bottom, I perceived that the whole tank was closely invested by a chain of these traps, which had been carefully covered over by my pygmy foes, the Bushmen. Having shot a springbok, I here roasted enough of the flesh to satisfy the cravings of hunger, and slinging a fine fat leg on either side of the saddle, took up my night's lodging in the manner already described, without having been able to discover the smallest traces of the road.

The night was serene and starlit. From the apex of my stronghold did I look forth upon the tranquil expanse beneath, and listen for hours to catch some friendly melody that might direct my bewildered footsteps. Where, alas! was the busy hum of men? The shrill neighing of the wild ass, the bleat of the timid springbok, or the hoarse bellow of the gnoo, with the deep-drawn distant sighing of some prowling lion, occasionally borne along upon the breeze, alone disturbed the grave-like stillness of the wilderness! Most seriously did I now debate with myself upon the propriety of making for the Colony, instead of prolonging my fruitless search. It is true that everything betwixt me and it was wrapped in the deepest uncertainty, and that to arrive there I should have to pass over a great extent of unknown and inhospitable soil; but on the other hand, I seemed to have already done all that human ingenuity could devise, and without the smallest success. I estimated my distance from New Hantam to be little more than two hundred miles; and having fortunately a good supply of ammunition, there existed a fair prospect of my being able to reach that district in six or seven days, unless driven by scarcity of game to sacrifice my steed. Taking into consideration, however, the long and dismal state of uncertainty that the measure must entail upon my companion, I finally resolved to make one more huntsman-like cast before giving up the search in despair.

Another day dawned, and once again having saddled my trusty beast, I struck into the pathless waste, intending to make a wide sweep to the northward and westward, where it was possible that rain might not have fallen. Far and wide, however, the enamelled carpet glistened beneath the reviving effects of the recent showers; the sun as he rose imparting to the face of nature a more than magic beauty, which seemed but to laugh at my wretched and forlorn condition. Well do I recall to memory that resplendent sunrise — that canopy of purple clouds retiring before the splendour of the golden orb, and resolving itself into ten million fantastic figures; whilst by the roseate and crimson ground disclosed beyond it, the surrounding heavens were tinted with every variety and depth of shade. About noon, lifting up my eyes from the ground, on which they had long and despondingly sought for some indication of the party having passed, what was my joy and delight to recognise the identical reed encircled fountain at which we had broken our fast on Christmas morning! Vaulting with nerves new braced into the saddle, I eagerly dashed towards the spot, unable almost to convince myself of the reality of the discovery; but having instantly hit upon the trail of our caravan, the fancied dream was dispelled, and following up the traces steadily, I shortly fell in with a party of Lihoya who were busily feasting upon a blesbok that had been taken in a pitfall. The potent agency of a broken cigar enabling me to negotiate with these terrified savages, female as well as male, a treaty of perpetual alliance, I pointed to the wheel-ruts, and giving by signs to understand what I required, struck merrily across the broad plain under their willing guidance, and in less than another hour was within sight of the white tilt of our wagons! Jaded and way-worn, it was with the most profound gratitude to an all protecting Providence that I thus found myself restored to the cafila, after three days of anxious and weary wandering over an unexplored and inhospitable wilderness.

Great was the anxiety, and many were the dismal forebodings to which my mysterious absence had given birth. A general gloom had pervaded the camp. There being no fuel with which to kindle a beacon-fire, whips had been cracked and muskets discharged at intervals, both during the day and night; and my horse's *spoor* having been completely effaced by the rain, three separate parties had gone out in search of me, in different directions, but in vain. Those only who have experienced the warm cordiality which grows up between partners in so wild and adventurous an expedition as that in which my companion and myself had embarked, are capable of fully understanding the nature of the welcome I received — the sensations created by my safe and unhoped-for return, even extending themselves to the disaffected to our followers. On comparing notes with my fellow-traveller, I was concerned to find that in many respects he had scarcely fared better than myself; the knuckle-bone of a tainted ham having supplied the place of a smoking sirloin and richly dotted plum pudding — and, with a cupful of dirty water, constituted, alas, his Christmas dinner.

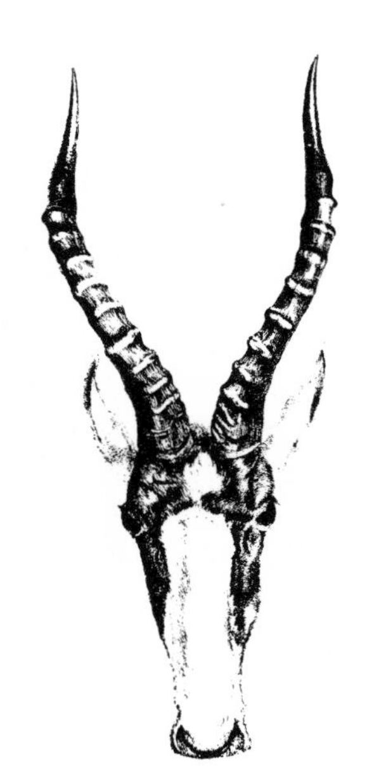

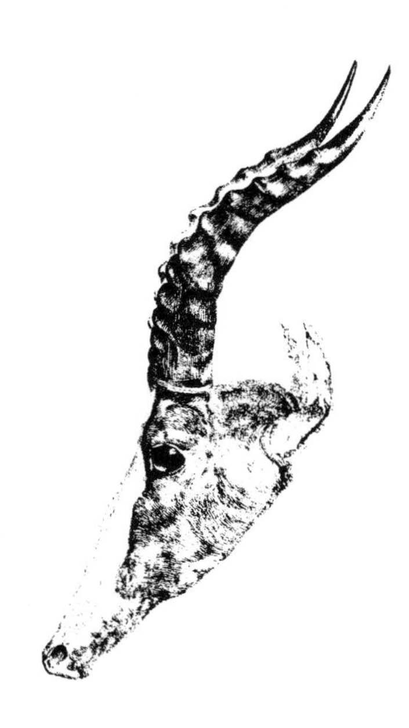

Head of the blesbok, as preserved by Captain Harris

22

African Elephant

On comes the elephant, to slake
His thirst, at noon, in yon pellucid, springs.
Lo! from his trunk upturned, aloft he flings
The grateful shower; and now,
Plucking the broad-leaved bough
Of yonder plume, with waving motion slow
Fanning the languid air,
He waves it to and fro.

Throughout the more remote and unfrequented portions of the African continent which have yet been explored, the elephant, mightiest and most peaceful of all the denizens of the woods, has been found in far greater abundance than in any other quarter of the globe. Many of the southern regions are still teeming with vast herds; and the unwholesome, though fertile borders of the almost inaccessible rivers on the eastern and western coast, have ever formed its chosen habitat. Since the first establishment of the Portuguese settlements about the close of the fifteen century, man has waged against this lordly animal, a ruthless and exterminating war. Hunted and persecuted for the sake of its costly ivory, it has been driven farther and farther from the haunts of civilization, and is only now to be found in multitudes, amid regions to which its arch enemy seldom penetrates. Delighting especially in wide and secluded savannahs, where sluggish streams are skirted by a congenial vegetation, this giant among quadrupeds resides towards the southern tropic in stately troops, comprising many hundred individuals. There, fearless of danger, he wanders with calm solemnity amid the groves of aged mimosas, with which the broad meadows are sprinkled — leisurely prizing out of the ground, by means of his huge tusks, used upon the principle of the crowbar those which please him best, and inverting them with his single hand, the more readily to browse upon the soft and juicy roots that constitute his favourite food. Social in habits, and secure in his own strength from every four-footed foe, the wisest of brutes luxuriates in the waters of the lone stream that he has troubled, and, unless when man invades his repose, passes a lengthened life of tranquil enjoyment:

Calm amid scenes of havoc, in his own
Huge strength impregnable, the elephant
Offendeth none, but leads a quiet life,
Amongst his own contemporary trees,
Till nature lays him gently down to rest
Beneath the palm which he was wont to make
His prop in slumber. There his relics lie,
Longer than life itself had dwelt within them.
Bees in the ample hollow of his skull
Fill their wax citadels, and store their honey.
Thence sally forth to forage through the fields,
And swarm in emigrating legions thence.
The little burrowing animals throw up.
Hillocks beneath the over-arching ribs;
While birds within the spinal labyrinth
Contrive their nests.

With the image of the elephant we are apt to associate the idea of the gorgeous and stupendous vegetation of an Indian forest — to imagine trees of a growth and foliage proportioned to the bulk of the gigantic tenants which they screen. Such at least was my own impression, and I was therefore not a little amazed to find countless herds inhabiting the most open tracts, embellished with occasional straggling woods, so stunted in growth, that a host of colossal backs were not infrequently to be seen above the tops of them. The face of the verdant hills, that in time of danger form the stronghold of the species, usually terminate in an abrupt scarp, resembling a coronet, whence a number of ravines arising, are encumbered with rocks and precipices o'ershadowed by heavy forests — the intervening rounded space being quite destitute of trees. Through the denser covert, in parts impervious to man, the monstrous inmates have cleared many a path that would do credit to the pioneers of an army, and even by them would not have been accomplished without infinite labour. Marching in the van of his troop, the great bull elephant bursts through the heaviest jungle, with the same facility that a bullock would make its way through a hop-garden, trampling under his heavy foot the thorny brushwood, and with his sinewy proboscis summarily wrenching off the larger branches, and tugging away the parasitic web that obstructs his progress; whilst the females, with the younger members of the herd, bringing up the rear in single file, complete the Herculean labour which their lord has so ably commenced.

But, notwithstanding the extravagant traditions that have been handed down of the colossal stature attained in Africa by nature's great masterpiece, I am strongly disposed to the belief, that twelve feet form the maximum height of the male, and nine that of the female. Readily might the stupendous bulk of such an animal deceive an eye unaccustomed to its contemplation; but twice the circumference of none of the many footprints I measured, among the hundreds which were daily seen, yielded a product in excess of this standard. In Africa the tusks of the male unquestionably attain a much greater size than is usual in Asia, and nearly all of the cows are possessed also of these accessories, measuring from three to four feet in length. The enormous magnitude of the ears — which in the subject before us not only cover the whole of the shoulder, but overlap each other at the neck to the complete exclusion of a driver — together with the increased volume and prominence of the forehead, constitute the most striking external features of difference between the two species. Nor will those who have been accustomed to the sight of a groomed and well-greased elephant in his stall, fail to view with astonishment the brick dust complexion of the animal's hide in its native forest — this latter fact being attributable to the collection of adventitious matter by rubbing against trees and rocks, no less than to the habit peculiar to the whole race, of dusting the carcase after a cold bath, with a shower of earth and gravel cast up by the aid of the trunk.

On first entering the haunts of the elephant, nothing surprised me more than the extraordinary facility with which, in a wild state, unencumbered by the howdah, the unwieldy quadruped contrives to clamber to the very rigging of the steepest and most

XXII. ELEPHAS AFRICANUS. – THE AFRICAN ELEPHANT.

inaccessible hills dexterously traversing narrow mountain paths, descents and gullies, over which a horse can follow with extreme difficulty — and like a sculptured monument, standing out at last in the boldest belief against the clear blue sky. Solemn and dignified in his ordinary gait, the long slouching amble to which he has recourse when pursued, covers the ground at an inconceivable rate, and will at first keep a good steed at a round gallop; but the tracts over which we usually hunted, being flinty, and strewed with loose pointed stones, it was only necessary to press the herd a mile beyond their speed, to render them so tender-footed that they were glad to seek shelter in the first wooded ravine that fell in their way — up and down which they might be driven, and murdered from the banks *ad libitum.* That portion of the forehead lying immediately above the eyes, consists of two walls or tables, between which a wide cellular space intervening, a bullet hardened either with tin or quick silver readily penetrates through the honeycomb to the cavity of the brain — proving so instantaneously fatal that the unfortunate animal often passes from life to death, without either a groan or a struggle. Guided usually by some monstrous male, long standing in years, it is not easy to separate the herd; and whether they attack, march or fly they appear to act with discipline, and in concert. Their enormous bulk and power considered, there is probably no creature in the creation possessed of a smaller share of animal courage; yet, if easily terrified and routed, they never hesitate when roused into fury to charge the assailant with persevering hostility, and although turning clumsily upon a wide circle, not infrequently conclude the pursuit by playing a game of football with his lifeless body.

From the very outset of our campaign against the wild beasts, and long before we had obtained from his Amazooloo Majesty the freedom of his tropical preserves, our respectable acquaintance, Andries Africander, had gratuitously assumed unto himself the office of lecturer on the intricate science of elephant hunting, wherein, during three successive expeditions with ivory traders from the Colony, he flattered himself to have acquired no ordinary skill. A day never elapsed without some gasconade of his bygone or coming exploits; but although perpetually thrusting upon us his code of sage laws on the subject, we subsequently found that the impostor was uniformly the first to infringe it. Whilst winding through a grand and extensive forest which covered a slight acclivity leading to the Cashan Mountains, we for the first time beheld the *vestigia* of the noble object of our search. Mimosa trees were there up-torn by the roots; sturdy branches rent from the parent stock overhung the path, or stripped of their foliage were strewed upon the ground; and hundreds of deep holes, impressed during some recent heavy rain by the feet of a gigantic drove, together with great heaps of their fresh excrement, were visible in every direction. Heretofore our sapient tutor had affected to consider beneath his notice all animals that had been found; and at the near prospect now presented of displaying his science to advantage, he became perfectly frantic. Checking the team of the wagon which he was leading, he waved aloft his greasy blue cap, tossed a mass of dung into the air, and huzzaed till he was hoarse.

Not an hour was lost in setting fire to the grass on the hills, and making other customary preparations for forcing the elephants into the more open plains; but although the ravages committed by their foraging parties became hourly more and more apparent, and their footprints more recent and numerous, many days were still passed in fruitless search. During one excursion a gigantic savage of a subordinate tribe of the Baquaina nation, accidentally joining our party, confidently volunteered to lead us to a troop out of whose ranks he had the preceding day speared a large calf — an act, be it observed, of which no one could be better capable, seeing that he was a perfect ogre in dimensions, six feet four inches without his boots and built in proportion. On reaching a sequestered valley at the opposite foot of the range, we found the recently evacuated cantonment of the herd, wherein was a portion of the victim's skull, being all that the hyenas had left of the little that this Goliath of Gath had deemed too hard for his own digestion. But after following the trail of the receding column nearly the whole day, and twice passing across and through the mountains — from the summit of which was presented an extensive prospect over on of the wildest and most savage regions that the whole universe can produce — the main body was ascertained to have marched eastward, in which direction it was deemed necessary that the camp should forthwith be shifted. Like small specks in the distant valley, our white wagon could be discerned from the bare and sterile rocks which crown the highest elevation, and form a strong contrast to the middle and lower regions, so thickly covered with verdure and forest. The latter occupies the ravines and hollows only, whilst the whole plain beyond on either side is studded with detached pyramidical stony hills, interspersed with dilapidated cattle enclosures, and with crumbling 'cities of the dead'.

Wild elephants make the most extraordinary forced marches, invariably travelling in troops during the night, and with all military precaution. We followed on their route during the day, and thus it happened, that although frequently coming upon the bivouac or encampment which they had evacuated only a few hours previously, their retreating forces were always in advance. On the third day of our pursuit, hugging the base of the mountains, we passed through high coarse grass, betwixt two conical hills of singularly twin-like appearance, which stood like sentinels on either hand, and were called by our guides the *Cloguncolo* and *Clogunpalma* — gaining at length the vicinity of a remarkably abrupt aperture in the range which, through a telescope promised to afford a practicable road for wagons to the northward. The heat had gradually waxed intense — not a breath stirred — and heavy black clouds fast collecting bade us prepare for a deluge. We accordingly formed the camp in a sheltered but elevated position under the lee of a high stone enclosure, which only required the entrance to be stopped with

Plate XXII: *Elephas Africanus* — African elephant — *olifant* of the Dutch colonists — *'clou* and *maclou* of the Bechuana

Generic Character — Male attains the height of twelve feet at the shoulder; droops considerably behind. Extreme length between eighteen and nineteen feet. Provided with a flexible proboscis and finger. Skin solid, black, rough and nearly destitute of hair. Tail moderately long, and tufted with long hair of the thickness of common iron wire, set round the edges of the flattened extremity. Head rounder, forehead more convex, and ears four times larger than in the Asiatic variety. The latter appendages extremely flat, reaching to the setting on of the legs, and overlapping each other at the top of the neck. Legs pillar-like and shapeless. Five toes on all the feet, so encrusted in the callous skin which envelopes them, that their existence is only indicated externally by the nails. Double the circumference of the foot invariably denotes the height at the withers. Tusks two, composed of solid ivory, arched and springing from immediately before the eyes; eight or nine feet in length, and often weighing each more than one hundred pounds. No canine or incisorial teeth. Two enamelled molars or grinders in each jaw, marked with lozenge-shaped ribands. These teeth are shed and renewed during the whole life, as occasion requires by a lateral process — a new tooth growing from behind, gradually forcing the old one forward, and eventually taking its place, so that at certain periods the total number in the head may be eight instead of four.

Female from eight to nine feet high, usually provided with tusks about four feet in length. Mammae two, placed between the forelegs. Male sometimes found alone, but the species usually gregarious in large troops. Still said to exist in the forest of Zitzikamma and is common in the extensive plains, woods and hills of the interior.

bushes to become a secure pound for the cattle. Scarcely were these arrangements completed, when a stream of liquid fire ran along the ground, and a deafening thunder clap, exploding close above us, was instantly followed by a torrent of rain, which 'came dancing to the earth' not in drops, but in continuous streams, and with indescribable violence, during the greater portion of the night; the thunder now receding, and rumbling less and less distinctly, but more incessantly, among the distant mountains — now pealing in echoes over the nearer hills, and again returning to burst with redoubled violence above our heads:

Far along
From peak to peak the rattling crags among,
Leapt the wild thunder; not from one lone cloud,
But every mountain soon had found a tongue.

The horses and oxen were presently standing knee deep in water, and the sheep were in imminent danger of being drowned. Our followers remained crowded all night in the baggage wagon which leaked immoderately; but our own vehicle being better covered, fortunately resisted the pitiless storm. Sleep was, however, perfectly out of the question, the swamped earth actually threatening to give way under us, and the lightning being so painfully vivid, that we were glad to hide our diminished heads beneath the pillow!

Those only who have witnessed the setting in of the south-west monsoon in India are capable of fully understanding the awful tempest that I have thus feebly attempted to describe. About an hour before dawn its fury began to abate, and at sunrise the weather was perfectly fine; but the mountain streams being quite impassable to the wagons, I proceeded on foot with some of the Hottentots to reconnoitre the pass. It proved to be nothing more than a narrow channel, flanked by perpendicular bulwarks, between which a small river wends its way to the parent stream, through a number of very abrupt windings created by a succession of steep acclivities:

Where the monarch of storm
Rears his giant form,
On some rock built throne
That he claims for his own.

Descending from the highest peak, whence, after prying with a telescope into every nook and corner of the vast landscape that lay expanded before us, several herds of buffaloes only could be descried, we came unexpectedly upon the deep sunken tracks of a monstrous bull elephant, that could not have passed above an hour before, and finding that the trail proceeded eastward along the chain, we recrossed the river — of which the waters had now considerably subsided — and without loss of time returned to the encampment for horses and ammunition.

Leaving the wagons to proceed to a spot agreed upon, we took the field about ten o'clock, and pursued the track indefatigably for seven or eight miles, over a country presenting every variety of feature. At one time we crossed bare stony ridges; at another threaded the intricacies of shady, but dilapidated forests; now struggled through high fields of waving grass, and again emerged into open downs. At length we arrived amongst extensive groups of grassy hillocks, covered with loose stones, interspersed with streams, and with occasional patches of forest, in which the recent ravages of elephants were more than ever surprising. Here, to our inexpressible gratification, we descried a large herd of those long-sought animals, browsing lazily at the head of a distant valley, to which our attention had first been directed by the strong, and not to be mistaken effluvia wherewith the wind was impregnated. Having never before seen the noble elephant in his native abode, we gazed on the sight before us with intense and indescribable interest, our own feelings on the occasion extending to the whole of our followers. As for Andries, he became so agitated, that he could scarcely articulate. The blood forsook his sallow cheek, while with open eyes and quivering lip he barely contrived to stutter forth; '*Daar stan de Olifant!*' Mohanycom and 'Lingap were immediately despatched by a circuitous route to head the herd back into the valley, up which we rode slowly and without noise against the wind — and arriving unperceived within one hundred and fifty yards, made our horses fast, and took up an elevated position in an old stone kraal. The shouting of the savages who now appeared upon the height, rattling their white ox hide shields, presently caused the huge animals to advance unsuspiciously towards us, and even within ten paces of our ambuscade. The group consisted of nine — all females with large tusks. Selecting the finest, with perfect deliberation, we fired a volley of five balls into her side. She stumbled, but quickly recovering herself, uttered a shrill note of lamentation, whereupon the whole party threw their trunks above their heads, and clambered up the rugged face of the adjacent hills with the incredible celerity, their huge fan-like ears flapping in the ratio of their speed. We instantly mounted our horses, and the sharp loose stones ill suiting the feet of the wounded lady, soon closed with her. Streaming with blood, and infuriated with pain, she turned upon us with uplifted trunk, her little eyes glowing like live coals — nor was it until after repeated discharges that a ball took effect in her brain, and cast her lifeless on the earth, which resounded with the fall.

Turning our attention from this exciting scene, we perceived that a second valley had opened upon us, surrounded by bare stony hills, and traversed by a thinly wooded ravine. Here a grand and magnificent panorama was before us, which baffles all attempt at description. The whole face of the landscape was actually covered with wild elephants! There could not have been fewer than three hundred within the scope of our vision. Every height and green knoll was dotted over with groups of them, whilst the bottom of the glen exhibited a dense and sable living mass — their colossal forms, at one moment partially concealed by the trees which they were disfiguring with giant strength, being seen the next majestically emerging into the open glades, bearing branches in their trunks with which they indolently defended themselves from the flies. The background was filled in by a limited peep of the blue mountain range which here assumed a remarkably precipitous character, and partly scathed by fire, completed a picture, at once soul-stirring and sublime!

The approach of our party being still against the wind, was unobserved, and created no alarm, until the vanguard of the herd that we had left behind, suddenly showed itself, recklessly thundering down the side of the hill to join the main body, and passing so close to us, that we could not refrain from pouring a broadside into the leader, who, however, bravely withstood it. Having secured our horses on the summit of a stony ridge, and stationed ourselves at an opportune place, on a ledge overlooking a portion of the wooded defile, we sent Andries to manoeuver so that as many of the elephants as possible should pass before us in order of review designing to ascertain, by a close inspection, whether there was not a male amongst them. Filing sluggishly along, numbers halted at intervals, and crossing their hind legs, stood at ease beneath an umbrageous tree, some fifteen yards below the rock on which we sat, lazily fanning themselves with their ample ears, blowing away the flies through their trunks pushing their enormous foreheads wantonly against the stem, and uttering that feeble and peculiar cry so familiar to an Indian. They all proved to be ladies, and most of them mothers — the little old fashioned calves trudging close to the heels of their dam, and mimicking all her actions. Thus situated, we might have slain any number we pleased, a score of heads being frequently turned towards us in such a position, and so close, that a single ball from our elevated position must have sufficed for each; but we still hoped to find a bull, and were yet hesitating when a shot fired by Andries suddenly whizzing past Richardson's ear, put the whole cohort to immediate flight. We had barely time to seek the shelter of a tree, before a party of about twenty adults, with several little ones in their wake, were close upon our heels, striding at their utmost speed, and trumpeting loudly with uplifted heads. I rested my rifle against the stem, and firing behind the shoulder of the leader, she dropped instantly. Another large detachment appearing in our rear at the same moment, we were again compelled to retreat, dodging from tree to tree, stumbling among stumps and stones, and coming ever upon fresh parties of the enemy. But this scene of ludicrous confusion did not long continue, and being soon enabled to approach the prostrate lady, we put an end to her struggles by a rifle shot in the forehead. Andries now came puffing up in high good humour at his achievements, and under the pretence that the animal was shamming, in the most bravado manner discharged his cumbrous piece into the dead carcase. The villian's object evidently was, however, to confound the shots — for thrusting his middle finger into the orifice made by my two ounce ball, he with the most modest assurance declared himself to be the author of the deed, being pleased altogether to overlook the fact of the mortal wound having been inflicted on the side opposite to that on which he was stationed, whilst his own bullet, whether designedly or otherwise, had all but expended my worthy and esteemed fellow traveller.

On our way back to the camp, of the exact position of which we were rendered somewhat uncertain, owing to the difficulties opposed to the advance of the wagons by the late inundation, we passed three other large herds. One of them standing directly in our route, we attacked and pursued the fugitives about a mile over loose stones. Much has been said and written of the attachment of elephants to their young, but neither on this nor on any subsequent occasion could we perceive that the mothers evinced the smallest concern for the safety of their offspring. On the contrary, they left them to shift for themselves, and Mohanycom with 'Lingap being behind us, assegai'd one little fellow whose tail they brought in. Another old female was slain as we ascended the brow of an eminence, and at the same moment our wagons were revealed within a few hundred yards of the spot. The whole drove dashed through the middle of the camp, causing indescribable confusion both amongst cattle and followers; but fortunately no accident occurred, and after the fatiguing day's work that we had undergone, we were not sorry to find ourselves again at home.

Watery clouds hung about the sun as he set heavily behind the mountains. Loud peals of crashing thunder rent the air, and before nightfall we had a repetition of yesterday's storm — the river roaring past us with frightful fury. Troops of elephants flying from the scene of carnage, passed close to our wagons during the darkness, their wild voices re-echoing amongst the mountains, and sounding like trumpets above the tempest.

It was not possible to keep the fires burning, and the oxen and sheep were alarmed to so great a degree, that they broke from the kraal, and sought safety in the wilderness. Tired as I was, the excitement of the recent proceedings banished sleep from my eyes. I ruminated on the spirit-stirring events of the day and burned with impatience to renew them. Heedless of the withering blast that howled without, I felt that my most sanguine expectations had been realized, and that we had already been more than amply repaid for the difficulties, privations and dangers, that we had encountered in our toilsome journey towards this fairyland of sport. It was still raining heavily when the day slowly and gloomily broke; and the mountain torrents having overflown their banks, had rendered the valley in which we were encamped one continuous pool of water. High roads had been ploughed through the mire by the passage of the giant army; and whole acres of grass by which we had been surrounded the preceding evening were trampled level with the ground. The weather clearing up as usual, shortly after sunrise, and the truant cattle having been recovered, we armed a party with hatchets, and proceeded to collect the ivory. After a little brush with a crusty rhinoceros, and a long and tedious trudge through deep black mire, from which our feet were extricated with extreme labour, we again sought the living picture — but upon all the plain which was yesterday so teeming with noble quadrupeds, not one was to be seen. On reaching the glen, however, which had been the scene of our exploits during the earlier part of the action, a calf some three and a half feet high, walked forth from a bush, and saluted us with mournful piping notes. The unhappy little wretch had been observed hovering about its mother for some time after she fell, and having probably been unable afterwards to overtake the flying herd, it had passed a dreary night in the woods. Entwining its pliant proboscis about our legs, the sagacious creature, after demonstrating its delight at our arrival by a thousand ungainly antics, accompanied the party to the body of its dam, which, swollen to an enormous girth, was surrounded by an inquest of vultures. Seated in gaunt array with their shoulders shrugged, these loathsome fowls were awaiting its decomposition with forced resignation — the tough hide having defied all the efforts of their beaks, with which the eyes and softer parts had been vigorously assailed. The conduct of the quaint little calf now became so affecting as to elicit the sympathy of everyone present. It ran round its mother's corpse with touching demonstrations of grief, piping sorrowfully, and vainly striving to raise her stiff limbs with its tiny trunk. I confess that I had not been without compunction when committing the murder, and now felt so bitterly reproached by this moving behaviour, that I half resolved never to be found aiding or abetting in another.

The operation of hewing out three pairs of tusks occupied several hours, their roots, embedded in massive sockets, spreading over the greater portion of the face. After considerable labour we also succeeded in extracting the ball which Andries pretended to have fired; and the grooves of my rifle being conspicuous upon it, that worthy but unabashed 'squire was not only constrained to relinquish his claim to the merit of having secured the prize, but, which was the unkindest cut of all, to forego his fancied right to the ivory. During the whole operation the miniature of its prostrate mother was scanning our proceedings with the most intense interest, and finding at length that she heeded not its caresses as of yore, voluntarily accompanied our party to the wagons, where it was received with shouts of welcome from the people, and by a band of all sorts of melody from the cattle. But in spite of every care, the little wretch pined to death in the course of a few days, as did two others, much older, that were subsequently captured.

Arriving next in the valley of the Limpopo, I went out alone one afternoon, shortly after the caravan had halted, and having ascended the hill by a narrow path trodden by wild animals, entered a strip of forest occupying an extensive ravine. Several elephants had been seen from the wagons during the morning, clambering with the agility of chamois to the very summit of the chain; and I had now not advanced many yards, before I perceived a solitary bull posted on the outskirts of the wood, upon one of the lower steppes — his ponderous trunk wreathed around his white tusk, and but for the measured flapping of his ample ears, motionless as a marble statue. Securing my dapple grey mare to a convenient tree, I crept noiselessly behind a huge red block of stone; and from this ambush, which completely concealed and protected me, levelled my rifle at his ample forehead:

Like a whole town
Clean undermined, the slain beast tumbled down;

the very earth trembling under his stupendous weight as he

subsided with a heavy crash, and uttering one deep groan expired without a struggle! The echoes of the report, reverberating through hill and dale, whilst they caused the mare to break her tether and abscond, brought forth a whole colony of pig-faced baboons from their sylvan haunts to afford me by their ridiculous grimaces, anything but sympathy; and so long was it before I recovered my truant steed, that I did not regain the party until some hours after nightfall.

We were now in the very heart of the elephant country, but the perils of wagon travelling were hourly so materially increased by the more rugged character of the ground as we advanced, that in order to follow a retreating herd it was found requisite to leave the camp standing — a measure to which we were further impelled by a positive refusal on the part of the rebellious guides to accompany us one step to the eastward of the Limpopo. Crossing that river, therefore, we skirted the mountain chain on horseback, overtaking the rearguard of the fugitives at the close of the second day, below the highest point where the sources of the *Bekane* and *Umpeban* mark the site of the last bloody conflict betwixt the savage forces of Moselekatse and Dingaan. Speedily becoming confluent these rivers describe a nearly semi-circular course before joining the Limpopo considerably to the northward of the range, where the country, intersected by detached stony hills, and by mountain spurs of barren and forbidding aspect, assumes a more rugged character than ever. Open and level to the southward, it is dotted with clumps of forest literally swarming with elephants; but although the rich black soil continues, vegetation become visibly less and less abundant.

Seated the following morning upon a grey rock, we were discussing our frugal meal on the summit of a lofty knoll which overlooked a wild tract of this broken forest, when some of the Hottentots, shading their squinting eyes with one hand, pointed with the other to certain sable objects upon an eminence about two miles in advance, the which, on being reconnoitred through a glass, proved as conjectured, to be the outlying pickets of the vast troop of which we were in search. The unconsumed portion of our coarse repast being hastily thrust into our pockets, we saddled up, and having with some difficulty eluded the officious attention of a rhinoceros, who was at hand as usual, were presently ascending the brow on the opposite side of which stood the van of the enemy. As our figures rose to view, the bull, startled by the unwonted sound of a horse's footfall in his quiet valley, flourished his great trunk above his head, and having gazed a moment in mute astonishment at the intrusion of such a cavalcade — whilst the females crowded up as if to claim his protection — erected his enormous ears, and moving his column-like legs after the fashion of seven league boots, strode rapidly past. Crossing Andries first in order, that skillful Nimrod, anxious probably to accelerate his pace, dismounted nimbly, and marked the hindquarters of the quarry with a four-to-the-pound bullet, the heavy pat of which was instantly followed by a copious flow of blood. A shrill scream of mingled rage and dismay gave token of the pain occasioned by this wound, as, curling his trunk in the air, and clapping his flail-like tail betwixt his legs, the giant pressed on at his utmost speed — the wrathful voices of his associates, mingled with the crackling of broken branches, resounding meanwhile in the hollow, as they burst through the wood in various directions. Alternately galloping up on either flank, Richardson and myself then saluted him by turns, each with two barrels — the one keeping sight of him among the trees, until the other had reloaded. Every discharge was succeeded by a fresh stream of gore, and his noble form was shortly bathed in crimson; but still the gallant beast held on his course at a swinging pace, until, being obscured for an instant by the brow of an intervening ridge, he was suddenly rejoined by his flying comrades, and could no longer be distinguished in the crowd.

Conceiving that he had broken away with a small section to the lower ground, I left the Hottentots completely at fault, seeking to retrieve the *spoor,* and leading my horse, attempted to force my way on foot through a ravine at its base, tangled with trees and undergrowth. Confused and unintelligible shouts from the height presently warned me of the proximity of danger: '*Daar stan he! Daar lope he! Daar com he!*' but who or what he was, or in what direction he stood, ran, or came, I had not the most remote idea; and being consequently unable to extricate myself — hearing at the same time a fearful crash among the branches, accompanied by a sound resembling the rolling of numerous large stones, I abandoned my horse to his fate, and hastily ascended the nearest tree, whence I obtained a bird's eye view of the broad red backs of a large detachment of females, emerging with heavy tramp from the defile not twenty yards from my secure position. Andries had in the meantime been descried scouring over the plain below, with the wounded bull in front, and having fired two dozen shots in rapid succession before anyone could arrive to his aid, he finally left the ivory standing, and came blustering back to say his 'powder was out.' This terrible piece of mismanagement affording the animal a fresh start, we were compelled to follow the bloody trail a full mile, and having been again delayed by the attack of a rhinoceros, the lengthened shadows plainly told that it was late in the afternoon, when from a rising ground we once more obtained a partial view of the colossus, standing sulkily in the very middle of an isolated scrub, banging to and fro his broad ears, and occasionally, by way of interlude, trumpeting forth a challenge to advance an we dared.' Having fired several salvoes without the slightest effect, and long waited in the vain hope of the Philistine coming forth to do us battle, Richardson, as a *dernier resort,* proposed that before it grew too dark, we should cut business short by going in to him in a body. Andries, upon hearing this rash proposal, began to foam and stutter like a maniac, stating so soon as his powers of articulation had returned, that in event of our entering the jungle we should certainly '*kill de olifant.*' 'That' remarked my companion 'is the very thing we are ambitious of doing so come along.' 'No, no, no, no,' screamed our vaunting ivory hunter, with much painful blinking of the eyes to accelerate his delivery, 'I fra dat de olifant shall undoubtedly kill de Sieur; he's, he's, he's — vary quaad' [Angl. 'I say that the elephant will surely kill you, for he's very angry!'].

This was indeed a clean different affair, and after some deliberation it appeared so highly probable that Andries' last position was correct, that seeing the poor beast was in no condition to travel far, we bivouacked in a snug situation, hoping to find him somewhat the worse of his wounds when hostilities should be renewed in the morning. But no! The moment the badgered animal again perceived his persecutors, like a champion knight of old entering the lists to cast down the gauntlet to all comers, his little twinkling red eyes glaring under the fire of madness like lenses of glass — out he burst into the open space, grinding his heavy foot along the soil, brandishing his ponderous trunk aloft, and screaming forth his shrill note of rage and defiance! Charge succeeding charge, volley after volley, was poured into the moving mountain of flesh, now completely begrimed with dirt and clotted gore. Frenzied by pain, he rushed recklessly in every direction, squirting the crimson tide from his nostrils, and appearing to be almost suffocated with rage — until, covered with wounds and with glory, and fairly exhausted by exertion and loss of blood, he quietly sank upon his knees after a last desperate lunge, and receiving another shower of balls in the broad forehead, rolled over like a falling tower! Great as was our triumph, and loud and long though the cheering that followed the reduction of this most invincible of his race, the manner of his death could not fail to recall somewhat unpleasantly to mind the foul murder in Exeter 'Change of the unfortunate *Chunee,* upon whose luckless carcase were expended more than a bushel of rifle bullets, in addition to the entire ammunition possessed by a strong detachment of the military.

Long ere retracing our steps from the Tropic through this menagerie of elephants, both the wagons were so crammed with *spolia opima,* that we were compelled to cast out a number of the teeth, and leave the ground strewed with ivory. After all, the greatest difficulty was experienced in getting the heavily laden vehicles clear of the formidable belt of wooded hillocks, which, intersected by deep ravines, form the suburbs of the Cashan range. In some places, the paths worn by the huge tenants of this almost trackless region being too narrow, it was found requisite to send a party of pioneers to widen them — thus literally cutting our way through the country, and making the aged and hitherto silent forests ring to the unwonted sound of the axe. Our concluding day's elephant hunting was scarcely less full of incident than the first. From the top of a commanding eminence overlooking a lone valley in which they had long been cantoned, many hundreds of the stately beasts burst at once upon the vision, and we for the last time saw the face of the highly picturesque landscape literally alive with their scattered forces — some bathing in the pellucid stream — others browsing in indolent security 'like the cattle upon a thousand hills.' It is no exaggeration to say that a verdant glen some two or three miles in length, was completely studded over with clumps of them. Wheresoever we gazed, there a party of elephants was to be seen, and upon our attacking a column consisting of one hundred at least, the whole rushed frantically down a ravine, with ears upraised, and tossing trunks, screaming wildly, and levelling everything before them. A shot fired from the bank, whilst it sealed the fate of the leader, headed the division back again; and again, like a fleet tossing the opening waves from before their gallant bows, they crashed through the yielding branches, snapping like small twigs the largest that opposed their progress, and strewing them on either side of their headlong course — the persecution being repeated after this manner until they had become fairly stupefied. On one occasion the generals attempted to retrieve the lost day by a reckless and simultaneous charge from several quarters; but although we were often so surrounded by small detachments that it appeared extremely doubtful which party would be eventually obliged to retire from the field, the sound of the human voice uniformly turned the scale, and proclaimed man the victor.

A stupendous army of elephants thus ranging in native dignity amid the primeval magnificence of an African landscape — their sagacious appearance giving earnest of their exalted intellectual endowments amongst quadrupeds, and their very attitude and motion so in unison with the majestic solemnity of their deportment, as to inspire sentiments approaching to veneration — doubtless forms a most uncommon and imposing spectacle; and both to my companion and to myself, the first view of a herd under such circumstances — now industriously working among the aromatic trees with their ivory crowbars, and now with lithe proboscis idly culling the succulent shoots:

> *upon the flowery lap*
> *Of some irriguous valley,*

afforded infinitely greater gratification than the wholesale butchery of the noble quadruped which might have ensued. In most instances, this chase is followed as an avocation solely for the profits arising from the ivory; but as we possessed not the means of bringing away this valuable commodity, had we even been so minded, the chief incentive to continued pursuit was obviously wanting; and after the novelty of the excitement had worn off, I do not hesitate to confess, that although the tracking among scenery of the wildest and most romantic character, backed by the various turns and accidents of the spirit-stirring chase, possessed a never fading charm in my eyes, I could not at any time thoroughly divest myself of the idea that the half reasoning quadruped against whose voluminous carcase I had turned my deadly weapons, was none other than mine own stalwart ally, my tried and trusty favourite *Mowla Buksh,* from whose gallant back I had during many happy years vanquished my feline foes in western India, and whose fancied presence — how idle soever the impression must appear — detracted not a little from the satisfaction that I experienced.

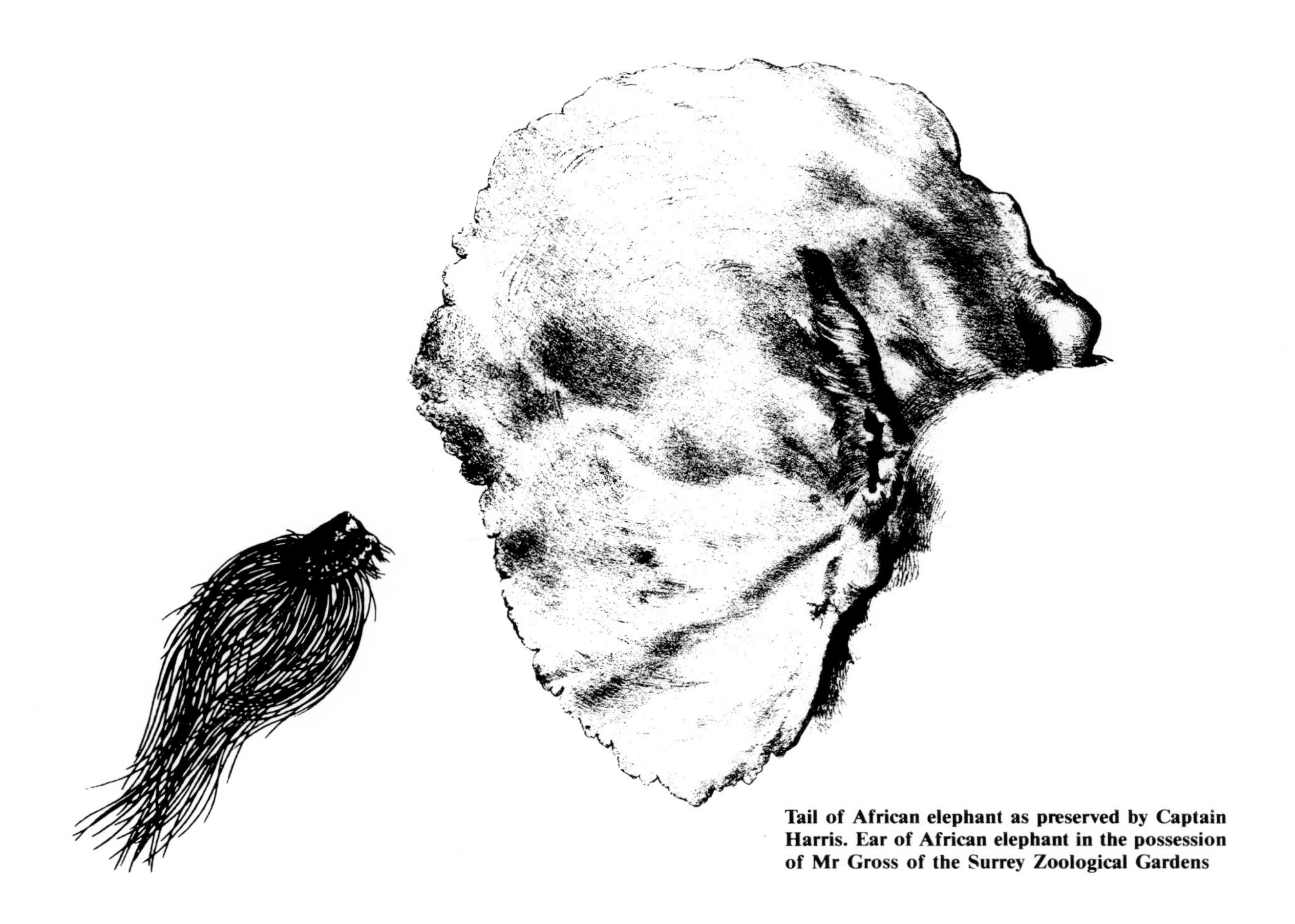

Tail of African elephant as preserved by Captain Harris. Ear of African elephant in the possession of Mr Gross of the Surrey Zoological Gardens

23

Sable Antelope

His beams seemed great, in good proportion led,
Well barred and round, well pearled near his head.
He seemed fayre 'tween blacke and berrie brounde,
He seems well fed by all the signes I found
The toes were great, the joynt bones round and short,
The shine bones large, the dewclawes close in port;
Short ioynted was he, hollow-footed eke,
And hart to hunt as any man can seek
The Noble Art of Venerie or Hunting

Africa was justly looked upon by the ancients as the land of zoological prodigies. It is not possible to open the works of those among them who have treated of the natural productions of the country, without finding some passage in unison with the general opinion of the time, that in this wild quarter of the globe, nature sported even to prodigality, and was profuse of monsters in her chartered libertinism. Her wildernesses formed the principal source whence was drawn the stream of animal life that soaked the Roman arena, where the cross now towers as if to expiate the deeds of blood done on its site; and from her innumerable wonders, natural as well as unnatural, it passed into a Greek byword, that she was always producing something new.

Next to the slaughter of the proud giraffe, the desire nearest to my heart from the very outset of our campaign against the *ferae naturae* had been to discover something new. Not a new lizard, nor a new rat, no, nor even — by which to immortalise myself as a naturalist — a new weasel; but an entirely new something or other, I cared not what whereupon an humble disciple of the chaste Huntress might reasonably pique himself; some stately quarry whose portrait might not be the least conspicuous in the well-filled gallery of African 'beastis of enchase', and whose spoils — unknown to science and adorning no museum of trophies saving mine own, might fill some prominent niche in halls:

with woodland honours grac'd.

The catalogue of large animals humbled, had already exceeded four hundred head of various sorts and sizes — many of them passing rare and *recherché* — novelties altogether even to the dwellers in the Colony; and excepting a few of the smaller antelopes which are restricted to certain portions of the coast that we subsequently proposed to visit on our return to civilization — my collection of *exuviae* had extended to every species of game quadruped known to inhabit the continent south of the Tropic. But *Africa semper alquid novi offert* — the proud trophy that I coveted was yet in abeyance; and the truly splendid addition to the *mammiferes* which forms the subject of the portrait annexed, was shortly to be realized:

To crown our triumph and our toils reward.

My double-barrelled rifle having, under the influence of an evil star, again suffered in a fall with my horse, I took the field on the 13th of December, with a heavy weapon built upon the primitive principle of flint and steel, the which, as a *pis aller,* I had obtained whilst at Litakoo from our kind friend Mr Moffat. Our whole party, with exception of Piet, who was still laid up with the shot through his leg, were in full pursuit of a wounded elephant on the southern side of the Cashan Mountains, when a clump of unusually swarthy looking antelopes attracted observation in an adjacent valley which stretched away at the foot of the steep grassy ridge that we were ascending. One great fellow, evidently the chief, looking as black as an undertaker's mute, and appearing to be covered with long shaggy hair, was standing nearest, his head and forehand only protruded beyond a thick green bush, from a siesta in which the alarm occasioned by our advent appeared to have disturbed him. Whilst the apathetic Hottentots were pointing and carelessly inquiring of each other, *'Vat swart bok is dat?'* [Angl. What black buck is that?]. I reconnoitred the group through a pocket telescope, and as they slowly emerged from the covert into the open glade, at a glance convinced myself that they were perfectly new to science. Hastily announcing this fact, together with my determination of pursuing them, if requisite, to the world's end — my heart thumping like a sledge hammer, I dashed down the slope, followed by the derision of all the Hottentots for my unsportmanlike desertion of the trail of a wounded *olifant,* in favour of a *lelyke,* or ugly buck, one specimen of which I assured them in reply, I would rather possess than all the ivory in Africa! In an instant I was in the middle of the herd, which was then crossing the valley. All had scimitar-shaped horns — nine chestnut coloured does leading, and two superb coal-black and tan bucks, whose sable coats vied in depth with the team of a hearse, bringing up the rear in Indian file, with all the pomposity and self importance of village billy-goats, to which, although some five times superior in stature, they appear to bear considerable resemblance in general *contour.* Dismounting, and drawing the bridle over my horse's head, I was delighted to observe the funeral procession stand for a few seconds within fifty yards, and as if unable to account for so sudden an intrusion, stare at me with amazement. No opportunity could have been more favourable, and properly equipped, I must have secured a brace at least; but in vain was it that I pulled the trigger of my clumsy artillery at the fellow who carried the finest head. Three times did the heavy machinery of the lock descend with alarming vehemence, but no report following the clattering concussion; and the herd having in the meantime taken the hint, and clambered up the face of a steep hill, I fairly rode my horse to a stand, in a desperate but hopeless, attempt to overtake them. Cursing my hard fate as I dashed the treacherous weapon to the ground, I planted a stick at the last *spoor* left by the troop, as it disappeared over the stony brow, and hastening to the wagons, devoted half an hour to the splicing of my broken rifle — being armed with which, and mounted upon my freshest steed, I returned with my companion to the scene of discomfiture. Taking up the footmarks, we followed them among the hills with unwearied perseverance during the residue of that luckless day — the shadows shifting, the sun setting, and night finally casting her murky mantle around us, without our having retrieved the object of our search. Being still within reach of the camp, we marked the spot where the tracks had been relinquished, and returned home with the determination of resuming them on the morrow — the near view I had obtained of the magnificent quarry having, if possible, strengthened my previously formed resolution never to relinquish the pursuit until I had succeeded.

Scarcely one wink did I sleep during the whole of that tedious night. Visions of strange unearthly looking beasts, as inconstant in their exterior as the changeable chameleon, appeared in quick succession during my broken dozings, but uniformly vanished upon pursuit like the *ignis fatuus.* Alone and bewildered in the bosom of pathless mountains, I found myself at one moment wandering up and down, seeking vainly to recover the lost track of some double-headed monster disguised in widow's weeds, that like an eel had slipped through my fingers when I fancied I was most sure of him; at the next I was straining every muscle in an abortive attempt to draw the unyielding trigger of an obstinate blunderbuss — the giant hobgoblin at whose carcase the tube was levelled, waxing momentarily larger and blacker and more shaggy, until, presuming upon the harmless nature of my rebellious weapon — which, when it at last exploded spontaneously, proved to have been loaded without a bullet — he finally strutted up like a great bully, and kicked me over a precipice into the yawning abyss below. Then came a sudden start to terminate my unpleasant bumping, and behold! it was a dream. At length the irksome shadows of night beginning to dissipate:

Ere yet the morning peep
Or stars retire from the first blush of day.

our eager feet are again in the stirrup. Resuming the tracks the moment it was light enough to read the ground whereon we trod, again did we carry them during the live-long day over hills and through valleys — now casting about at fault, now hurrying on upon the hot trail — but still without obtaining so much even as a distant glimpse of the gem for which we panted. More than once we came upon the spot where, under the shade of some projecting crag, the roaming herd had sojourned for an hour during the heat of the day; and the footprints became then so fresh that they were for a time abandoned, and a cast made ahead in the hope of viewing the quarry in the very next valley. All other game, how much coveted soever under ordinary circumstances, was suffered to pass unheeded. Sometimes a solitary bull koodoo carrying a noble head, would lay his corkscrew horns along his grey shoulders, burst through the brake, and bring our hearts; into our mouths, yet was he permitted to proceed unmolested. Repeatedly, too, the *spoor* had been crossed either by a waterbuck or by a roan antelope, both of which animals were observed in unusual abundance — their slot so closely resembling that of the new species, that much valuable time was invariably lost in deciding which was the true one — the Matabili who had not been present when the herd was first viewed, cunningly availing themselves of each check to assure me that the chase was no other than *Etak* [Angl. The roan antelope], hoping that I might be thus tempted to discontinue the [to them] wearisome pursuit. But the day had ended before it would appear to me to have commenced; and this second night closing when we were far from the encampment, we lighted a fire, and made ourselves snug under a projecting ledge of rock near the summit of a spur from the great range.

During the early part of the night there was no moon, but the stars shone out in brightness and beauty upon a dark blue sky, whilst the nocturnal sounds peculiar to such savage solitudes were ever and anon wafted to our ears. The wind as it moaned dismally by in fitful gusts, sounded at times like the measured tramp of a hundred elephants marching across the opposite hill; then all was silent as the tomb, until the startling *who-oop* of the fetid hyena, or the discordant baying of a troop of hungry jackals, burst from the gloom like spirit- warnings from the past. Again the stealthy footfall of some carnivorous prowler might be heard approaching the spot on which we lay, and once more all would become hushed at the indistinct and lurid gleam cast upon the surrounding bushes by our watch-fire, as we heaped on the dry wood. At length:

Like a queen came forth the lovely moon
From the slow opening curtain of the clouds,
Walking in beauty to her midnight throne;

and after a sound sleep of some hours, 'the bright morning star, day's harbinger', shooting above the dark brow of the mountain range to the eastward, was speedily followed by the white glimmering of dawn. Seizing our rifles we at once quitted this lone bivouac, and descending towards the valley, passed over one of our battlefields, whereon lay the mortal remains of three huge elephants and a rhinoceros, whose white bones, bleached by the sun and shower, showed in the twilight, through the black, shroud-like shrivelled skin, by which the skeletons were partially enveloped. Once more the sun has risen, but the air is still misty and chill. Again he touches each mountain peak successively with fiery light, whilst the lower range, including the deep valleys at its foot, are yet shadowy and undefined. Every minute now produces a change in the face of the landscape, and every change is more beautiful then the last. To the westward alone, all is veiled under cloud, which the eye vainly attempts to penetrate, unless when partial openings in the sweeping curtain afford glimpses of cliff or forest, whose rainbow hues, sunny and soft, are scarcely more substantial than the gauze-like vapour which is again closing its fleecy folds around them. As the red orb mounts upwards, these mists bow before his power, still, however, lingering about the craggy summits as though reluctant to quit their old resting place, until, curling up one by one into the calm blue sky, they gradually melt away into thin air. And now the last wreath has disappeared, and we are looking forth upon a boundless and savage expanse of grey mountains and ravines, far below which the sinuous course of the river can be traced by the bordering of trees that shelter and conceal it.

Towards noon of this, the third day, the hoof-marks of the herd denoted its having divided into packs, and it became evident that we were fast closing with the fugitives. Following upon the largest track, and peeping cautiously over a rocky eminence, our laudable assiduity was in half an hour more rewarded by the gratifying sight of the two bucks, clad in their 'blacke attyre' like the chief mourner at a funeral, and grazing by themselves, quite unconscious of our approach, in a stony valley some five or six hundred yards in advance! I was the first to make the discovery, and my sensations, as I quickly withdrew my head to whisper to my companion. 'There they stand', were positively sickening — for although at last fortunately found, the quarry had yet to be secured. Fresh caps were instantly applied to our own rifles, while the Hottentots renewed their damp priming, and wiped their clumsy gun flints. One moment's consultation sufficed so to dispose our forces, as to afford the best chance of intercepting the game from a tangled labyrinth of ravines which terminated in an impenetrable defile. A simultaneous equestrian attack from different quarters was then directed against the handsomer of the two, the order being given:

Whoever meets him, shoot him dead,
Five hundred nobles on his head.

Bang, bang, bang — went the rifles, and in an instant, with one hind leg dangling from the hip, the cripple had dashed into a scrub of flowering proteas, above the gay blossoms of which

XXIII. AIGOCERUS NIGER:- THE SABLE ANTELOPE.

his sweeping horns alone were visible. Pressing him on horseback through the copse, he broke within a few yards of me, when another shot through his body laid him sprawling on his black side. Quickly recovering himself, however, he was again on his feet, and before anyone had reloaded, was making the best of his way towards the defile at the neck of the valley. Aware that if he once gained this covert, he was lost to me and my heirs forever — without waiting to drive the bullets down my rifle, I sprang into the saddle, and exhorting Andries to follow upon the mare instead of stopping to reload, crammed in the rowels and dashed after the fugitive. I have before remarked, that the genus antilope should have been created with three instead of four legs, inasmuch as they invariably appear to run faster upon the odd, than upon the even number; and here was indeed a case in point. Although upon the first discovery of the herd on the morning of the 13th, I had made my way into the middle of them almost without an effort, it was now with the utmost difficulty that I could even preserve my place. Swinging his tasselled tail from side to side without one symptom of distress, and squinting at me occasionally over his swarthy shoulder, as if to say: 'Pray catch me if you can', the wounded quarry rattled gallantly along over broken ground, beset with buffalo holes and strewed with pointed stones. Fast gaining the jungle, he appeared to be gaining heart also, as each strides brought him nearer and nearer to his citadel; but at the termination of a mile, when close at home a yawning nullah arresting his career, he was compelled to swerve. During the progress of the chase to this point, my sorel *Gallaway* had twice kissed the ground, but twice cleverly recovered himself, after I had laid my account for a severe fall. Clearing the obstacle now presented at a bound, he brought me well on the quarter of the prize, which, little inferior to himself in stature, faced instantly about lowered his great horns, and charged. Ramming down the balls as I retreated, I presently approached again. Again he tilted at me, and receiving both shots through the shoulder, was overthrown and slain!

Vain were it to attempt a description of my sensation, when thus after three days of toilsome tracking and feverish anxiety, unalleviated by almost any incident that could inspire confidence, or even hope of ultimate success, I at length found myself actually standing over the prostrate carcase of so brilliant an addition to the catalogue of game quadrupeds — so bright a jewel amid the riches of zoology! Turning it over and over, I thought I could never have scanned the prize sufficiently, and my companion, after long feasting his eyes in silence, exclaimed, that 'the sable antelope would doubtless become the admiration of the world!' A minute description was written with its own red blood, and a portrait having been completed on the spot, while the victim was still warm, the *spolia* were carefully removed, and conveyed upon a pack-horse to the wagons — the night which succeeded to that most fortunate day of the whole campaign — my last in the bonny mountains of Cashan — being passed in preparing the skin for the long journey that was before us. After having been thoroughly salted, it was folded up and enclosed in an empty meal-bag — a place being allotted to it at the foot of my bed, which it occupied during the greater portion of our return pilgrimage. A highly unenviable bed-fellow and a source of perpetual anxiety, it finally reached Cape Town in a state of the highest preservation; and having been elegantly set up by Monsieur Verreaux, the French naturalist, now graces the collection of the British Museum.

From the very first glimpse I had been thoroughly persuaded that the sable antelope would prove to be a member of the Aigocerine group, nor was I mistaken in my conjecture. Nearly equal in stature to the *Equina,* it appeared in point of general contour to be more closely allied to that splendid species than to any other with which we are yet acquainted. The horns, upwards of three feet in length and perfectly flat, swept gracefully over the back in the form of a crescent — a bushy black mane rising behind them, and extending betwixt the lively chestnut coloured ears to the middle of the back. The tail — both tasselled and fringed — resembled that of no other known antelope; and the glossy jet black hue of the greater portion of the coat, whilst it formed a most vivid and remarkable contrast with the snowy whiteness of the lower parts, imparted the appearance of a suit of the deepest mourning. During my first interview, I had ample opportunity of remarking, that the females, like their lords, were all provided with scimitar-shaped horns; and although somewhat smaller in stature, that they were similarly marked — a deep chestnut brown, verging upon black, taking the place of the intense sable and tan. Judging from the compact form of the hoof, the habitat of the species should be limited to hilly districts; and it seems probable from many circumstances, that the herd from which my specimen was obtained, had wandered to the spot in which we found it, from mountains lying to the northward and eastward, which may perhaps form their headquarters. Be this as it may, by none of the natives within our reach was the animal recognised — although some, to conceal their ignorance pronounced it to be *kookaama,* which in the Sichuana dialect signifies the oryx or true gemsbok — an animal of such extremely rare occurrence within Moselekatse's country, that they had in all probability never even seen one.

On our return to Grahamstown, several months after the realization of the new antelope, I sought the trader Scoon, who had given us many valuable hints connected with the expedition now so successfully terminated. The poor fellow was confined to his bed with an acute attack of rheumatism, which he had contacted during his last *smouching* [Angl. Itinerant traders in the Colony are not inappropriately termed 'smouches'] journey to Litakoo; and mistaking me at first for one of his hard-hearted creditors, my visit naturally enough appeared to afford him

Plate XXIII: *Aigocerus niger* — sable antelope — undescribed by naturalists — unknown to the Matabili

Generic Character — Adult male four feet six inches high at the shoulder; nearly nine feet in extreme length. Horns thirty seven inches over the curve, placed immediately above the eyes; flat, slender, sub-erect, and then strongly bent back scimitar-wise; at first gradually diverging, and then running parallel to each other; three fourths annulated with about thirty strongly pronounced incomplete rings, more rigid on the edges, but chiefly lost on the outside of the horn; the remaining one fourth smooth, round, slender and pointed. Head somewhat attenuated toward the muzzle and compressed laterally. Carcase robust. Withers elevated. Neck broad and flat. Hoofs black, obtuse and rather short. Hair close and smooth. General colour of the coat, intense glossy black, with an occasional cast of deep chestnut. A white streak commencing above each eye, and continued by a pencil of long hairs, covers the place of the suborbital pouch, (of which cavity no trace is to be found), and then runs down the side of the nose to the muzzle, which is entirely white — the same colour pervading the throat and one half of the cheek. Ears ten inches long; narrow, tapering and pointed; white within, lively chestnut without, with black pencilled tips. A broad half crescent of deeper chestnut at the base of each ear, behind. A small entire sharp black muzzle. A copious standing black mane, somewhat inclined forwards, five and a half inches high, extending from between the ears to the middle of the back. Hair of the throat and neck longer than that of the body. Belly, buttocks and inside of thighs, pure white. A longitudinal dusky white stripe behind each arm. Forelegs jet black inside and out, with a tinge of chestnut on and below the knees. Hind legs black, with a lively chestnut patch at and below the hocks. Tail black; long hair skirting the posterior edge, terminating in a tuft which extends below the hocks.

Female smaller than the male, with smaller but similarly shaped horns. Colour deep chestnut brown, verging upon black. Very rare. Gregarious in small families. Inhabits the great mountain range which threads the eastern portion of the Matabili country.

anything but pleasure. 'You hae see,' said he, after several uneasy allusions to the crippled state both of his frame and finances, 'You hae seen the twa gentlefolks, Sir, wha cam last oot o' Sillekat's land? I canna for the vary life o' me think on their names. Sure one was a Captun Harrison, or some Captun or anither o' the Indy Company's airmy and he had wi' him Sir William Richards, the Juidge, or I'm sair mistaen. Its noo mair nor a twalmonth syne, Sir. They cam up frae the Bay wi' auld Mathew's lang waggin, on their road oot to pit a muckle topcoat on the black shoulders o' that naked cairl Sillekat; and noo I'm tell't they're coom back into the toon.' 'You probably allude to myself,' I returned, 'and to my fellow traveller, Mr Richardson, whom you were so good as to visit at Parke's Hotel.' 'Eh, Captun Harrison,' he exclaimed, snatching from off his head the foot of old stocking, which was doing duty for a nightcap, at the same time that he extended his bony hand, 'an is it yoursel? aweel I thoght ye was Misther Smeeth. I'm varry glad to see ye safe returned again, Sir, frae amang a' thae cut throat kaffirs, an Sir William, too,' — taking a pinch of snuff with renewed confidence — 'I hope he's uncommmon hearty. Andhries has been tellin' me, Sir, that ye hae broucht doon in the waggin wi' ye that unco fine black boke that I made sartain wad hae been the makin' o' ma fortine ane o' thae days, whan the rheumatiz had left me ould banes. Ech, Sirs, that's aye the gait; them that has mair siller nor they ken what to do wi', are sure to hae a' the luck and them puir deevils that's starvin' o'want, is everlastingly unfortnit. Why, Sir, its twa year syne that I was huntin o' yeelephants in thae same muntains, whan I foregathered wi' thae varry troep o'bonnie bokes wi' that yaedentical black spunkie that I'm tell't ye've felled, and rale keen to be sure I was to hae fired amaingst them; but thae Hottentot loons — ye ken the obstinit and thrawn natur o'them — they wad hear o' nathing o' the sort. I wad na say ma heed was ma ain whan a bul yeelifant was a-fit; and as it turned oot, the loons lost the ivory, an I let ma guid fortin slip atween ma fingers. The flees played the mischief wi' ma oxes, or ma certie I'd hae lookit oop the black deevil aince mair in the Morl muntains that lies ower agin the tither side o' Sillekat's; but bad luck to thae stupit Hottentots, I was forced to coom awa wioot him.'

'And we should gave come away without him too,' I replied 'had we listened to what the Hottentots had to say upon the subject; but from the moment I first obtained a glimpse of that buck, I swore that he should die. All the flies in the Murál should never have driven me out of those hills without his black hide; and had we not obtained it as we did, instead of now talking about him to you at Grahamstown, I should at this very moment have been still upon his trail.'

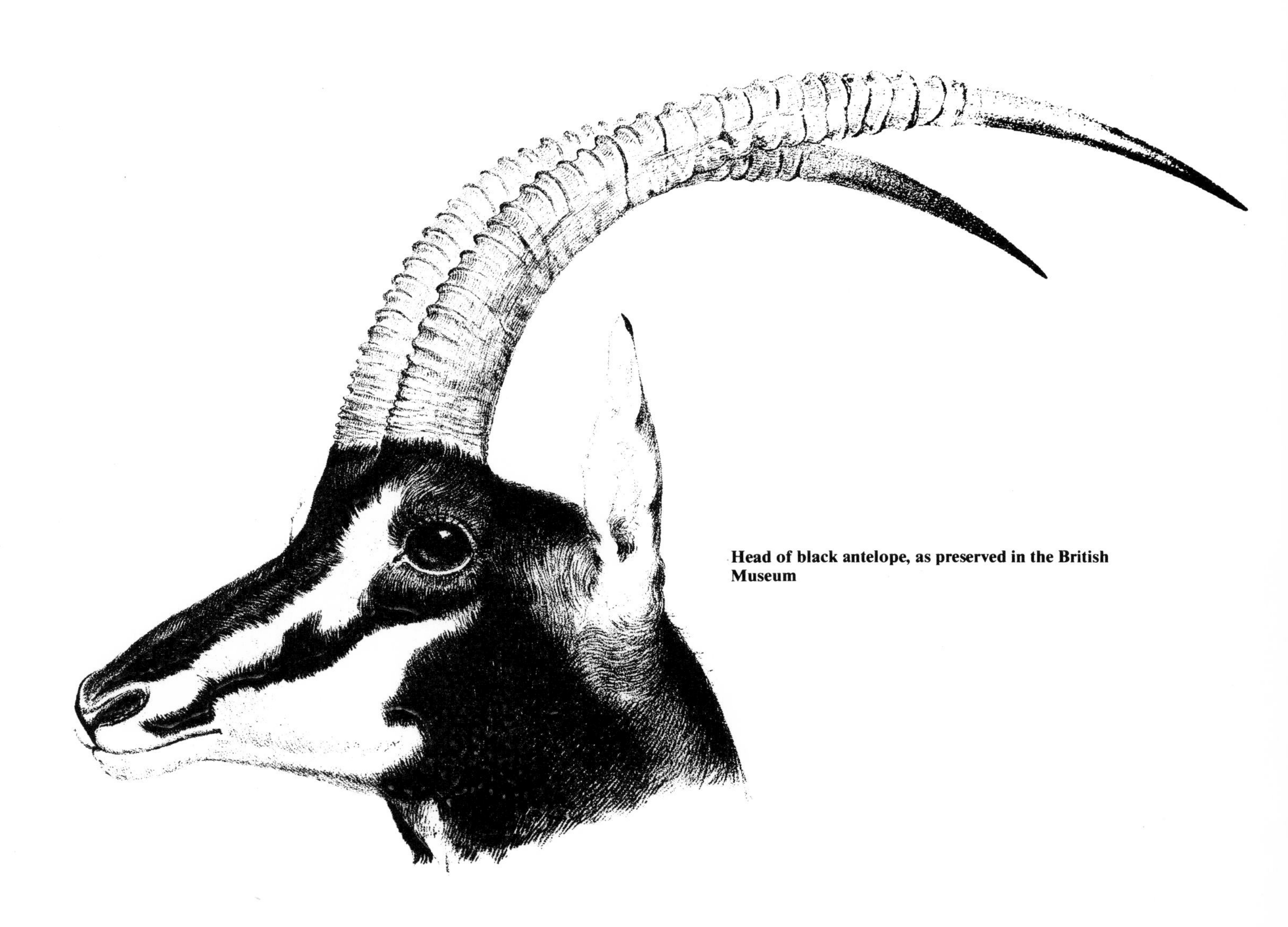

Head of black antelope, as preserved in the British Museum

24

Zebra And Klipspringer

I plant no herbs nor pleasant fruits,
Nor toil for savoury cheer;
The desert yields me juicy roots,
And herds of bounding deer,
The buffalo bends beneath my yoke,
And the wild horse to my rein,
My yoke is the quivering assegai,
My rein the tough bowstring.
Song of the wild Bushman.

Third and last of the African solidungula, but less equine in appearance than either of the species which have already been portrayed, the zebra of modern naturalists — its limbs wreathed, sable and silver — is amongst quadrupeds one of the most symmetrically formed, as well as the most sumptuously arrayed by the liberal hand of nature. 'With the figure and graces of the horse,' observes M le Compte de Buffon, 'it combines much of the lightness and elegance of the cervine race — the black and white ribbons which decorate every part of its sleek yet muscular figure, being arranged with such apparently artificial precision, that one might almost imagine the rule and compass to have been employed in their distribution.' Brilliantly contrasted, and placed alternately in parallel stripes, they extend over the fetlocks to the very coronets — following the contour of every part of the body — or widening, or becoming more narrow, according to the muscular development, and presenting under the glossy smoothness of the coat, a picture of such sparkling beauty that of all the motley:

Denizens of wood and wild
Nature's free race,

it would seem to be pre-eminently fitted both to gratify the pride, and to contribute to the service of the vain lords of the creation.

Since the first part of this work has appeared, I have discovered that I have been misled by the most distinguished naturalists, in hitherto calling the animal here portrayed the true zebra. Zebra is a native name of an animal of this genus on the plains of Congo, and first described by Pigafetta in his account of that part of Africa. He says it is regularly striped with three colours — white, black and brown, all over. He has given an engraving, in which these strips run diagonally across the animal, parallel with the collar line of the shoulder. He also says, it is commonly found in Barbary, and some other parts of Africa.

Cavazzi, whose description of the same country is also given by Labat, but the original of which I have not been able to consult, calls it the 'Zebra of the size of a mule. The skin is white, with black stripes, *égales et bien compassées.* This animal is very swift and if it could be tamed, there is no doubt it would be a *monture admirable,* and capable of carrying burdens. They are found in great herds in the kingdom of Benguela. The negroes hunt them because their flesh is good to eat, and that they may sell their skins to the Europeans.'

The distance at which I am placed from Europe has unfortunately prevented my examining other authorities, to which I have been referred, and from this circumstance I have not been able to discover any other account of this animal, nor has any zebra from Congo, or skin of one, ever been seen in England, that I can discover. But the description and plate of Pigafetta have been repeatedly copied by various persons, naturalists as well as others. When Dr Burchell found the bonti quagga on the plains of southern Africa, having black and brown, or lighter and darker stripes upon a ground varying from nearly white, through pale yellow, to rich brown, he suggested that it might be the true zebra; but in the meantime the *wilde paard,* which Dr Burchell called *equus montanus* had been sent to Europe from the mountains of the Cape, and had usurped the title. The great Cuvier in his work *Menagerie du Muséum* professing to correct Dr Burchell's nomenclature, and possibly concluding that a zebra being a striped *Equus,* the *wilde paard* being the most striped, was therefore the most a zebra, added his sanction to the old error, called the animal of the mountains of the Cape, *equus zebra,* the name of the animal of the plains of Congo, and committed the second error, of applying *equus montanus,* and *daow,* the Hottentot appellation of the *wilde paard*, to the bonti quagga or Burchell's zebra, the animal of the plains. Frederick Cuvier, in his great work upon the *Mammiferes,* has repeated his brother's errors, one of which has been corrected by some naturalists; but the original confusion between the zebra from Congo and the subject of the present plate, still exists.

Restricted to the mountainous districts of Africa, from Abyssinia to the southernmost portions of the Cape of Good Hope, this beautiful and wary animal, never of its own free will, descends into the plain, as erroneously asserted by all naturalists, and it therefore never herds with either of its congeners, the quagga and Burchell's zebra, whose habitat is equally limited to the open and level lowlands. Seeking the wildest and most sequestered spots, the haughty troops are exceedingly difficult to approach, as well on account of their watchful habits and extreme agility and fleetness of foot, as from the abrupt and inaccessible nature of their highland abode. Under the special charge of a sentinel, so posted on some adjacent crag, as to command a view of every avenue of approach, the chequered herd, whom 'painted skins adorn,' is to be viewed grazing on the steep hillside, or perambulating some rocky ledge, on which the rifle-ball alone can reach them — many a keen-eyed vulture sailing majestically at their feet, over the bosom of the deep blue valley. No sooner has the note of alarm been sounded by the vedette, than, pricking their long ears, the whole flock hurry forward to ascertain the nature of the approaching danger:

On high their glittering crests they toss,
As springs the wild-fire from the moss,

and having gazed for a moment at the advancing hunter, whisking their brindled tails aloft, helter-skelter, away they thunder down craggy precipices, and over yawning ravines, where no less agile foot could dare to follow them.

Although inhabiting the lofty and broken mountain chains to the eastward, that divide Kaffraria from the country of the

XXIV. I. EQUUS MONTANUS.- THE MODERN ZEBRA.
II. OREOTRAGUS SALTATRIX.- THE KLIPSPRINGER.

Bechuana, the zebra occurred in none of the more tropical hills that we visited, and thus proved one of the few game quadrupeds of which no specimen was observed by our party. Small herds still exist within the colonial limits, among the rugged environs of Graaff-Reinet especially, as well as in the mountainous districts of George, which notoriously form one of the chosen cantons of the species; and it was during a visit to the proprietor or a farm in the latter neighbourhood, that I realized, on our homeward journey, the gay spoils of the *wilde paard* which now grace my collection of trophies. The capture and sale of the foals forms no inconsiderable addition to Mynheer's revenues, his numerous sturdy scions devoting a large portion of their time to the chase of the shy herds — forcing the stragglers occasionally from the mountain fastnesses, and annually disposing of the fruits of their skill with the lasso, for exportation, chiefly to the Mauritius, where they are often whimsically trained to harness. Under these circumstances, it was not without some difficulty that I obtained permission to invade the haunts of the quarry, whose humiliation I desired to encompass — Mynheer finally granting the same; but reserving to himself the conviction of my total inability, as a 'reght Engelschman' [Angl. A real Englishman], to approach within rifle-range of the wild troops, much less:

> *To fright the animals, and kill them up*
> *In their assigned and native dwelling place*

Ill, therefore, could he conceal his surprise and disappointment, when, on the third morning, I returned from the rugged hills which bound his demesnes, laden with the painted spoils of a stallion and a mare — the numerical extent to which my depredations had been permitted.

Mine host of Attaqua's Kloof, whom I must positively introduce to the reader, was one of those patriarchal characters so frequently met with in the Cape Colony, who, like those of old, described in Scripture, possess extensive tracts of land, whereon are located their children and their children's children, with their bondsmen and bondswomen, their flocks of sheep, and their herds of cattle. The entire country, in fact, for miles around his primitive abode, was tenanted by the old man's married progeny, the proprietor each of as good a farm and as extensive flocks as himself, whilst all possessed in the same rude abundance, the good things of this life which are there esteemed the essentials of happiness. Rough, but courteous, Mynheer fortunately entertained less of that hatred towards an English *Heer* [Angl. Gentleman] which now so commonly sours the once vaunted hospitality of the Dutch African boer; yet did he not fail to complain long and loudly of taxes and the abolition of slavery, invariably concluding his harangue with the reproach, that in him I beheld a once wealthy man, reduced to positive penury by the British Parliament. In this, as in every other asseveration, he was stoutly toadied by two most interesting personages, whom gratitude for a fund of diversion will not suffer me to pass without special notice. The one was a taciturn butcher's rider, who, under the high-sounding title of *slagter kneght,* was performing an equestrian tour through the grazing districts, to make extensive purchases for the shambles. The other worthy was a diminutive itinerant pedagogue, of French extraction, who was honoured by the domestic circle with the title of *meester;* and who inheriting all the grimace and vivacity of his progenitors, afforded by his drollery a ridiculous contrast to the staid demeanour and phlegmatic gravity of the knight, whom he was pleased to consider his especial butt. Pedantic, disputatious, and garrulous to the most wearisome extent, Monsieur's tongue rattled on in mixed Dutch and French, without the smallest cessation; and having only lately made his way into the family for the purpose of affording to some of its juvenile members the benefit of his erudition, he deemed it requisite on all occasions to refer to myself for confirmation of his boasted talents for the task he had undertaken, and for which, he told me in the strictest confidence, he was boarded and remunerated in cattle. *'Et cela monsieur, n'est il pas vrai?'* the little man would exclaim in a shrill querulous voice, accompanied by a confident expansion of the paws, after every assertion that had curled the lips of his feminine auditors with a smile of incredulity — *'dat is ney var mynheer.'* A loud guffaw at the tutor's expense invariably followed each of these appeals, the young ladies choosing to be especially sceptical on all points connected with the boasted charms of the fair Parisians, a specimen of whose accomplishments their champion volunteered at a dance given, during my visit, by a neighbour, in honour of his third wedding. To the equal amazement and delight of all beholders, the little tutor, after dancing with every female in the assembly, until there

Plate XXIV (1): *Equus montanus* — zebra of modern naturalists — *wilde paard* or wild horse of the Cape colonists — *daow* of the Hottentots

Generic Character — About four feet high at the withers, and eight feet two inches in extreme length. Shape light and symmetrical. Legs clean, wiry and slender. Feet small, terminating in a compact solid castled hoof. Head light and bony. Ears and tail asinine — not equine as in the quagga and Burchell's zebra — the latter sixteen inches in length, transversely banded at the root, and tufted with black hair at the extremity. Ground colour of the coat pure white, the whole of the head, neck, legs and body the lower portion of the belly excepted, striped with glossy jet black bands, some narrower, some wider and placed close together or farther apart, according to the position they occupy; the upper portions connected with the dorsal line, and forming a plait over the crupper. Those on the neck continued through the bushy upright mane, which is thus alternatively checked black and white. Legs gartered by narrow ribbons, which extend both within and without, down to the coronets. A bare spot inside of each arm, a little above the knee. Two transverse bay bands on the ears. Lively brown stripes on the face, terminating in a bay patch above the nose, which is black.

Female similar, with two inguinal mammae. Gregarious in small troops. Found within and beyond the Cape Colony, but in mountainous regions only.

Plate XXIV (2): *Oreotragus saltatrix* — *klipspringer* of the Dutch colonists — *kainsi* of the Hottentots

Generic Character — Adult male about twenty two inches high at the shoulder, and thirty six in extreme length. Tail three inches long, almost rudimental, and only visible by the brush of hair which clothes it. Form robust and square. Head short and broad; compressed at the sides; suddenly contracting immediately in front of the orbits, and terminating in a pointed black muzzle. Ears large, open and rounded; margined with black and filled with long white hair. Eyes of the darkest hazel; full, lively and surrounded by a black edging, as if collyrium had been applied. Arch of the orbits unusually prominent. Horns about four inches long; round, distant, vertical and parallel, but slightly inclined forwards; obscurely wrinkled at the base, and annulated in the middle. Legs robust and caprine; long and broad in the arm, with short shanks or canon bones. Pasterns extremely high and rigid, preserving the same line as the canons. Hoofs upright and cylindrical; each subdivided into two segments, so jagged at their edges as to impart the power of adhering to the steep side of the smoothest rock — no portion of the toe touching the ground excepting the tip. Callosities on the knees. Fur of the upper parts extremely thick, long and quill-like; hard, brittle, spirally twisted and standing off the skin vertically, so as to form a natural pad; at base ashy, brown in the centre, and yellow at the ends; forming in their combination, an agreeable olive green. Under portions of the body sandy, tinged with ochre. Below the knees and hocks, buff. Suborbital sinus circular and conspicuous. Muzzle naked.

Female hornless; in other respects similar to the male. Mammae two. Common in and out of the Colony. Inhabits rocks and precipices in pairs.

was not one who could dance longer, volunteered a waltz with the surly *slaughter knight;* and being indignantly repulsed, suddenly commenced a most energetic *pas de seul* upon his own private account — whirling round upon his proper centre, after the manner of a teetotum, and flying from corner to corner of the room like a parched pea, until the perspiration streamed over his bald forehead. Fairly worn out at last with his exertions, he strove, with the aid of a chair to climb on to the back of a tall restive mare that was to convey him home — but throwing up her head, she struck the bookworm so violent a thump on the nose, that a torrent of blood forthwith sullied the lustre of his white waistcoat. Nor could he be satisfied of the escape from total annihilation of his prominent feature, until one of the damoiselles had obligingly enabled him to view its true condition in a cracked pocket mirror, when he acquired sufficient confidence to inhale a pinch of snuff, and finding the organ fit for the discharge of its most important duty, took his leave amid peals of merriment.

In Attaqua's Kloof I was greeted with scenery of a wilder and more romantic character than is usually to be met with in the Cape Colony, whose, cold, forbidding, and almost woodless mountains present an appearance strikingly bleak, as contrasted with those of other quarters of the globe especially.

During the pursuit of the zebra which was confined to the most steep and elevated parts of this rugged range, I repeatedly fell in with and killed the klipspringer, of which singular little species the portrait is here given. Once extremely abundant in the Cape Colony, it is now daily becoming more rare — the venison being deservedly reputed among the first that the country affords, whilst the elastic hair is sought above all other materials for the stuffing of saddles. Long, padded and standing out vertically from the side, it resembles moss in texture, and constitutes, as in the chamois of the Alps, a natural cushion to protect the animal from the contusions to which its habits must render it constantly liable. No antelope possesses more completely the lively gambolling manners of the young kid — none bound with greater force or precision from rock to rock, or clear the yawning abyss with more fearless activity. Found usually in pairs among the most precipitous rocks, and inaccessible summits, the klipspringer would appear in southern Africa to supply the place of the ibex and chamois; and such is the rigidity of its stiff pasterns and the singular formation of the high cylindrical hoof, that even when at speed there is no track left but by the tips of the toes, whereas every other class of ruminant would leave, under similar circumstances, some trace also of the spurious hoof. The most trifling obliquity or ruggedness of surface thus affording a secure foothold, the little animal, 'whose house is on the hilltop' entertains a sense of self-security which oftentimes proves its ruin. Looking down from some craggy pinnacle, as if in derision of the vain efforts of its pursuer, it presents to the rifle the fairest of targets; and tumbled headlong from its elevated perch, pays the penalty of its rashness. Missed, it bounds from ledge to ledge, on which the human eye can mark no footing — balancing at one moment upon the giddy verge of a precipice where barely sufficient space exists for the hoof to rest — at the next casting itself recklessly into the bottomless chasm, and pitching, as if by miracle, upon some projecting peak, where all four feet appeared to be gathered into the space of one. Another spring, and, clear of the intervening gulf, it is nimbly scaling yon perpendicular barrier, that resembles the wall of a lofty citadel — and now it is sweeping securely away over the naked and polished tablets of granite which pave the summits of those elevated regions, where:

We listen and hear but the wild river sounding,
We gaze, but see only the klipspringer bounding,
And the eagle of Winterberg, high o'er the woods,
Sailing supreme 'mid his still solitudes.

Skin of zebra of modern naturalists, as preserved by Captain Harris

25

Rheebok And Steenbok

O'er the plains where the bright bulbs lie,
Through the kloofs where the zephyrs sigh,
O'er the heath whose flowery head
Trembles scarce beneath his tread,
Wildly bounds the rheebok by,
In the love of liberty!

Although both of the elegant species of antelope here portrayed, are to be met with in many of the open and rugged portions of the interior that we visited, they are far better known to me as denizens of the Cape Colony, throughout even the better inhabited cantons of which, the rheebok especially is extremely common. Never entering the forest, but residing chiefly among rocky glens and mountain passes, it haunts the vicinage of little stagnant pools that have been left by the winter torrents; and small families, comprising one old male and five or six females, with their fawns, may there frequently be seen grazing quietly on the bare hillside, or gambolling amongst the dwarf trees and underwood with which the lower declivities are scantily fringed. To guard against surprise, a vedette is on these occasions invariably on the alert; and should a human figure or other suspicious object be descried nearer than is judged to be safe, the wary sentinel forthwith extends her slender neck, and gives warning to her companions by a sharp sneeze. Away they all bound, lightly as the wind, tossing their graceful heads, whilst their dainty feet scarcely seem to touch the earth; and never slackening their pace until they have gained the summit of some distant eminence, they halt as if by word of command, and suddenly facing half round, reconnoitre the enemy. Exceedingly shy, and possessed of a keen scent and a hawk-like vision, it is difficult enough to approach within rifle range; but the little herd when thus in motion, usually winding round the base of a hill instead of taking directly up the acclivity, an opportunity is often presented to the pursuer to gallop across the path they have selected, and thus obtain an easy snapshot. Of lighter proportions than almost any other African antelope, with long taper legs, and a singular raking neck, the rheebok moves with no less smoothness than velocity, keeping its graceful figure close to the ground, which it covers by long easy strides, with a motion so rapid and uniform, that it would seem rather to glide than gallop:

Rough are those rocks, yet down their slope
The silvery-footed antelope
More gracefully and gaily springs
Than in the marbled courts of kings.

In the woolly quality of the fleece, which resembles the fur of a wild rabbit, and is often beautifully curled and frizzled into distinct locks, consists one of the most remarkable features of this singular species. Nor is the position of the horns less eccentric. They are straight, set perpendicularly upon the cranium, and withal so slender and sharp at the tips, that the savage tribes employ them in lieu of awls and bodkins for piercing holes during the manufacture of their skin cloaks.

Another member of the Reduncine group, likewise a denizen of the Colony but of which no figure will appear among these portraits, is the Oribi; *redunca scoparia.* This antelope is most commonly found to the eastward, about Algoa Bay, ranging over the more open tracts, and it may frequently be descried at the distance of a mile, grazing or diverting itself in the barren plain:

Where stunted heath is patched with ruddy sand.

Without being positively gregarious, it is fond of the society of its fellows — ten or a dozen being sometimes detected together, although straggling so confusedly that they would appear to be in company rather by accident than by design. Neither, when alarmed, do the whole retreat together — each individual selecting its own line of country, and flying off in the direction which it deems to be the most secure. In point of colour and general appearance, this animal differs little from the steenbok, but it may be readily distinguished by its superior stature, by conspicuous brushes on the knees, and by white arches above the orbits, neither of which latter peculiarities, it will be seen, have existence in the smaller of the annexed figures.

Often solitary, and never congregating even in small families, the delicate little steenbok is common enough within the colonial limits, where it resides chiefly in pairs among stony plains and mountain valleys — uniformly eschewing very elevated or abrupt localities. Dry open flats, scantily strewed with large red rocks and boulder stones, shaded here and there by scraggy underwood, or clumps of stunted thorn bushes, form its favourite haunt — this being indeed the prevailing character of the tracts lying about the gorges of secondary hills within the Colony.

More timid than a hare, the tailless steenbok conceals its imperceptible figure among piles of stone and broken ravines, its colour and diminutive stature enabling it most successfully to elude observation so long as it remains upon its form. High on the legs in proportion to its length, its motions when aroused are swift, and if pursued it will bound without exertion over a space of ten or fifteen feet; but when closely pressed, or deprived of the hope of escape, it is wont to hide its diminutive head in the first hole or corner, where it patiently awaits its doom. 'Twas no uncommon event for the Bechuana of our party to knock these little bucks off their legs by squaling at them with knob-sticks or clubs of rhinoceros horn; and we once fell in with a party of hunting Corannas who had doubled up no fewer than seven in this fashion. Numbers are destroyed by vermin and by the larger birds of prey, and within the colony the species is greatly persecuted on account of the delicacy of its venison, which is as universally esteemed as the dry insipid flesh of the rheebok is deservedly despised.

Colony of the Cape of Storms! How often during the cold bracing mornings of winter, with my good rifle across my shoulders, have I roamed over thy wild mountains. Fanned by thy elevating zephyrs how elastic and buoyant are our bodily sensations. The tip of each finger tingles to the warm current of our blood, and as the clustering heath-bell crisps beneath the tread from the white hoar wherewith its hair-like leaves are embossed, we feel as though we could leap forth out of ourselves:

XXV. I. REDUNCA CAPREOLUS: THE RHEEBOK.
II. TRAGULUS RUPESTRIS: THE STEENBOK.

Come up the hill and smell the breath
Of the purple mountain heath,
Sweeter than the painted flowers
Reared in artificial bowers.

The sun is just rising from his slumbers, and the steaming slopes are enveloped in the grey filmy veil of the departing mist. Viewed from the higher altitudes, it rests on the bosom of the deep valleys like a vast inland lake, the reflection of surrounding objects so sleeping upon the mirror as to perfect the resemblance to a sheet of water. And at every step we take, what thousands and tens of thousands of gay flowers rear their lovely heads around us. Of a surety, the enthusiasm of the botanist has not painted the wonder of these regions in colours more brilliant then they deserve, for Africa is the mother of the most magnificent exotics that grace the greenhouses of Europe. Turn where we will, some new plant discovers itself to the admiring gaze, and every barren rock being decorated with some large and showy blossom, it can be no exaggeration to compare the country to a botanical garden left in a state of nature. To the brilliant and sweet-smelling *ixia* and to the superb species of the iris there is no end — the moraea, the cornflag, the amaryllis, the *hoemanthus* and *pancratium,* being countless as the sands upon the sea shore. After the autumnal rains, their gaudy flowers mixed with those of the brilliant *orchidae,* impart life and beauty for a brief season to the most sandy wastes, and covering alike the meadows and the foot of the mountains, are succeeded by the *gnaphalium,* the *xeranthemum,* and a whole train of everlastings, which display their red, blue or silky white flowers among a host of scented geraniums, flourishing like so many weeds. Even in the midst of stony deserts arise a variety of aloes and other fleshy plants — the *stapelia* or carrion flower with square succulent, leafless stems and flowers resembling star fish, forming a numerous and highly eccentric genus, in odour so nearly allied to putrescent animal matter, that insects are induced to deposit their larvae thereon. The brilliant *mesembryanthemum,* or fig marigold, comprising another genus almost peculiar to South Africa, extends to nearly three hundred species, and whilst they possess a magazine of juices which enables them to bear, without shrinking, a long privation of moisture, their roots are admirably calculated to fix the loose shifting sands which form the superficies of so large a portion of the soil. But amid this gay and motley assemblage, the heaths whether in number or in beauty, stand confessedly unrivalled. Nature has extended that elegant shrub to almost every soil and situation — the marsh, the river brink, the richest loam and the barest mural cliff, being alike.

Upwards of three hundred and fifty distinct species exist, nor is the form of their flowers less diversified than are their varied hues. Cup-shaped, globular and bell-shaped, some exhibit the figure of a cone, others that of a cylinder; some are contracted at the base, others in the middle and still more are bulged out like the mouth of a trumpet. Whilst many are smooth and glossy, some are covered with down, and others again are encrusted with mucilage. Red, in every variety and depth of shade, from blush to the brightest crimson, is their prevailing complexion; but green, yellow and purple, are scarcely less abundant, and blue is almost the only colour whose absence can be remarked:

In emerald tufts, flowers purple, pink and white
Like sapphire, pearl and rich embroidery,
Buckled below fair knighthood's bending knee
Fairies use flowers for their charactery.

Flora may here indeed be said to hold her court, surrounded by all the gayest and most elite of her varied train, yet is she usually more imposing than beautiful. Her caprices are greatly in excess of her charms, and the rich treasures which she has thus cast into the lap of rugged rocks and arid sands, thoroughly satisfy neither our eye nor our ideas. An isolated plant, how intrinsically beautiful soever it may be, is seen but to poor advantage on a mass of otherwise barren clay; and too often does it happen, that amid the rich tints and elegant structure which have been lavished on the vegetable kingdom of the Cape, we seek in vain for that perfume, whose aroma fills the gardens of our native lands.

Advancing among the inanimate novelties just described, one of the first living objects that meets our gaze is the tall secretary bird; *falco serpentarius,* either formally seated upon an ant hill, or stalking upon stilts with grave and measured strides in quest of his morning meal. Clad in the parish uniform of grey jacket and black breeches, observe how ceremoniously the pompous villain struts along with his quill jauntily stuck behind his ear like a lawyer's clerk. See! he has found a puffadder, from whose poisonous glance all save himself recoil. Darting like lightning upon his mortal foe, he wages active war with his armed pinions, leaping frequently into the air after the manner of a game-cock, while sparring vigorously with his long scaly legs and eagle-like talons. Now seizing the reptile by the writhing tail:

The snake-fed bird his silver wings unfolds,

and soaring away with his prize, lets it fall from a great height

Plate XXV (1): *Redunca capreolus* — rheebok of the Cape colonists — *peeli* of the Bechuana and Matabili

Generic Character — Adult male two feet five inches high at the shoulder, and about five feet in length. Body very slender and long. Neck attenuated and light. Head small and ears pointed. A conspicuous black spot at the angle of the mouth. Horns about nine inches in length; straight, slender, vertical and pointed; highly polished, with from ten to fifteen rings at the base. Hair very soft and villous, disposed in curls like the fleece of a lamb. General colour of the coat ashy grey, with a cast of buff in the older subjects; beneath white. Tail about five inches long, full and bushy like that of a rabbit; grey, lined and turned up with white. Muzzle naked and moist. Suborbital sinus low down, but distinct.

Female similar, though smaller and without horns. Mammae four. Found in small troops, chiefly among the hills and rocks of the colony.

Plate XXV (2): *Tragulus rupestris* — steenbok of the Cape colonists — *eoolah* of the Matabili — the vlacte steenbok *(T Rufescens)* and the bleekbok *(T Pediotragus)* appear to me simply varieties of this antelope and not distinct species

Generic Character — About twenty inches high at the shoulder, twenty two at the croup and thirty five in length. Very high on the legs. Head short and oval; snout pointed; muzzle black, ending in an angular gusset upon the ridge of the nose. Eyes high in the head, with black eyelashes. Horns vertical, parallel and nearly straight; four inches in length, slender, round and pointed, with two or three rudiments of wrinkles at the base. From the root of each, a remarkable black horseshoe passes backwards, and unites between the ears so as to form an obtuse angle on the occiput. Ears large, round and open; of a pale fawn colour edged with black. Tail barely an inch long and almost imperceptible, being a mere stump or tubercle, beyond which the hair does not protrude. General colour tawny or rufous, with occasionally a cast of brown or crimson. Breast, belly and buttocks white. Groin naked and black. Legs of a uniform fawn colour. Small callosity on the knees. No accessory or spurious hoofs. Pasterns very rigid. A small black detached suborbital sinus beneath the inner canthus of the eye.

Female similar, but without horns; the black horseshoe on the occiput being however as conspicuous as in the male. Mammae four. Monogamous or solitary among the stunted bushes of elevated tracts of ground. Common in the colony.

to the earth — as instantly resuming his grip and successively going through the same manoeuver until the life of his victim having become extinct, he swallows it without more ado.

So engrossed have we been with this singular piece of venerie, that we have only now perceived yonder herd of rheeboks grazing among a scraggy copse of the succulent *speckboom; portulacaria Afra* — most useless of all trees, whose pithy branches, refusing to burn, are not even serviceable for fuel. The wary animals are hugging the inumbrated side of the hill; but although our head has barely appeared above the brow, it has been observed by the lynx-eyed sentinel, and stamping petulantly with her light forefoot, she has already given the note of alarm, by sending down the breeze a sharp and not to be mistaken whistle. Ceasing to graze, the whole group forthwith elevate their white rabbit-like scuts, and pay us the compliment of devoting to our proceedings their exclusive attention — one and all being fully prepared to start at score whenever the danger shall appear sufficiently imminent. Whilst all eyes are riveted on the spot we occupy, crouching low, we place our hat and jacket in effigy upon a staff, and the herd being fascinated thereby, we steal quietly round to the rear, and arrive unobserved within sure rifle range. The rest is lowered, and the fatal aim taken; the fine drawn sights cover the lord of the sergalio who is readily to be distinguished by his bodkin horns; and a gentle pressure of the forefinger being applied to the well-balanced hair trigger, the billeted missive speeds through the air with unerring precision. All shaggy with heather, the frost-bound hills echo again to the sharp crack of the explosion, and the stricken quarry is plunging in his last throes. Every living object within earshot is now instantly in motion. Yonder troop of white-rumped springboks, which have hitherto been quietly distributed over the plain in straggling groups, is suddenly collected, and in full retreat. Scores upon scores of red-backs form at each leap one sheet of snow, displayed but to disappear again in an instant; whilst the little herd of widowed rheeboks, puzzled by the echo, having described the segment of a wide circle, come racing round the base of the very slope on which we are stationed, and leave one more of their number weltering in her red gore to the crack of our reserve barrel.

The ruse which has proven so successful in this instance, is again practised with a similar result upon a troop of younger and less wary bucks, which have been forced by their late jealous sire to separate themselves from the herd, and are next descried through a glass feeding at the foot of a stony ridge. Winding out of the glen with three woolly carcases corded to the back of a stout pony, we trudge back, well pleased with the morning's work, towards the farmhouse in which we have taken up our week's quarters; and striking into the high road, are presently hailed in a strain highly complementary to our skill in woodcraft by the Dutch inmates of a light horse wagon which comes whirling past at a rapid rate. The corpulent owner is holding the rude reins in both his hands, whilst those of an activity Hottentot are flourishing about the ears of the reeking team of ten, a whip some five and thirty feet in extreme length, beside which two of Crowther's rolled into one, would seem but a sprig of jasmine. Springing ever and anon from the driving box to the ground, and coursing alongside the rudely-harnessed steeds, he lustily flogs up the sluggards, and when all are at full gallop, vaults again into his seat with the agility of a monkey. Such, gentle reader, is the more luxurious mode of travelling within the Colony of the Cape, the equestrian order in which we are ourselves about returning to the metropolis, now that our sport is over, being of a character scarcely less novel. Shouldst thou possess leisure and inclination to accompany us a few miles on the road, we doubt not of thy returning diverted by the peep that will be afforded at Dutch African men and manners.

We have equipped ourselves with four ragged raw-boned steeds, not one of which, unless his uncouth exterior doth strangely belie him, has ever been within the precincts of a stable, or felt the grateful titillation of a curry-comb. The best are bestrode by ourselves and by our Hottentot henchman or *agterryer,* whilst the others, which quarter the Cape arms upon their deeply-cut knees are led with light packs, that may, in the absence of relays, be shifted every eight or ten miles to the backs of the saddle horses. The bits and stirrup irons of our travel-stained furniture are embrowned by the accumulated rust of ages! A sheepskin coverlet which serves as a saddle cloth during the day, takes the place of bedding by night, and on a pinch, the bags may possibly produce a change of raiment; but in all other respects are we solely dependent upon the boers, whose bare unsheltered dwelling, few and far between along our route, are each the very duplicate of the last. Built with scarcely any variation in size, with fantastic white stuccoed gables, a thatched roof and an elevated *stoep* or platform along the front — the latter screened by half a dozen poplars which form a line betwixt it and the road — to see one of these bleak abodes is to see all. A cattle-fold near to which stands a wagon divested of its white awning; a conical cooking house surrounded by a group of dirty half naked children; a tanning vat formed of an ox hide slung between four stakes; and a soap boiler, wherein a decrepit old witch is brewing a nosegay that may be scented a league off, are the never-failing concomitants. Nor do the manners and habits of the half civilized proprietors possess a less remarkable similarity than their domiciles. In the more remote portions of the Colony, no deviation is made under any circumstances, from the primitive custom of dining at noon; so that if we propose to satisfy the appetite which our ride has doubtless engendered, we shall do well to time our visit accordingly. Not heeding a surly reception, let us wait with patience until the board groans under greasy viands, and then, taking our seats as a matter of course, without tarrying for an invitation, harpoon with our double pronged steel fork, whatever edible within reach we may have taken a fancy to — bestowing no unnecessary attention upon the fair ladies, who, we may rest assured, will never fail to take proper care of themselves.

Arrived at the termination of our first fifty mile stage, let me introduce thee to the inmates of that old fashioned cottage in which we have resolved to pass the night. They are fortunately of the more civil order, and we will hope that their's may prove a sample of the hospitality which we are to experience throughout our journey. Having ridden up to the everlasting *stoep,* we remain seated during the process of shaking hands, or more correctly speaking of touching palms in a cold unmeaning manner, with the phlegmatic *baas.* His meerchaum stuck in the corner of his mouth, the good man is lounging over the half hatch of his front door, calmly surveying the operation of plucking the down from a cackling flock of geese, the which is being performed with no very tender hand by a possé of Hottentot urchins. Mynheer Dikkop is a substantial apoplectic looking burgher of passing grave deportment — his chin beset with stubble of a fortnight's growth, which imparts an admirable finish to the general slovenliness of his uncouth exterior. The lower edge of a greasy night-cap which once may have been white, protrudes under the broad brim of an ample drab hat, positively smothered in crepe — a band of which material, you are of course aware is permanently attached to every *hoed* in the Colony. A shaggy woollen jacket composed of duffel cloth, and the upper portion of a pair of sheepskin trousers of no stingy dimensions, completes the portrait so far as the closed lower door will at present admit of our surveying it.

'Goen dag mynheer' is our opening salutation; *'Hoe vaart gij — gij wil afklimm?'* the civil reply. And having climbed down accordingly, and been further invited to *afzadel,* our meagre steeds have their heads lashed to their broken knees, and are turned out with full permission to forage for themselves — the first advantage

they take of their restored liberty being to indulge in a hearty roll upon the green sward.

'Kom binnen' continues our new acquaintance, thrusting his lighted pipe into his waistcoat pocket, and leading the way into his bleak *voorhuis. 'zit'* taking his own seat at the same time — *'zie hier myn vrow, en myn dogteren'* pointing comprehensively to a party of six plump, flaxen-haired, queen-ant-looking damsels at the farther end of the room, who, each with her dropsical feet upon a warming pan, are staring at us with all their eyes. They are seated at a small table covered with green baize, and garnished with sundry broken cups and saucers — a small chafing dish upon the ground, above which a tea kettle is perpetually humming, together with an old fashioned coffee urn in constant use, serving to distinguish the mistress of the house, who, to judge by her looks, is several years younger than her married step daughters. She is fluently issuing her commands from an easy chair to a number of female slaves who are ironing clothes on an adjoining dresser; and she possesses in an eminent degree the rudiments of that *sine qua non* of Dutch feminine loveliness, elegantly expressed by her doting lord in the emphatic phrase *'dik en vet' 'keek nu mynheer,* he repeats several times with proud exultation, *'zic nu mynheer, is zij nict een mooiste jonge vrouw'*.

From the centre of the ceilingless roof dangles the inviting carcase of a sheep, with a noble tail, now in the very act of being flayed by the family butcher — a heterogeneous assemblage of raw hides, dried flesh and beef sausages, so festooning the rafters as almost to conceal from view a coffin, which has been prudently provided for the use of the first of the family that may happen to require such accommodation.

'En daar is komt mijn zoons,' resumes the host, turning towards half a dozen hulking lads of the self same pattern, all dressed precisely like each other, and like their progenitor, who may truly be said to have 'his quiver full of them.' Filing mechanically into the room, and each extending one hand for a shake, whilst they slightly raise their crepe-enveloped hats with the other, they seat themselves in succession upon the rude wooden bottomed chairs that are ranged around the cheerless white walls, against which they sit like so many statues in their niches. Quaker-like, not one of these hopeful scions uncovers his matted head, or has a single word to say for himself — the dead silence which their entrance has caused, being presently broken by an order from Mynheer, directing the youngest, his favourite cup-bearer, to *'schenk een zoopje,'* whereupon a case bottle of *brandywyn* or rather of downright *aqua-fortis* is produced form a cupboard containing various nostrums, and a fiery draught handed round, which is finally tossed off by the host himself with a hearty smack of the lips, and many jeers at the bad taste of us his guests in rejecting *'de lakkerest ding wat in al de waereld is!'*

It is now high meridian, for all the shadows have vanished; and taking this as the sign and signal, the slave girls drag into the middle of the hall a dresser capable of accommodating some twenty persons, and then *exeunt* to *opschep* the dinner; whilst mine host, whose dormant curiosity has been considerably stimulated by the exhilarating *zoopje'* proceeds to put the customary interrogatories to his hungry guests. The preliminary question of *'Wel nu mynheer, gij kan Hollandsch spreeken?'* is followed by an elaborate catechism, whereof, *'Hoe is uwe naam?' — 'Waar komt gij van daan?' — 'Waar trek gij nu toe?' — 'Hoe veel kinderen hebt gij?' — 'Waar nu is uwe vrouw?' — 'Almagtig, gij hebt niet een vrouw! zij dood is?'* invariably form the leading points, and are intended to be couched in a familiar colloquial idiom, adapted to our limited comprehensions; but ere the good man has had time to recover from the surprise into which he has been thrown by the last astounding intelligence that we have positively never been married in the whole course of our lives, re- enter the whole feminine group, bearing each a dish or utensil of some sort. *'Kom, zit bij'* exclaims the master, losing sight of his cross examination, suddenly dragging in his chair, and suiting the action to the word — when his excellent example being followed by everyone present, the revel commences with an earnest. Sheep's tail fat form the basis of every mess and even the vegetables are swimming therein. Mutton basted with its own grease, mealies or Indian corn soused in milk, together with stewed apricots and boiled pumpkins, are rapidly disappearing. Five minutes prove amply sufficient to settle the whole business; and the portly baas having then reproduced from the pocket of his waistcoat, that never failing pipe of half smoked tobacco, calls for another dram. The rest of the party meanwhile drench themselves with jorums of tea water at the good wife's side table, and disperse to re-assembled at dark, when the same process repeated, is followed by a general foot-washing, according to seniority, in one and the same tub; and the dirty table cloth having duly discharged the office of a napkin, we are bid to *slaap geruste* or soundly rest, and rolling ourselves up in our kaross accordingly, proceed to look out for a warm corner. When taking our departure betimes the following morning, a present to the hostess of a little tea or snuff will not fail to be considered an equivalent for our board and lodging; but I may not venture to affirm that the rude hospitality which we have experienced, will be accorded in every instance with so good a grace as by Mynheer Dikkop and his *'mooey jonge vrouw.'*

Head of rheebok, as preserved by Captain Harris

26

Bushbuck, Grysbok, Cerulean Antelope

Though a thousand branches join their screen,
Yet the broken sunbeam glance between,
And tip the leaves with lighter green,
With brighter tints the flower;
Dull is that heart that loves not then
The deep recess of the wild-wood glen,
Where roe and red-deer find sheltering den,
When the sun is in his power.

'Voici encore,' writes the enthusiastic Buffon, in allusion to the largest of the three figures annexed, *'une trés jolie gazelle, auqelle les Hollondois du Cap de Bonne Esperance donnent le nom de bosbok. Ce mot que j'ai conservé signifie le bouc de bois, et cette effectivement dans les forêts qu'on le trouve.'* And aptly enough has this elegant and game looking antelope been designated the bushgoat; since, concealing itself during the day in the deepest glens of wooded mountains, it quits not its retreat except during the matin hours, when it warily sallies forth to graze along the outskirts of the forest, or tempted by the bright moonlight nights, makes a foray upon the neighbouring gardens and cultivation. Slow of foot, and easily overtaken if surprised in open situation, it is wise to lie thus close in its native jungles, the thickest of which it traverses with ease — darting from one shubbery to another, and forcing its elastic form through the plaited undergrowth, with its horns so couched along the neck as to prevent their impending progress by becoming entangled in the sylvan labyrinth. So perfectly does the voice of this singular species counterfeit the barking of a dog, that the benighted wayfarer is said to have been decoyed by it into the most lonely depths of the forest, vainly hoping to discover some human habitation, whereas every step has but removed him farther from the abodes of man. Combining singular elegance and vigour with the most marked and decided colouring, the bushbuck stands quite by itself among the antelopes of southern Africa, and is to be found only in those parts of the Colony and of Kaffraria, where sufficient cover exists to afford it a safe asylum. Naturally preferring solitude, the buck is nevertheless frequently found in the society of the doe, accompanies during the breeding season by one or two kids, but never by adult individuals. Every specimen that I have seen, displayed a bare ring around the neck, from which by some process not satisfactorily explained, the hair had been removed as if through long confinement by a chain and collar. Very old subjects wear white stockings gartered above the knee, and it is usual to find a narrow white tape along the back, partially concealed by the goat-like mane which bristles from the ridge of the spine. But of these characters, none are constant, all being often absent in the female, and even in the non-adult male, whose lighter coloured coats are never so prominently picked out as the dark robes of the patriachs. When wounded these latter are usually extremely pugnacious, and their sharp horns render them by no means pleasant adversaries in a narrow path. During our sojourn at George, a hoary old buck made his way one moonlight night into a vineyard lying in the very middle of the village, and menacing all who attempted to eject him in the morning, was finally mobbed by every mongrel that could be collected, hunted down the main street, and run into at the end of it, after making a successful resistance for a considerable time upon its knees, and wounding several of its canine assailants.

A party of boers, residing not far from the banks of the Knysna, have consented to give us a day's shooting over one of their best preserves. As few portions of the vast belt of eternal verdure which skirts the eastern coast can present such magnificent scenery as this romantic river, along whose verdant borders:

the wild buck bells from his thorny brake,

we will take our guns, although it wants still some hours of the appointed time, and ride through the forest to the place of rendezvous. Tranquil and solemn is the scene — the stillness of ages which sits upon the wilderness rendering its silence almost oppressive. Stupendous trees of the yellow-wood and wild cedar, shielded from the ruthless violence of the tempest by yon cloud-capped mountains, heave their fringed boughs against a sky of transparent azure, and spreading far and wide their venerable arms, are linked together by many a parasitic wreath. The shadow of this canopy has encouraged the growth of various trailing plants, in parts so woven into a matted undergrowth as to be impervious to the morning sun, which now streams through the lower branches, and causes the pearly dew-drops to glisten upon every leaf. Each open vista reminds us of a ride through a noble park, the very ground upon which we tread being enamelled with myriads of little wax-like flowers, daisies and harebells, whilst many of the stately trees that tower on either hand, are hung with perfumed garlands blue, white, crimson and yellow:

See you that rock
Where the moss tuft has thrown
A fairy like beauty
Around the grey stone
See you that tree
Where the wild vine has braided
With cluster of green
Its foliage faded?

Already is the amorous wood-pigeon cooing softly to his partner above our heads, and the glancing host of birds which people the sylvan shades are displaying their gay plumage in the sunbeams. The painted lori, the laughing *epimachus,* and the cuckoo, robed in gold embroidery, make the forest re-echo to their wild screech; whilst the honey-bird, fluttering before our path, would fain tempt us by reiterated whistles to the dangerous task of plundering a stack of hives which are glued to that lofty branch. Ever and anon may be heard the speckled woodpecker — most laborious of winged artisans — rattling his hard chisel against the hollow limbs of some shattered trunk, whose withered crest tells of many a tempest that has assailed it; and hark! in the distance the funeral *campanero* or bell-bird perched in sad solitude upon a distant treetop, is tolling forth at broken intervals its deep and solemn chime, like the grave-knell from a village spire.

We have shortly opened a full view of the stupendous chain

of mountains, a portion of whose steep grassy acclivity must next be ascended. Whilst their bases are clothed with dwarf evergreens, each deep cleft ravine and towering eminence is shaggy with masses of sombre foliage, which seem almost to touch the skies:

Majestic woods of ever vigorous green
Stage above stage high waving o'er the hills,
Or to the far horizon wide diffused,
A boundless, deep, immensity of shade.
Here lofty trees to ancient song unknown
The noble sons of potent heat and floods
Prone rushing from the clouds, rear high to heaven
Their thorny stems, and broad around them throw
Meridian gloom.

And having finally toiled to the summit, behold stretching away to the far horizon the broad bosom of the dark blue sea — its long line of coast, indented with spacious bays, traced like a chart before us, and lashed by a thick misty spray. Those twin pyramidical rocks defining the entrance to the Knysna, form a Scylla and Charybdis, whence issues the stunning thunder of never-ceasing breakers that whirl and bellow with convulsive shocks — a bare, black, broken surface, emerging at one moment like the many-headed Hydra — at the next drinking up the white waves, and vomiting forth into a thousand fantastic cascades a frothy spume which reflects the prismatic colours of the iris.

The sun has mounted high above our heads, and reiterated blows from the ponderous hatchet of the wood cutter ring in cheerful echoes through the primeval forest. Many a prostrate trunk that we have passed has borne testimony to the havoc he commits, and the stately ironwood tree, to whose root the axe is now laid, soon quivering above its arboreal companions, falls too from its prosperous estate with a mighty crash, which resounds far and wide amid the valley. Alarmed by the sound, two or three of those most Lilliputian of all sylvan denizens, the slate-coloured antelopes, have crossed our path like a ray of light, and skipping over the intervening shrubs, have dived like rabbits among the rank vegetation. A pair that have emerged from betwixt two banks:

where the lady-fern grows longest

are yet to be seen at the extremity of yonder avenue engaged in a thousand kid-like gambols, and in mimic strife butting at each other with their tiny horns. Stealing behind that tall straight stem, we are in the act of making one of the pygmies our own, when the voices of the party of whom we are in search, burst in upon our ears — and through the wood they come, a goodly group, armed *cap-a-pie,* and escorted by such a motley train of curs as may rarely be witnessed out of Africa.

The sequestered habits of the bushbuck putting the exercise of wood-craft out of the question, the guns are presently so disposed around the first promising clump of detached covert, as to beleaguer every avenue by which it appears probable that the inmates may break. In go the pack, to the number of two dozen, and each dog running by scent with a most clamorous tongue, the echoing solitudes are speedily rendered too hot to hold anything larger than a mouse. Scarcely have they opened, before the light bounding footstep of an animal is heard advancing pit-a-pat through the wood, and a fine speckled buck, bursting through the leafy screen, turns up the path immediately in front of the stand below us. Bang! the clumsy Dutchman has missed his mark, and like a meteor, on dashes the quarry, undaunted and unscathed. He is ours beyond a doubt. The gun is at our shoulder, and a dull flat sound, resembling the tap of a muffled drum, following the crack of the first barrel, an ancient buck, in whose fat carcase the bullet is fleshed, springs a considerable height into the air, and coming headlong to the earth, rolls over and over several times with its own velocity.

And a noble fellow he is, with horns as sharp as cambrich needles. His consort having run the gauntlet on the opposite side of the grove, has died under a general salvo of buckshot; and the brake being now completely drained, it is necessary, in order to arrive at the next covert, that we should force our way through that dense thicket occupying the very heart of the forest, where tangled grapevines oblige us to creep upon our hands and knees. A hugh mouldering trunk, freckled with fungus, and half hid by rank vegetation, opposes our progress, and in the act of scrambling over it, our Batavian confederate, taking the lead, obligingly lets fly in our face the elastic twigs of two stubborn saplings betwixt which he has squeezed his apoplectic figure, and whether designedly our otherwise, has thus done his best to distort our aim during the residue of the day. Emerging from the copse, we attain the black boggy margin of a spring, which, during the wet season doubtless exhibits a mimic torrent, by now, under the drought of summer, is creeping sluggishly along the level land, just saturating its mossy covering, and occasionally disappearing so completely through some hidden channel, that its existence is only to be traced by the exuberance of the high fern which it nourishes. Sombre trees flourish on either side — their naked roots, as well as the lower portions of their arrow-like stems, wrapped in dark green mosses, whilst their overhanging boughs support luxuriant clusters of unsunned creepers, whose tendrils almost dip into the stream. The chill and darksome character of this lone spot, which would indicate that even at his noontide height the sun sends not one solitary ray through the gloom, has rendered it a chosen resort of the forest denizens. Already have we disturbed a bushbuck from his lair beneath that thicket of twisted grapevines, wherein unmolested he has long been wont to pass the heat of the day. Yonder he goes, right in front of us, his bristly back arched, his muzzle down, and his weapons laid along his bare neck. Nor is his lady far behind him. Away fly a dozen cartridges at their dappled flanks, and both are fairly on the ground, but after plunging a few seconds they have become obscured by a redundant clump of evergreens. Hurrying to the spot on which they fell, we find it bespattered with blood, the sharp hoofs of the stricken pair having left deep impressions as they bounded up under the smarting of their wounds. The red drops that trickle from their hazel sides do not fail to reveal the course they have severally taken, and tracking on, the doe is presently found lying across a log of decayed timber, over which she has stumbled, her bright sloe-like eyes already glazed in death, and the tongue hanging out of her half open mouth. But the breath has not so easily forsaken the nostrils of her mate. Carrying a charge of buckshot under his ribs, he has lain him down among the long weeds, and having the impudence forsooth, when discovered, to make a show of resistance, is speedily on his way out upon a stick.

Clear of the wood, we have packed the slain, and mounting our horses, proceed to cross a shelving bank, destitute of trees and completely overgrown with dry matted ferns, when a ridiculous contingency occurs which for some time retards our progress. Our fat Dutch friend of the morning, who, be it remarked *par parenthese,* rides not an ounce under two and twenty stone without his furniture, has incontinently disappeared; and after some search is found to be so completely jammed with his steed in a deep narrow water gully, rejoicing in a boggy bottom, that he is extricated with inconceivable difficulty upon our part, and no small hazard of suffocation on his own. But to release the unhappy quadruped, which is trembling in its strait waistcoat as if under a fit of the ague, defies every effort, and the purchase of sundry long levers thrust under its girth, added to the hauling of some dozen Hottentot domestics at the uncombed mane and tail, having completely failed, no alternative remains but to send to the nearest farmhouse for spades and pickaxes, in order that

XXVI. TRAGELAPHUS SYLVATICA. THE BUSHBUCK.
TRAGULUS MELANOTIS. THE GRYSBOK.
CEPHALOPUS CŒRULA. THE CERULEAN ANTELOPE.

the prisoner may be dug out. Numbers of these mossy and treacherous tracts which here exist, can be recognised by little standing pools of discoloured water, whereon floats a metallic scum; but the firm valley at our feet, as well as the base of the heights that embosom it are clothed with luxuriant verdure, partially studded with forest trees which cast their umbrage over many a flowering *parterre.* Proteas and large plots of scarlet geraniums are especially conspicuous, interspersed with patches of purple heath, the favourite harbour of the roan grysbok. Squatted like a hare upon its snug form, this beautiful little animal is rarely to be dislodged until well nigh trodden upon; but the dogs had pushed one out of that bed of fern, and are hunting it directly towards us. Returning again and again upon its old track, it bounds now over the head of the clustering heather, now doubles round the corner of a bush, and now, darting aside into the narrow footpath by which we are advancing, stands a moment with averted head to listen for its pursuers. Finding them close upon its heels, away it flies again, and making a desperate plunge into the heart of a thick shrub, vainly that it may have found an asylum. But thine enemies have again ferreted thee out, cunning one! and disabled by a stray buckshot from the *roer* of that ruthless Hollander, thou art circling round with dizzy brain and drooping head in quest of a corner wherein thou mayest lie down to die. Alas! Mynheer's rude hand has seized thee, innocent! and whilst he is fumbling for a knife wherewith to terminate they helpless struggles, who that hears thy plaintive cries, like those of a new-born babe, or witnesses the infantile simplicity expressed in they large melting black eye, brimful of dewy tears, can fail inwardly to curse his barbarity?

Another isolated clump of wood is now invested, and again the pack are busy at their work within; but a sly buck that has gained wisdom from experience, breaking where least looked, for is first viewed racing over the open glade well on his way towards the next shelter. Hot on the scent, and eager in their cry, the dogs are still however pottering about the same spot, and from the little progress they make, it is evident that they are hunting one of the little bluebucks, of whose musky odour they are so strangely enamoured that nothing will induce them to leave it. Running round and round in a limited circle, dodging backwards and forwards from bush to bush, the dwarf defies their utmost efforts to expel it from the covert, nor would they catch it in another month, did we not creep in upon all fours to their assistance. The sport has now terminated. It has been a lovely day, but the soft zephyrs whisper that it is drawing to a close. White fleecy vapours are flitting across the bosom of the more distant hills, the long shadows fast approaching have spread their grey mantle over a large portion of the valley, and ere we reach our home night has involved the whole landscape in mourning weeds.

The reader has already been initiated into some of the mysteries of an equestrian journey in the Cape Colony; let me here afford a peep at the even greater delights which attend him who travels through these hospitable regions with a heavy ox wagon. Great as the difficulties of moving with wheeled carriages had sometimes appeared in the interior, yet when compared with those encountered on our homeward journey to the metropolis, they proved utterly unworthy of a record. In regions where the name of MacAdam is unknown, we are left full liberty to select a rout for ourselves, and rarely does a little perseverance fail to reveal a practicable one; but when a high road is already prepared to the hand, infamous though it obviously be, we hold ourselves in honour bound to follow it. Beyond the limits of civilization, accidents were thus of comparatively rare occurrence, but during our return pilgrimage across the rugged regions of the eastern coast, a complete capsize, or the fracture of some important portion of the vehicle, formed weekly entries in our log, the former invariably proving lamentably fatal to our worldly possessions. It was during the descent of one of the mountain passes leading out of Outeniqualand to dorp of George, that the most ruinous smash of all occurred — the slippery path having there been by some skillful engineer led by a series of zigzags over a succession

Plate XXVI (1): *Tragelaphus sylvatica* — bushbuck — *boschbok* of the Cape colonists

Generic Character — Adult male about five feet two inches in length and two feet eight inches high at the shoulder; more at the croup. Form elegant: receding somewhat from the typical structure of true antelopes, and assuming that of the goat. Limbs robust and clean. Hoofs small and pointed. Horns about twelve inches long; erect, spiral and sublyrate, being so twisted in their ascent upon their own axis, as to diverge from each other in the middle. They are marked with an obsolete ridge in front, and one in the rear, forming a wreath; are black, and closely wrinkled at the base, and have sharp, smooth and polished points, a little bent forward. General colour a brilliant chestnut black above, marked usually with a narrow white streak along the spine, partially concealed by long brown hair four or five inches in length, which forms a mane. Two round white spots on each cheek, and several larger ones on the flanks, groins and haunches, forming unconnected lines. A white patch on the gullet, and two on each fetlock. Chin and inside of thighs white. Forehead intense sienna. A broad naked black band generally encircles the neck, as if the hair had been worn off by a collar. Tail nine inches long, shaped like that of the fallow-deer; brown above and white beneath. Ears large and round. A moist naked muzzle. No lachrymary opening.

Female similar, but without horns. Mammae four. Monogamous or solitary. Inhabits chiefly the forests bordering on the sea coast.

Plate XXVI (2): *Tragulus melanotis* — grysbok

Generic Character — Adult male from twenty to twenty two inches high at the shoulder, and rather more at the crupper. Length about thirty two inches. Head very broad and short, contracting suddenly before the orbits. Snout obtusely pointed. Horns about three and a half inches long, smooth, round, slender and vertical, or very slightly inclined forwards. Eyes full and melting; surrounded by a black border which likewise encircles the detached suborbital sinus. Ears round, open and broad; black, and nearly naked on the outside and marked on the inner side with three dark striae. A black horseshoe on the occiput. Colour deep chocolate or crimson red; the long coarse coat being stippled with numerous single hairs of the purest white, which impart a hoary appearance. Beneath rufous. Tail tuberculous, and concealed among the surrounding hair of the buttock.

Female similar but hornless. Mammae two. Habits monogamous or solitary. Common in the Colony among the wooded tracts which skirt the coast.

Plate XXVI (3): *Cephalopus caerula* — cerulean antelope — *blauwbok* or *kleenebok* of the Cape colonists — *noumetje* of the Hottentots

Generic Character — Adult male seldom more than twelve inches high, by twenty five inches in length. Head very long and pointed, with a sharp spacious muzzle resembling a rat's both in shape and expression. A naked fleshy spot around the eyes, which have a cunning cast. Ears short and round like those of a rat. Horns black, conical, reclined; slightly turned inwards and forwards; two inches in length closely and strongly annulated. General colour dull brownish buff, or mouse-colour above; beneath white. The upper part of the body has often a slaty purplish blue complexion. Legs and rump rufous. Hoofs oval, three quarters of an inch in length and of a light horn colour. Tail two inches long; dark above, white beneath. No suborbital sinus, but a suborbital sack lower down, marked by a lengthened streak upon the cheek.

Female similar, but hornless and even more diminutive. Solitary, in the forests along the sea coast.

of formidable acclivities and perilous descents — barely fit for baboons to travel — along the verge of yawning chasms so many hundred feet in perpendicular height, that the contemplation turned the head dizzy. Not a living creature was to be seen, save a grey vulture sometimes sweeping in mid-air below us. All around for miles, far as the eye could scan, was a billowy sea of mountains — wild, boundless, desolate; one range melting into the other, until the airy outline of the last fairly mingled with the clouds that rested upon their lofty peaks. We took the usual precaution of hiring an extra team from a surly boer residing at the foot of the range; but the honest man affecting to mistrust our solvency, doggedly insisted upon receiving in advance every stuiver of his exorbitant demand; and had no sooner touched *de gelt* than he secretly instructed his inebriated Hottentot driver not to assist us one step beyond the summit. True to his orders, the fellow accordingly prepared to desert us at a late hour, in the most dangerous part of the whole road, having first obligingly thrown the wagon on its side against a rock, which fortunately abutted just sufficiently far to prevent the vehicle from going over, so that with the aid of a tackle it was restored to equilibrium. Threats, coaxing, bribery, aye and even brandy, failing in turn to shake the ruffian's determination, and the steep stony descent, crossed by numerous deep gullies, having been rendered slippery as a glacier by recent heavy rain, I felt convinced that with the cattle unaccustomed as our own were to any but a champaign country, it could scarcely fail to go hard with us. Amply indeed were my fears verified. Four of the leading oxen having been removed from the yoke in order to render the rest more manageable, three of the wheels were chained; yet many and frightful were the hair breadth escapes that preceded the final catastrophe! Perched upon the pinnacle of some lofty crag, as if actually suspended in the air, with one hind wheel resting on an almost perpendicular slope, and the other buried in a deep hollow, the vehicle often leaned over at an angle of forty four degrees, the sport of every breath that stirred. Again in motion, it was launched, tottering from side to side, along some narrow undefended ridge, where the turn of a feather would have sufficed to decide its fate — a sharp angle at the foot of one of them leading directly over a polished pavement, which sloped to the very verge of a frightful precipice. Barely had I effected the removal of my artillery from their place within the awning, when a portion of the saturated bank gave way, and down went team and all into the abyss below — the wagon cutting three separate somersaults and wheels uppermost, finally resolving itself with an appalling crash into one shapeless heap, while the motley contents flew forth and displayed themselves in admirable disorder. Paltry, merchandise and hunting trophies, camp furniture, tin man's wares and oil man's stores, were simultaneously scattered over the hillside; several thousand leaden bullets — returned from the campaign in the interior — being liberated by the sudden jerk from the sacks wherein they had been sewn up, emulated each other in a wall contested race towards the lower ground. The two wheel oxen were killed on the spot; a third had its shoulder dislocated, and whilst few indeed escaped without bumps and bruises of some sort, the vehicle to which they had so recently been harnessed, had assumed in one single moment the hopelessly shattered appearance of a total wreck!

A heavy grey mist had hung over the crest of the mountain during our ascent, and now, as if to increase the weight of our misfortune, a deluge of rain descended, which promised to last throughout the moonless night that was to ensue. It being presently discovered that Sillekat and Kalipi, two favourite dogs, so named after the Matabili king and his prime minister, had been abstracted by the vagabond Hottentot, a party was sent in pursuit, and no shelter of any kind presenting itself, Richardson and myself resolved to turn to account the remaining half hour of daylight by walking to the village, said to be no more than four miles distant, and to boast of a respectable inn. Leaving the two domestics in charge of the soaking remnants of our chattels, we accordingly set forward under the auspices of our driver, who being a native of George, was not discredited when he professed himself well acquainted with the road thither. Braving a most pitiless storm, besides wading waist-deep through divers frantic mountain torrents, we reached the lower ground long after it had become pitch dark, and then proceeded to grope our way on among heavy black mire. But after tramping up and down for two mortal hours, losing first our shoes and then our stockings, tumbling into fifty holes, and leaving one half of our apparel upon the bushes — hopes alternately raised and disappointed by some will-o-the-wisp which glimmered at intervals through the murky darkness, Jacob, our guide, finally astounded with with the intelligence, that he had 'forgot the road!' No alternative presented itself under such circumstances but to fall back upon an encampment of Hottentot recruits whom we had passed near the foot of the mountain, and to whose unenviable bivouac their fire at last directed us. There, without even straw for bedding, in a miserable hovel hastily constructed of the branches of trees, through which the rain found ready admission, we contrived to pass the night in a series of abortive efforts to dry our saturated clothes — our combined dinner and supper consisting of a small mouldy crust of coarse brown bread, obtained as a great favour from one of our monkey-faced entertainers, upon the promise of an unlimited treat at the gin-shop the following morning.

Resuming our journey with the dawn, our hatred of Jacob was not a little increased by the mortifying discovery, that we had during the night actually wandered to within a few hundred yards of the outskirts of the village, and even of the identical inn of which we had heard such promising accounts — an intervening ridge having unhappily concealed its lights from view. Arriving at length, however, our misfortunes appeared but to be commencing:

All haggard from the midnight watch,

begrimed from head to foot, and destitute of flowered satin waistcoats, an item of apparel without which no rational being who hopes for civility will venture to visit George, mine host of the hotel stoutly declined to concede the shelter we sought beneath his roof, and wearied by our importunity did finally slam the door in our faces. In quest of an asylum we then wandered like paupers up and down the streets, bandied from one house to another — experiencing equal incivility at all — and at each receiving a fresh lesson in the great truth, that in the Cape Colony a gentleman is not recognizable in a homely garb. One old widow lady, to whom we came strongly recommended from the next house, subjected our persons to a minute scrutiny through a deadly pair of horn spectacles; which she removed from her nose after an elaborate catechism, evidently very ill-pleased with the view she had obtained of our patriarchal beards and travel-stained exteriors; and shaking her head in a determined manner, stated in round terms that she had no room. Mr Ebenezer Grubbe, a consequential, pot-bellied little man, with such a nose, and so red, who kept a *negotie winkel* or retail shop, and moreover set up for an Englishman, received us with a formal bow, and after listening to our woes, regretted that he was quite full. A certain young lady at last prove so compassionate as to promise that she would 'go and ask Pa' who was said to be in bed with the mumps, and our drooping hopes then began to revive; but alas, the malady had produced the usual effect upon the good man, and his fair daughter returned with a surly negative. As a *dernier ressort,* we were fain to take up our abode in a cobbler's stall, adjoining the most filthy of all pot-houses, the Irish landlady whereof did consent, after much coaxing, to produce a mess of garlic pottage, which we were directed to share with a radical carpenter, who 'took his meals there regular', she said, and had the run of his teeth. Neither did it require any extraordinary share of acumen to discover that this worthy chip had the run of the tap also, for in less than five minutes after favouring us with a spontaneous burst of melody, he was alarmingly drunk, and mounted on a chair, attempting to expound a set of political caricatures, bearing reference to remote proceedings in the Emerald Isle, and gracing the walls of the room. From this state of abject yet laughable misery, we were at length most providentially relieved by a gentleman who obligingly made us a tender of hospitality, which was joyfully accepted. And then followed the harvest. No sooner had the good people of George discovered who were their visitors, than every sharper stepped forward to volunteer his assistance in bringing out the *waar* which we were told with ill-concealed exultation, had carried away an axle-tree, and was completely disabled. I need scarcely add, that these obliging offers did not propose services of a wholly gratuitous nature; and each newcomer appeared to consider the *Indians* such fair game, that to avoid being plundered to the uttermost farthing, I was at last compelled to go and bring down the wagon myself.

Young and old, the hospitable denizens of the *dorp* now flocked to our place of residence, some to take a peep at my museum, or as they termed it 'mynheer's rarities te kek', and others to express regret, that having not sooner been made aware of our arrival, they had been prevented from offering us a lodging. Of the number of these latter were the old lady with the horn spectacles, and the damoiselle with her Pa, who had his head carefully wrapped in flannel bandages, and rejoiced in the name of Smith shorn of its final letter. Unfortunately for me, a rumour quickly got abroad that I was by profession a portrait painter, and there was no end of feminine applicants to know: *'Hoe fel gelt mynheer sal crie, mijn schilder aff taaken?'* In an evil hour was it, that upon certain conditions I indulged the *Juffrouw* Smit with a sight of her pretty features upon paper; for the very next morning I was waited upon by a perfect Daniel Lambert of a boer — a very mountain of obesity, who informed me after a vast deal of puffing and blowing, that his *kinderen,* twenty one in number — the fruits of three happy unions — being so scattered over the face of the globe, that little prospect, as he feared, existed of his being able to exhibit his paternal figure to all, if any, of them again, he had some to me with the determination of having his 'head taken off' in order that it might be circulated to his dutiful offspring by the very next pedlar's wagon that should be travelling in the proper direction. Upon expressing my inability to delineate the male subject, the monster produced a bait of thirty Rix dollars and bitter indeed was his disappointment when I assured him once for all, that I possessed no paper sufficiently large to admit of my doing justice to his voluminous proportions!

Head of bushbuck, as preserved by Captain Harris

27

African Boar And Reitbok

Whose eyeballs glare with fire suffused with blood,
Whose neck shoots up a thickset thorny wood;
Whose bristled back a trench impaled appears,
And stands erected like a field of spears.
Froth fills his chaps, he sends a grunting sound
And part he churns and part befoams the ground;
For tusks with Indian elephants he strove
And Jove's own thunder from his mouth he drove.

The Indian hog-hunter, who has dimmed the lustre of his flashing spear blade in the heart's blood of many a venerable boar, cannot fail to be sorely disappointed in both the African varieties of the genus *sus* to the more deserving whereof he is here respectfully introduced. Hideous to a surprising extent, but far inferior in pith to his Asiatic relative; slightly built, and of very insignificant stature, his chaps are armed with lancets which in many instances attain the most astounding dimensions; and four goodly sized fleshy protuberances, which resemble nodes or carbuncles, adorning his bewhiskered muzzle, he apes a Hottentot in physiognomy, and stands confessed a most unsightly swine! The wart-hog is extremely common in the interior, where early in the morning, or at eventide, after the sun had declined, large herds or *sounders* were daily to be seen, rooting in the open plain; and being possessed of a passing inquisitive disposition, the approach of our novel cavalcade often excited it to their own destruction, and to the supply of our larder with most sumptuous pork. Carrying their whip-like tails erect, and led by some unseemly white-tusked patriarch, they were wont to approach within point blank range of our battery, and peer pryingly at our line of march, until the incontinent demise of one of the party by a gun shot wound, first made the survivors acquainted with the fatal effects of firearms, and somewhat unpleasantly warned them that it was high time to decamp. Returning one drizzly morning from the banks of the Limpopo, with the spoils of three noble water-bucks packed upon my horse, I chanced upon a very large drove of the unclean beasts, feeding unconcernedly on the slope of a hill; and the sleet obscuring my rifle sights, I projected no fewer than three bullets at the diabolical looking boar without touching a bristle — the whole party, with a general grunt, scampering off after each discharge to a little distance — then wheeling about to show a menacing front, exalting their whiplash-tails at the same time, and screwing horrible faces at me. But the fourth missive tripped up the hoary general, and although shooting a pig may sound somewhat oddly in the sporting ears of my brother Nimrods, I can assure them that whilst we had no horses to spare, the head of that ilk swine proved a prize well worth the lead and gunpowder that had been expended on it. It most unfortunately happened, however, that the wagon which carried my hunting trophies was upset the very next day; and on sending back to the scene of the disaster so soon as the absence of this treasure was discovered, the lower jaw had disappeared, and the snout had ben so mangled by the strong teeth of a hyena, that the upper tusks only were saved. Gigantic, and protruding like those of an elephant, they were quite sufficiently hooked to admit of the wearer hanging himself up by them to roost, as did his ancestors of yore, if the ancients are to be believed. By all who saw these trophies in the Colony they were invariably mistaken for the ivories of a *zeekoë*, the best that I afterwards realised measuring less than half their length. Of these the finest belonged to a solitary fellow whose sinister red eyes had been fixed upon me at a moment when I fancied myself perfectly alone. Our camp was formed under the lee of the Cashan Mountains, in an extensive mimosa grove, that skirted the banks of a little rivulet overgrown with tangled flags and tassel grass; and a reitbok, of which species no specimen had previously been obtained, having crossed our path in the morning, I long coaxed the Matabili to accompany me for the purpose of beating up his quarters; but failing to overcome their laziness, I was fain at last to sally forth by myself. The buck being soon found, was slain of course, and his measure having been taken in the usual way, I proceeded to decapitate the victim, and looking suddenly up was startled to perceive the gentleman whose portrait adorns the annexed plate — his bristles erect like the quills of a porcupine, and evidently just risen from his stye among the dry reeds, diligently scanning my proceedings round the corner of a bush! Dearly did he pay for his curiosity. A shot broke one foreleg at the elbow, but hobbling along upon the three that remained, he contrived to lead me a great foot chase among the covert ere I could secure him. Arriving with his tusked trophies late in the afternoon at the wagons, it was with no small gratification that I witnessed the chagrin of the savages, who would have begrudged no labour to obtain a slice of the bacon. But not a morsel did the wretches taste; for my turn having now fairly arrived, I purposely so misdirected them, that they came back late at night, sulky and empty handed, after a fruitless hunt for the carcase.

The second of the annexed figures, whereof the name points strongly to its locale is that of the identical reitbok, slain on the occasion above referred to. This species resides either in pairs or in very small families along the margins of springs and swampy ground abounding in flags and rushes, or among the sedges that choke the channel of desiccated torrents which flow only during the winter season. Specimens occurred throughout our route, chiefly to the eastward of the Colony, and in the tropical streams:

'mongst reeds and willows that o'erhung the flood;

but owing to the shy and secluded habits of the animal, it was not often seen, nor is it in fact anywhere so common as on the western coast, where the attraction of water a rare element in those barren regions — sometimes causes it to congregate in the open plain. This fact indeed once came under my own observation on the Chooi desert. Moving with considerable rapidity by lengthened stretches, close to the ground, its galloping action resembles that of the horse — its colour rendering it so imperceptible that 'twould seem to stand on the wilderness like a mirage, or to glide over it like a mist driven before the wind, until lost altogether to the sight. Of this antelope there is said to exist a variety which has been styled the red rheebok or nagor; *redunca lalandii* — and is usually met with on open rocky mountains, along the dry channels of upland streams. I killed one specimen in the Cashan range, whose hair, feathering and whirling in various directions, less resembled that of the kangaroo, than does the fur of the adult reitbok, whilst its horns were smaller, and not so much approximated in form to a button hook. In every respect, however, it bore so close a resemblance to the figure here given, that I am disposed to doubt whether the imaginary species may not be made up of younger individuals, driven forth into the world by the old reitsboks, who brook the presence of no adult of their own sex.

For the traveller in southern Africa, it is in some respect a fortunate circumstance that rivers of any magnitude are of such extremely rare occurrence; since he who may never have essayed their passage with a lumbering ox wagon and its long train of cattle, where neither beaten ford nor ferry exists, can form but an imperfect idea of the manifold difficulties connected with such an undertaking. In the European acceptation of the term, perhaps the only stream really entitled to be called a river, is the Gareep [Vaal River]; and after a weary pilgrimage over tracts characterized by desolation and sterility, the first glimpse obtained of its beauties, fully justifies the eulogies of Dr Burchell. The alluring fancies of a fairy fiction, or the fascinating imagery of a romance, being suddenly brought into actual existence, realized those idea of elegant and classic scenery which occupy the minds of poets. A majestic volume of water, three hundred yards in breadth, flowing on in one unbroken expanse, resembled a smooth translucent lake; and as its gentle waves glided past on their way to join the restless ocean, bearing on their limpid bosom as in a polished mirror, the image of the wood-clothed borders, they seemed to kiss the shore ere bidding it farewell. Babylonian willows, clad in their yellow vest of vernal freshness, leaned over the bank, and dipping their dishevelled tresses into the tide, which glistened under the last rays of the setting sun, seemed fain to follow — whilst at intervals, the wrecks of stately trees, that had been torn from their roots by the violence of the torrent during some vast inundation, whereof the traces on the shore gave ample evidence, reared their dilapidated arms in token of the resistless fury of this smooth and tranquil flood at seasons when:

The glorious stream
That late between its banks was seen to glide
Hath wide sent forth its waters, and o'er plain
And valley, like a giant from his bed
Rises with outstretch'd arms superbly spread.

It was many months afterwards, on our exit from the game preserves of the Amazooloo tyrant, that we crossed the Likwa, one of the principal arms of the Gareep, a little above the scene annexed. Forming the southern limit of the territory to which he lays claim, it rises in a lofty range nearly opposite to the Bay of Delagoa, and like a great artery, traversing the continent from east to west, discharges its waters, after a course of one thousand miles, into the Atlantic Ocean. Long shall I remember the joy with which the reappearance of this formidable obstacle to advance was hailed by our little band. Deserted by guides, escort and interpreter, we were shaping our lone course through an unknown wilderness, the recent scene of bloody strife betwixt the king and emigrant boers, looking with hourly increasing anxiety for the friendly stream which should place us beyond the outposts of the contending parties in a position of comparative safety. Our compass was the tortuous Chonapas, a silver thread winding betwixt fringes of sighing bulrushes, and traversing verdant meadows upon which great droves of the impoofo were grazing like tame cattle. In constant expectation of an attack from the plumed and kilted warriors, we pressed on by forced marches, leaving numbers of our toil-worn oxen to perish by the wayside — the envious sun setting upon us the second day while one wagon was fast locked in a quagmire, whence, with the assistance of spades and pickaxes, it was at length extricated by double purchase, at the expense of trek touw wrought of:

the wilde bull's treble hide.

To replace this essential piece of furniture, a tax was forthwith levied upon a herd of elands that were espied in the neighbourhood, several having already suffered, although at too great a distance to admit of their spoils being brought in. A few minutes sufficed to reduce two dropsical subjects to submission; and having been made to carry their own skins to the wagons, the victims were there despatched. Piet had in the meantime slain a sow from his coach box, and we then drew up in a strong position before an old stone enclosure, the rear of which was fortified by an isolated tumulus, when Andries the Bold confidently predicting some coming evil, *Coeur de Lion* voluntarily perched himself upon the summit of this eminence, and during the whole night maintained a weary vigil.

The third day was fast drawing to a close, after merciless applications of the whipcord and double thong had enabled us with some further loss to achieve twenty five miles. The blue mountain range now on our left, in which the river was known to rise, had gradually assumed a deeper and deeper tint; and as we advanced over the broad bosom of the trackless plain like ships through the ocean, was fast developing its rugged character. At length, lifting up our eyes, we beheld before us afar off, a long dark streak of *karree* bushes stretching parallel to the horizon, and clearly marking the course of the waters of which we were in search. Shouts of exultation burst from the lips of the Hottentots, as they sprang nimbly from the wagon-boxes whence they had been earnestly gazing, and cracked their long whips with increased energy. The patient oxen broke into a trot — the object upon which all eyes were riveted became better and better defined — our friendly pilot stream increased rapidly in breadth, and as the sun disappeared once again below the horizon, we were standing on the osiered banks of the Likwa. At the spot where we had reached it, the breadth did not exceed one hundred and fifty yards, but the fresh deposition of slime, with the water wrack dangling from the tall trees, showed plainly enough that it had very recently risen at least ten feet above its present level. From the strength and muddiness of the turbid current, on which portions of driftwood were occasionally whirled past, we were not without apprehensions that it might be again flooded during the night, and perhaps obstruct our passage for many days; but the absence of anything like a practicable ford compelled us to take our chance.

The dimness of evening had already stolen over the distant mountains, and the harsh voice of the roosting pintado arose from the shadowy fringe of Chaldean willows, that bent enamoured over the opposite shore. The river was absolutely teeming with Hippopotami:

Which here and there, in many a scattered band,
Stretched their huge limbs, and slept along the strand;

nor, until we had set the example in person, could our perverse followers be induced to suspend hostilities against them, in order to construct a thorn fence for the better security of the cattle. Numerous lions had been disturbed by our arrival, and together with their wild music we were serenaded during the drenching and dismal night that followed, by the bellowing of crocodiles, accompanied by a loud noise produced by the slamming together of several huge pairs of jaws — broad sheets of lightning, followed by darkness that could be felt, and peals of deafening thunder, completing the gloomy terrors by which we were surrounded. No sooner had the morning broke, than Andries started on horseback in quest of a ford, the rest of the Hottentots sallying forth with unusual alacrity to seek the oxen, which had burst out of the

XXVII. 1. PHACOCHŒRUS AFRICANUS: THE AFRICAN WILD BOAR.
2. REDUNCA ELEOTRAGUS: THE REITBOK.

pound; and all but one having by the most unlooked for good fortune been recovered, we moved down the river, the waters of which had risen upwards of a foot since the preceding evening. Crossing many perilous ravines, we became at length alarmed at the protracted non-appearance of our scout, and had just determined to send back in search of him, when he rejoined us, triumphantly bearing the teeth of a sea-cow, whilst extracting which for his own private advantage, he had fortunately suffered us, his honoured employers, to overshoot by several miles what he was pleased to term an 'admirable drift'. Upon retracing our steps with some difficulty:

along the wild and willowed shore,

to this ford of promise, we had the gratification of finding the current more than waist-deep, the banks acclivitous, and the bed strewed with large blocks of granite; but having first taken the precaution of sending a horseman repeatedly across, to ascertain the soundings, it was finally resolved to attempt the passage.

After much violent bumping the leading wagon by a miracle reached the opposite side without any material damage, but not so its consort. Owing to some mismanagement on the part of the driver, the luckless 'onmibus' deviating from the track when about half way over, became so firmly jammed between two masses of rock, that although everyone stripped to the skin, and applied his shoulder to the wheel, three hours were provokingly passed in abortive attempts to extricate it. Whips, shin-bones and new *trek-touw* were alike fruitlessly broken, and fresh oxen repeatedly yoked, without the smallest advantage; and the river rising rapidly every instant, we had almost despaired of saving our property, when cracks and yells followed by the simultaneous struggling of twenty four of our sturdiest beasts, were responded by the grating of a wheel. An interval of intense anxiety succeeded. One after another the fore and hind nave on the same side rose slowly above the surface of the water, and the fall of the slanting vehicle appeared inevitable. To our joy, a sudden jerk restored it tottering to the perpendicular — pair after pair of the long string of oxen obtained their footing on the bank, once again the whips resounded cheerily in the hollow, and the dripping van emerged in safety from the flood. Another hour then passed away before the wayward flock of sheep could be reclaimed. These stubborn animals having in the first instance been only forced into the stream by dint of much pelting and persecution, had been carried down a considerable distance by the current, and whilst all hands were engaged in extricating the wagon, had strayed as a matter of course into the thick grove. At length, however, everything was ready; and the Hottentots, little dreaming of the distance that still divided them from their beloved gin shop, huzzaed and fired a salute as they turned their backs upon the waters of the 'yellow river' and upon the execrated dominions of his beer drinking majesty.

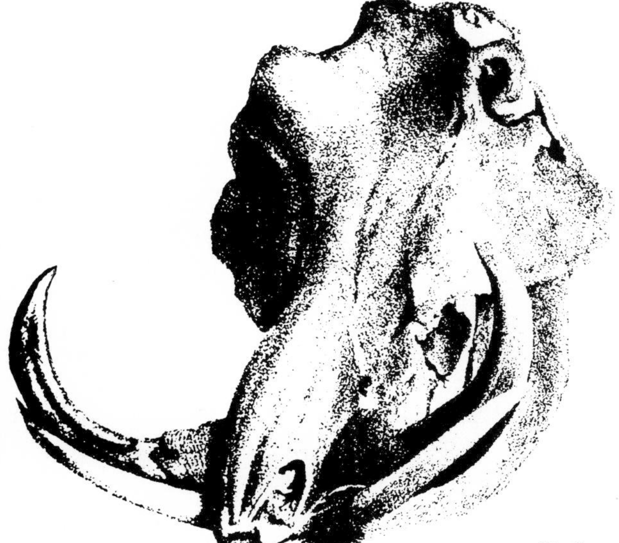

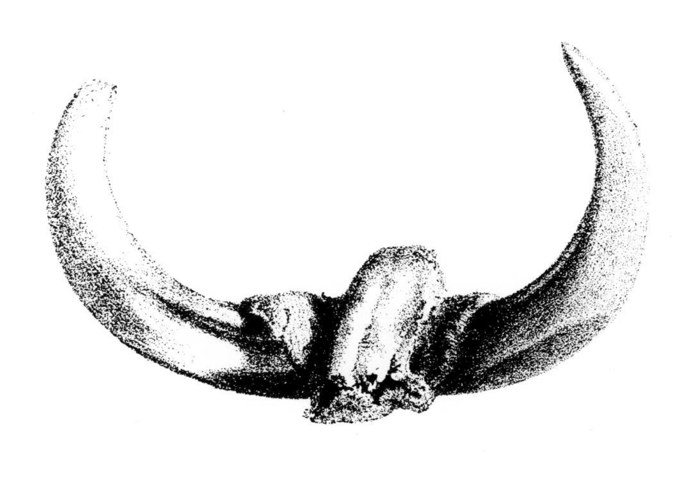

Skull and teeth of boar, as preserved by Captain Harris

Plate XXVII (1): *Phacochaerus Africanus* — African boar — *vlacke vark* of the Cape colonists — *ingooloob* of the Matabili

Generic Character — Height at the shoulder about two feet six inches. Skin reddish brown or earth colour, scantily beset with bristles. The top of the head, upper part of the neck, shoulders and back, covered with long rigid bristles, rising in tufts, those on the cranium diverging like the radii of a circle. Long white whiskers under the canine teeth, which are very large, long and directed upwards. Head extremely large, and muzzle very broad. A large fleshy wen behind each eye, and a prominent warty excrescence on each side of the snout behind the tusks. Ears bordered with strong hair. Eyes small and sinister, placed very high in the head, with black lashes and long brows, and a tuft of bristles behind them. Tail tufted with bristles, twenty inches in length, straight and thin like the lash of a whip. Loose accessory hoofs, and a piece of protuberant thick hard skin on the fore feet.

Gregarious. Inhabits the plains and forests.

Plate XXVII (2): *Redunca eleotragus* — reitbok of the Cape colonists — *inghalla* of the Matabili

Generic Character — Adult male about two feet ten inches high at the shoulder, and four feet ten inches long. Form slender and elongated. Neck raking. Horns ten or twelve inches in length, placed above the eyes, and advanced beyond the plane of the face; divergent and moulded by a bold and regular sweep to the segment of a circle, with the points hooked forward; wrinkled at the base, and annulated with obsolete rings in the middle. Ears six inches, tail ten inches long: the latter grey, tipped with white, remarkably bushy and covered with a profusion of woolly hair. General colour of the coat ashy grey, tinged with ochre, in substance soft and silky, like that of the kangaroo; beneath white. Hair of the throat white and flowing. Head, neck and legs usually tawny. A small muzzle and imperfect suborbital opening.

Female similar; but smaller and hornless. Mammae four. Solitary or gregarious in small troops. Resides variously, but chiefly amongst long reeds.

28

Leopard And Hunting Pard

My kingdom is the forest green,
'Tis strong and old and wide;
By the swift torrent's shelvy brink,
Or by the mountain's side.
The lion knows me in his path;
The spotted leopard hies
To seek the thicket's closest shade,
When my red arrow flies.
Song of the Mountaineer

In open defiance of Pliny, Buffon, Cuvier and the whole fraternity of natural historians, whether ancient or modern, the Dutch colonists of the Cape of Good Hope have set up for themselves a classification and nomenclature which, whilst it is certainly no improvement upon the old system, is in most instances sufficiently preposterous. The proud *Otis* of bustard, for instance, is made to represent a peacock; they have dubbed the hyena, a wolf and the subject of the annexed portrait, forsooth, a tiger! I need hardly state that the striped Bengal Royal cat of the travelling menageries has no existence in Africa, but the leopard, as well as the cheetah or hunting pard, are generally distributed, nor do they differ in any respect, that I could discover, from their Asiatic brethren. Both species occur chiefly in mountainous districts, where they prey upon the coney or rock rabbit of the Dutch zoologists, upon baboons and such of the antelopine race as they are able to surprise. Common throughout the Colony, the leopard is much dreaded by the farmers on account of the ravages he commits amid their sheep, and during the breeding season, also among the foals and calves:

Fierce from his lair springs forth the speckled pard,
Thirsting for blood, and eager to destroy;

and nightly may his low half-smothered growl be heard, as he prowls around the fold, whence, in spite of the baying troops of watchdogs that are maintained for the protection of the flocks, he not infrequently contrives to purloin mutton.

Viewed in a wild state, few animals can surpass the lurking leopard in point of beauty; his brilliant orange and white skin, which shines like silk, being richly studded with open rosettes, sometimes of the most intense sable, at others disposed as if a cat had been walking over it with her paws tarred. Nor is he less distinguished for elegance and grace. His every motion easy and flexile in the highest degree, he bounds among the rocks and woods with an agility truly amazing; now stealing along the ground with the silence of a snake, now crouching with his forepaws extended, and his spotted head laid betwixt them, whilst his chequered tail twitches impatiently, and his pale gooseberry eyes glare mischievously upon his unsuspecting victim. But the nocturnal depredator is not infrequently outwitted, and being ensnared in a cage constructed of stones and timber, upon the principle of the rat trap, is sentenced without trial by judge or jury to be worried by every dog that the country round can contribute; for no Dutchman choosing to hazard an attack upon the intruder, when at large, unless he be backed by some dozen canine coadjutors, it is of course desirable to give these latter a foretaste of the animal's tactics. Accidents in the chase are frequent in those districts which abound most in this species, and during my short sojourn in the Colony, I heard of the occurrence of more than one. On our way across the Sneuwbergen, we encountered a Hottentot, wearing a battered hat almost smothered in ostrich plumes, and riding as if for a wager against time. Inquiring as he bumped past with legs and arms going, whither he sped in so desperate a hurry, we were informed, 'to Graaff Reinet in order to fetch Doctor Krebbs to *myn jong baas,* whose *kop* has been nearly pulled off by *de Tiger!'* And we afterwards ascertained that the young boer in a clumsy attempt upon the life of the spotted prowler of the wild, had in truth been so severely dealt with, that the eventually lost his own.

One leopard only suffered at the hands of our party, and his demise; in a hole, being simultaneous with the discharge of the first rifle I may be allowed to draw upon tradition for an anecdote better illustrative of the sport. 'Two African farmers' writes Pringle 'returning from hunting the Hartebeest, happened to rouse a leopard in a mountainous ravine on the frontier, and forthwith gave him chase. The animal endeavoured to effect his escape by clambering up a steep precipice, but being hotly pressed and wounded, presently turned upon his pursuers with the frantic ferocity peculiar to the species in such emergencies. Springing first on the man who had fired at him, he tore him from his horse to the ground, bit him through the shoulder, and severely lacerated his face with his claws. The other, observing the disastrous situation of his comrade, leapt from his saddle, and essayed to shoot the brute through the head, but whether from trepidation and the fear of wounding his friend, or whether from the quick motions of the animal, he unfortunately contrived to miss his mark. Then came the tug of war. Abandoning his prostrate enemy, the enraged beast darted like lightning upon his second assailant, and ere the boer could stab him with his knife, had actually torn the scalp over his eyes. In this frightful position, the hunter grappled with his savage antagonist, and both struggling for the mastery, away they rolled together down a steep declivity. The whole was but the work of an instant, and ere the man who had been abandoned could start upon his feet or resume his weapon, the combatants were tumbling one over the other in their descent. Reloading his gun, he rushed forward to save the life of his companion, but it was too late. The leopard had seized the wretched victim by the windpipe, and so fearfully mangled him, that death was inevitable, nor had his severely wounded comrade more than the melancholy satisfaction of completing the destruction of the feline foe already exhausted with loss of blood from divers deep wounds inflicted by the knife of the expiring huntsman.'

The only hunting pard seen during our expedition, was detected by my companion at the foot of the Cashan Mountains in the very act of tearing out the reeking entrails of a water-buck. This animal differs in no respect from the cheetah so commonly trained in the East to hunt the black antelope of the plains; and although not very abundant, is found throughout the Amazooloo country. Moselekatse's state apron, entirely composed of tails of the *felinae,* exhibited a large proportion borrowed from the *'Nquane,* while the skins sent by the hands of 'Um Nombate together with other costly gifts from his illustrious master, belonged also to this species, and were crowded with round black dots in place of open rosettes. Although the air and manner of the *Jubata* are unquestionably those of the cat, it doubtless forms the link with the canine group. Slender and elastic in build, and high on its attentuated legs, it presents the fine drawn figure of a greyhound, wearing a feline head and tail, the latter appendage being, however, extremely bushy towards the extremity. The claws are semi-retractile only, and although the wiry limbs are fitted for the strong muscular exertion required by the miraculous vigour and velocity of the animals's bounds, which impart a lightning-like speed that can laugh at the fleetest antelope, and for a few hundred yards, far exceeds that of the swiftest racehorse they are yet altogether deficient in that remarkable weight and substance which render so formidable a pat even, from the paw of the true-leopard. Both these species are the deadly enemies of the pig faced baboon, large colonies of which people the rugged regions of southern Africa. Great, hairy, athletic villains, forming the outposts of some mountain garrison, often advanced towards our party with an inquisitive look, and deliberately seated themselves on the rocks above us, as if debating over the propriety of what they were evidently pleased to consider a trespass upon their legitimate domain.

In point of personal attractions the pig-faced baboon odious and disgusting though he be, has, if anything, perhaps rather the advantage of the genuine Bushman, who most decidedly forms the connecting link with *Homo sapiens,* but in the scale of creation is barely one grade removed from the 'beasts that perish'. Meagre, bow-legged and ill-made the stature of these wild aborigines rarely exceeds four feet. High cheek bones, blear eyes, crisp and coarse wool disposed over the head in detached tufts, together with prominences of fat, jutting out in parts of the body where they prove the least ornamental, render the pygmies sufficiently hideous; nor do they spare either pains or filth to perfect the disgusting exterior with which Dame Nature has invested them. Driven by the gradual encroachments of the European colonists to seek an asylum in the pathless desert, they subsist precariously from day to day upon bulbous roots, reptiles and the larvae of ants, abiding chiefly in holes and crannies:

Where flock nocturnal bats, and birds obscene.

Unblessed among the nations of the earth — heedless of futurity, and forgetful of the past, without either laws, arts or religion, only a faint glimmering ray of instinct guides their benighted path; whilst possessed of neither flocks nor herds, and unacquainted with agriculture, the most wealthy of the wandering outcasts can boast of no property beyond his rude weapons, and his starving dog — his hand being raised against every man, as is every man's hand against him.

The traveller might almost pass from end to end of a country infested by these troglodytic imps, without even suspecting that it was inhabited, were it not for occasional serious depredations committed upon his property. Although the men could sometimes be perceived scampering like so many Tom Thumbs towards their mountain fastnesses, or warily reconnoitring our cavalcade from some craggy summit, such is their general distrust of visitors, and of a troop of horsemen in the plain more especially, that they could seldom be induced to hazard an interview. During the night, their watch fires often burned brightly on the surrounding hills, and it was no uncommon event to come upon a nest of woman encamped near some stagnant pool. The gypsies usually approached with great familiarity, patting their shrivelled stomachs in token of their palpable emptiness, and importuning for tobacco, which luxury was invariably doled out to them by the inch. But it was written on the page of our destiny that our intercourse with these 'daughters of the desert' should bring upon us foul disaster. Almost within sight of the colonial hills, we halted one evening during our return pilgrimage, in the midst of a wide plain, whence arose an isolated tumulus in the figure of an Egyptian pyramid. Among some bluff rocks about its base, a knot of the witches held their orgies, and scarcely were the teams unyoked, before we were waited upon by a nymph whose foot measured barely four inches in length, and whose native charms enhanced, by copious unguents of red clay and fat, completely turned the heads of the Hottentots, that of the gallant Andries in particular. This Cinderella, who was followed by five wrinkled hags bringing fuel and wild roots for barter, gave us to understand in the mellifluous Dutch tongue, of which she was perfect mistress, that she had recently absconded from a farmer residing in the Sneuwbergen, whose slave she had been from infancy; and after receiving a suitable bribe of tobacco, she obligingly directed us to a dirty pool at some distance, whither the thirsty oxen were immediately driven to water. The unfortunate animals, having fasted the preceding day and night, were then left to graze in a verdant hollow, whence it did not appear probable that they would stray; but about midnight, the roar of a lion being followed by a general rush towards the wagons, Andries, who stood next to the roster for duty, was appointed to keep watch. Spent with fatigue, and possessing withal a most gentlemanly abhorrence of anything like trouble, the worthy did not long preserve his vigil, and as a natural consequence of his drowsiness, at break of day not an ox was to be seen. This being an event of very common occurrence, created small uneasiness, nor would it in all probability have booted much, had the culprit, in lieu of dallying with the pretty Bush girl, atoned for his past misdeeds by a suitable display of activity. But although the siren soon contrived to gull him with the assurance that she had seen the missing cattle hard by only a few minutes before, all that day, and a part of the next, were passed in a state of feverish anxiety, and in abortive attempts to recover the absentees — someone of the many of our scouts who had been despatched on the trail, dropping in occasionally with a blank face, and the information of his having also failed. At last it was ascertained that the whole drove had gone off at a gallop several miles towards some distant hills, and a conviction that they must have been chased either by lions or Bushmen, imparted to our situation an aspect so lowering, that I determined at once to proceed in person to the rescue. Accompanied by Piet, and provided with rations for two days, I had cantered less than half way towards the hills, when Andries and Cobus, who had been left to carry on the tracks, were descried plying the lash, and approaching at speed, with the dismal tidings that our herd was in the custody of a troop of Bushmen occupying the summit of the nearest eminence, whence one of the pygmies in broken Dutch had challenged the gallant equestrians to do them battle. Cobus, who the morning before, when he dreamed not of the real state of affairs, had ridden forth gasconading of his prowess in arms, now repeated several times emphatically that the contemptible spokesman had actually defied him in terms derogating from his valour. 'Here', said he, 'here stand your oxes, come up if you're a man, come! take them, ye poltroons an ye dare!' Yet although mounted, and abundantly equipped with ammunition, these hulking white-livered villains did not blush to acknowledge that their personal fears had induced them to decline the invitation:

But to avoid the foe's pursuit,
With spurring put their cattle to 't,
And till all four were out of wind,
And danger too, ne'er looked behind.

Neither was it now possible to persuade them to turn back with

XXVIII. 1. FELIS LEOPARDUS: THE LEOPARD.
2. FELIS JUBATA: THE HUNTING PARD.

me; the enemy, they averred, being so exceedingly numerous, and ensconced in so strong a position, that nothing could be attempted without a much larger force. *'Neen'* quoth Cobus, urging on his steed in the direction of our camp, *'neen ik wil niet. Ik is for de Boschmans bung.'*

Here then, like sailors who have foundered upon a rock when within sight of their destined haven, were we, after weathering many a storm, and safely accomplishing the most hazardous portion of our journey, left at last a wreck in the desert. The vindictive and improvident character of the *Troglodytes,* aptly surnamed the 'ox eaters' rendered it but too probable that the whole of our unfortunate beasts had already been sacrificed to their malice, and to their ogre-like appetites, but the day was at all events too far spent to admit of our disturbing their revels before dark and the night being moonless, it was necessary that our attack should be delayed until the following morning. Nor did it appear unlikely that a party of the marauders might be lurking in the hill, ready to fall upon the wagons during the anticipated absence of the owners, for the hateful squaws, with the flirt at their head, at their head had deserted their abode late the preceding day — a filthy area, fortified by masses of rock heaped together by the hand of nature, and overgrown with wild olives, being now inhabited by none save meagre curs, which had been left by the vindictive sprites, to guard from the assaults of vultures the garbage and putrid skins with which the trees were festooned. After much deliberation, therefore, it was resolved to leave Claas and Frederick, two perfect old women, who confessed their inability to fight, together with the two domestics, whose black beards, to say nothing of the broken muskets with which they were armed, were calculated to instill terror into the stoutest heart — starting ourselves with the other five Hottentots in the dead of night, in order, if possible, to avoid creating suspicion of our departure. All the preliminaries of a Bushman hunt thus skillfully arranged, the best horses were selected and fastened to the wagons, and one hundred rounds of ball cartridge having been served out to each of the little band, we retired to rest, leaving the chronometer in charge of *Coeur de Lion,* with instructions to observe his wonted vigilance, and keeping both his eyes steadily fixed upon the hands, not fail to arouse us when they pointed at the hour of twelve.

I was, however, still wide awake, conjecturing the success of our projected commando, when the watchful valet thrust his well-furnished chin under the canvas curtain of the wagon, and in a tremulous voice proclaimed that it was high time to be up and doing. With the design of inspiring chivalrous sentiments, a dram of ardent spirits was forthwith issued to each Hottentot knight-errant, and not a syllable having been spoken above a whisper, the skeleton steeds were silently caparisoned, and we commenced our stealthy march towards the enemy's position:

Most mighty hunters, for our prey was man.

The night was cold and clear, and withal gloriously starlight: and it was in truth a goodly sight to behold the dusky band of gay cavaliers, girded everyone about with his furniture of war, and carrying a heavy carbine on his shoulder, pricking jauntily over the plain. The distance of the Bushman castle being not less than eighteen miles, it was requisite, in order to arrive in proper time, that we should move on as briskly as possible. Ever and anon, whilst we cantered blindly along, in momentary apprehension of losing each other, some one of the party was to be seen floundering among the *meerkat* burrows by which the sandy soil was completely undermined. Herds of timid springboks, upon whose nocturnal repose we had unceremoniously obtruded, bounded panic-stricken across our path; and spectral gnoos, galloping inquisitively up at intervals, stood within pistol shot, whisking their snowy tails, and bellowing defiance. After three hours' journeying we arrived on the bank of a narrow stream, completely choked with high bulrushes and tangled sedge; shortly after forcing our way through which abode of lions, not without incredible difficulty and many casualties, we descried the Lilliputian fortress towering before us in dim perspective. There was yet no glimmering of dawn, but the whoop of the disappointed hyena returning to his lair, mingled with the waning cry of the jackal assuring us that the night was nearly spent, we halted for a few minutes to hold a council of war, whereat it was decided that we should ascend the hill from the opposite side, and having carried the enemy's position in reverse by a *coup de main,* should shoot all who made any show of resistance. Dismounting accordingly, and leading our steeds, we noiselessly groped our way among thorns and boulder stones to the summit of the ridge, which, although rather abrupt in front, was spread out behind into easy undulations. Here the horses, after having been fastened together by their bridles, were left in charge of Cobus, whose heart again began to sink within him; the rest of the Hottentots, with ourselves, creeping on all fours towards the table land occupied by the enemy of whose increasing proximity our noses began now to apprize us. Piet, who was in the van, presently made a warning sign, when peeping cautiously with uncovered heads over a natural parapet, we could perceive

Plate XXVIII (1): *Felis leopardus* — leopard — *tiger* of the Cape colonists

Generic Character — Adult male about two feet seven inches high at the shoulder, and seven feet six inches in extreme length. Claws retractile, chin, neck, breast, belly and inside of extremities, mottled black and white. The rest varying in different specimens between yellow, tawny, fulvous and reddish brown, irregularly marked with open black rings *en form de roses* which vary greatly in number, size and appearance, in different sexes, and at different ages or seasons and contract into full spots about the head, neck and limbs. Tail about two feet eight inches long, spotted and ringed with black. Ears round. Whiskers strong and white. Eyes yellow.

Female similar, but smaller. Monogamous or solitary. Inhabits thick coverts and rocky situations both within and without the Colony.

According to Dr Smith it is difficult to find any two individuals of this species which exactly resemble each other. The ground colour is subject to considerable variation, not only in the different sexes, but even in the same sex at different ages and at different times of the year. The spots are also found to vary in appearance and number, and the tail has seldom the colours arranged in the same way in any two specimens. The female as met with in South Africa, is commonly about a third smaller than the male, with the ground colour generally darker, at least upon the back and upper portions of the sides. The occurrence of such discrepancies may probably have given rise to the establishment of more species than actually exist in nature, and when the *felis leopardus, F Pardus* and *F Pardus antiquorum*, are compared together with attention, and the variations to which the first is known to be subject, are kept in view, it will probably be admitted that there are not three species but one species.

Plate XXVIII (2): *Felix jubata* — hunting pard — *luipaard* of the Cape colonists — *'nquane* of the Bechuana

Generic Character — Size of both sexes about that of a greyhound. Body slender; legs very long, claws semi retractile. Belly and insides of extremities white; the rest pale yellow, studded with small round black spots, larger on the back and outside of the thighs. Hair of the upper part of the neck and withers, rather long, forming a small mane. A black stripe on the ears and another from the corners of the eyes to the angle of the mouth. Tail annulated with black and white bars and tipped with white.

Inhabits open rocky situations. Not very common.

fires burning about two hundred yards in advance; and thus securely ambushed, scarcely daring even to breathe, we awaited the approach of dawn with a degree of nervous impatience which will be correctly estimated by those who reflect, that upon its successful issue the salvation of our wagons and property almost entirely depended.

Whilst still watching the cold darkness of night, which seemed as though it would have lasted forever, the bright morning star, that joyous herald whose appearance I had never hailed with greater delight, shot suddenly like a rocket above the horizon. A faint light immediately pervaded the eastern sky, before which, as it gradually increased the stars, already winking as if drowsy with their long vigil, fast faded away, though the earth still continued in night. Imperceptibly almost, this light had presently given place to a ruddy tint, which speedily extended itself over the whole vault of heaven; but although the outline of objects in the extreme distance could now be indistinctly traced in sombre brown, against the background of a sky cloudless to the zenith, those immediately about us were yet shrouded in darkness. Around, all was silent as the tomb, not a zephyr disturbing the death-like stillness that was reigning. As objects became gradually plainer, the shadowy forms of several conical reed huts could be distinguished; and lastly by a still less dubious light, the prostrate carcase of many of our pet oxen became visible, a surfeited old vulture, the genius of desolation, mounting sentry over them. Alas! it was then even as we had feared; but if indeed we were irretrievably ruined, it was some consolation to know that the moment for taking vengeance had arrived. Every rifle was noiselessly cocked, and a finger flew to every trigger, as with palpitating hearts and wary tread we stole over the parapet towards the wretched wigwams. Woe betided that luckless wight who had there been found sleeping — he would never have awoke again! But although smouldering fires were smoking in various directions, every cabin proved to be deserted; and after visiting each in succession, and diligently searching every nook and cranny without being able to discover a solitary human being, we turned for a moment to contemplate the tragic scene before us. Nineteen of our gallant teams, swollen almost to bursting from the operation of a subtile poison, and disfigured by many a wanton wound, lay stretch in the wild enclosures, from which arose the most sickening of savage odours. Lean dogs:

Gorging and growling o'er carcase and limb,

held their carnival over the half-devoured dead, but were far too busy even to bark at our intrusion; whilst torpid vultures distended to such a size that they could with difficulty hop out of our way, were perched like harpies upon the surrounding rocks.

It was by this time broad daylight. The blue mountain peaks to the southward arose like islands above the sea of mist which floated over the intervening valley, and as the sun's genial influence gradually raised the white veil, were each converted into an altar whence a cloud of incense ascended towards heaven. To our delight a few of the oxen being now perceived standing in a cleugh at the foot of the hill, a party was immediately detached to take possession of them. Seventeen drooping wretches, with glazed eyes and fallen crests, were here huddled together, some shivering in the last agonies of death, and others with staring coats barely able to rise. In addition to sundry wounds which had been inflicted by our merciless and malicious foes whilst urging them across the plain, the unfortunate animals had recently received many cold-blooded gashes bestowed apparently with the design of rendering them unserviceable to ourselves. Maddened with rage at the heart-rending prospect before us, again and again did we search every chink and rifted den, and unweariedly did we case about upon the hard soil for the trail of the marauders. Grim satyr-faced baboons railed hoarsely at us from their rocky clefts, and to which side soever we turned, the slope of the hill was strewed with mouldering human bones; but after the closest scrutiny, no object could be discovered upon which we might wreak our vengeance. A rheebok, disturbed by our matin approach, had unfortunately bounded through the encampment, and given the alarm to the dwellers with owls and bats who, thought doubtless spectators of all that we were doing, had effectually concealed themselves from view; and after the strictest scrutiny nine tracks only could be discovered. Of these six belonged to females, and one was that of our bewitching acquaintance! Barely four inches in length, but yet fully developed, there could be no mistaking her footmark; and whilst not a doubt now remained that Cinderella and her elfin colleagues had from our very first arrival been aiding and abetting the 'pirates of the desert' to our ruin, it became equally evident that our doughty followers must have fled — not from the overwhelming host which their heated imaginations had conjured into existence, but from the empty challenge of a woman!

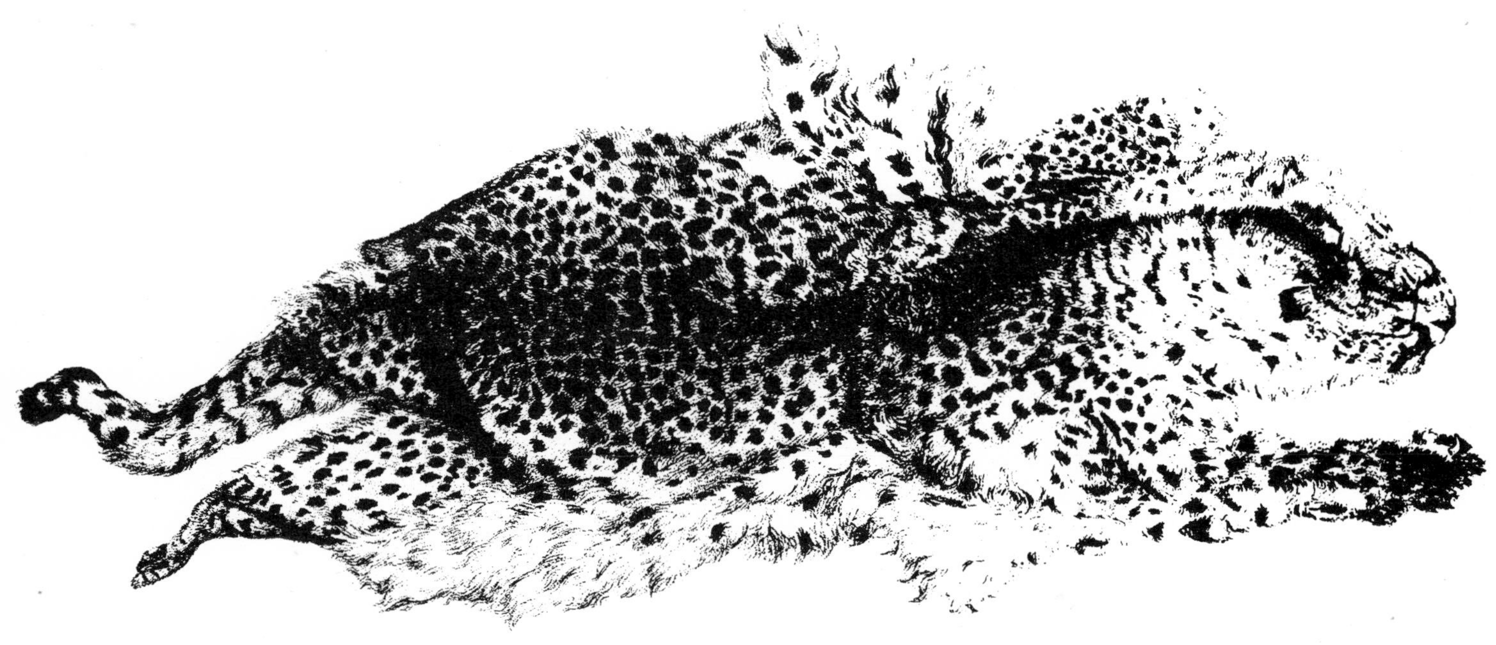

Skin of the African hunting pard, as preserved by Captain Harris

29

African Lion

Now while the shades
Of night hang lowering o'er the mountain's brow,
Ang hunger keen, and pungent thirst of blood,
Rouse up the slothful beast, he shakes his sides,
Slow rising from his lair, and stretches wide
His ravenous jaws with recent gore distain'd.
The forest trembles as he roars aloud,
Impatient to destroy.

You who have beheld the blood-seeking monarch of the forest but in crippling captivity, immured in a cage barely double his own length, until his brawny sinews have become relaxed by irksome confinement, have seen but the shadow of the lordly savage that wields the sceptre of the desert! The pen and the pencil are alike inadequate to do justice to the majesty of this terrible original as he appears when prowling at liberty over his native plains; and neither by verbal description, nor even by the most accurate of portraits can I hope to convey more than a feeble representation of him, beneath the gleam of whose tawny eye the brute creation quail. Side by side with the aristocratic unicorn:

the royal lion
Rampant in golden treasure,

a fit emblem of the courage of Britain's sons, has from time immemorial formed the most prominent figure of our national heraldry; and from the earliest periods of antiquity down to the present day, in his character of King of Beasts, he has maintained over the human mind an ascendancy, which his noble and imposing presence, his gigantic bodily powers, his undaunted resolution and his dignified self-possession, are alike calculated to inspire. That haughty growl, the deep-toned thunder of the roar, the fixed and steady gaze of his terribly expressive eye, proclaim him *facile princeps.* Combining the models of strength and of agility, his carnivorous regimen, his predatory habits and the tremendous machinery by which he is adapted for the work of destruction, have created Leo indisputable tyrant of the waste.

It is in the scorched and desolate regions of the torrid zone, whence mankind are excluded by the rigorous heat of climate, that the lion has established his headquarters, and may most properly be said to reign Lord Paramount. The desert of Zahara and the interior tracts of the vast continent of Africa, exhibit him in all his grandeur, and in uncontrolled abundance, his disposition partaking strongly of the ardour of his native soil. Residing in southern Africa chiefly on immense open plains which are in no way redeemed from the pristine sterility of any attempt at cultivation, the Prince of the Felinae, is an invariable attendant upon the great migratory herds of quaggas, gnoos and springboks which there abound; and to these, rather than to the genus *Homo,* he forms an object of unceasing dread; the number of bleaching skeletons wherewith the lone pastures are embellished; fully attesting the extent of the havoc he commits. After the sun had declined towards the western horizon, when the:

shades of eve come slowly down,
And woods are wrapt in deeper brown;

forth stalks the despot, attended by a knot of hungry vultures; and early in the morning, should his nocturnal foray have proved unsuccessful, may he be seen with taselled tail erect, chasing his dismayed subjects over the open plain. Twice I chanced upon the dropsical carcase of a fine fat eland whereon His Majesty had only the moment before completed an early repast, the entrails yet reeking, and the sand still moist which the prints of his heavy feet had displaced. No sooner is his appalling voice heard rolling along the ground like breakers of the sea, than every animal reposing upon the waste, starts upon its feet, and betaking itself to headlong flight, not infrequently rushes into the teeth of the very danger it is seeking to avoid:

there to the solitary lion's roar
So many echoes answer that there seems
Ten in the field for one; where'er they turn,
The flying animals from cave to cave,
Hear his voice issuing, and recoil aghast
Only to meet it nearer than before;
Or o'er they see his shadow, or his face,
Fall dead before his thunder-striking paw!

Scarcely a day passed towards the tropic without our party observing one or more either in deep repose amid the straggling thickets of brushwood and evergreens which skirt the 'green pastures by the quiet waters' issuing from their lair among clumps of reeds and mat rushes, or, resolute and slow, promenading over the open plain in troops to the number of four or five. A shaggy truculent-looking rascal was observed on one occasion to emerge from his hiding place as the twilight drew on, stretch himself like a drowsy tom cat, and walk steadily forward with a look that seemed to imply, 'know Sirs, that I'm not to be trifled with.' Yet, like the rest of the brute creation, Leo uniformly retreated when aware of the approach of man, seldom during the day manifesting the slightest inclination to be uncivil unless we first commenced hostilities. This fact, while it will not fail to astonish those who couple the idea of a violent and sudden death with the bare proximity of a lion, may readily enough be accounted for by the animal's nocturnal habits, and the consequent inability of his eye, in common with that of most others of the cat tribe, to bear a strong light. The inconvenience with which he may thus be supposed to support the glare of a tropical sun reflected from a sandy soil, naturally enough begets an unwillingness to measure his strength with man, should he happen to cross his path in the full blaze of day. 'Attitude, physiognomy and language,' remarks the eloquent Buffon, 'proclaim the rudest savage that traverses the desert, to be lord of the prone and mute creation;' nor does the character of supremacy which the Most High hath stamped upon the human brow, fail to instill dread into the stout heart of the King of Beasts, or to induce him to avoid an encounter, unless put upon his mettle, or urged to desperation by the qualms of hunger. Where animal food is so abundant as in the southern

W. C. Harris

XXIX. FELIS LEO: THE LION.

regions of Africa, this latter must be a contingency of somewhat rare occurrence; and although all feline obtruders within the precincts of our camp were saluted with a broadside from the top of the white canvas roofs of the wagons, those that could manage it were invariably suffered to effect their escape; the badness and low condition of our horses rendering us little disposed to throw down the gauntlet in the field, to 'beard the lion' in his den or to risk the issue of combat with so formidable an enemy when rendered desperate by the smarting of gunshot wounds.

But if the unmolested lion is little to be dreaded so long as daylight lasts, widely different is the case during the dark nights, when after a lowering evening, the clouds are wont to gather in every quarter and the most vivid flashes of lightning serve as the forerunners of a deluge. The thunder being vertical, there is no interval between the fire and the crash, which latter may be likened to the peal of a volley of heavy ordnance, discharged in a mountain gorge, where the repercussion from surrounding heights multiplies with terrific energy its deep and astounding echoes. During every night, the lion is abroad patrolling the wilderness in quest of prey; but it is at such dismal periods as these that he evinces particular activity; and the fury of the elements appearing to rouse him thoroughly from his ordinary indolence and torpidity, he was then wont to beleaguer us with less than his customary caution, and appeared in no way dismayed by the incessant barking of our canine companions. Whilst a cutting blast whistled through the unsheltered wagons with a violence that bid fair to overturn them, the foe prowled around our slender breastwork, and roaring in concert with the howling of the tempest, strove ever and anon to effect his entrance into the fold. No possibility existing of keeping up the usual fires for defence against such nocturnal invasion, our cattle became momentarily more restless and uncontrollable; and aware before ourselves of the advent of their blood-thirsty enemy, struggled to break away from the enclosure, in the vain hope of escaping by flight the danger that impended; repeated volleys of firearms alone serving to allay their uneasiness, or to avert the threatened attack. It was our practice to encamp, if possible, near to a grove of mimosas, and the felling two or three dozen of those thorny trees, whilst it was a work of little labour, formed the nucleus of a ring fence which was readily perfected by dragging outwards a few more that it was necessary to clear away from the interior; so that where wood was abundant, a tolerably substantial barrier could always be erected within half an hour of the formation of our camp. But when compelled to pass the night in the open plain without any such fortification, rarely indeed was it that we escaped the depredations of the chief of the carnivora, a sniff of whose odour, like a dram to the Hottentots, invariably put our jaded oxen into such marvellous spirits, that they were often enabled to complete a long march after having appeared too tired to advance another step.

The first impress of the cushioned foot of the lion, when discovered on the sandy plain, caused vast excitement among our followers, who crowded round the spot, and chattering long and incessantly, could at last with difficulty be persuaded that a grim fellow was not *looring* at them from every bush by the wayside. During the still evening that followed, shortly after the sun had ceased to shine upon us, the voice of the prowling savage, like the rumbling of an earthquake, came up repeatedly with the breeze; and about midnight, being encamped on the broken and jungle-cumbered banks of the Meritsane, he introduced himself in a mode befitting his rank and character. An unusual commotion causing us to start from our slumbers, we found that the whole of the cattle had burst through the thorn fence, and panic-stricken, were blindly charging they knew not whither — oxen, horses and sheep, tumbling headlong over the wagon poles, and over each other, in indescribable confusion. The night was intensely dark, and all the watch fires had gone out. *Coeur de Lion,* ever the first to take the alarm, had clambered upon the top of the omnibus, whence he was screaming like a woman for assistance; whilst each Hottentot, as he sprang from his sleep, was precipitately discharging his gun, loaded with a hard bullet, in any direction that the muzzle might happen to have assumed. Of our livestock, the horses were least dismayed; and after floundering about in the dark for a considerable time, and scratching ourselves considerably among the thorns, we succeeded in recovering all save one; but every endeavour to reclaim the oxen and sheep proving abortive, we retired again to our beds, having first ascertained by the light of the candle that the consternation had been caused by three lions, that had entered the fold, and slain two of the sheep.

The moment it was light enough to see, we despatched the Hottentots upon the tracks of the fugitives, escorted by a party of Batlapi who had passed the night in our camp. Some of these latter shortly returned with the flock, several more having however been devoured during their flight; but our own people did not make their appearance again until noon, when they imparted the exhilarating intelligence that the oxen had divided into two parties, and being dreadfully terrified, would not tarry in all probability until they should reach the Kuruman; adding, that if we were desirous or recovering a sufficient number to draw the wagons, each Hottentot must forthwith be provided with one of the best horses, and a week's supply of ammunition. Aware from sad experience of the mischief that would befall our steeds, upon whose well being our future sport entirely depended, we stoutly resisted this modest application, whereupon the whole gang, Claas and Ethaldur alone excepted, begged at once to throw up their commission. Andries, who looked especially out of humour, was evidently the ringleader of this mutiny, as indeed was he of all mischief; but it was not until after he had been bullied into taking his departure on one of the sorriest hacks, accompanied only by Cobus, that we discovered the wretch to have been the instigator of a plot, which had at first been joined by all, to desert us in the wilderness, and abscond to the Colony with the horses and whatever other property they could lay their hands upon. Apprehensive of another attack, we shifted our camp in the afternoon to the opposite bank of the river, clearing away the jungle around the wagons, which were so drawn up on the top

Plate XXIX: *Felis leo* — lion — *leuew* of the Cape colonists — *tao* of the Matabili and Bechuana

Generic Character — Adult male about three feet eight inches high at the shoulder and rather less at the rump. Extreme length usually about ten feet six inches. Figure noble and imposing; the model of activity and strength. Tail three feet long, tufted at the extremity with a tassle of black hair. Ears rounded and black. Five toes on the fore feet, four on the hind. Claws retractile, and each concealed by a tuft of blackish hair. Hair on the body and extremities, short and close, varying in colour, between yellow, tawny, brown and slate colour, according to the age of the animal; but uniformly darker on the upper parts, and lighter on the belly, where it is often dappled. The upper portions of the head, the chin, neck, shoulders and belly, covered with long silky hairs, forming a copious and shaggy mane, which sprouts during the third year, and increases in depth of shade, as the animal advances in age, until it becomes perfectly black. A tuft of black hair under the armpits. An angular black spot at each corner of the mouth on the lower jaw, which is white, bearded and projects beyond the upper. Whiskers and eyebrows strong and white, each hair set in a black spot. Eyeballs yellow, pupils capable of contraction and dilation.

Lioness smaller; more slender, agile and graceful, and destitute of any appearance of a mane. Gregarious in small troops, or solitary. Inhabits variously, but is most usually found on the open plains of the interior among reeds and long grass, or along the wooded banks of rivers. Very numerous towards the Tropic.

of a hillock as to flank the cattle enclosure — an arrangement that was ever afterwards observed with the greatest advantage. Much to our surprise, our friends the Batlapi returned about sunset with all the oxen, reporting that they had overtaken them about twelve miles off, for which signal piece of service they were rewarded, according to previous stipulation, with a yard of tobacco and a tinder-box. Cobus and Andries likewise straggled back during the night, after deeply galling the backs of both horses, as we had anticipated, without, however, obtaining the smallest tidings of the lost one; and it afterwards appeared, that instead of attending to the important business upon which they were sent, they had been engaged in an attempt to destroy a lion, that drove them fairly out of the field after nearly making an end of Cobus. The whole of the following day was passed in fruitless endeavours to recover the truant; and it was not until six months afterwards that we ascertained him to have found his way back to the farm on which he had been bred, in New Hantam, a distance of five hundred miles!

As our little party rolled farther and farther from the abodes of civilized man, few evenings passed during which we did not hear the solemn voice of Leo rumbling along the ground like the murmuring of distant thunder; and in return for our obtrusion upon his legitimate empire, many were the unwelcome visits that he paid us during that hour, when sleep is wont to 'knit up the ravelled sleeve of care'. My first and least agreeable interview with the Governor took place after the night's solitary bivouac on the banks of the Meritsane, detailed in a former chapter. Although long accustomed to the sound of his voice, and to the contemplation of his shaggy figure from the back of an elephant or of a fleet Arab horse, I confess that on the occasion in question, I neither felt soothed by his deep drawn nocturnal music, nor gratified when bestriding a jaded garron the next morning, by the bulldog aspect of his broad tawny muzzle, or the glance of his hazel eye, as he scowled at me over his shoulder. The Meritsane is a positive nest of *felinae* and during my rambles I one morning stumbled upon a den that must from time immemorial have been the lurking-place of a whole troop, presenting as it did the appearance of a perfect Golgotha, rife with emblems of mortality, and redolent of its unsavoury inmates, who, fortunately for me, were from home at the period of my accidental visit. We found the banks of the Bagobone equally infested by the species. Being engrossed with the contemplation of a dead elephant, and with conjectures as to the when and how it had departed this life, 'Lingap suddenly pointed with his assegai to a bush a few yards distant and whispered: *'Tao'* — when I immediately perceived through the umbrage, no fewer than three lionesses fast asleep. Ensconcing himself behind his shield, he made signs to me to fire, which I foolishly did into the middle of the party, springing at the same moment behind a tree which completely screened me. Thus unceremoniously aroused, the royal harem broke covert, roaring in concert, and bounding over brakes and bushes like so many cats over a footstool, darted into an adjacent thicket, whilst we continued our course in the opposite direction as expeditiously as our legs could carry us. I had killed a gallant water-buck the preceding evening not far from this spot, and the report of my rifle caused a lion with his sleek consort to bounce out of a coppice and slink into the dense jungle; Piet, who had been shooting a little higher up the river, also reporting on his return that whilst walking through a patch of long rank grass, he had narrowly escaped treading upon the tail of a huge black male, which he designated *'een groot zwart mannikin.'* The vast abundance of the feline race in this wild spot, induced us to bestow upon our fortifications more labour than usual; nor had we any reason to repent of the precaution, numbers roaring around in every direction until the day broke, and in the face of a blazing watch fire, making three ineffectual attempts to carry the stockade by storm.

Being encamped one moonlight night on the banks of the Machachochan, north of the Cashan Mountains, our slumbers were disturbed by sounds of desperate strife at no great distance, which elicited many surmises as to the nature of the noisy conflict. Proceeding at break of day to the spot, we found that the Emperor had done his pleasure upon an unfortunate cow giraffe, heavy in foal, that had come down to quench her thirst at a pool surrounded by tall green reeds, whence she was surprised, and overthrown on the spot.

The dark nights were unusually tempestuous, but how boisterous soever they might be, the weather generally cleared up with the dawn:

when the orient beam
With blushes paints the morn, and all the race
Carnivorous with blood full gorged retire
Into their darkest cells, there satiated snore
O'er dripping offals, and o'er mangled limbs.

Upon one occasion, however, whilst encamped near a rushy bottom, it continued until nine o'clock to pour with such violence that we were unable to open the canvas curtains of the wagon. Richardson and myself were the first astir, and peeping out during a temporary cessation to ascertain whether there existed any prospect of the rain holding up, we perceived three he lions insolently squatted on their hams in the open plain within one hundred yards of the cattle pound. Their round golden orbs were attentively fixed upon the oxen, whose wet coats stood on end with the cold; and watching their motions from the naked branches of a withered tree at the back of the kraal, sat a family of expectant vultures with drooping wings and ruffled plumage — their hang dog air of poverty and abject humiliation calling to mind a herd of wandering gypsies drying their rags. With a view to the dislodgement of this formidable foraging party our rifles were hastily unstrapped, but the excessive dampness of the atmosphere prevented either of them from exploding. One after another the Hottentots next sprang out of the pack wagon, and exclaiming, *'Almightig, kek daar de leuwen,'* snapped each his long gun at the unwelcome intruders, as they moved sulkily away at a good round trot, and took up their position on a stony eminence within point-blank range. Fresh caps and priming were quickly applied, and a general volley fired by word of command, was followed by the instantaneous demise of the largest, whose muffled cranium was perforated by two bullets at the same instant. His sinewy frame just quivered slightly — his huge head dropped upon the ground — and he was lying on his side a corpse. Swinging their tasseled tails over their backs, the survivors took warning by the fate of their companion, and dashed with a roar into a neighbouring mimosa grove. In another half hour the voice of Leo was again heard at the foot of the mountains, less than a quarter of a mile from the camp; and clambering on to the wagon top we could perceive a savage monster rampant, with his tail hoisted and whirling in a circle — charging vigorously along the base of the range — and in desperate wrath making towards John April who was tending the flock:

Loose in the gale his mane redundant play'd.

whilst everyone instinctively snatched his weapon and calling loudly to warn the expected victim of his danger, rushed to the rescue. But without taking the smallest heed either of the shepherd or his mutton, the infuriated monster, intent upon some urgent business best understood by himself, dashed past at a lumbering gallop, roaring and lashing his dun sides, until concealed behind the mist.

Having advanced one afternoon during our return route some twenty five miles over boundless plains covered with pale yellow dry grass, a long line of karree trees darkening the horizon, proclaimed our approach to some hidden stream; and at a late hour we struck upon a sudden bend of the Vaal River winding abruptly between willowed banks round a narrow peninsula, the neck of which scarcely exceeded six hundred yards in breadth. Whilst our cavalcade was in the act of drawing up near a cluster of deserted Bushman wigwams, three saucy lionesses, as lank and active as greyhounds, leaped out of a bush immediately on our flank; and the lynx-eyed Piet, who vowed that he could discern the tawny muzzle of a fourth, having lustily cracked his long whip into the bush, forth there stalked a venerable lion, evidently as much subdued and enfeebled by years as the poor fellow in *Aesop's Fables,* who was fain to set up for a physician. A bullet discharged from the wagon box as he walked leisurely off 'smote him with a great smiting;' and penetrating the patriach's shoulder, he bounded forward with a roar — thrust his hoary head into a clump of brushwood, and was gathered unto his fathers:

Set were his teeth, his faded eye
Was firmly fixed on vacancy;

and his demise having been tested by a volley directed against his protruded stern, his body was dragged out for inspection. There is much of repose and grandeur about the mortal remains of Leo, and I never recollect to have seen the asserted resemblance to the human face divine, more perfectly than in this subject, already in the last stage of imbecility. Years had robbed him of his pristine vigour, and the honourable scars of many a fierce conflict seamed his scabby hide. His once splendid mane had waxed scant and scraggy — his yellow fangs were worn away to their stumps — and so deeply had age furrowed his savage cheek, that with his overhanging brow and bearded under jaw, he might have furnished a handsome portrait for a toothless Jew. The weight of the lion's body as compared with its size is very remarkable, and is accounted for by the singular density of the muscles and the compactness of the principal bones; which latter, like the teeth of the hippopotamus, will produce fire with steel. The force with which he must alight after a bound of fifteen or twenty feet is therefore sufficiently obvious, and his massy paw will batter in the skull of an ox quite as effectually as if a sledge hammer has been employed.

Among the Dutch colonists it is a fashionable belief that there are two distinct species of the African lion, which they designate the *vaal* and the *zwart,* or the yellow and the black variety, maintaining stoutly that the one is infinitely less ferocious than the other. But I need scarcely inform the well instructed reader that both the colour and the size depend chiefly upon the animal's age — the development of the physical powers and of the mane also — which does not sprout until the third year, but continues to increase long after the wearer has arrived at maturity — being principally influenced by a like contingency. In point of size and complexion the South African subject differs in no respect from that found so abundantly in Guzerat — one of the only two provinces of India wherein the species exists — measuring usually between ten and eleven feet in extreme length, and varying in hue betwixt ash colour and tawny dun; but generally possessing a much more elaborate and matted mane, which peculiarity is attributable in a great measure to the less jungly character of the country that he infests, and to the more advanced age to which, from the comparatively small number of his mortal foes, he is suffered to attain. In India the lion is often compelled to establish himself in heavy jungles, which comb out a considerable portion of the long loose silky hair about his head and neck; but this is seldom the case on the arid plains of Africa, where the covert being chiefly restricted to the banks of rivers, or to isolated springs, he rests satisfied with a less impervious shade, and is often disturbed from a clump of rushes barely large enough to conceal his portly figure.

Although probably possessing none of those magnanimous qualities that have been attributed to the Royal Beast by the romantic imagery of poetical naturalists, yet when compared with the tiger — which it has already been said exists not in Africa — the lion is unquestionably a noble animal. He displays more confidence and self-possession, with a much larger share of intrepidity than the only other cat that can vie with him in point of size or power; and he is consequently less easily irritated, and far more resolute in his charge when fairly provoked to a combat. Wounds then enrage, but rarely serve to terrify him. A tiger in full career will frequently turn at the bare report of a rifle, and whether wounded or not by the discharge, will almost invariably retreat at the flash of gunpowder in his face — but a lion, never; and whether in Asia or in Africa, nothing short of death, or of a wound that places him completely *hors de combat,* will divert him from his object. In the Colony, the approved method of assailing this formidable quarry is to badger him with curs of every degree, until he abandons the covert, and stands at bay in the open plain; when the band of hunters march forward in a compact body, and fire deliberately by kneeling sections from under the girths of their horses, which with their cruppers turned towards the enemy, are drawn up in form of a crescent. The native tribes, and especially the warlike Matabili, contrive to work his destruction without the aid of firearms, but their victories are often dearly purchased. Should a lion attack the king's herds, either his death or that of the guardians invariably ensues. Armed only with a sheaf of assegais and an ox hide shield, they rush in upon the marauder, and generally at the expense of one or two of their lives, which are held of small account, retire from the conflict bearing with them the head and paws to their Royal master — trophies of their valour which are left to decompose within the area of the imperial kraal, every part whereof is strewed with the relics of wild animals.

The only instance in which I believe our party to have had a very narrow escape from the clutches of the *felinae,* was on the occasion adverted to in a preceding chapter, of our arrival at the source of the Likwa, immediately prior to our exit from Moselekatse's dominions. It was late in the afternoon when we prepared to unyoke, and two lions, with manes like new mops, were observed actively shifting their quarters among the labyrinth of ravines, and seemingly vastly disposed to assert their pretensions to the dominion of the desert, and to dispute our right to encamp thereon. My whole attention being shortly afterwards directed towards the slaughter of a hippopotamus that was ploughing up the turbid waters, and making directly for the shore, the first I observed of a couchant lioness was her tufted tail vibrating angrily among the grass within a yard only of my foot. Happily her buttocks were turned towards me, and her ladyship's thoughts were so full of beef, that I had time to retreat and to draw back Piet, who was even still nearer than myself, without her being aware of our intrusion; and she would have retired quietly enough, had not another of the Hottentots stupidly fired at, and turned her. Roaring, brandishing her tail, and ripe for any mischief, she dashed impetuously through the middle of our party, and had she been wounded by the discharge, there would doubtless have been a casualty amongst us; but as usual, the ball had fortunately missed the mark, and finding that we all stood to our arms, she merely favoured each with a good natured glance *en passant,* curling up her wrinkled nose, and exhibiting her white fangs, until being joined by her Royal mate, they both dived into the thick jungle, with which portions of the river bank were clothed.

I have already cited one instance of the King of Beasts having been detected in the act of carousing over game that had not fallen to his own talons. Returning with Maphook on another occasion to the theatre of my morning's sport, in order to take up the horns of a koodoo which I had concealed in a bush, I was not a little surprised to find an enormous fellow, rougher than a French poodle, banqueting upon the headless trunk, whilst an odious assemblage of eager vultures garrisoned the adjacent trees, and awaited their turn when the gorged monarch should make way for them. Immediately upon my appearance, His Majesty walked heavily off, expressing by a stifled growl his Royal displeasure at being thus unceremoniously disturbed at his meals. It was not, however, destined that our acquaintance should terminate here; for passing the scene of this introductory interview the following morning, Richardson and myself were suddenly made aware of the monster's presence, by perceiving a pair of round gooseberry eyes, with small jet black pupils, glaring upon us from beneath the screen of a shady bush; and instantly upon reining up our horses, out the grim savage bolted with a roar like thunder, and bounded across the plain with the agility of a greyhound. The luxuriant beauty of his shaggy black mane, which in its full and bushy grandeur almost swept the ground, tempted us, contrary to established rule, to offer him battle with the design of appropriating his *regalia* — and on putting spurs to our horses, he no sooner felt himself hotly pursued, than he swung round like a cutter letting go her anchor under full press of canvas, and standing at bay in a mimosa grove, measured the strength of his assailants with a port the most noble and imposing. Disliking our appearance, however, and not relishing the smell of gunpowder, he soon abandoned the grove and took up a strong position on the summit of an adjacent stony hill, of which the base was so thickly clothed with thorn trees, that we could only obtain a clear view of him from the distance of three hundred yards, and were thus compelled to open battery at long range. Crouched on this fortified pinnacle like the sculptured figure at the entrance of a nobleman's park, the enemy disdainfully surveyed us for several minutes, daring us to approach with an air of conscious power and pride which well beseemed his grizzled form. As the rifle balls whizzed about his ears, and ploughed up the ground nearer and nearer at each discharge, his wrath, as indicated by his glistening eyes, increased roar and more impatient switching of the tail, was clearly getting the mastery over his prudence. Presently a shot broke his brawny leg. Down he came upon the other three with reckless impetuosity, his tail straight out and whirling on its axis, his mane bristling on end, and his lurid eyeballs flashing rage and vengeance. Unable, however, to overtake our horses, he shortly retreated under a galling fire, limping and discomfited to his stronghold. Again we bombarded him, and again, exasperated, he rushed into the plain with headlong fury — the blood now streaming from his open jaws, and dyeing his clotted mane with crimson:

To his bold charge the savage turns alone,
He murmurs fury with a hollow groan;
He grins, he foams, he rolls his eyes around,
Lashed by his tail his heaving sides resound;
Calling up all his rage, he grinds his teeth,
Resolved on vengeance, or resolved on death.

It was a gallant charge, but it was to be his last. A well directed shot arrested him in full career, he sprang into the air as if seized with vertigo — pitched with violence upon his ample skull, and throwing a complete somersault, subsided amid a cloud of dust!

In the year 1705, half a century after the first establishment of the Dutch at the Cape, Jos Sterreberg Kupt, the Landdrost, proceeded on a journey into the interior to purchase oxen for the Dutch East India Company; and the following curious adventure, at which I have enjoyed many a hearty laugh, is thus quaintly related in the journal of his proceedings. Modern lions do not require so heavy an expenditure of ammunition.

'We pitched our tent about a musket shot from the kraal, and went to rest, but were soon disturbed; for about midnight the cattle and horses which were standing between the wagons, began to start and run, and one of the drivers to shout, on which everyone hurried out of the tent with his gun. About thirty paces from it stood a lion, which on seeing us, walked very deliberately about thirty paces farther, behind a small thorn bush, carrying something with him, which I took to be a young ox. We fired more than sixty shots at the bush, and pierced it stoutly, without perceiving any movement. The south-east wind blew strong, the sky was clear and the moon shone very bright, so that we could perceive everything at that distance. After the cattle had been quieted and I had looked over everything, I missed the sentry from behind the tent, Jan Smit, from Antwerp, belonging to the Groene kloof. We called as loudly as possible, but in vain — nobody answered; from which I concluded that the lion had carried him off. Three or four men then advanced very cautiously to the bush, which stood right opposite to the door of the tent to see if they could discover anything of the man, but returned helter-skelter, for the lion who was still there, rose up and began to roar. They found there the musket of the sentry, which was cocked, and also his cap and shoes.

'We fired again about a hundred shots at the bush (which was sixty paces from the tent and only thirty from the wagons, and whereat we were able to point as at a target), without perceiving anything of the lion, from which we concluded that he was killed, or had run away. This induced the marksman, Jan Stamanz, to go and see if he was there still or not, taking with him a firebrand. But as soon as he approached the bush, the lion roared terribly and leapt at him; on which he threw the firebrand at him, and the other people having fired about ten shots, he retired directly to his former place behind that bush.

'The firebrand which he had thrown at the lion, had fallen in the midst of the bush and favoured by a strong south-east wind it began to burn with a great flame so that we could see very clearly into and through it. We continued our firing into it without the least intermission; the night passed away and the day began to break, which animated everyone to aim at the lion, because he could not go from thence without exposing himself entirely, as the bush stood directly against a steep kloof. Seven men, posted on the farthest wagons, watched him to take aim at him if he should come out.

'At last before it became quite light, he walked up the hill with the man in his mouth, when about forty shots were fired at him without hitting him, although some went very near. Every time this happened he turned round towards the tent and came roaring towards us; and I am of opinion that if he had been hit, he would have rushed on the people and the tent.

'When it became broad daylight, we perceived by the blood and a piece of the clothes of the man, that the lion had taken him away and carried him with him. We also found behind the bush, the place where the lion had been keeping the man, and it appeared impossible that no ball should have hit him, as we found in that place several balls beaten flat. We concluded that he was wounded and not far from this. The people therefore requested permission to go in search of the man's corpse in order to bring it, supposing that by our continual firing, the lion would not have had time to devour much of it. I gave permission to some, on condition that they should take a good party of armed Hottentots with them and made them promise that they would not run into danger, but keep a good look out and be circumspect. On this, seven of them, assisted by forty three Hottentots followed the track, and found the lion about half a league farther on, lying behind a little bush. On the shout of the Hottentots he sprang up and ran away, on which they all pursued him. At last the beast turned round, and rushed, roaring terribly, amongst the crowd. The people, fatigued and out of breath with their running, fired and missed him, on which he made directly towards them. The captain or chief head of the Kraal, here did a brave act in aid of two of the people whom the lion attacked. The gun of one of them misfired, and the other missed his aim, on which the captain threw himself between the lion and the people, so close, that the lion struck his claws into the kaross or skin cloak of the Hottentot. But he was too agile for him, doffed his mantle, and stabbed him with an assegai. Instantly the other Hottentots hastened on and adorned him with their assegais, so that he looked like a porcupine. Notwithstanding this he did not leave off roaring and leaping, and bit off some of the assegais, until the marksman, Jan Stamanz, fired a ball into his eye, which made him turn over, and he was then shot dead by the other people. He was a tremendously large beast, and had but a short time before carried off a Hottentot from the kraal and devoured him.'

Skin of African lion, as preserved by Captain Harris

30

Hyenas And Wild Dog

And their white trunks crunch'd o'er the whiter skull,
As it slipp'd through their jaws when the edge grew dull,
As they lazily mumbled the bones of the dead,
Where they scarce could rise from the spot where they fed,
So well had they broken a lingering fast
With those who had fallen for that night's repast.

With a view of correctly obtaining the synonyms of the various species of game quadrupeds that form the subjects of the foregoing portraits, it was my wont, whensoever a savage crowd of either sex assembled round our caravan, to display the drawings from the end of the wagon; and the exhibition, whilst it fully answered my purpose, was invariably attended with diverting theatric effect. Although in India, even well educated natives are extremely slow in recognising objects upon paper, each animal was in its turn acknowledged by the sable daughters of Africa, who did not fail to pronounce the native name, or with animated gestures to invite the attention of their neighbours to the sight. This fact will appear the less extraordinary when it is considered how constantly the originals are before the eyes of these unsophisticated damsels, and moreover that upon the success of the chase every savage is dependent for both food and raiment. The names of the *ferae naturae* are in fact ever in their mouths; and a long line of women and girls may often be seen working in the fields, their *piochs* or mattocks raised like a company of Amazons under arms, ready to be stuck into the ground at a given signal, and their toil animated by a ditty which comprises the name of every useful animal that their country can afford. Among my motley audience the production of the 'noble elephant' conjuring up recollections of the reigning despot, was followed by an involuntary elevation of the eyelids, but no lips dared to profane the royal title. On beholding the towering giraffe, all clapped their hands together, exclaiming in an ecstasy of delight: *'Intootla! Intootla! Intootla!'* mounting at the same time on tiptoe, and craning their greasy necks in order to make the most of their dumpy figures. *'Imfoobo,'* the apoplectic-looking hippopotamus, caused all beholders to inflate their cheeks and distend their stomachs, ladies who happened to be in a certain delicate condition being forthwith selected as objects of universal merriment; whilst *'Impatoomo'* induced those of the wanton party whose animal spirits were most buoyant, to frisk and caper about in humble imitation of the absurd pranks of that madcap amongst beasts, the gnoo. But upon the production of *the Emperor,* the excitement became even more universal, a general flourish of weapons and thumping of shields on the part of the hitherto silent warriors, being accompanied by an application of fair hands to averted faces, and by exclamations of *Tao*, delivered in a subdued and piano tone. A liberal distribution of snuff and tobacco, together with a peep at their own umber faces in the looking-glass — that never-failing source of surprise and delight to uncivilised beings — for the most part concluded the entertainment; and this latter 'merrye disport' to use the words of old Holinshed, 'so highly pleased them that they expressed their inwardly conceived joy and delight with shrill shouts and variety of gestures.'

Every four-footed denizen of southern Africa that is fairly entitled to a place in the game catalogue, having now passed before the reader in order of review, it remains but to introduce those inseparable attendants upon the sportsman, the scavengers, who complete the work of demolition which the bullet from his grooved rifle shall have commenced. In a wild land where there exist such thronging legions of herbivorous quadrupeds, and where such a goodly host of the more formidable *carnivora* are arrayed against them, it may well be conjectured that there lack not those more humble in the scale, who are at hand to gather up the scraps; and indeed, the multitude of birds of prey, as well as of the carrion-eating *mammiferes,* with which the country is overrun, fully attest the extent of the terrific carnage that must daily be committed.

Less addicted to putrefactions than either of the larger hyaenas, is the *wilde hond* or wild dog, already briefly noticed in these pages as taking the field in large organised bands, and without the aid of a whipper-in, committing extensive havoc among the antilopine tribes. The ravages of this diminutive but formidable species extends also to the flocks and herds of the colonists; an ox, when detected asleep, being as surely deprived of more or less of its tail; whilst the flock of sheep upon which they may fall, whether at pasture or in the fold, is invariably mangled and mauled to an extent ten times exceeding the present wants of the predators, who snap right and left, without the smallest respect either to age or sex. In the jungles of western India I once witnessed the chase of a noble stag by a troop of these self hunting hounds; and although not so fortunate as to see a pack in full cry over the desert plains of Africa, I very frequently disturbed them feasting upon the quarry which had rewarded their industry. On such occasions they were wont to retire sulkily to a little distance, and squatting on their hams, to utter a petulant sort of growl, which ended in a suppressed bark; their ample semi circular ears, neatly rounded as if with the cropping scissors — their black cheeks, bloated as though of the mumps — and their crooked spindle shanks, appearing to have been broken and clumsily spliced — imparting altogether an aspect sufficiently ludicrous. A shot fired into the middle of the kennel was on more than one occasion attended with fatal results; whereupon the survivors, clapping their bushy tricoloured tails betwixt their hinder legs, exhibited a set of snow-white teeth, and grinning repeatedly over their blotched shoulders, as if seeking to ascertain whether any further mischief were meditated, went slouching off with a general howl.

Of the larger species of hyaena, the *straand wolf* of the colonists, covered with long, coarse, shaggy, grey hair, brindled, clouded and barred, most nearly resembles the fetid resurrectionist found in Asia. Solitary in its habits, this animal is better known to residents along the southern coast, where it banquets upon dead whales, and whatever offal may be rejected by the ocean, concealing its beauties during the day in some dormitory within the thick bush which extends in clumps throughout the districts which form its limited habitat.

But the 'real indomitable laughing hyaena', whose spotted figure is ever conspicuous among his carrion-eating confederates, is by far the most formidable and rapacious of this foul-feeding class. Superior in size to the largest mastiff and possessing under his bulldog muzzle a power of jaw, which, whilst it is adapted for grinding the hardest bones, is exceeded in few of the *carnassiers,* all fish come alike to his net. He is, in fact, the vulture of quadrupeds. Feeding chiefly at night, he prowls about the country in sulking gangs, which often comprise twenty or more individuals, committing serious depredations, and eagerly revelling in all kinds of putrescence. Concealed during the day in some loathsome den, amid ruins, craggy rocks and solitary thickets, as evening draws on, the gaunt bone-cracker commences its nocturnal foray, haunting the streets of inhabited villages after bedtime, strolling up and down the lanes in search of offal, carrying off dogs and not infrequently young children or infirm persons; its appetite for human flesh being so sharpened by the practice which obtains among the savage tribes of exposing their dead to be entombed in the maw of beasts of prey, that to pass the night in the open fields, and especially near the confines of a town, could not fail to prove a somewhat hazardous experiment.

The diet, deformity and fierceness of the hyaena having ever rendered it an object of extreme aversion to mankind, few animals have been more misrepresented, or few placed in a more odious light. Credulity has echoed the words of superstition, and the writings of the Greek and Roman naturalists, whilst they furnish abundant proof of the acquaintance of the ancients with the dastardly species, evince also that their knowledge was mixed up with a thousand absurdities which have been too currently received. Owing to a certain glandular pouch beneath the tail, it was believed that the animal could change its sex at pleasure — Pliny and other writers stoutly maintaining that the bone of the neck was jointless, on which account it was considered to possess a peculiar efficacy in magic incantations. Throughout southern Africa, the sullen brute prowls through the crumbling relics of human dwellings — once thronged by busy thousands, but now chiefly tenanted by beasts of darkness; and during the ruthless wars which continually pull down the strength of her barbarous sons, and depopulate her soil, numbers follow the contending armies, escorted by the jackal and the vulture, with whom they would seem to have established a league of perpetual amity. Constant attendants upon the field of battle, these scavengers relieve the living from the trouble of disposing of the dead — the flap of the eagle's wing, and the howl of the hyaena forming the only death note of the fallen warrior:

There as the fierce hyaena stalks
Through the lone desert's dreary walks,
At midnight, and his carnage plies,
Woe to the half dead wretch who spies
The glaring of those large blue eyes,
Amid the darkness of the skies.

Although more in awe of the superior weapons which it has to encounter within the colonial limits, de wolf is yet a perfect bugbear in the eyes of the Batavian. The hand of every man is raised against him, and wheresoever his ill-favoured face may be seen, a mob collects at his heels to hunt him down like a mad dog. Nightly may his long dismal howl be heard, answered from the farmhouses by troops of dogs trolling up with him in full chorus — an unhappy wight being occasionally taken in a trap constructed with a hanging door, and baited with some tempting *morceau,* such as a dead dog or the entrails of a sheep. Miserable indeed is the fate that then awaits the captive. Bent on retaliating upon the hapless delinquent the misdeeds of his pilfering kindred, the Dutchmen indulge in a most savage pastime at his expense. A hind leg having been drawn betwixt the bars of the cage, is perforated above the hock, and a heavy wagon chain being hooked to the sinew, the victim is turned loose and baited till he dies. The carcase uniformly decomposes within a few hours, and so mephitic is the stench of the foul feeding beast, that its remains are invariably left untouched save by its own all-devouring fraternity.

These hideous animals frequently annoyed us all night long by grunting round our fortifications, and by funereal moans aiding 'the Jackal's troop' in too successful endeavours to scare the sheep out of the enclosure. But we often had our revenge, and whilst in pursuit of other game, I several times accidentally knocked up the vagabond's quarters. His bowed hind legs and drooping crupper impart an awkward and shuffling gait when first roused from his lair, and it is some time before his stiff and rheumatic joints acquire suppleness; but after hobbling and limping a little distance he is enabled to scamper over hill and dale with ludicrous alacrity. Whilst his round blue tapers served during the dark nights as an excellent mark, the extreme clearness of the atmosphere, added to the brilliancy of the stars, usually favoured an accurate aim; and the largest of several slain during the campaign was by the clear light of the moon, shot through the broad cranium as he was in the act of skulking under our sheep pen. So timid had the little flock at last become from repeated depredations, which on more than one occasion extended to no fewer than three victims in a single night, that the slightest noise was sufficient to put the whole to flight — their truancy invariably resulting in the further diminution of their numbers. But the hardihood of the survivors became daily more the theme of admiration, an instance of footsoreness rarely occurring during the longest march. When we did, the unhappy cripple either rode in the omnibus, or was consigned to the *Fireworshipper,* at whose hands, for good and substantial reasons already assigned, he had little mercy to expect. Their timidity increasing in the ratio of their reduction in numerical strength, the remnant took alarm one night on the plains of the River Vaal, where no materials for a fence could be collected, and dashing off for the last time, ran into the embraces of a lurking gang of Bushmen.

Popular fable has assigned to the yelping jackal the place of the lion's provider; but the only part he actually sustains in the drama is that of gleaner up of the crumbs that fall from the Royal table.

Pukoli abounds in many varieties from Barbary to the Cape of Good Hope, his soft silky skin being in high demand among the native tribes for the manufacture of cloaks, whilst the animal contributes no less essential service when living by assisting to clear the country, the suburbs, of villages especially, from carrion in every stage of putrefaction. Scarcely had the sun sunk below the horizon, than attracted by the smell of the larder to the very limit of our camp, the impertinent intruders were wont to serenade us with a squall not very dissimilar from a concert of metropolitan cats on the house top — their dismal laugh uttered at intervals throughout the night, responded to, bark for bark, by our dogs, and re-echoed back by all their own more remote companions who happened to be within hearing — together producing the most discordant and lugubrious of all possible music, and often eliciting a well merited volley of bullets in the direction whence their sad voices arose. The ears of my Indian readers are all sufficiently familiar with that:

mix'd and mournful sound
'Twixt crying babe and beaten hound.

An opening note which serves as a signal for a general chorus, is frequently succeeded by a sudden yell from a hundred throats at once — the long protracted scream, resounding through the solitudes during the still darkness, like the roll of the thunderclap immediately succeeding the flash — its effects being finest when the first shriek is faintly heard in the distance, and the answer bursts from several points at once, within a few yards of the elbow

PLATE XXX. 1. HYÆNA CROCUTA: THE SPOTTED HYÆNA.
2. HYÆNA FUSCA: THE FUSCOUS HYÆNA.
3. HYÆNA VENATICA: THE WILD DOG.

of the dozing auditor.

But the office of carrion scavenger is principally borne by various species of the vulture, which are always collected near the abodes of man, and render excellent service to the community at large by removing offal and putrescent matter that would by accumulating corrupt the air with pestilential exhalations. There are several varieties of this obscene bird, to all of which the term *aasvogel* is indiscriminately applied by the colonists — the most common being the small white species with yellow head and neck, one of the sacred birds of the Egyptians, known by the title of Pharaoh's hen. The solemn, slow and measured movements of the large black species with sooty plumage, and bare livid rose-coloured head, has a funereal affect well adapted to its cadaverous employment; and there is in the gait and looks of all a heaviness which makes one feel half inclined to regard them as beasts rather than as birds of prey. Accustomed to feed in the society of the former, they are little disturbed by the presence even of dogs, and when driven away by a canine charge, walk round with the greatest ease and familiarity, returning immediately to the repast. Almost unable after a surfeit to rise from the ground, the harpy waddles round the bones which it has picked with an air of sombre and sinister gravity, a fetid discharge exuding from its nostrils, until at last, taking wing slowly, it retires to some inaccessible crag, where it perches phlegmatically for whole days together, motionless, in melancholy silence.

During the progress through the wilderness of our little band, we were instinctively attended by a relief of these gaunt and ravenous harpies, ever ready to pounce upon the carcases of cattle that might perish by the wayside, or summoned by the well known crack of the rifle, to take possession of the quarry that had fallen — the promptitude they evinced in discovering booty, being scarcely less surprising than their alacrity in disposing of it. Roused from their torpor by the progress of digestion, and stimulated by the qualms of hunger, they have again mounted aloft to a vast aerial altitude until lost to human gaze; and sustained in the serene atmosphere upon outstretched but motionless pinions, scanning the surface of the earth from their towering elevation, they soar in wide and buoyant circles, reviewing at a glance the boundless tract of country which is to furnish them with prey, and inhaling with keen nostrils the odours that are wafted from the lower regions.

A herd of naked aborigines, besmeared and bedaubed with copious defilements of red clay, their hair clogged with fat and shining with *sibilo,* are usually the first to take possession of a newly fallen carcase, tearing and devouring which — tooth, nail and assegai — with all the voracity of half famished barbarians, they at length succeed in stuffing themselves *usque ad nauseam,* and within an ace of suffocation. To these greasy men, of whom the sole aim and object in life may be said to be eating raw bowels and sleeping succeed a host of vultures, followed by a train of hyaenas and jackals; their banquet which affords the subject of this my concluding scene, forming no inappropriate type of the scrambling carousal which has so recently terminated. Although the azure vault of heaven, free from all speck and blemish, may present no indication of the presence of these ubiquitous and filthy birds, yet no sooner has the quarry fallen, than a whizzing like that of the cloth yard from the bow, accompanied by a fusty and noisome effluvia, announces the descent upon earth of three or four *avant couriers*, who directing with their pointed beaks an impatient attack at the eyes and softer parts of the skin, speedily force in their way to:

the reeking entrails and yet quiv'ring heart.

Conjured into existence as if by some magic agency, multitudes are presently to be seen pouring to the repast — and hundreds still gathering from afar, are wheeling round and round at a prodigious height — a succession of intersecting circles, each sweeping lower than the last, constantly importing additional legions to the banquet. Then commences such fighting and sparring and snuffling, such tugging and tearing and gobbling, that half an hour is generally sufficient to reduce the largest carcase to mere skin and bones — the latter being picked as clean as if they had been boiled and scraped with a knife; until, gorged at last to the throat, and their portion of the business accomplished, they leave the residue to find a ready sepulchre in the voracious maw of the grave diggers, who thrust their broad bulldog-muzzles, and with the assistance of their brother scavengers so complete the work, as often to leave upon the wide plain scarcely one bone to attest the slaughter:

From the mountains fall
The lengthening shades — and the shrill jackal
Shrieks forth his hymn to the horned moon,
And says that his master will follow soon;
And the wolf replies from his bone-strew'd brake,
And tells that the leopard is also awake
And the lynx and hyaena join in the train
All chanting to Hecate a joyful strain,
For the rout is oe'r and the carnage ceased,
And the vulture hath bidden them all to the feast.

Plate XXX (1): *Hyaena crocuta* — spotted hyena — *wolf* of the Cape colonists — *impeese* of the Matabili

Generic Character — Height of both sexes at the shoulder about two feet six or eight inches; much less at the rump. Extreme length about five feet ten inches. Feet with four toes; nails non retractile. Head short and very broad; muzzle and nose black. Lower part of the head, throat, and belly and inner surfaces of the extremities, dingy white. General colour of the other parts fulvous brown, irregularly blotched with circular black spots. Tail sixteen inches; the lower two thirds of its length furnished with long black hairs forming a tassel. Hair on the back of the neck and withers, long, forming a reversed mane. Both sexes furnished with a glandular pouch below the tail.

Very common everywhere.

Plate XXX (2): *Hyaena fusca* — fuscous hyena — *straand wolf* of the Cape colonists

Generic Character — Usual height at shoulder, about two feet four inches; much lower behind. Extreme length about four feet ten inches. Hair very long and shaggy on the upper parts of the neck, back and tail. General colour reddish grey, brindled with brown and black stripes and spots. Extremities yellowish, with deep black transverse bands. Tail twelve inches; black, with red hairs towards the tip.

Female similar. Less abundant than the preceding, but common along the sea coast.

Plate XXX (3): *Hyaena venatica* — wild dog — *wilde hond of the Cape colonists*

Generic character — Height at the shoulder under two feet; rather lower behind. Length about four feet three inches. Form slight. Legs slender and crooked; muzzle pointed. Ground colour of the hair sandy bay, or ochraceous yellow, irregularly blotched and brindled with black and white variegated spots of exceedingly irregular shape. Face, nose and muzzle, black. Ears ample, and rounded. Tail bushy, like that of a fox, divided about the middle by a black ring, above which the colour is sandy, and below white.

Common. Hunts in large organised packs.

Huntsman rest! Thy chase is done

SPOLIA OPIMA,

Spolia opima, as preserved by Captain Harris

Finis Coronat Opus